Lecture Notes in Computer Sci

Commenced Publication in 1973
Founding and Former Series Editors:
Gerhard Goos, Juris Hartmanis, and Jan van Leeuw

T0259852

Abhik Roychoudhury
Meenakshi D'Souza (Eds.)

Theoretical Aspects of Computing – ICTAC 2012

9th International Colloquium
Bangalore, India
September 24-27, 2012
Proceedings

 Springer

Volume Editors

Abhik Roychoudhury
School of Computing
National University of Singapore
13 Computing Drive
117417 Singapore, Singapore
E-mail: abhik@comp.nus.edu.sg

Meenakshi D'Souza
International Institute of Information Technology
26-C, Electronics City
560100 Bangalore, India
E-mail: meenakshi@iiitb.ac.in

ISSN 0302-9743   e-ISSN 1611-3349
ISBN 978-3-642-32942-5   e-ISBN 978-3-642-32943-2
DOI 10.1007/978-3-642-32943-2
Springer Heidelberg Dordrecht London New York

Library of Congress Control Number: 2012944719

CR Subject Classification (1998): D.2.4, D.3.1, F.1, F.3, F.4

LNCS Sublibrary: SL 1 – Theoretical Computer Science and General Issues

Typesetting: Camera-ready by author, data conversion by Scientific Publishing Services, Chennai, India

Printed on acid-free paper

Springer is part of Springer Science+Business Media (www.springer.com)

Preface

This volume contains the proceedings of the 9th International Colloquium on Theoretical Aspects of Computing (ICTAC) 2012. The event was held in Bangalore, India, during September 24–27, 2012. The ICTAC 2012 colloquium was organized jointly by the International Institute of Information Technology Bangalore (IIIT-B) and United Nations University - International Institute for Software Technology (UNU-IIST) at Macau.

One of the new features of ICTAC 2012 was the holding of an Industry Day to encourage greater communication and co-operation between academic researchers and industrial researchers. We would like to thank Satish Chandra (IBM Research) and Sriram Rajamani (Microsoft Research India) for chairing the first ever Industry Day at ICTAC. We are also thankful to Formal Methods in Europe (FME) for providing partial support for the Industry Day.

ICTAC 2012 received 73 submissions. Each submission was reviewed by at least three members of the Program Committee, along with help from external reviewers. Out of the 73 submissions, the Program Committee accepted 16 full-length papers, and three tool papers. The three tool papers accepted for ICTAC 2012 were presented on the Industry Day.

ICTAC 2012 featured three invited talks by Luke Ong (University of Oxford), Gernot Heiser (NICTA and UNSW Australia), and Ganesan Ramalingam (Microsoft Research India). Gernot Heiser was the invited speaker for the Industry Day, while Luke Ong was the UNU-IIST 20th anniversary speaker.

Luke Ong's invited talk focused on automated verification of actor-style message passing concurrency. Gernot Heiser's invited talk provided an overview of trustworthy systems and focused on how to provide safety and security guarantees to real-world systems including operating systems. Ganesan Ramalingam's invited talk focused on formalizing process failures and achieving failure-free computations in modern distributed platforms.

Apart from the paper presentations and invited talks, ICTAC 2012 continued the tradition of previous ICTAC conferences in holding a school on Software Engineering. The speakers at the Software Engineering school were Supratik Chakraborty (IIT Mumbai), Peter Mueller (ETH Zurich), K.V. Raghavan (IISc), and Nishant Sinha (IBM Research).

On behalf of the Program Committee we would like to thank the authors of the submitted papers, as well as the external reviewers whose expert reviews helped us build up the program.

July 2012

Abhik Roychoudhury
Meenakshi D'Souza

Organization

Program Committee

Ana Cavalcanti	University of York, UK
Supratik Chakraborty	IIT Mumbai, India
Satish Chandra	IBM T.J.Watson Research Center, USA
Yifeng Chen	Peking University, China
Meenakshi D'Souza	IIIT Bangalore, India
Thao Dang	Verimag, France
Frank deBoer	CWI, The Netherlands
Xinyu Feng	USTC, China
John Fitzgerald	University of Newcastle, UK
Susanne Graf	Verimag, France
Lindsay Groves	Victoria University, New Zealand
Zhenjiang Hu	NII, Japan
Lei Ju	Shandong University, China
Moonzoo Kim	KAIST, Korea
Daniel Kroening	Oxford University, UK
Kim G. Larsen	Aalborg University, Denmark
Martin Leucker	TU Munich, Germany
Zhiming Liu	UNU-IIST, Macau, SAR, China
Kamal Lodaya	Institute of Mathematical Sciences, India
Annabelle McIver	Macquarie University, Australia
Madhavan Mukund	Chennai Mathematical Institute, India
Kedar Namjoshi	Bell Labs, USA
Jun Pang	University of Luxembourg
Sanjiva Prasad	IIT Delhi, India
Geguang Pu	ECNU, China
Zongyan Qiu	Peking University, China
Anders P. Ravn	Aalborg University, Denmark
Abhik Roychoudhury	National University of Singapore, Singapore (Chair)
Diptikalyan Saha	IBM Research, India
Augusto Sampaio	UFPE, Brazil
Bikram Sengupta	IBM Research, India
R.K. Shyamasundar	TIFR, India
Sofiene Tahar	Concordia University, Canada
Kapil Vaswani	Microsoft Research, India
Wang Yi	Uppsala University, Sweden
Naijun Zhan	Chinese Academy of Sciences, China
Jianjun Zhao	Shanghai Jiao Tong University, China

Steering Committee

John Fitzgerald, UK
Martin Leucker, Germany
Zhiming Liu, Macau SAR China (Chair)
Tobias Nipkow, Germany
Augusto Sampaio, Brazil
Natarajan Shankar, USA
Jim Woodcock, UK

Executive Committee

Program Chair

Abhik Roychoudhury   National University of Singapore, Singapore

General Chair

Meenakshi D'Souza   IIIT Bangalore, India

Industry Day Chairs

Satish Chandra   IBM Research
Sriram Rajamani   Microsoft Research India

Publicity Chair

Jun Pang   University of Luxembourg, Luxembourg

Referees

Naeem Abbasi	Maissa Elleuch	Yongjian Li
Bharat Adsul	Santiago Escobar	Wanwei Liu
Vincent Aravantinos	Johannes Faber	Fabrizio Maria Maggi
Amitabha Bagchi	Uli Fahrenberg	Manuel Mazzara
Benedikt Bollig	Jing Fan	Matthijs Melissen
Svetlana Boudko	Yu Fan	Swarup Mohalik
Peter Bulychev	John Field	Partha Mukhopadhyay
Haopeng Chen	Raghavan G.S.	Seokhyeon Mun
Yuting Chen	Vinicius Garcia	Mikael H. Moller
Deepak D'Souza	Amjad Gawanmeh	Raja N.
Cristina David	Rajeev Gore	Gopalan Nadathur
Stijn De Gouw	Michael Greenberg	Michele Pagani
Normann Decker	Thomas Hildebrandt	Paritosh Pandya
Benoit Delahaye	Mathai Joseph	Nafees Qamar
Yuxin Deng	Josva Kleist	Jan-David Quesel
Thomas Dinsdale-Young	Piotr Kordy	C. Ramanathan

R. Ramanujam	Traian Serbanuta	Hongli Yang
Stefan Rieger	Volker Stolz	Miaomiao Zhang
Krishna S.	Qiang Sun	Hengjun Zhao
Martin Sachenbacher	Michael Tautschnig	Lixiao Zheng
Prahalad Sampath	Louis-Marie Traonouez	Jiaqi Zhu
Rudolf Schlatte	Christian Urban	
Martin Schaf	Shuling Wang	

Sponsoring Institutions

- International Institute of Information Technology Bangalore (India)
- United Nations University - International Institute for Software Technology (Macau SAR, China)

Table of Contents

Symbolically Bounding the Drift in Time-Constrained MSC Graphs*

S. Akshay[1], Blaise Genest[1,2], Loïc Hélouët[1], and Shaofa Yang[3]

[1] IRISA, INRIA Rennes - ENS Cachan Bretagne - CNRS, France
[2] CNRS, UMI IPAL joint with NUS and A*STAR/I2R, Singapore
[3] SIAT, Chinese Academy of Sciences, China
{akshay,bgenest}@irisa.fr, loic.helouet@inria.fr, sf.yang@siat.ac.cn

Abstract. Verifying systems involving both time and concurrency rapidly leads to undecidability, and requires restrictions to become effective. This paper addresses the emptiness problem for time-constrained MSC-Graphs (TC-MSC graphs for short), that is, checking whether there is a timed execution compatible with a TC-MSC graph specification. This problem is known to be undecidable in general [11], and decidable for some regular specifications [11]. We establish decidability of the emptiness problem under the condition that, for a given K, *no path* of the TC-MSC graph *forces* any node to take more than K time units to complete. We prove that this condition can be effectively checked. The proofs use a novel symbolic representation for runs, where time constraints are encoded as a system of inequalities. This allows us to handle *non-regular specifications* and improve efficiency w.r.t. using interleaved representations.

1 Introduction

In a distributed system, several processes interact to implement a protocol. One way to describe these interactions is through scenarios, formalized using Message Sequence Charts (MSCs) [13]. MSCs describe finite interactions among agents that communicate asynchronously. A protocol is described by allowing choices and repetition of these MSCs. To specify these main characteristics while abstracting away details of implementation, the formal methods community often considers *MSC graphs*, which are directed graphs whose nodes are labeled by MSCs. Protocol specifications also include timing requirements for messages as well as descriptions of how to recover from timeouts. To specify how time and concurrency influence each other, MSCs and MSC graphs have been generalized to *time-constrained MSCs* (TC-MSCs) and *time-constrained MSC graphs* (TC-MSC graphs) [2]. The timing information is captured by adding timing constraints between pairs of events, and transitions have additional timing constraints.

We consider decidability issues for TC-MSC graphs. This is a challenging task due to the presence of both time and concurrency. First, the set of executions of a TC-MSC graph is not regular in general. Even checking whether there exists a timed execution that is consistent with all the constraints of a model

---

* Funded by the French Consulate at Guangzhou, ANR IMPRO, and the DST project.

A. Roychoudhury and M. D'Souza (Eds.): ICTAC 2012, LNCS 7521, pp. 1–15, 2012.
© Springer-Verlag Berlin Heidelberg 2012

is non-trivial. This question, called the *emptiness problem*, is undecidable for TC-MSC graphs in general [11]. However, it is decidable for (sequential) timed automata [4]. Extending decidability results to distributed systems has been done in two particular and limited settings. In the first setting [15,10], clocks are local to a process, and so, one cannot specify time taken by a communication (message or synchronization). This limitation makes the specification formalism very weak. The second setting can relate clocks from different processes and specify how long a communication takes, but the specifications can only exhibit regular behaviors [2,3,7,8,18], which is a significant restriction in a concurrent setting where even the simple producer-consumer protocol is not regular. To obtain regularity (and hence decidability), these papers restrict the concurrency in a structural way, for instance considering only locally synchronized (see [16,5,12]) MSC graphs (in [2,3]) or only safe Petri Nets (in [7,8]). In [1], the language is restricted to being representable by a regular set, using both K-drift-boundedness — that we use in this paper and define below — *and* a restriction on Zeno behaviors. Decidability of checking K-drift-boundedness was however left open. Last, the procedures for TC-MSC graphs in [2,3,11,1] construct an interleaved timed automaton, leading to a combinatorial explosion. This could be seen as going against the spirit of MSCs, which try to avoid interleavings. Further, the approaches in [2,3,11,18,1] add another blow-up in complexity through the use of zone construction [4].

   In this paper, we prove a novel decidability result for timed concurrent systems with global clocks having a possibly *non-regular* set of behaviors. We investigate the emptiness problem for TC-MSC graphs, and prove it to be decidable in the setting where a TC-MSC graph is prohibited from *forcing* any TC-MSC appearing along one of its paths to take an arbitrarily long amount of time to complete. More precisely, for a given integer K, for any path ρ of a TC-MSC graph, if there exists at least one execution of ρ, then we require that there exists one in which the occurrence times of any two events from the same TC-MSC differ by at most K. Such a TC-MSC graph is said to be K-*drift-bounded* [1]. We further show that given K, one can effectively test whether a TC-MSC graph G is K-drift-bounded. Both results are established without constructing an interleaved timed automaton or relying on the seminal result on decidability of emptiness of timed automata [4], avoiding both state space explosions. Instead, we translate the set of time constraints of a path into a *symbolic profile*, in the form of a system of inequalities. We show how to manipulate this system symbolically using Fourier-Motzkin elimination [9]. We approximate symbolic profiles by a bounded system of inequalities whose coefficients are integers in $[-K', K']$ for some integer K' depending on G and K. This does not hinder checking consistency of K-drift-bounded TC-MSC graphs. This forms the cornerstone of our decidability results, as finite state automata can keep track of bounded systems of inequalities.

   The paper is organized as follows: Section 2 recalls basic definitions. Section 3 discusses drift-boundedness and its relevance. Section 4 shows how to check emptiness for K-drift-bounded TC-MSC graphs and Section 5 shows that checking K-drift-boundedness is decidable, for a given K. Omitted proofs are available in an extended version (http://perso.crans.org/~genest/AGHY12full.pdf).

2   Preliminaries

Let $\mathbb{R}_{\geq 0}$ denote the set of non-negative reals, $\mathbb{N}$ the set of integers and $\mathcal{I}$ the collection of open and closed intervals with end points in $\mathbb{N}$ as well as intervals of the form $[c, \infty), (c, \infty)$, where $c \in \mathbb{N}$. Throughout this paper, we fix a finite set $\mathcal{P}$ of processes and let p, q range over $\mathcal{P}$. Let $\Sigma = \{p!q, p?q \mid p, q \in \mathcal{P},\ p \neq q\}$ be the *communication alphabet*. The letter $p!q$ represents p sending a message to q, while $p?q$ signifies p receiving a message sent by q. We define the map $loc : \Sigma \to \mathcal{P}$ via $loc(p!q) = p = loc(p?q)$, and call $loc(a)$ the *location* of a. We define Message Sequence Charts (MSCs) and time-constrained MSCs (TC-MSCs) as usual. We do not require FIFO ordering among messages.

Definition 1. *An* MSC *is a tuple* $(E, (<_p)_{p \in \mathcal{P}}, \mu, \lambda)$. *The set of events is* E *and* $\lambda : E \to \Sigma$ *labels events with letters. For each* p, $<_p$ *is a total order over* $E_p = \{e \in E \mid loc(\lambda(e)) = p\}$. *The message function* $\mu \subseteq E_S \times E_R$ *is a bijection, such that* $f = \mu(e)$ *implies* $\lambda(e) = p!q$, $\lambda(f) = q?p$ *for some* $p, q \in \mathcal{P}$, *with* $E_S = \{e \in E \mid \exists p, q \in \mathcal{P}, \lambda(e) = p!q\}$ *and* $E_R = \{f \in E \mid \exists p, q \in \mathcal{P}, \lambda(f) = q?p\}$. *We require that the transitive closure* $\leq$ *of* $\lessdot = \bigcup_{p \in \mathcal{P}} <_p \cup \mu$ *is a partial order.*

The relation $\leq$ reflects causal ordering of events. We will write $e < f$ when $e \leq f$ and $e \neq f$. Notice that E_p has a unique $<_p$-maximal event (respectively, minimal event), which we refer to as the last (respectively, first) event of E on p.

Definition 2. *A* TC-MSC *is a tuple* $(E, (<_p)_{p \in \mathcal{P}}, \mu, \lambda, \delta)$ *where* $(E, (<_p)_{p \in \mathcal{P}}, \mu, \lambda)$ *is an MSC and* δ *is a function associating an interval* $\delta(e, e') \in \mathcal{I}$ *to each* $e \lessdot e'$.

For each pair of events $e \lessdot e'$, the interval $\delta(e, e')$ constrains the range in which the difference between the occurrence time of e' and the occurrence time of e can lie. For clarity, we shall refer to occurrence times as *dates*. A TC-MSC T defines a collection of MSCs with dates such that the relative differences of dates fulfill the constraints asserted in T.

Definition 3. *Let* $T = (E, (<_p)_{p \in \mathcal{P}}, \mu, \lambda, \delta)$ *be a TC-MSC. A* dated MSC *generated by* T *is a tuple* $(E, (<_p)_{p \in \mathcal{P}}, \mu, \lambda, d)$ *where* $d : E \to \mathbb{R}^+$ *is such that for each* $e \lessdot e'$, $d(e') - d(e)$ *is in the interval* $\delta(e, e')$.

We denote by $\mathcal{L}(T)$ the set of dated MSCs generated by T. To capture infinite collections of TC-MSCs, we define TC-MSC graphs as in [2,11], which are finite graphs whose nodes are labeled by TC-MSCs. Each path ρ of a TC-MSC graph G induces a TC-MSC by concatenating TC-MSCs labeling nodes of ρ. Transitions of G are labeled by interval constraints, one for each process, that act as constraints on the timing between the last and first event of each process in consecutive nodes of ρ.

Definition 4. *A* TC-MSC graph *is a structure* $G = (N, \mathcal{T}, \Lambda, n_{in}, N_{fi}, \longrightarrow, \Delta)$ *where* N *is a finite non-empty set of nodes,* $\mathcal{T}$ *a finite set of TC-MSCs,* $\Lambda : N \to \mathcal{T}$ *labels each node with a TC-MSC,* n_{in} *is the initial node,* N_{fi} *the set of final*

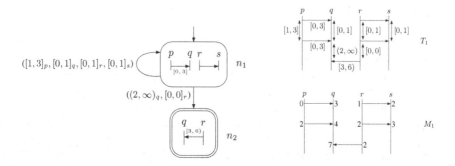

Fig. 1. A TC-MSC graph G_1, a TC-MSC T_1 and a dated MSC $M_1 \in \mathcal{L}(G_1)$

nodes, $\longrightarrow \subseteq N \times N$ is the transition relation, and Δ is a labeling function which associates an interval $\Delta_p(n{\rightarrow}n') \in \mathcal{I}$ to each transition $n{\rightarrow}n'$ and each process p, such that $\Delta_p(n{\rightarrow}n') = [0, \infty)$ if $\Lambda(n)$ or $\Lambda(n')$ has no event on process p.

A *path* ρ of the TC-MSC graph G is a sequence $n_0 n_1 \ldots n_\ell$ such that $n_0 = n_{in}$ and $n_i{\rightarrow}n_{i+1}$ for $i = 0, \ldots, \ell - 1$. The path ρ is said to be *final* if $n_\ell \in N_{fi}$. For each $n{\rightarrow}n'$, the *concatenation* of TC-MSCs $\Lambda(n)$, $\Lambda(n')$ is defined with respect to $\Delta(n{\rightarrow}n')$, and is denoted $\Lambda(n) \circ \Lambda(n')$. Roughly speaking, this consists of putting $\Lambda(n')$ after $\Lambda(n)$ and for every process p, attaching to the pair (e_p, f_p) the constraint $\Delta_p(n{\rightarrow}n')$, for e_p the last event of $\Lambda(n)$ on process p and f_p the first event of $\Lambda(n')$ on p. Formally, let $\Lambda(n) = (E, (<_p)_{p\in\mathcal{P}}, \mu, \lambda, \delta)$, $\Lambda(n') = (E', (<'_p)_{p\in\mathcal{P}}, \mu', \lambda', \delta')$. Then $\Lambda(n) \circ \Lambda(n') = (E'', (<''_p)_{p\in\mathcal{P}}, \mu'', \lambda'', \delta'')$ where E'' is the disjoint union of E and E', $<''_p$ is the transitive closure of the union of $<_p$, $<'_p$ and $E_p \times E'_p$, and λ'' is given by: $\lambda''(e) = \lambda(e)$ for $e \in E$, $\lambda''(e) = \lambda'(e)$ for $e \in E'$. We also set $\mu''(e) = \mu(e)$ when $\mu(e)$ is defined, and $\mu''(e) = \mu'(e)$ when $\mu'(e)$ is defined. At last, δ'' is given by: $\delta''(e, f) = \delta(e, f)$ for $e \lessdot f$, $\delta''(e, f) = \delta'(e, f)$ for $e \lessdot' f$. For each p, if both E_p and E'_p are nonempty, we set $\delta''(e_p, f_p) = \Delta_p(n{\rightarrow}n')$ for e_p the last event of E_p and f_p the first event of E'_p.

We emphasize that by definition, $\Delta_p(n{\rightarrow}n') = [0, \infty)$ if E_p or E'_p is empty. It follows that for $n{\rightarrow}n'{\rightarrow}n''$, $(\Lambda(n) \circ \Lambda(n')) \circ \Lambda(n'')$ is the same as $\Lambda(n) \circ (\Lambda(n') \circ \Lambda(n''))$. Thus, we unambiguously define the TC-MSC T^ρ *induced* by a path $\rho = n_0 \ldots n_\ell$ of G to be $\Lambda(n_0) \circ \ldots \circ \Lambda(n_\ell)$. A path ρ of G is called *consistent* if $\mathcal{L}(T^\rho) \neq \emptyset$. From now on, we will speak interchangeably of a node n and its associated TC-MSC $\Lambda(n)$. We write $\mathcal{L}(G)$ for the union of $\mathcal{L}(T^\rho)$, ρ ranging over *final* paths of G. We call a dated MSC in $\mathcal{L}(G)$ a *timed execution* of G. An example of a TC-MSC graph G_1 is in Figure 1. The TC-MSC T_1 is induced by path $n_1 \cdot n_1 \cdot n_2$ of G_1, i.e., $T_1 = T^{n_1 \cdot n_1 \cdot n_2}$. Further, M_1 is a dated MSC generated by T_1. As n_2 is final, $M_1 \in \mathcal{L}(G_1)$.

The emptiness problem for TC-MSC graphs is: given a TC-MSC graph G, determine whether $\mathcal{L}(G) = \emptyset$, that is, whether it has no *consistent* and *final* path. This is a fundamental verification problem that must be addressed. Indeed, a TC-MSC graph with an empty language should be considered ill-specified and such an exception should be caught at an early stage of design. In [11], it is shown that this problem is undecidable in general, and decidable for some regular specifications. We show in the following that checking emptiness for TC-MSC graphs is decidable under an arguably mild restriction on time constraints which does not impose regularity. Furthermore, we will show that one can test whether a given TC-MSC graph satisfies this condition.

3   Drift-Boundedness

In this section we define our mild restriction, namely *drift-boundedness*. Let us fix a TC-MSC graph G. Let $\rho = n_0 \ldots n_\ell$ be a consistent path of G and $M = (E, (<_p)_{p\in\mathcal{P}}, \mu, \lambda, d)$ be a dated MSC generated by T^ρ. For an integer K, we say that M is a K-*drift-bounded* dated MSC of ρ iff for each $i = 0, \ldots, \ell$, for any two events e, e' in $\Lambda(n_i)$, it is the case that $|d(e) - d(e')| \leq K$. We say that ρ is K-*drift-bounded* iff there *exists* a K-drift-bounded dated MSC in $\mathcal{L}(T^\rho)$. We emphasize that $\mathcal{L}(T^\rho)$ may also contain dated MSCs which *are not* K-drift-bounded. We say that G is K-drift-bounded iff every *consistent* (but not necessarily final) path of G is K-drift-bounded. In other words, for each *consistent* path ρ, we can find a dated MSC in $\mathcal{L}(T^\rho)$ such that the difference between the dates of any two events from the same instance of a node is at most K. Notice that we can have $\mathcal{L}(G) = \emptyset$ even though G is K-drift-bounded. In fact, G is vacuously K-drift-bounded for any K if it has no consistent path.

As an example, consider the TC-MSC graph G_1 from Figure 1. G_1 is 3-drift-bounded since in every timed execution, we can be sure that all events in node n_1 or n_2 can be completed within a delay of 3 time units. But if we change the constraints on the loop on n_1 from $([0, 1]_r, [0, 1]_s)$ to $([4, 5]_r, [1, 2]_s)$ then for any integer K, G_1 is not K-drift-bounded. Note that G_1 is not locally synchronized (as defined in [16,5], and lifted in [3] to a timed setting). In fact, we can simulate the producer-consumer protocol and obtain non-regular behaviors. Thus, this example cannot be handled by the decidability result in [3].

We believe that drift-boundedness is a practical notion. Interpreting a node of a TC-MSC graph as a phase or a transaction of a distributed protocol, we expect any scenario labeling the node to be executable in a bounded time, say K. A protocol specified as a TC-MSC graph that is not K-drift-bounded should thus be considered as ill-formed. Indeed, while a TC-MSC graph specification is usually incomplete (as it abstracts away some events and constraints used in the actual implementation), if it is not K-drift-bounded, then every implementation of this specification will not be K-drift-bounded either.

3.1   The Main Results

We can now state our main results. The first result establishes the decidability of the emptiness problem for K-drift-bounded TC-MSC graphs.

Theorem 1. *Let $K \in \mathbb{N}$ and G be a K-drift-bounded TC-MSC graph. Then checking whether $\mathcal{L}(G)$ is empty is decidable in PSPACE.*

We next show that the drift-boundedness hypothesis of Theorem 1 can be effectively checked, giving rise to an effective decidability procedure.

Theorem 2. *Let $K \in \mathbb{N}$ and G be a TC-MSC graph. Then checking whether G is K-drift-bounded is decidable in PSPACE.*

We can show that the decidability result in Theorem 2 is in fact at the boundary of undecidability. Recall that the definition of K-drift-bounded considers every path of a TC-MSC graph, including paths that cannot be extended to consistent final paths. Instead, if we consider the problem of checking whether every consistent *final* path of a TC-MSC graph is K-drift-bounded, this turns out to be undecidable. We assume K fixed for the next proposition.

Proposition 1. *It is undecidable, given a TC-MSC graph G, to determine whether every consistent final path of G is K-drift-bounded.*

Proof. The proof is by a reduction from the emptiness problem of TC-MSC graphs, shown undecidable in [11]. Let G be a TC-MSC graph. We construct another TC-MSC graph G' from G such that there does *not* exist a consistent final path of G iff every consistent final path of G' is K-drift-bounded, which shows the result. G' is obtained from G with the following modifications. Firstly, add a new node n_{new} and for every final state n_f of G, add a transition (n_f, n_{new}). Secondly, define the set of final nodes of G' to be the singleton set $\{n_{new}\}$. Thirdly, n_{new} is labeled with a TC-MSC consisting of a single message (e, f) from p to q. The time constraint on (e, f) is $[K+1, K+1]$. Lastly, for every final state n_f of G and every process, the time constraint of transition (n_f, n_{new}) is $[0, \infty)$. If there does not exist a consistent final path of G, then there does not exist a consistent final path of G', and it is vacuously true that every consistent final path of G' is K-drift-bounded. On the other hand, assume that there exists some consistent final path ρ of G. Then $\rho \cdot n_{new}$ is a consistent final path of G' (timing of a consistent dated MSC of ρ can be easily extended). But it is not K-drift-bounded because of the constraint $[K+1, K+1]$ on the last node n_{new} of the path, which impose e, f to be $K+1$ time units away. Hence not every consistent final path of G' is K-drift-bounded.   □

Next, we introduce *full* TC-MSC graphs and show that any TC-MSC graph can be transformed into a *full* TC-MSC graph, while preserving consistency and drift-boundedness of paths. This enables us to check both the emptiness of a K-drift-bounded TC-MSC graph G, and the K-drift-boundedness of any TC-MSC graph G, by working with a full TC-MSC graph constructed from G.

3.2   Full TC-MSC Graphs

We call a TC-MSC graph G *full* if each node of G has at least one event on each process $p \in \mathcal{P}$. We will now show how to "augment" a TC-MSC graph G to obtain a full TC-MSC graph $\widehat{G}$ by adding "dummy events" to nodes of G. For notational convenience, we assume that TC-MSCs may contain internal events. We denote by $p(int)$ the label of such an internal event on process $p \in \mathcal{P}$.

Given $G = (N, \mathcal{T}, \Lambda, n_{in}, N_{fi}, \longrightarrow, \Delta)$, the *augmented graph of G* is defined as $\widehat{G} = (N, \widehat{\mathcal{T}}, \widehat{\Lambda}, n_{in}, N_{fi}, \longrightarrow, \Delta)$ differing only in the labeling set of "augmented" TC-MSCs and the labeling function assigning nodes to them. More precisely, any TC-MSC $T = (E, (<_p)_{p \in \mathcal{P}}, \mu, \lambda, \delta)$ in $\mathcal{T}$ is replaced by the TC-MSC $\widehat{T} = (E', (<_p)_{p \in \mathcal{P}}, \mu, \lambda', \delta)$ in $\widehat{\mathcal{T}}$ where E' is obtained from E by adding a new event e_p with $\lambda(e_p) = p(int)$ for each process p such that $E_p = \emptyset$. Every $<_p$ and δ are unchanged, so e_p is an isolated point in the partial order $\leq$. Such events e_p will be called *dummy events*. Events already in $\Lambda(n)$ will be called *concrete events*. Note that $\Delta(n \rightarrow m)$ is unchanged for each transition $n \rightarrow m$. In particular, recall that for each transition (n, m) in G, if either n or m has no concrete event on p, then $\Delta_p(n, m) = [0, \infty)$. For each $\Lambda(n) = T$, we set $\widehat{\Lambda}(n) = \widehat{T}$. Obviously, $\widehat{G}$ is full for any G.

Let H be any full TC-MSC graph with events partitioned as dummy or concrete. That is, in every TC-MSC labeling a node of H, there is a mapping from the set of events to $\{dummy, concrete\}$. For instance, $\widehat{G}$ is such a full TC-MSC graph. Let $Y \leq Y' \in \mathbb{N}$. Now, for a path $\rho = n_0 \ldots n_\ell$ of H, we say that a dated MSC $M = (E, (<_p)_{p \in \mathcal{P}}, \mu, \lambda, d)$ generated by T^ρ is (Y, Y')-*drift-bounded* if for each $i = 0, \ldots, \ell$, for any two events e, f in the TC-MSC $\Lambda(n_i)$, we have: (i) if both e and f are concrete events, then $|d(e) - d(f)| \leq Y$; (ii) if one or both of e, f are dummy events, then $|d(e) - d(f)| \leq Y'$. We say that a consistent path ρ of H is (Y, Y')-*drift-bounded* if there exists a (Y, Y')-drift-bounded dated MSC generated by ρ. At last, H is (Y, Y')-*drift-bounded* if all its *consistent* paths are.

Proposition 2. *For a TC-MSC graph G, a path ρ of G and $K \in \mathbb{N}$, (i) ρ is consistent in G iff $\widehat{\rho}$ is consistent in $\widehat{G}$, (ii) ρ is K-drift-bounded in G iff $\widehat{\rho}$ is $(K, \widehat{K})$-drift-bounded in $\widehat{G}$, with $\widehat{K} = (|\mathcal{P}| - 1) \cdot K$.*

Hence, we are able to restrict to full TC-MSC graphs when checking for emptiness using (i), and when checking for K-drift boundedness using (ii):

Corollary 1. *Given a TC-MSC graph G, (i) $\mathcal{L}(G) \neq \emptyset$ iff $\mathcal{L}(\widehat{G}) \neq \emptyset$, and (ii) G is K-drift-bounded iff $\widehat{G}$ is $(K, \widehat{K})$-drift-bounded, where $\widehat{K} = (|\mathcal{P}| - 1) \cdot K$.*

4   Emptiness for K-Drift-Bounded TC-MSC Graphs

We now prove Theorem 1. We assume G to be a K-drift-bounded TC-MSC graph. By Corollary 1, we can build $\widehat{G}$, a $(K, \widehat{K})$-drift-bounded full TC-MSC graph with $\mathcal{L}(\widehat{G}) \neq \emptyset$ iff $\mathcal{L}(G) \neq \emptyset$. It then suffices to check the emptiness of a finite automaton that accepts the set of $(K, \widehat{K})$-drift-bounded *final* paths of $\widehat{G}$.

Let H be a full TC-MSC graph, with events partitioned as dummy or concrete. To avoid clutter, we assume that constraints in H are only of the form $[a, b]$ and $[a, \infty)$. Extending proofs to handle other constraints is straightforward and all statements hold in general, but additional notations are needed to remember whether each inequality is strict or not. We first describe intuitively the key ingredients of the proof, which will be developed in the rest of this section.

– First, we observe that checking consistency of a path ρ of H, i.e., $\mathcal{L}(T^\rho) \neq \emptyset$, is equivalent to checking for the existence of a solution to a system of inequalities over (real-valued) variables x_e depicting the dates of events e of T^ρ.
– Next, we show that checking whether a dated MSC can be extended by a node by assigning appropriate dates to events of this node can be done with information only on the relative difference of dates of the last event of the dated MSC on each process. This motivates us to associate a symbolic profile $PF(\rho)$ to each path ρ. A symbolic profile is a system of inequalities whose solutions correspond to the dates of final events of dated MSCs generated by T^ρ, and vice versa. In particular, $PF(\rho)$ has a solution iff ρ is consistent.
– We remark that constants appearing in symbolic profiles can be chosen as integers. Restricting constants to be within $[-\widehat{K}, \widehat{K}]$ does not exclude any consistent $(K, \widehat{K})$-drift-bounded path of H. We can then represent with a finite automaton the set of consistent $(K, \widehat{K})$-drift-bounded paths of H.

Systems of Inequalities and Fourier-Motzkin Elimination. We first fix basic terminologies for systems of difference inequalities. Let X be a finite nonempty set of real-valued variables. A *(difference) inequality* is an inequality of the form $x - y \leq a$, where x, y are two different variables in X.

Definition 5. *A system of (difference) inequalities ϕ over X is $\wedge_{(x,y) \in R} x - y \leq a_{xy}$ where $R \subseteq X \times X$ is an irreflexive relation. We say that ϕ has integral coefficients whenever a_{xy} is a (possibly negative) integer for all $(x,y) \in R$.*

From now on, we assume that the system is *simplified*, that is, for each $x, y \in X$, there is at most one inequality of the form $x - y \leq a$. This involves no loss of generality as $x - y \leq a \wedge x - y \leq a'$ is equivalent with $x - y \leq min(a, a')$. If $x - y \leq a$ appears in ϕ, we say that ϕ contains an *edge* (x, y), and the weight of this edge is a. We say that two systems ϕ, ψ of inequalities are *equivalent* when ϕ has a solution (in the real domain) iff ψ has a solution (in the real domain).

A key idea is to propagate constraints concerning variables in a subset $Y \subsetneq X$ on variables in $X \setminus Y$, and then safely remove variables in Y while keeping an equivalent system. This is done using the *Fourier-Motzkin* elimination method (see extended version, or [9,14]).

For $F \subseteq X$, let $\phi_{|F}$ denote the (unique) system of inequalities over variables F obtained by performing Fourier-Motzkin elimination of variables in $X \setminus F$ following a fixed order. We have that ϕ and $\phi_{|F}$ are equivalent. If ϕ has *integral coefficients*, then so does $\phi_{|F}$.

Symbolic Profiles. Let $T^\rho = (E, (<_p), \mu, \lambda, \delta)$ be the TC-MSC associated with some path $\rho = n_0 \ldots n_\ell$ of H. We denote by x_e a $\mathbb{R}_{\geq 0}$-valued variable, standing for the date of event $e \in E$, and let $X_E = \{x_e \mid e \in E\}$. We associate path ρ with a system of linear inequalities $\Phi(\rho)$ *with integral coefficients* as follows:

Definition 6. *The system $\Phi(\rho)$ associated with ρ is the smallest system of inequalities over the set of variables X_E*
    such that, for any $e, f \in E$ with $e \lessdot f$,

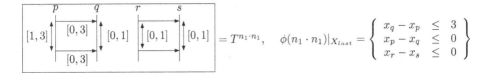

Fig. 2. The TC-MSC induced by path $n_1 \cdot n_1$ of G_1 and its profile

- if $\delta(e, f) = [L, U]$, then $\Phi(\rho)$ contains both $x_f - x_e \leq U$ and $x_e - x_f \leq -L$;
- if $\delta(e, f) = [L, \infty)$, then $\Phi(\rho)$ contains $x_e - x_f \leq -L$.

We easily have that ρ is consistent iff $\Phi(\rho)$ has a solution. Let e_p be the last event of T^ρ on p, for each process p. Let E_{last} be the set $\{e_p \mid p \in \mathcal{P}\}$. Using Fourier-Motzkin elimination of variables $X' = \{x_e \mid e \notin E_{last}\}$, we obtain a system $\Phi(\rho)|_{X_{last}}$ over variables $X_{last} = \{x_e \mid e \in E_{last}\}$, with integral coefficients, equivalent with $\Phi(\rho)$. Once simplified, this system has at most $|\mathcal{P}|^2$ inequalities with integral coefficients. We encode this system as a *symbolic profile*.

Definition 7. *A symbolic profile σ is a function from $\mathcal{P} \times \mathcal{P}$ to $\mathbb{Z} \cup \{\infty\}$. We denote by $\mathcal{PF}$ the (infinite) set of all profiles.*

Notice that symbolic profiles are *syntactically* similar to Difference Bounded Matrices (DBMs) [6] over $|\mathcal{P}|$ clocks. However, unlike a DBM, a symbolic profile may not correspond to a timed linearization, and the update function (defined below) is very different when compared to DBMs.

Let ϕ be a system of inequalities with integral coefficients over $X_{last} = \{x_p \mid p \in \mathcal{P}\}$. We define the symbolic profile $PF(\phi)$ induced by ϕ as $PF(\phi)[p, q] = a_{pq}$ if $x_p - x_q \leq a_{pq}$ belongs to ϕ, and $PF(\phi)[p, q] = \infty$ otherwise. Intuitively, $PF(\phi)[p, q] = \infty$ means that there is no inequality of the form $x_p - x_q \leq a_{pq}$ in ϕ. We abusively use $PF(\phi)$ as a system of inequalities in the following, and denote x_p for x_{e_p}. For a path ρ, we denote $PF(\rho) = PF((\Phi(\rho))|_{X_{last}})$. We say that a symbolic profile $\sigma \in \mathcal{PF}$ is *satisfiable* if it has a solution. It is easy to check whether $PF(\rho)$ is satisfiable, either by using Fourier-Motzkin elimination till reaching a trivial equation, or by using Shostak characterisation [17].

Proposition 3. *$PF(\rho)$ is satisfiable iff ρ is consistent.*

As an example, consider the TC-MSC $T^{n_1 \cdot n_1}$ in Figure 2, generated by path $n_1 \cdot n_1$ of G_1 from Figure 1. Let e^i_j denote the ith event on process j and E be the set of events of $T^{n_1 \cdot n_1}$. We obtain $\Phi(n_1 \cdot n_1)$ to be the set of inequalities over $X = \{x_e \mid e \in E\}$, where for instance the inequations $x_{e^2_p} - x_{e^1_p} \leq 3$ and $x_{e^1_p} - x_{e^2_p} \leq -1$ capture the timing constraint $[1, 3]$ between e^1_p and e^2_p. Now eliminating variables $x_{e^1_p}, x_{e^1_q}, x_{e^1_r}, x_{e^1_s}$ results in a set of equations on $X_{last} = \{x_{e^2_p}, x_{e^2_q}, x_{e^2_r}, x_{e^2_s}\} = \{x_p, x_q, x_r, x_s\}$ as shown. E.g., $PF(n_1 \cdot n_1))[p, q] = \min(3, -1 + 3 + 1) = 3$ and $PF(n_1 \cdot n_1))[s, r] = \infty$. This system of inequalities has many solutions.

Bounded profiles. Notice that the set of symbolic profiles as defined above is not finite in general (the coefficients range over $\mathbb{Z}$), and so, it cannot be recorded by a finite state automaton. Instead, we use the *finite set* of L-bounded profiles, where $L \in \mathbb{N}$ is some integer.

Definition 8. *For $L \in \mathbb{N}$, a L-bounded profile σ is a function from $\mathcal{P} \times \mathcal{P}$ to $\mathbb{Z} \cap [-L, L]$. We denote by $\mathcal{PF}_L$ the set of L-bounded profiles.*

Let $Y \leq Y' \in \mathbb{N}$. Notice that the set $\mathcal{PF}_{Y'}$ is finite. We denote by $\Phi_{Y,Y'}(\rho)$ the system of inequalities obtained from $\Phi(\rho)$ by the following modification: for each $i = 0, \ldots, \ell$, for any two different events e, f in the same node n of ρ, if $\Phi(\rho)$ contains $x_e - x_f \leq a_{e,f}$, then replace it by $x_e - x_f \leq min(a_{e,f}, Y)$ if both e, f are *concrete*, and by $x_e - x_f \leq min(a_{e,f}, Y')$ otherwise (that is if at least one of e or f is *dummy*); if $\Phi(\rho)$ does not have an edge (e, f), then add the inequality $x_e - x_f \leq Y$ if both e, f are *concrete*, and $x_e - x_f \leq Y'$ otherwise. Clearly, ρ is consistent and (Y, Y')-drift-bounded iff $\Phi_{Y,Y'}(\rho)$ has a solution. If $\Phi_{Y,Y'}(\rho)$ has a solution, we set $PF_{Y,Y'}(\rho) = PF(\Phi_{Y,Y'}(\rho)|_{X_{last}})$. In a full TC-MSC graph H, by definition of $\Phi_{Y,Y'}(\rho)$, we have $PF_{Y,Y'}(\rho) \in \mathcal{PF}_{Y'}$. If $\Phi_{Y,Y'}(\rho)$ has no solution, it is possible that $PF(\Phi_{Y,Y'}(\rho)|_{X_{last}}) \notin \mathcal{PF}_{Y'}$. In this case, we set $PF_{Y,Y'}(\rho)$ to be a particular profile $\perp \in \mathcal{PF}_{Y'}$ without solution, e.g. $\perp[p, q] = 0, \perp[q, p] = -1$ (which would require $1 \leq x_p - x_q \leq 0$).

Proposition 4. *Let ρ be a path of a full TC-MSC graph H. Then $PF_{Y,Y'}(\rho) \in \mathcal{PF}_{Y'}$, and $PF_{Y,Y'}(\rho)$ is satisfiable iff ρ is consistent and (Y, Y')-drift-bounded.*

Notice that $PF_{Y,Y'}(\rho)$ *cannot* be obtained from $PF(\rho)$. An intuitive (but wrong) idea would be to set $PF_{Y,Y'}(\rho)[p, q] = Y'$ for all $PF(\rho)[p, q] > Y'$ and else $PF_{Y,Y'}(\rho)[p, q] = PF(\rho)[p, q]$. However, setting $PF_{Y,Y'}(\rho)[p, q] = Y'$ for all $PF(\rho)[p, q] > Y'$ only constrains the dates of the last events on each process. So, the bound Y' in $\Phi_{Y,Y'}(\rho)$ must be imposed for every node of ρ, and these constraints on past nodes can have implications for the profile of ρ.

We now explain how to compute $PF_{Y,Y'}(\rho)$ in an inductive way, by defining an extension function $\theta_{Y,Y'}^{n^- \to n} : \mathcal{PF}_{Y'} \to \mathcal{PF}_{Y'}$ for all transitions $n^- \to n$. For $\sigma \in \mathcal{PF}_{Y'}$ and a transition $n^- \to n$, we define the profile $\theta_{Y,Y'}^{n^- \to n}(\sigma)$ as follows:

- Form the system $\Psi = \psi_\sigma \wedge \psi_{n^- \to n} \wedge \psi_n$ over $X = \{x_p \mid p \in \mathcal{P}\} \cup \{x_e \mid e \in E_n\}$ (x_p represents the date of process p in σ, E_n the events of T^n), where:
  - ψ_σ consists of $x_p - x_q \leq \sigma[p, q]$ for every $p, q \in \mathcal{P}$, such that $\sigma[p, q] \neq \infty$.
  - $\psi_{n^- \to n}$ contains, for each p with $\Delta_p(n^- \to n) = [L, U]$, two inequalities $x_p - x_{f_p} \leq -L$ and $x_{f_p} - x_p \leq U$, where f_p is the first event of n on p. For each p with $\Delta_p(n^- \to n) = [L, \infty)$, $\psi_{n^- \to n}$ contains $x_p - x_{f_p} \leq -L$.
  - ψ_n is $\Phi_{Y,Y'}(n)$, the system associated with the singleton path n.
- Perform Fourier-Motzkin elimination on Ψ to remove all variables but $\{x_{\hat{e}_p}\}_{p \in \mathcal{P}}$ where $\hat{e}_p$ is the last event of $\rho \cdot n$ on p. Denote by Π the resulting system (after simplification) of inequalities over $\{x_{\hat{e}_p} \mid p \in \mathcal{P}\}$. Set $\theta_{Y,Y'}^{n^- \to n}(\sigma) = PF(\Pi)$. If at any stage of Fourier-Motzkin elimination, the system is not satisfiable, then set $\theta_{Y,Y'}^{n^- \to n}(\sigma)$ to be the un-satisfiable profile $\perp \in \mathcal{PF}_{Y'}$.

Lemma 1. *For a path ρ ending in n^- and a transition $n^- \to n$, we have that $PF_{Y,Y'}(\rho \cdot n)$ and $\theta_{Y,Y'}^{n^- \to n}(PF_{Y,Y'}(\rho))$ have the same set of solutions.*

Construction of a Symbolic Automaton. We now construct a symbolic automaton $\mathcal{A}(H)$ accepting the final (Y, Y')-drift-bounded paths of H.

Proposition 5. *Let H be a full TC-MSC graph with $|H|$ nodes. Then there exists an automaton $\mathcal{A}(H)$ with at most $|H| \times (2 \cdot Y' + 1)^{|\mathcal{P}|^2}$ states, such that $\mathcal{L}(\mathcal{A}(H)) \neq \emptyset$ iff H has a (consistent) final (Y, Y')-drift-bounded path.*

Proof (sketch). The states of $\mathcal{A}(H)$ are pairs (n, σ), with n a state of H and $\sigma \in \mathcal{PF}_{Y'}$. The initial state is $(n_{in}, PF_{Y,Y'}(n_{in}))$. A state (n, σ) is final if n is final, and σ is satisfiable. There is a transition labeled by n' from (n, σ) to (n', σ') iff both σ, σ' are satisfiable, there is a transition from n to n', and $\sigma' = \theta_{Y,Y'}^{n \to n'}(\sigma)$. The proof now follows from Lemma 1 and Proposition 4. □

The proof of Theorem 1 follows from this: as every path of $\widehat{G}$ is $(K, \widehat{K})$-drift-bounded, taking $H = \widehat{G}, Y = K, Y' = \widehat{K}$ implies $\mathcal{L}(\mathcal{A}(\widehat{G})) \neq \emptyset$ iff $\mathcal{L}(\widehat{G}) \neq \emptyset$ (iff $\mathcal{L}(G) \neq \emptyset$ by Corollary 1). Now, checking that $\mathcal{L}(\mathcal{A}(\widehat{G})) \neq \emptyset$ is decidable in space logarithmic in $|G|, K$ and polynomial in $|\mathcal{P}|$.

Compared with [3], which builds an automaton accepting every timed linearizations of a regular TC-MSC graph, we end up with a much smaller automaton in the worst case (exponential in $|\mathcal{P}|^2$ instead of exponential in $|G|$ for [3]). Further, being symbolic, we believe that the worst case is seldom reached, contrary to constructions based on zones of timed automata [3,1,2,18]. Indeed, consider a path ρ made of one node, labeled by a TC-MSC with one event e_p for every $p \in \mathcal{P}$, and without constraints, hence allowing events to occur at any date. Without symbolic encoding, this path would give rise to $|2K|^{|\mathcal{P}|}$ configurations of the form $(x_p)_{p \in \mathcal{P}}$, with $x_p \in \{0, (0,1), 1, \cdots, K\}$ the clock associated with e_p. Our solution only memorizes the unique symbolic profile $PF_{K,\widehat{K}}(\rho)$ such that $\forall p, q \in \mathcal{P}, PF_{K,\widehat{K}}(\rho)[p, q] = \widehat{K}$, meaning that $-\widehat{K} \leq x_p - x_q \leq \widehat{K}$ for all p, q.

5   Checking K-Drift-Boundedness of TC-MSC Graphs

The construction of automaton $\mathcal{A}(\widehat{G})$ in Section 4 allows to decide the emptiness of $\mathcal{L}(\widehat{G})$ (and hence of $\mathcal{L}(G)$), under the hypothesis that G is K-drift-bounded. We show here that given K, one can decide whether G is K-drift-bounded. We use Proposition 2 to create a full TC-MSC graph $\widehat{G}$. The main idea is that if $\widehat{G}$ is not $(K, \widehat{K})$-drift-bounded, then there must be a path of "minimal" length which is consistent but not $(K, \widehat{K})$-drift-bounded. The idea is then to look for such a *minimal witness*. We call a path $\rho \cdot n$ of $\widehat{G}$ a *minimal witness* iff:

1. The path ρ is $(K, \widehat{K})$-drift-bounded, and
2. The path $\rho \cdot n$ is not $(K, \widehat{K})$-drift-bounded, and
3. The path $\rho \cdot n$ is consistent.

Remark 1. G is not K-drift-bounded iff $\widehat{G}$ is not $(K, \widehat{K})$-drift-bounded iff there exists a minimal witness in $\widehat{G}$.

Now we build a finite automaton recognizing exactly the set of minimal witnesses of $\widehat{G}$ which from the remark above immediately proves Theorem 2. Requirements 1. and 2. are easy to check with the automaton built in the previous section. Requirement 3. is harder to check on its own as there is no effectively constructible finite state automaton accepting all consistent paths, (since it is undecidable to know whether there exists a consistent final path [11]). However, we will prove that thanks to requirement 1., requirement 3. can be replaced by: the path $\rho \cdot n$ is consistent and K_2-drift-bounded, for some contant K_2 depending on G and $\widehat{K}$. Notice that fixing $K_2 = \widehat{K}$ may not be enough.

The bound K_2 is chosen as follows. For a node n in $\widehat{G}$, set D_n to be the sum of lower bounds of $\delta(e, f)$, for every pair (e, f) with $e \lessdot f$. For a transition (n, n') in $\widehat{G}$, set $D_{(n,n')}$ to be the sum of the lower bounds of $\Delta_p(n, n')$ for p ranging over $\mathcal{P}$. Set $D(\widehat{G})$ to be the maximum of $D_{(n,n')} + D_{n'}$ where (n, n') ranges over transitions of $\widehat{G}$. Finally, we let $K_2 = (|\mathcal{P}|/2 + 1) \cdot \widehat{K} + D(\widehat{G})$.

Proposition 6. *Let $\rho \cdot n$ be a path of $\widehat{G}$ such that ρ is $(K, \widehat{K})$-drift-bounded. Then $\rho \cdot n$ is consistent iff $\Phi_{K_2,K_2}(\rho \cdot n)$ is satisfiable.*

The technical proof uses the characterisation of consistent systems of equations given by Shostak lemma [17], which we explain now.

Recall that consistency of a path ρ in $\widehat{G}$ is equivalent to satisfiability of the associated system of inequalities $PF(\rho)$. Let φ be a (simplified) system of inequalities. A *cycle* in φ is a sequence $x_1 \ldots x_m$ such that for all $i \in \{1, \ldots, m-1\}$, $x_{i+1} - x_i \leq a_i$ appears in ϕ for some a_i, and $x_m = x_1$. The *weight* of this cycle is $\sum_{i \in \{1,\ldots,m-1\}} a_i$. A cycle is simple if all variables, except the first and last one, are pairwise distinct. According to Shostak lemma [17], *a system of inequalities φ has a solution iff every cycle in φ has non-negative weight iff every simple cycle in φ has non-negative weight.* Detection of cycles of negative weight can be efficiently performed with the Bellman-Ford algorithm.

Proof (of Prop. 6.). We will consider three systems of inequalities.

1. The first one is $\phi_1 = \Phi(\rho \cdot n)$.
2. The second one is $\phi_2 = \Phi_{K_2,K_2}(\rho \cdot n)$. By definition, ϕ_2 is obtained from ϕ_1 by adding inequalities $x_e - x_f \leq K_2$ for all e, f from the same node of $\rho \cdot n$.
3. Finally, $\phi_3 = \Phi_{K,\widehat{K}}(\rho)$. Since $K \leq \widehat{K} \leq K_2$, ϕ_3 can be obtained from ϕ_2 by deleting the events from n, and adding inequalities $x_e - x_f \leq K$ for all concrete e, f from the same node of ρ, and adding inequalities $x_e - x_f \leq \widehat{K}$ for all events e, f from the same node of ρ s.t. e or f or both are dummy.

We know that $\rho \cdot n$ is consistent iff ϕ_1 is satisfiable. Hence, we just need to prove that ϕ_2 has a solution iff ϕ_1 has a solution to yield the statement of the proposition. Clearly, if ϕ_2 has a solution, then this solution is also a solution for ϕ_1. Conversely, assume that ϕ_1 has a solution. By Shostak lemma, it implies that every cycle in ϕ_1 has weight at least 0. Now to prove that ϕ_2 has a solution, it suffices to show that every simple cycle of ϕ_2 has weight at least 0. Let $x_1 \ldots x_m$ be a simple cycle in ϕ_2. That is, for all $i \in \{1, \ldots, m-1\}$, $x_{i+1} - x_i \leq b_i$ appears in ϕ_2 for some b_i, and $x_m = x_1$. We want to prove that $\sum_i b_i \geq 0$.

Let a_i be the associated coefficients in ϕ_1, i.e such that there is an inequality in ϕ_1 of the form, $x_{i+1} - x_i \leq a_i$ (if a_i does not exist, fix $a_i = +\infty$). Let c_i be the associated coefficients of ϕ_3 (we fix $c_i = -\infty$ if it corresponds to events in n, i.e., events not represented in ϕ_3).

Observe that $c_i \leq b_i \leq a_i$ by definition of ϕ_1, ϕ_2, ϕ_3. Now, if $a_i = b_i$ for all i, then the cycle $x_1 \ldots x_m$ in ϕ_2 is also a cycle in ϕ_1 and $\sum_i b_i = \sum_i a_i$. As every cycle in ϕ_1 has weight at least 0, we are done. Else, we have $a_j \neq b_j$ for some j. Let $J \neq \emptyset$ be the set of indices j such that $a_j \neq b_j$. Hence $|J| \geq 1$. Further, e_j, e_{j+1} are in the same node m of $\rho \cdot n$ for all $j \in J$, because ϕ_2 only adds constraints on pairs of events of the *same node*. Last, $b_j = K_2$ for all $j \in J$, as the only additional constraints in ϕ_2 w.r.t. ϕ_1 are of the form $x_e - x_f \leq K_2$.

Now, we partition the indices $\{1, \ldots, m\} = I_\rho \cup I_n \cup J_\rho \cup J_n$ where,

$J_\rho = \{j \mid b_j = K_2$ and both x_j and x_{j+1} belong to $\rho\}$,

$J_n = \{j \mid b_j = K_2$ and at least one of x_j or x_{j+1} belongs to $n\}$.

$I_n = \{j \mid b_j \neq K_2$ and at least one of x_j or x_{j+1} belongs to $n\}$, and

$I_\rho = \{j \mid b_j \neq K_2$ and both x_j and x_{j+1} belong to $\rho\}$.

With this $\sum_i b_i = \sum_{i \in I_n} b_i + \sum_{i \in J_n} b_i + \sum_{i \in I_\rho} b_i + \sum_{i \in J_\rho} b_i$. Now, observing that $J = J_\rho \cup J_n$, we have $\sum_{i \in (J_n \cup J_\rho)} b_i = K_2 \cdot (|J_\rho| + |J_n|) = K_2 \cdot |J| \geq K_2 \cdot 1$.

Further, we also have $\sum_{i \in I_n} b_i \geq -D(\widehat{G})$ by definition of $D(\widehat{G})$ and because the cycle is simple. Now, we bound the sum $\sum_{i \in I_\rho} b_i$ (the remaining weights) using ϕ_3. Indeed, since each $i \in I_\rho$ is an index such that x_i and x_{i+1} are events of ρ, we have $b_i \geq c_i$ where c_i is the coefficient of ϕ_3. And therefore it suffices to bound $\left(\sum_{i \in I_\rho} c_i\right)$. It immediately yields the bound for $\sum_i b_i$.

For this, the set I_ρ is first partitioned into *pieces*. Each *piece* $I' \subseteq I_\rho$ is made of "consecutive" indices, i.e., either $I' = \{i, i+1 \ldots, j\}$ or $I' = \{i, \ldots, m, 1, \ldots, j\}$, such that $(e_{i-1} \in n$ or $b_i = K_2)$ and $(e_{j+1} \in n$ or $b_j = K_2)$. There are at most $|J_\rho| + |\mathcal{P}|/2$ pieces (because the cycle is simple). Each piece begins and ends either with the last event on some process of the node before n or with an event e_i or e_{i+1} such that $b_i = K_2$.

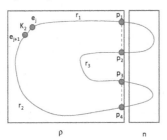

For instance, the picture above depicts a cycle (in ϕ_2) with 3 pieces r_1, r_2, r_3, involving 4 processes. r_1 begins with the last event on some process p_1 of ρ and ends with an event e_j such that $b_j = K_2$. r_2 begins with e_{j+1} and ends with the last event on some process p_4 of ρ. r_3 begins and ends with the last events on some processes p_2, p_3 of ρ.

As ρ is $(K, \widehat{K})$-drift-bounded and consistent, we know that ϕ_3 has a solution, that is every cycle in ϕ_3 has weight at least 0 by Shostak lemma. Let $I_1, \cdots, I_r$ be the pieces of I_ρ. Recall that $r \leq |J_\rho| + |\mathcal{P}|/2$. For all $i \leq r$, denoting $I_i = \{s, \ldots, t\}$, we rename $e_s \cdots e_t$ into $y_1^i \cdots y_{m^i}^i$. We now build a cycle of ϕ_3 using every piece, and with some additional edges connecting these pieces. More precisely, we define $\xi = y_1^1 \cdots y_{m^1}^1 \cdots y_1^r \cdots y_{m^r}^r y_1^1$, made by gluing all the pieces together. Comparing the weight of ξ with $\sum_{i \in I_\rho} c_i$, there is an additional weight d_i in ξ with $y_1^{i+1} - y_{m^i}^i \leq d_i$, for each i. We have that both $y_{m^i}^i$ and y_1^{i+1} are in the same node (either the last node before n, or some node where there were a K_2 edge). In ϕ_3, there is an edge between any two events of the same node, hence this connecting edge $y_1^{s+1} - y_{m^s}^s \leq c_s$ exists (that is ξ is a cycle), and $c_s \leq \widehat{K}$, by definition of ϕ_3. By Shostak lemma, the weight w of ξ in ϕ_3 is at least 0. We thus have $(\sum_{i \in I_\rho} c_i) + (|\mathcal{P}|/2 + |J_\rho|) \cdot \widehat{K} \geq w \geq 0$. We then have $\sum_{i \in I_\rho} b_i \geq \sum_{i \in I_\rho} c_i \geq -(|\mathcal{P}|/2 + |J_\rho|) \cdot \widehat{K}$. Thus, we get $\sum_i b_i \geq K_2 \cdot (|J_\rho| + |J_n|) - (|\mathcal{P}|/2 + |J_\rho|) \cdot \widehat{K} - D(\widehat{G}) = K_2 + (|J_\rho| + |J_n| - 1) \cdot K_2 - (D(\widehat{G}) + |\mathcal{P}|/2K) - |J_\rho|) \cdot \widehat{K} = \widehat{K} + (|J_\rho| + |J_n| - 1) \cdot K_2 - |J_\rho| \cdot \widehat{K} = (|J_\rho| + |J_n| - 1) \cdot K_2 - (|J_\rho| - 1) \cdot \widehat{K} \geq 0$, as $|J_\rho| - 1 \leq |J_\rho| + |J_n| - 1$, $0 \leq |J_\rho| + |J_n| - 1$ and $\widehat{K} \leq K_2$. □

We can now build an automaton accepting minimal witness paths of $\widehat{G}$.

An Automaton for Minimal Witnesses. We search for a minimal witness path $\rho \cdot n = n_0 \cdots n_\ell \cdot n$ in $\widehat{G}$ using an automaton $\mathcal{B}(\widehat{G})$. The first component of a state of $\mathcal{B}(\widehat{G})$ keeps track of the current node n. The second component will test for $(K, \widehat{K})$-drift-boundedness, which needs to hold for ρ but not for $\rho \cdot n$. This is done by keeping track of a $\widehat{K}$-bounded profile. The last component keeps track of $PF_{K_2,K_2}(\rho)$ which is sufficient to check consistency of ρ according to Proposition 6. Theorem 2 is obtained using the following proposition (where $|\widehat{G}|$ is the number of nodes of $\widehat{G}$):

Proposition 7. *Let G be a TC-MSC graph. Then there exists an automaton $\mathcal{B}(\widehat{G})$ such that $\mathcal{L}(\mathcal{B}(\widehat{G})) = \emptyset$ iff $\widehat{G}$ is $(K, \widehat{K})$-drift-bounded. Further, $\mathcal{B}(\widehat{G})$ has at most $|\widehat{G}| \times (2\widehat{K}+1)^{|\mathcal{P}|^2} \times (2K_2+1)^{|\mathcal{P}|^2}$ states, where $K_2 = (|\mathcal{P}|/2+1) \cdot \widehat{K} + D(\widehat{G})$.*

Proof (Sketch). The states of $\mathcal{B}(\widehat{G})$ are triples (n, σ, τ), with n a node of $\widehat{G}$, σ a $\widehat{K}$-bounded profile of $\widehat{G}$, and τ a K_2-bounded profile of $\widehat{G}$. The initial state of $\mathcal{B}(\widehat{G})$ is $(n_{in}, PF_{K,\widehat{K}}(n_{in}), PF_{K_2,K_2}(n_{in}))$. A state (n, σ, τ) of $\mathcal{B}(\widehat{G})$ is final if σ is not satisfiable, but τ is. Last, there is a transition labeled by n' from (n, σ, τ) to (n', σ', τ') iff $\widehat{G}$ contains a transition $n \to n'$, $\sigma' = \theta_{K,\widehat{K}}^{n \to n'}(\sigma)$, $\tau' = \theta_{K_2,K_2}^{n \to n'}(\tau)$, and *both σ and τ' are satisfiable*. Notice that τ is satisfiable when σ is, as $K_2 \geq \widehat{K} \geq K$, and that σ' is not required to be satisfiable. □

6   Conclusion

This paper has addressed the emptiness problem for TC-MSC graphs. We have shown that emptiness can be checked under the restriction that a TC-MSC graph is K-drift-bounded, for some K, and we established the decidability of checking this restriction. The decision procedure does not consider linearizations of TC-MSC graphs, nor rely on the seminal result of [4]. Instead, a finite automaton keeps track of a system of inequalities describing symbolically constraints over dates on each process. As future work, we plan to consider checking whether a TC-MSC graph is drift-bounded (without the bound K), and if so computing the bound. It seems that tackling this problem needs new ideas and concepts.

References

1. Akshay, S., Genest, B., Hélouët, L., Yang, S.: Regular set of representatives for time-constrained MSC graphs. Inf. Proc. Letters 112(14-15), 592–598 (2012)
2. Akshay, S., Mukund, M., Kumar, K.N.: Checking Coverage for Infinite Collections of Timed Scenarios. In: Caires, L., Vasconcelos, V.T. (eds.) CONCUR 2007. LNCS, vol. 4703, pp. 181–196. Springer, Heidelberg (2007)
3. Akshay, S., Gastin, P., Kumar, N.K., Mukund, M.: Model Checking Time-Constrained Scenario-based Specifications. In: Arvind, V., Prasad, S. (eds.) FSTTCS 2007. LNCS, vol. 4855, pp. 290–302. Springer, Heidelberg (2007)
4. Alur, R., Dill, D.L.: A theory of timed automata. Theoretical Comp. Sci. 126(2), 183–235 (1994)
5. Alur, R., Yannakakis, M.: Model Checking of Message Sequence Charts. In: Baeten, J.C.M., Mauw, S. (eds.) CONCUR 1999. LNCS, vol. 1664, pp. 114–129. Springer, Heidelberg (1999)
6. Bengtsson, J.E., Yi, W.: On Clock Difference Constraints and Termination in Reachability Analysis of Timed Automata. In: Dong, J.S., Woodcock, J. (eds.) ICFEM 2003. LNCS, vol. 2885, pp. 491–503. Springer, Heidelberg (2003)
7. Bouyer, P., Haddad, S., Reynier, P.-A.: Timed Unfoldings for Networks of Timed Automata. In: Graf, S., Zhang, W. (eds.) ATVA 2006. LNCS, vol. 4218, pp. 292–306. Springer, Heidelberg (2006)
8. Cassez, F., Chatain, T., Jard, C.: Symbolic Unfoldings for Networks of Timed Automata. In: Graf, S., Zhang, W. (eds.) ATVA 2006. LNCS, vol. 4218, pp. 307–321. Springer, Heidelberg (2006)
9. Dantzig, G., Eaves, B.C.: Fourier-Motzkin Elimination and Its Dual. J. Comb. Theory, Ser. A 14(3), 288–297 (1973)
10. Dima, C., Lanotte, R.: Distributed Time-Asynchronous Automata. In: Jones, C.B., Liu, Z., Woodcock, J. (eds.) ICTAC 2007. LNCS, vol. 4711, pp. 185–200. Springer, Heidelberg (2007)
11. Gastin, P., Kumar, K.N., Mukund, M.: Reachability and boundedness in time-constrained MSC graphs. In: Perspectives in Concurrency – A Festschrift for P. S. Thiagarajan. Universities Press, India (2009)
12. Henriksen, J.G., Mukund, M., Kumar, K.N., Sohoni, M., Thiagarajan, P.S.: A theory of regular MSC languages. Inf. and Comp. 202(1), 1–38 (2005)
13. ITU-TS Recommendation Z.120: Message Sequence Chart (MSC 1999) (1999)
14. Korte, B., Vygen, J.: Combinatorial Optimization: Theory and Algorithms, 3rd edn. Springer (2006)
15. Lugiez, D., Niebert, P., Zennou, S.: A partial order semantics approach to the clock explosion problem of timed automata. Theoretical Comp. Sci. 345(1), 27–59 (2005)
16. Muscholl, A., Peled, D.: Message Sequence Graphs and Decision Problems on Mazurkiewicz Traces. In: Kutyłowski, M., Wierzbicki, T., Pacholski, L. (eds.) MFCS 1999. LNCS, vol. 1672, pp. 81–91. Springer, Heidelberg (1999)
17. Shostak, R.: Deciding linear inequalities by computing loop residues. JACM 28(4), 769–779 (1981)
18. Zhao, J., Xu, H., Li, X., Zheng, T., Zheng, G.: Partial Order Path Technique for Checking Parallel Timed Automata. In: Damm, W., Olderog, E.-R. (eds.) FTRTFT 2002. LNCS, vol. 2469, pp. 417–432. Springer, Heidelberg (2002)

A Compositional Hierarchical Monitoring Automaton Construction for LTL

Deepak D'Souza and Raj Mohan Matteplackel

Department of Computer Science and Automation
Indian Institute of Science
Bangalore, India

Abstract. In this paper we give a compositional (or inductive) construction of monitoring automata for LTL formulas. Our construction is similar in spirit to the compositional construction of Kesten and Pnueli [5]. We introduce the notion of hierarchical Büchi automata and phrase our constructions in the framework of these automata. We give detailed constructions for all the principal LTL operators including past operators, along with proofs of correctness of the constructions.

1 Introduction

Linear-Time Temporal Logic (LTL) was proposed by Pnueli in [8] as a language for specifying temporal properties of program executions. It has since become a popular specification language with widespread use in practical verification.

In recent years, the most popular approach to solving the verification problem (or the so-called model-checking problem) for LTL is the automata-theoretic approach of Vardi and Wolper [9]. The central idea in this approach is the construction of a formula automaton $\mathcal{A}_\varphi$ for a given LTL formula φ, which is a Büchi automaton that accepts precisely the models of φ. Given a finite-state system model $\mathcal{T}$ and an LTL specification φ, one can check whether $\mathcal{T}$ satisfies φ (ie. whether all runs of $\mathcal{T}$ satisfy φ) by checking whether $\mathcal{T}$ and $\mathcal{A}_{\neg\varphi}$ have a joint accepting run. If they do have a joint accepting run, then we have a witness to the fact that $\mathcal{T}$ does not satisfy the formula, and if not we know that $\mathcal{T}$ does indeed satisfy the formula. This technique is implemented in popular explicit-state model-checking tools like Spin [4] as well as symbolic model-checking tools like Sal [2].

The Vardi-Wolper formula automaton construction is "monolithic" in that it directly (as against "compositionally") constructs an automaton for the given formula. While the transition relation of the automaton has a simple description, the set of valid atoms (which play the role of states) do not. In fact many techniques (for example [3]) focus on generating the set of valid next states efficiently. This can be an impediment to applying symbolic model checking. Further, the automaton can have a number of states that is exponential in the size of the given formula. Verifying systems with large state spaces and reasonable sized specifications in this "one-shot" technique is often a problem, with model-checking tools running out of memory.

A. Roychoudhury and M. D'Souza (Eds.): ICTAC 2012, LNCS 7521, pp. 16–29, 2012.

In the face of this problem, an interesting "compositional" alternative for both deductive and algorithmic verification for LTL (and more generally for CTL*) was proposed by Kesten and Pnueli in [5]. Here the task of verifying whether $\mathcal{T}$ satisfies a temporal logic φ is broken up into several sub-tasks of verifying sub-formulas of φ. The key step in this approach is a compositional construction of a "monitoring" automaton (or a "temporal tester" as termed in [5]) for a given LTL formula. A monitoring automaton for a formula φ is similar to a formula automaton for φ, except that it "monitors" the truth of φ at *all* points along an accepting run of the automaton on any candidate model for φ. The technique is compositional in that the monitoring automaton for a formula of the form $\psi U \eta$ is constructed purely from monitoring automata for ψ and η. The monitoring automaton is constructed as a composition of component automata, where the communication between component automata is through shared state variables, in a manner similar to modelling languages like Z [10] and Event-B[1]. The monitoring automaton so constructed is linear in the size of the given LTL formula, though of course the explicit Büchi automaton corresponding to it may have an exponential number of states. This linear-sized representation is also conducive for symbolic model-checking.

In this paper, our focus is on a compositional construction of a monitoring automaton for an LTL formula. We present such a construction which is similar in spirit to that of Kesten and Pnueli, though in the framework of Hierarchical Büchi Automata (HBA's) which we introduce for this purpose. HBA's are similar to synchronous products of Büchi automata, except that component automata can have "edge guards" which may disallow certain joint transitions in the product. Thus the communication in these automata is only through edge guards.

Our work differs from Kesten and Pnueli in several ways. Our constructions are more concise than those in [5]. In general our constructions can be seen to use an optimal number of states and transitions. We formalize the notion of "monitoring" in terms of universal and unambiguous Büchi automata, and explicitly show that our constructions conform to this restriction. Unlike [5], which do not address the issue of correctness of their constructions, our constructions are accompanied by detailed proofs of correctness.

Finally our framework of HBA's is useful in generalising the compositional construction to timed temporal logics like MITL [7]. Such a generalisation has been done earlier in [6] though in the setting of signals (rather than timed words, for which we find HBA's more convenient).

The rest of this paper is organised as follows. We begin with preliminary definitions in the next section, and then introduce hierarchical Büchi automata in Section 3. In Section 4 we define the notion of a monitoring automaton for LTL formulas, and go on to give our inductive constructions for monintoring automata in Section 5. In the following section we discuss the optimality of our construction. We finally close with a conclusion section.

2   Preliminaries

For a finite alphabet of symbols Σ, an *infinite* word over Σ is an infinite sequence of symbols from Σ. We denote the set of infinite words over Σ by Σ^ω and the empty word by ϵ. We use standard notations for regular expressions denoting languages over finite and infinite words. We use $\mathbb{N}$ for the set $\{0, 1, \ldots\}$ of natural numbers.

Let us fix an alphabet Σ for the rest of this paper. The syntax of an LTL formula over Σ is given by:

$$\varphi ::= \top \mid a \mid \neg\varphi \mid \ \varphi \mid \ \varphi \mid \varphi \vee \varphi \mid \varphi U \varphi \mid \varphi S \varphi,$$

where $a \in \Sigma$. The natural interpretation of LTL is over words in Σ^ω. Let $\sigma \in \Sigma^\omega$ be a word of the form $a_0 a_1 \cdots$. Let $i \in \mathbb{N}$. Then the satisfaction relation $\sigma, i \models \varphi$ is given by:

$$
\begin{aligned}
&\sigma, i \models \top \\
&\sigma, i \models a &&\text{iff}\quad a_i = a \\
&\sigma, i \models \neg\psi &&\text{iff}\quad \sigma, i \not\models \psi \\
&\sigma, i \models \psi \vee \eta &&\text{iff}\quad \sigma, i \models \psi \text{ or } \sigma, i \models \eta \\
&\sigma, i \models \ \psi &&\text{iff}\quad \sigma, i+1 \models \psi \\
&\sigma, i \models \ \psi &&\text{iff}\quad i > 0 \text{ and } \sigma, i-1 \models \psi \\
&\sigma, i \models \psi U \eta &&\text{iff}\quad \exists k \geq i : \sigma, k \models \eta, \text{ and } \forall j : i \leq j < k, \ \sigma, j \models \psi \\
&\sigma, i \models \psi S \eta &&\text{iff}\quad \exists k \leq i : \sigma, k \models \eta, \text{ and } \forall j : k < j \leq i, \ \sigma, j \models \psi.
\end{aligned}
$$

We say that a word σ satisfies the LTL formula φ, written $\sigma \models \varphi$, if and only if $\sigma, 0 \models \varphi$, and set $L(\varphi) = \{\sigma \in \Sigma^\omega \mid \sigma \models \varphi\}$.

A *Buchi automaton* $\mathcal{B}$ is structure of the form (Q, Σ, S, E, F) where Q is a finite set of states, Σ is an alphabet, $S \subseteq Q$ is the set of initial states, $E \subseteq Q \times \Sigma \times Q$ is the set of transitions (or edges), and $F \subseteq Q$ is the set of final states.

Let $\sigma = a_0 a_1 \cdots$ be an infinite word over Σ. Then a *run* of $\mathcal{B}$ over σ is a map $\rho : \mathbb{N} \to Q$ satisfying the following conditions:

1. $q_0 \in S$.
2. For each i, $(\rho(i), a_i, \rho(i+1)) \in E$.

We call the run ρ *accepting* if $\rho(i) \in F$ for infinitely many i. In other words an accepting run visits a set of final states infinitely often. We say a word σ is accepted by $\mathcal{B}$ if $\mathcal{B}$ has an accepting run over σ. We define the language accepted by $\mathcal{B}$, denoted $L(\mathcal{B})$, to be the set of all words which are accepted by $\mathcal{B}$. We say $\mathcal{B}$ is *universal* if $L(\mathcal{B}) = \Sigma^\omega$ and *unambiguous* if $\mathcal{B}$ has at most one *accepting* run over each in Σ^ω.

It will be convenient to use a variant of Buchi automata in which the edges are marked initial and final. We call these *edge Buchi automata*. Formally, an *edge Buchi automaton* $\mathcal{B}$ is a structure of the form (Q, Σ, S, E, F) where Q is a finite set of states, Σ is an alphabet, $S \subseteq E$ is the set of *initial edges*, $E \subseteq Q \times \Sigma \times Q$ is the edge set, and $F \subseteq E$ is the set of *final edges*.

Let $\sigma = a_0 a_1 \cdots$ be an infinite word over Σ. Then a run of $\mathcal{B}$ over σ is a sequence of edges $\rho : \mathbb{N} \to E$ satisfying the following properties:

1. $\rho(0) \in S$.
2. There exist states $q_0 q_1 \cdots$ such that for each i, $\rho(i) = (q_i, a_i, q_{i+1})$.

We call the run ρ *accepting* if $\rho(i) \in F$ for infinitely many i. In other words an accepting run visits a set of final edges infinitely often.

Fig. 1 shows an example edge Buchi automaton $\mathcal{B}$ with two states. In the figure and the others that follow we adopt the following conventions. We write the action labels of the edges after the name label. Absence of an action label indicate that the edges can be taken on any action in Σ. The initial edges will be given as bold edges and the non-initial edges will be given as non-bold edges. For the final edges we use normal edges (non-dashed) and for the non-final edges we use dashed edges. The automaton has two initial edges labelled f_1 and f_4 and two final edges labelled f_1 and f_3. The edges f_1 and f_4 are enabled when the action a occurs and f_3 enabled when a b occurs. The edge f_2 is enabled on every action in Σ. The automaton accepts the language $(a^+(a+b)^*b)^\omega$.

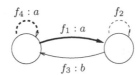

Fig. 1. An example edge Buchi automaton $\mathcal{B}$ accepting the language $(a^+(a+b)^*b)^\omega$. Bold face indicates initial edges, and full (as against dashed) edges indicate final edges.

It is not difficult to see that for a Buchi automaton one can construct a language-equivalent edge Buchi automaton and vice-versa. So these classes of automata are expressively equivalent.

3   Hierarchical Buchi Automata

We now introduce the notion of hierarchical Buchi automata which we will use in our constructions for LTL. Let $L = [\mathcal{B}_n, \ldots, \mathcal{B}_1]$ be a list of edge Buchi automata, where $\mathcal{B}_i = (Q_i, \Sigma, E_i, S_i, F_i)$ for each i. Then we define the syntax of an *edge guard* w.r.t. L as follows:

$$g ::= \top \mid \mathcal{B}_i.e \mid \neg g \mid g \vee g \mid g \wedge g,$$

where $e \in E_i$. We denote the set of all edge guards w.r.t. L by $\mathcal{E}(L)$.

The semantics of an edge guard is defined as follows: an edge guard is evaluated over a joint transition of $\mathcal{B}_n, \ldots, \mathcal{B}_1$. Let $(e_n, \ldots, e_1)$, where $e_i \in E_i$, be a joint transition of $\mathcal{B}_n, \ldots, \mathcal{B}_1$ and let $g \in \mathcal{E}(L)$. Then we define the satisfaction relation, $(e_n, \ldots, e_1) \models g$, inductively as follows:

- $(e_n, \ldots, e_1) \models \top$.
- $(e_n, \ldots, e_1) \models \mathcal{B}_i.e$ iff $e_i = e$.
- Boolean combinations are handled in the expected manner.

A *hierarchical Buchi automaton* (or HBA) over Σ is a structure of the form $[\mathcal{C}_n, \ldots, \mathcal{C}_1]$ where each $\mathcal{C}_i$ is of the form $(\mathcal{B}_i, G_i)$ with $\mathcal{B}_i = (Q_i, \Sigma, S_i, E_i, F_i)$ an edge Buchi automaton and $G_i : E_i \rightarrow \mathcal{E}([\mathcal{B}_i, \ldots, \mathcal{B}_1])$ a labelling of edges of $\mathcal{B}_i$ with "level i" edge guards.

Let $\sigma \in \Sigma^\omega$. Then a run of $\mathcal{H}$ over σ is a joint run of $\mathcal{B}_n, \ldots, \mathcal{B}_1$ except that at each position the edge guards have to be satisfied. Formally, a run ρ of $\mathcal{H}$ over σ is a tuple $(\rho_n, \ldots, \rho_1)$ satisfying the following two conditions:

1. Each ρ_i is a run of $\mathcal{B}_i$ on σ.
2. For all $j \in \mathbb{N}$, $(\rho_n(j), \ldots, \rho_1(j)) \models \bigwedge_{i=1}^{n} G_i(\rho_i(j))$.

For a run $\rho = (\rho_n, \ldots, \rho_1)$ over $\mathcal{H}$ and a point $i \in \mathbb{N}$ we henceforth use $\rho(i)$ to mean the tuple $(\rho_n(i), \ldots, \rho_1(i))$.

The run ρ of $\mathcal{H}$ on σ is called *accepting* if each ρ_i is an accepting run of $\mathcal{B}_i$ on σ. A word σ is accepted by $\mathcal{H}$ if $\mathcal{H}$ has an accepting run over it. We define $L(\mathcal{H})$, the language accepted by $\mathcal{H}$, to be the set of all words which are accepted by $\mathcal{H}$. We say $\mathcal{H}$ is *universal* if $L(\mathcal{H}) = \Sigma^\omega$ and *unambiguous* if $\mathcal{H}$ has at most one accepting run for every word in Σ^ω.

Example 1. Fig. 2 shows the HBA $\mathcal{H}_1 = [\mathcal{C}_2, \mathcal{C}_1]$ over the alphabet $\{a, b\}$. It accepts the language, $L(\mathcal{H}_1) = \{b^i a^\omega \mid i \in \mathbb{N}\}$. In the figure the guards $\mathcal{C}_1.e_1$ and $\mathcal{C}_1.e_2$ of the automaton $\mathcal{C}_2$ refer to the edges e_1 and e_2 in the automaton $\mathcal{C}_1$. By convention we write the edge guards after the action labels of the edges, if any.

We now show that the class of ω-languages accepted by edge Buchi automata and HBA coincide. Clearly every edge Buchi automaton is an HBA. To see

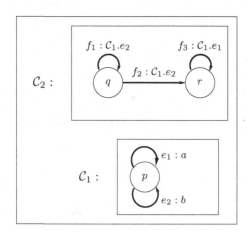

Fig. 2. HBA $\mathcal{H}_1$

that every HBA-definable language is Buchi-definable too, let $\mathcal{H}$ be an HBA as defined above. Then we define an edge Buchi automaton $\mathcal{B}_\mathcal{H}$ as follows: $\mathcal{B}_\mathcal{H}$ is essentially the product of $\mathcal{B}_n \ldots, \mathcal{B}_1$ except that some edges in the product are disallowed based on the edge guards present on the edges of these automata.

- $Q = Q_1 \times \cdots \times Q_n \times \{0, \ldots, n\}$.
- $S = S_1 \times \cdots \times S_n$.
- $E \subseteq Q \times \Sigma \times Q$ is the set of edges defined as follows: for each $a \in \Sigma$, an edge $((p_n, \ldots, p_1, l), a, (q_n, \ldots, q_1, m)) \in E$ iff for all $i \in \{1, \ldots, n\}$ there exists an $e_i \in E_i$ of the form (p_i, a, g_i, q_i) such that the following conditions are satisfied:
  - $(e_n, \ldots, e_1) \models \bigwedge_{i=1}^{n} G_i(e_i)$.
  - $m = \begin{cases} (i+1) \bmod (n) & \text{if } i \geq 1 \text{ and } e_i \in F_i. \\ 1 & \text{if } i = 0. \\ i & \text{otherwise.} \end{cases}$
- $F = \{((p_n, \ldots, p_1, 0), a, (q_n, \ldots, q_1, 1)) \in E \mid a \in \Sigma\}$ is the set of final edges.

It is not difficult to see that $L(\mathcal{B}_\mathcal{H}) = L(\mathcal{H})$.

Example 2. Fig. 3 shows the language equivalent edge Buchi automaton $\mathcal{B}_{\mathcal{H}_1}$ corresponding to the HBA $\mathcal{H}_1$ of Example. 1.

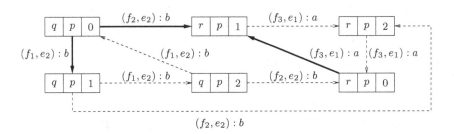

Fig. 3. Language-equivalent Buchi automaton $\mathcal{B}_{H_1}$ of the HBA $\mathcal{H}_1$

4   Monitoring HBA for LTL

In this section we define the notion of a monitoring HBA for an LTL formula.

Let $\mathcal{H} = [C_n, \ldots, C_1]$, where each C_i is of the form $(\mathcal{B}_i, G_i)$, be an HBA. Then by an *edge guard* over $\mathcal{H}$ we will mean an edge guard over the list of automata $\mathcal{B}_n, \ldots, \mathcal{B}_1$.

Definition 1. *Let φ be an LTL formula over Σ. Let $\mathcal{H}$ be an HBA over Σ and let g be an edge guard over $\mathcal{H}$. Then $(\mathcal{H}, g)$ is called a monitoring HBA for φ iff for every word $\sigma \in \Sigma^\omega$ the following conditions are satisfied.*

- *There exists a unique accepting run of $\mathcal{H}$ over σ. We denote this run by ρ_σ.*

- *The edge guard g monitors the truth of the formula along ρ_σ in the sense that $\sigma, i \models \varphi \iff \rho_\sigma(i) \models g$. We call g the monitoring guard for φ.*

We note that such an HBA $\mathcal{H}$ is necessarily unambiguous and universal.

The notion of a monitoring automaton for a formula is useful in verification because one can easily build a formula automaton for the formula from it. To see this consider an LTL formula φ. Let $(\mathcal{H}, g)$ be a monitoring automaton for φ and let $\mathcal{B}_\mathcal{H}$ be the language-equivalent edge Buchi automaton constructed as mentioned above. Let $\mathcal{C}$ be the automaton $\mathcal{B}_\mathcal{H}$ with the following restriction on its initial edges: an edge $(e_n, \dots, e_1)$ of $\mathcal{C}$ is an initial edge if it is an initial edge in $\mathcal{B}_\mathcal{H}$ and $(e_n, \dots, e_1) \models g$. It is not difficult to see that $L(\mathcal{C}) = L(\varphi)$, and hence $\mathcal{C}$ is a required formula automaton for φ.

5 Monitoring Automaton Construction for LTL

We now give a constructive proof showing that for any LTL formula φ we can construct a monitoring HBA for φ. In the proof, for an HBA $\mathcal{H} = [\mathcal{C}, \mathcal{C}_n, \dots, \mathcal{C}_1]$ and a word $\sigma \in \Sigma^\omega$, if we are only interested in the run of $\mathcal{C}$ over σ then we use the compact notation (π, ρ) where π is a run of $\mathcal{C}$ over σ and ρ is a joint run of $\mathcal{C}_n, \dots, \mathcal{C}_1$ over σ. And we also use the notation $(\pi(i), \rho(i))$ to refer to the edge tuple at position i in the run. For a list of edge Buchi automata $\mathcal{H} = [\mathcal{C}_n, \dots, \mathcal{C}_1]$ and an edge Buchi automaton $\mathcal{C}$ we write $[\mathcal{C}, \mathcal{H}]$ to mean the list $[\mathcal{C}, \mathcal{C}_n, \dots, \mathcal{C}_1]$.

In the figures that follow, the transitions are assumed to be labelled by Σ unless otherwise mentioned. Also, for convenience we write "ψ" instead of a monitoring guard for ψ.

Theorem 1. *Given an LTL formula φ we can effectively construct a monitoring HBA $(\mathcal{H}_\varphi, g_\varphi)$ for φ.*

Proof. We prove this theorem by induction on the structure of φ.

Case: $\varphi = a$, $a \in \Sigma$. For this case the monitoring HBA is $([\mathcal{C}_a], \mathcal{C}_a.e_a)$ where $\mathcal{C}_a$ is as shown in Fig. 4.

$e_a : a$

$\Sigma - \{a\}$

Fig. 4. Automaton $\mathcal{C}_a$

Clearly the automaton $\mathcal{C}_a$ is deterministic and universal. Also, along the run of the automaton over a word σ, the guard e_a monitors the truth of the formula "a".

Case: $\varphi = \neg\psi$. By the induction hypothesis we have a monitoring HBA $(\mathcal{H}_\psi, g_\psi)$ for ψ. Then $(\mathcal{H}_\psi, \neg g_\psi)$ is a monitoring HBA for $\neg\psi$.

Case: $\varphi = \psi_1 \vee \psi_2$. Let $(\mathcal{H}_{\psi_1}, g_{\psi_1})$ and $(\mathcal{H}_{\psi_2}, g_{\psi_2})$ be the monitoring HBAs for ψ_1 and ψ_2 respectively. Then $([\mathcal{H}_{\psi_1}, \mathcal{H}_{\psi_2}], g_{\psi_1} \vee g_{\psi_2})$ is a monitoring HBA for φ.

Case: $\varphi = \bigcirc \psi$. By induction hypothesis we have a monitoring HBA $(\mathcal{H}_\psi, g_\psi)$ for ψ. Let $\mathcal{C}_{\bigcirc\psi}$ be the automaton shown in Fig. 5. Let $\mathcal{H}_{\bigcirc\psi} = [\mathcal{C}_{\bigcirc\psi}, \mathcal{H}_\psi]$ and $g_{\bigcirc\psi} = \mathcal{C}_{\bigcirc\psi}.(e_1 \vee e_2)$.

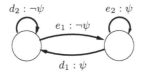

Fig. 5. Automaton $\mathcal{C}_{\bigcirc\psi}$

We prove that $(\mathcal{H}_{\bigcirc\psi}, g_{\bigcirc\psi})$ is indeed a monitoring HBA for $\bigcirc\psi$. Let $\sigma \in \Sigma^\omega$ and let ρ be the unique accepting run of $\mathcal{H}_\psi$ over σ. Let π be a sequence of edges of $\mathcal{C}_{\bigcirc\psi}$ given by

$$
\pi(i) = \begin{cases}
e_1 & \text{if } \sigma, i \models \neg\psi \wedge \bigcirc\psi \\
e_2 & \text{if } \sigma, i \models \psi \wedge \bigcirc\psi \\
d_1 & \text{if } \sigma, i \models \psi \wedge \neg\bigcirc\psi \\
d_2 & \text{if } \sigma, i \models \neg\psi \wedge \neg\bigcirc\psi.
\end{cases}
$$

We now show that the edges in the sequence π connect up to form a valid run of $\mathcal{C}_{\bigcirc\psi}$ over σ. For example, consider the case when $\pi(i) = e_1$. Since $\pi(i) = e_1$ it must be the case that $\sigma, i + 1 \models \psi$ and therefore $\pi(i + 1)$ should be either e_2 or d_1, both of which are valid successor edges of e_1. So the transition relation of $\mathcal{C}_{\bigcirc\psi}$ is respected by π at position i. Other cases can be handled similarly. Finally, since all the edges of $\mathcal{C}_{\bigcirc\psi}$ are initial π is a valid run of $\mathcal{C}_{\bigcirc\psi}$ and since all the edges final too π is an accepting run of the automaton.

We now prove that (π, ρ) is an accepting run of $\mathcal{H}_{\bigcirc\psi}$ over σ. For this we need to show that the edge guards along π are satisfied at each position i. Consider the case when $\pi(i) = e_1$ once again. Then by the construction of π it must be the case that $\sigma, i \models \neg\psi$. Since ρ is the accepting run of $\mathcal{H}_\psi$ over σ, by the definition of a monitoring automaton $\rho, i \models \neg g_\psi$ and therefore $(\pi(i), \rho(i)) \models \neg g_\psi$. So the edge guard $\neg\psi$ is satisfied at position i in the run (π, ρ). Other cases can be handled similarly and we conclude (π, ρ) is an accepting run of $\mathcal{H}_{\bigcirc\psi}$.

Now, it remains to prove that (π, ρ) is the *only* accepting run of $\mathcal{H}_{\bigcirc\psi}$ over σ. Consider any accepting run of $\mathcal{H}_{\bigcirc\psi}$ over σ. Then it must be the form (π', ρ). We argue that $\pi' = \pi$. Consider any position i, and suppose $\pi'(i) = e_1$. Since the edge guard on e_1 must be satisfied at $(\pi'(i), \rho(i))$ we have that $\rho(i) \models \neg g_\psi$ and $\rho(i + 1) \models g_\psi$, i.e. $\sigma, i \not\models \psi$ and $\sigma, i + 1 \models \psi$ By the construction of π, $\pi(i)$ should be e_1. Other cases can be handled similarly and we conclude $\pi' = \pi$.

Next we need to show that the guard g_φ monitors the truth of $\bigcirc\psi$ over (π, ρ). Consider any position i. Suppose $\sigma, i \models \bigcirc\psi$. Then:

$$\sigma, i \models \psi \iff \sigma, i+1 \models \psi$$
$$\iff \pi(i+1) = e_2 \text{ or } d_1$$
$$\iff \pi(i) = e_1 \text{ or } e_2.$$

Case: $\varphi = \psi_1 U \psi_2$. Let $(\mathcal{H}_{\psi_1}, g_{\psi_1})$ and $(\mathcal{H}_{\psi_2}, g_{\psi_2})$ be the monitoring HBA for ψ_1 and ψ_2 respectively (which exist by induction). Let $\mathcal{C}_U$ be the automaton shown in Fig. 6. Let $\mathcal{H}_\varphi = [\mathcal{C}_U, \mathcal{H}_{\psi_2}, \mathcal{H}_{\psi_1}]$ and $g_\varphi = \mathcal{C}_U(e_1 \vee e_2 \vee e_3)$.

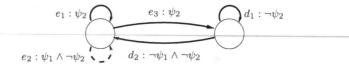

Fig. 6. Automaton $\mathcal{C}_U$

We first prove that for any word $\sigma \in \Sigma^\omega$, $\mathcal{C}_U$ has an accepting run over it. Towards that end let us define a sequence of edges π of $\mathcal{C}_U$ as follows: for all $i \geq 0$ we define:

$$\pi(i) = \begin{cases} e_1 & \text{if } \sigma, i \models \psi_2 \text{ and } \sigma, i+1 \models \psi_1 U \psi_2 \\ e_2 & \text{if } \sigma, i \models (\psi_1 \wedge \neg\psi_2) \wedge (\psi_1 U \psi_2) \\ e_3 & \text{if } \sigma, i \models \psi_2 \text{ and } \sigma, i+1 \not\models \psi_1 U \psi_2 \\ d_1 & \text{if } \sigma, i \models \neg\psi_2 \text{ and } \sigma, i+1 \not\models \psi_1 U \psi_2 \\ d_2 & \text{if } \sigma, i \models \neg\psi_1 \wedge \neg\psi_2 \text{ and } \sigma, i+1 \models \psi_1 U \psi_2. \end{cases}$$

We now prove that π is an accepting run of $\mathcal{C}_U$ over σ. Observe that as all the edges in $\mathcal{C}_U$ are initial the edge $\pi(0)$ is initial. Now to show that the consecution relation is respected by the run at every position consider a position i in π. Suppose, if $\pi(i) = e_2$ then by the condition associated with e_2 we have that $\sigma, i \models \psi_1 U \psi_2$. This implies either $\sigma, i+1 \models \psi_1 U \psi_2$ or $\sigma, i+1 \models \psi_2$. Clearly $\pi(i+1)$ cannot be d_2 because if it were then neither $\psi_1 U \psi_2$ nor ψ_2 is true in σ at $i+1$. If $\psi(i+1) = d_1$ then by construction we have that $\sigma, i+1 \models \neg\psi_2 \wedge \neg(\psi_1 U \psi_2)$. This contradictions the assumption that $\sigma, i+1 \models \psi_2 \vee (\psi_1 U \psi_2)$. Thus the edge at position $i+1$ in π must be e_1, e_2 or e_3 all of which are valid consecutions e_2. Other cases can be handled similarly and we conclude that π valid run of $\mathcal{C}_U$.

To see that π is an accepting run of $\mathcal{C}_U$ note the only non-final edge is e_3. So if $\pi(i) = e_2$ for some i then it must be the case that there exists a $j > i$ such that $\sigma, j \models \psi_2$ which by the construction implies that $\pi(j)$ should be either e_1 or e_3. Thus every e_2 edge is followed by an e_1 or an e_3 both of which are final in π and therefore π accepting. This completes the proof of the claim that π is an accepting run of $\mathcal{C}_U$ over σ.

We now construct an accepting run of $\mathcal{H}_\varphi$ on σ using π. By the induction hypothesis there exist unique accepting runs ρ_1 and ρ_2 of $\mathcal{H}_{\psi_1}$ and $\mathcal{H}_{\psi_2}$ respectively, along which g_{ψ_1} and g_{ψ_2} monitor the truth of the formula ψ_1 and ψ_2.

Consider the run (π, ρ), where ρ is the joint run ρ_1 and ρ_2. To show that (π, ρ) is an accepting run of $\mathcal{H}_\varphi$ on σ it is sufficient to show that the external guards of π are satisfied in (π, ρ). Again taking e_2 as an example, suppose $\pi(i) = e_2$. Then by the construction π, we know that ψ_1 and $\neg\psi_2$ are true at i in σ. Since g_{ψ_1} and g_{ψ_2} monitor ψ_1 and ψ_2 along ρ, it must be the case that $\rho, i \models g_{\psi_1} \wedge \neg g_{\psi_2}$. Hence the edge guard of e_2 is satisfied in ρ.

Next we show that (π, ρ) is the unique accepting run of $\mathcal{H}_\varphi$ over σ. Suppose it were not. Then there exists an accepting run π' of $\mathcal{C}_U$ such that (π', ρ) is an accepting run of $\mathcal{H}_U$. Let i be the first position such that $\pi(i) \neq \pi'(i)$. From the construction of $\mathcal{C}_U$ we observe that for any run the only plausible non-deterministic choices are between the edges e_1 and e_3, and between the edges d_1 and d_2. So let us assume that $\pi(i) = e_1$ and $\pi'(i) = e_3$. Then by the construction of π we have that $\sigma, i + 1 \models \psi_1 U \psi_2$. Since π' is an accepting run it must be the case that $\pi'(i + 1) = d_1$ or d_2. In either case we have that $\sigma, i + 1 \not\models \psi_1 U \psi_2$, a contradiction. Similarly we can handle the other cases and we conclude that (π, ρ) is the unique accepting run of $\mathcal{H}_U$ over σ.

To prove that g_φ monitors the formula $\psi_1 U \psi_2$, consider a position i. Suppose $\sigma, i \models \varphi$. Then either $\sigma, i \models \psi_2$ in which case $\pi(i)$ should be either e_1 or e_3. Otherwise $\sigma, i \models \psi_1 \wedge \neg\psi_2$ and therefore $\pi(i) = e_2$. For the proof in the converse direction, if $\pi(i)$ is e_1 or e_3 then $\sigma, i \models \psi_2$ and if $\pi(i)$ is e_2 then $\sigma, i \models \psi_1 U \psi_2$.

Case: $\varphi = \quad \psi$. Let $(\mathcal{H}_\psi, g_\psi)$ be a monitoring HBA for ψ. Let $\mathcal{C}_\psi$ be the automaton shown in Fig. 7 and let $\mathcal{H}_\psi = [\mathcal{C}_\psi, \mathcal{H}_\psi]$. It is not hard to see that if $\mathcal{H}_{\psi_1}$ is unambiguous and universal so is $\mathcal{H}_\psi$. It is also easy to verify that $\sigma, i \models \quad \psi \iff \rho(i) \models \mathcal{C}_\psi.(e_1 \vee e_2)$ where ρ is the unique accepting run of $\mathcal{H}_\psi$ over σ. Therefore $(\mathcal{H}_\psi, \mathcal{C}_\psi.(e_1 \vee e_2))$ is monitoring HBA for $\quad \psi$.

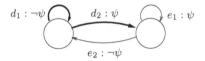

Fig. 7. Automaton $\mathcal{C}_\psi$

Case: $\varphi = \psi_1 S \psi_2$. Let $(\mathcal{H}_{\psi_1}, g_{\psi_1})$ and $(\mathcal{H}_{\psi_2}, g_{\psi_2})$ be monitoring HBA for ψ_1 and ψ_2 respectively. Let $\mathcal{C}_S$ be the automaton shown in Fig. 8 and let $\mathcal{H}_S = [\mathcal{C}_S, \mathcal{H}_{\psi_2}, \mathcal{H}_{\psi_1}]$. We observe that as both the HBA $\mathcal{H}_{\psi_1}$ and $\mathcal{H}_{\psi_2}$ are unambiguous and universal by induction, $\mathcal{H}_S$ also is unambiguous and universal. Once again, it is easy to verify that $\sigma, i \models \psi_1 S \psi_2 \iff \rho(i) \models \mathcal{C}_S.(e_1 \vee e_2)$ where ρ is the unique accepting run $\mathcal{H}_S$ on σ. Therefore $(\mathcal{H}_S, \mathcal{C}_S.(e_1 \vee e_2))$ is monitoring HBA for $\psi_1 S \psi_2$.

$\square$

Example 3. Fig. 9 shows an HBA $\mathcal{H}_U = [\mathcal{C}_U, \mathcal{C}_b, \mathcal{C}_b, \mathcal{C}_a]$ which along with the monitoring guard $\mathcal{C}_U.(e_1 \vee e_2 \vee e_3)$ monitors the LTL formula $aU(\quad b)$.

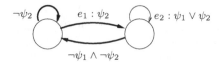

Fig. 8. Automaton $\mathcal{C}_S$

We note that size of our monitoring automaton is linear in the size of the given LTL formula. More precisely the number of states in the monitoring HBA is bounded by $2 \cdot len(\varphi)$ and number of edges is bounded by $5 \cdot len(\varphi)$. Though the size of the induced Büchi automaton may still be $2^{O(len(\varphi))}$ in the worst case (as in the Vardi-Wolper automaton), the HBA is a linear-sized representation that is conducive to symbolic model-checking techniques.

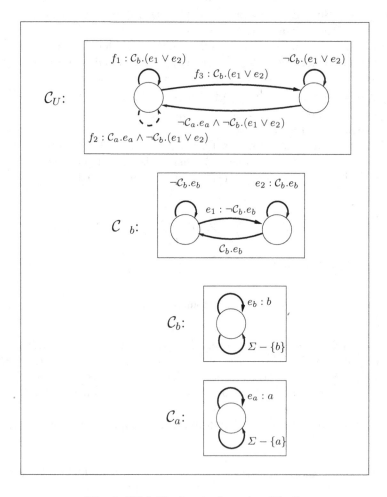

Fig. 9. HBA $\mathcal{H}_U$ for the formula $aU(\ b)$

6   Optimality of Our Constructions

We now prove that in general our constructions are optimal in terms of the number of states as well as edges used. To be precise, we prove that the component C_U of the monitoring automaton for a formula aUb, where $a, b \in \Sigma$, uses an optimal number of states and edges.

First let us argue that to monitor the formula aUb we require at least two states. Suppose there exists an automaton $\mathcal{A}$ with a single state such that $(\mathcal{A}, g)$ monitors aUb. Consider the accepting runs $\rho_1 = e_0 e_1 e_2 \cdots$ over the word $\sigma_1 = aaba^\omega$ and $\rho_2 = d_0 d_1 d_2 \cdots$ over $\sigma_2 = a^\omega$ of the automaton. Clearly $\sigma_1, 0 \models aUb$ and $\sigma_2, 0 \not\models aUb$. Since g monitors the truth of aUb we have that $\rho_1, 0 \models g$ and $\rho_2, 0 \not\models g$. This implies g in its most simplified form should be of the form $e_0 \vee g_1$, and should *not* be of the form $d_0 \vee g_2$, for some edge guards g_1 and g_2.

Let us now consider the run $\rho = e_0 d_1 d_2 \cdots$ of $\mathcal{A}$. It is not difficult that see that ρ is also an accepting run of $\mathcal{A}$ over σ_2. But this contradicts with the assumption that g monitors the formula as $\rho, 0 \models g$ and $\sigma_2, 0 \not\models aUb$.

In a similar way we can prove that in general our constructions for the remaining cases also use an optimal number of states.

To prove that any monitoring automaton for the formula aUb requires at least five edges let us assume, without loss of generality, that there exists an automaton $\mathcal{A}$ with four edges and a guard g over $\mathcal{A}$ such that $(\mathcal{A}, g)$ is a monitoring automaton for the formula. Let us first handle the case when, among the four edges, the formula is true when two of them say e_1 and e_2 are taken.

Now, consider an accepting run $\rho = f_0 f_1 \cdots$ of $\mathcal{A}$ over the word $\sigma = (ab)^\omega$. We first prove that there exists infinitely many i such that $f_i = e_1$ and infinitely many j such that $f_j = e_2$. Suppose that there exists a k such that for all $i \geq k$ $f_i = e_1$. Since ρ is accepting it must be the case that e_1 is final. Now consider the run $f_l f_{l+1} \ldots$ where $l > k$ and is even. It is not difficult to see that this is a valid accepting run of $\mathcal{A}$ over $(ab)^\omega$. But this implies that $\mathcal{A}$ has multiple accepting runs over σ, a contradiction to the assumption that $\mathcal{A}$ is unambiguous. Similarly we can handle the other case.

To prove that for all even i the edge $f_i = f_0$ ($=e_2$ say), suppose it were not. Then there exists an even position j such that $f_i \neq f_0$. Now consider the sequence of edges obtained from ρ by replacing the edge f_i with e_2. It is not difficult to show that this sequence is also an accepting run of $\mathcal{A}$ over σ, a contradiction as $\mathcal{A}$ is unamiguous. Similarly we can prove that prove that for all odd i, $f_i = f_1$ ($=e_1$ say).

We also observe that the edge f_0 is non-accepting because if it were then $f_0 f_0 \cdots$ is an accepting run of $\mathcal{A}$ over the word a^ω along which g does not correctly monitor the formula. Further, we also deduce that the edge f_1 is final as ρ is an accepting run of $\mathcal{A}$. Since e_1 and e_2 are the only monitoring edges we can also conclude that both the edges e_1 and e_2 are from p to p for some state p.

We have proved above that any monitoring automaton for aUb requires at least 2 states. Since there are only two more edges, say d_1 and d_2, other than

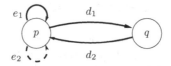

Fig. 10. Automaton $\mathcal{A}$

e_1 and e_2 it must be the case that d_1 is from state p to another state q and d_2 from q to p. Fig. 10 shows the edge transitions of $\mathcal{A}$.

It is not difficult to verify that this automaton cannot monitor the formula on any of its run over the word $(cccb)^\omega$, where c is another action in Σ. We can handle other cases similarly and hence we conclude that $(\mathcal{A}, g)$ is not a monitoring automaton for aUb.

Once again, on a similar note we can prove that in general our constructions for the remaining cases also use an optimal number of edges.

We would like to point out here that the monitoring automaton for the formula aUb (where a and b are actions) in the setting of Kesten and Pnueli [5] has has 8 states (of which 3 are dead states) and 27 edges. In contrast our monitoring automaton for the formula has 2 states and 5 edges, which we argue is optimal.

7   Conclusion

In this paper we have given a compositional construction for a monitoring automaton for arbitrary LTL formulas, in the framework of hierarchical Büchi automata. As pointed out in the introduction we depart from the similar construction given by Kesten and Pnueli in [5] in several aspects.

In addition, we would like to mention that in our construction it is easy to see by inspection that for a pure past LTL formula, the monitoring automaton is deterministic.

We also believe that our construction is useful from a pedagogical point of view, as each inductive step is fairly simple and intuitive, with simple and direct automata constructions.

References

1. Abrial, J.-R.: Modeling in Event-B - System and Software Engineering. Cambridge University Press (2010)
2. de Moura, L., Owre, S., Rueß, H., Rushby, J., Shankar, N., Sorea, M., Tiwari, A.: SAL 2. In: Alur, R., Peled, D.A. (eds.) CAV 2004. LNCS, vol. 3114, pp. 496–500. Springer, Heidelberg (2004)
3. Gerth, R., Peled, D., Vardi, M.Y., Wolper, P.: Simple on-the-fly automatic verification of Linear Temporal Logic. In: Dembinski, P., Sredniawa, M. (eds.) PSTV. IFIP Conference Proceedings, vol. 38, pp. 3–18. Chapman & Hall (1995)
4. Holzmann, G.J.: The model checker SPIN. IEEE Trans. Software Eng. 23(5), 279–295 (1997)

5. Kesten, Y., Pnueli, A.: A compositional approach to CTL* verification. Theor. Comput. Sci. 331(2-3), 397–428 (2005)
6. Maler, O., Nickovic, D., Pnueli, A.: From MITL to Timed Automata. In: Asarin, E., Bouyer, P. (eds.) FORMATS 2006. LNCS, vol. 4202, pp. 274–289. Springer, Heidelberg (2006)
7. Matteplackel, R.M.: Automata Constructions and Decision Procedures for Real-Time Logics. PhD thesis, CSA Department, Indian Institute of Science (2012)
8. Pnueli, A.: The temporal logic of programs. In: FOCS, pp. 46–57. IEEE (1977)
9. Vardi, M.Y., Wolper, P.: An automata-theoretic approach to automatic program verification (preliminary report). In: LICS, pp. 332–344. IEEE Computer Society (1986)
10. Woodcock, J., Davies, J.: Using Z: Specification, Refinement, and Proof. Prentice-Hall (1996)

How to Translate Efficiently Extensions of Temporal Logics into Alternating Automata

César Sánchez[1,2] and Julian Samborski-Forlese[1,*]

[1] IMDEA Software Institute, Madrid, Spain
[2] Institute for Applied Physics, CSIC, Madrid, Spain
{cesar.sanchez,julian.sf}@imdea.org

Abstract. This paper presents results that enable efficient translations of extensions of linear temporal logic (LTL) into alternating automata, which can be applied to improve algorithms for the automata-theoretic approach to model-checking. In particular, we introduce—using a game theoretic framework—a novel finer grain complementation theorem for the parity condition. This result allows simple and efficient translations of extended temporal operators into pairs of automata accepting complementary languages, using only up to 3 colors. Our results: (1) allow to translate directly operators from LTL and different extensions (2) that can be combined without restriction; and (3) does not require to eliminate negation upfront, or to start from formulas in negation normal form.

1 Introduction

We study the problem of temporal verification of reactive systems, in particular the automata approach to model-checking [16,17]. Given a finite system and a specification in LTL [13,11] the problem consists in deciding whether all runs of the systems are accepted by the specification. The automata-theoretic approach to model checking reduces this verification problem to automata constructions (like product and complementation) and decision problems (like non-emptiness and language containment). First, one builds an automaton on infinite words for the negation of the formula, which is then composed with the system using a synchronous product. Finally, an emptiness check concludes whether the resulting product admits some trace (counter-example) or the system is correct with respect to the specification.

In recent years, specifications are translated into alternating automata. The richer structure of alternating automata enables a more direct translation than non-deterministic automata, and allows to postpone a potentially exponential blow-up. Another advantage of alternation is the easy dualization (see Muller and Schupp [12]) provided by the availability of both conjunctive and disjunctive

---

[*] This work was funded in part by the EU project FET IST-231620 *HATS*, MICINN project TIN-2008-05624 *DOVES*, CAM project S2009TIC-1465 *PROMETIDOS*, and by the COST Action IC0901 *Rich ModelToolkit*.

A. Roychoudhury and M. D'Souza (Eds.): ICTAC 2012, LNCS 7521, pp. 30–45, 2012.

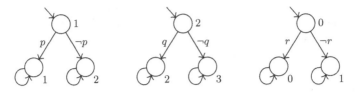

Fig. 1. Alternating automaton for the formula $\neg(p \wedge \neg q) \vee r$

transition relations. However, to obtain an automaton accepting the complement language, one also needs to complement the acceptance condition (e.g., [15] studies the complementation of weak alternating automata by dualization).

In this paper we study complementation constructions for parity automata and applications to translate formulas from LTL and extensions into automata more efficiently. We use APW to refer to alternating parity automata on words and NBW for non-deterministic Büchi automata on words. The parity acceptance condition allows a simple and well-known complementation construction: increment the color assigned to every state. This operation preserves the relative order between the colors of any two states, and inverts the parity of the maximum color in any given sequence of states. This way, accepting traces become non-accepting traces, and non-accepting traces become accepting traces. Even though this construction is simple and elegant, it suffers the drawback that the number of colors in the resulting automaton grows with every complementation step. If this construction is used to translate the logical negation operator, the total number of colors used in the resulting automaton can grow linearly in the size of the formula. Consider, for example, the expression $(\neg(p \wedge \neg q) \vee r)$. The number of colors generated in the translation using the standard complementation construction is 4 (see Fig. 1). The best known algorithms [3] for translating APW into NBW becomes less efficient as the number of colors grow, requiring $O(2^{nk \, log \, nk})$ states for an automaton with n states and k colors. Hence, many researchers [9] have suggested translations of LTL into automata with weaker acceptance conditions at the cost of manipulating formulas in the logical level. Gastin et al. [6] is the closest work to ours, but their approach is tailored for LTL and is not immediately applicable to extensions of LTL, like regular expression operators, which seem to preclude the use of simpler forms of automata.

In this paper we alleviate the problem of the inefficient translation into APW by exploiting the following intuition. The classical parity complementation construction complements all sequences of states in the automaton, while only a subset of these sequences are allowed by an automaton and its dual. We show that the set of traces of an automaton and its dual are identical, and that to complement an automaton it is enough to provide a pair of parity assignments with opposite outcomes on these traces. The second contribution of this paper is a translation of temporal logic operators into automata based on the complementation results. Each operator is translated into a pair of complement automata, starting from a pair of complement automata for the operands.

The rest of the paper is structured as follows. Section 3 presents the notion of specular frame and specular automata pairs, and show that they accept complement languages. Section 4 shows translations of some temporal operators from LTL and extensions into specular automata pairs. Finally, Section 5 concludes.

2 Preliminaries

Positive Boolean Formulas: We use $\mathcal{B}^+(X)$ for the positive boolean formulas over a set of propositions X. These formulas are built from **true, false** and elements of X, combined using $\wedge$ and $\vee$. A model of a formula θ is a subset of X that makes θ true. A minimal model M of a formula θ is a model of θ such that no strict subset of M is a model of θ. For example, given the set $Q = \{q_0, q_1, q_2, q_3\}$, the formula $\theta_1 = (q_1 \wedge q_2) \vee q_3$ is a $\mathcal{B}^+(Q)$ formula. The sets $\{q_1, q_2\}$ and $\{q_3\}$ are the minimal models of θ_1. We use $MOD(\theta)$ for the set of models of θ and $mod(\theta)$ for the set of minimal models.

Every positive boolean formula can be expressed in disjunctive normal form, as disjunction of conjunctions of propositions. Given a positive boolean formula θ there is a dual formula $\widetilde{\theta}$ obtained by switching $\wedge$ and $\vee$, and switching **true** and **false**. Some easy properties of dual formulas are:

Proposition 1 (Duals). *For every θ and $\widetilde{\theta}$, and for every $M \in MOD(\theta)$:*
1. *For every $M' \in MOD(\widetilde{\theta})$, $M \cap M' \neq \varnothing$.*
2. *Let $q \in M$. There is an M' in $MOD(\widetilde{\theta})$ with $q \in M'$.*

For example, the dual of θ_1 above is $\widetilde{\theta}_1 = (q_1 \vee q_2) \wedge q_3$, or equivalently in disjunctive normal form $\widetilde{\theta}_1 = (q_1 \wedge q_3) \vee (q_2 \wedge q_3)$. The minimal models of $\widetilde{\theta}_1$ are $\{q_1, q_3\}$ and $\{q_2, q_3\}$. A *choice function* is a map f that chooses, for a model M of θ an element of M, i.e., $f : MOD(\theta) \to X$ such $f(M) \in M$. Some interesting properties of choice functions follow:

Proposition 2 (Choice Functions). *Let θ be a formula and $\widetilde{\theta}$ its dual. Then*
1. *If f is a choice function for θ, then $Img\ f \in MOD(\widetilde{\theta})$.*
2. *If $M \in mod(\theta)$ then there is a choice function f of $\widetilde{\theta}$ such that $Img\ f = M$.*

Proof. We prove 2.1 (2.2 follows similarly). Consider θ in disjunctive normal form. Each child subexpression of the root expression corresponds to a conjunction of states that form a model. The choice function f chooses one state from each model of θ. Expressing $\widetilde{\theta}$ dualy, each child subexpression of $\widetilde{\theta}$ is a disjunction of the corresponding set of states. Hence, the element that f chooses in each child satisfies the corresponding disjunction, and $\left(Img\ f = \bigcup_{M \in MOD(\theta)} f(M)\right)$ is a model of $\widetilde{\theta}$. $\square$

Clearly, not every choice function has a minimal model as image (2.1 states that it must be a model but not necessarily minimal). Those choice functions whose images are minimal models are called *proper choice functions*. We will later focus our attention on proper choice functions as strategies for players in certain classes of parity games.

3   Specular Automata Pairs

3.1   Alternating Frames

We study now the layout of alternating automata. An automaton *frame*, or simply a frame, is a tuple $\mathcal{F} : \langle \Sigma, Q, \delta, I \rangle$ where Σ is an alphabet, Q is a finite set of states, $\delta : Q \times \Sigma \to \mathcal{B}^+(Q)$ is the transition function, and $I \in \mathcal{B}^+(Q)$ is the initial condition of the frame. A frame determines the legal traces for a given input word. We will later introduce automata as frames equipped with an acceptance condition, which will determine which traces allowed by the frame are "good". A frame is *non-deterministic* whenever I, and $\delta(q, a)$ for all states q and input symbols a, have singleton sets as minimal models. In other words, I and $\delta(q, a)$ are equivalent to disjunctive formulas. A frame is called *universal* if I, and $\delta(q, a)$ for all states q and symbols a, have a unique minimal model. In other words, I and $\delta(q, a)$ are equivalent to conjunctive formulas. A frame is deterministic if it is both non-deterministic and universal, that is if both the initial condition and transition functions correspond to **true**, **false** or a single successor state. In general a frame is neither universal nor non-deterministic, but fully alternating.

Run and Trace. Given a word $w \in \Sigma^\omega$, a *run* of a frame $\mathcal{F} : \langle \Sigma, Q, \delta, I \rangle$ on w is a DAG (V, E) with nodes $V \subseteq Q \times \omega$, such that:

1. The set $\{m \mid (m, 0) \in V\}$ is a minimal model for I.
2. for every (q, k) in V, the set $\{q' \mid (q', k+1) \in V \text{ and } ((q, k), (q', k+1)) \in E\}$ is a minimal model for $\delta(q, w[k])$.

A *trace* of a run is an infinite path in the run, following edges. A non-deterministic frame may admit multiple different runs for a given word, but each run contains a unique trace. A universal frame admits just one run for each word, but this run may contain multiple traces. In general a frame admits multiple runs each with multiple traces.

Given a frame $\mathcal{F} : \langle \Sigma, Q, \delta, I \rangle$, the *specular frame* is the frame $\widetilde{\mathcal{F}} : \langle \Sigma, Q, \widetilde{\delta}, \widetilde{I} \rangle$, where $\widetilde{I}$ is the dual formula of I and $\widetilde{\delta}$ is the dual transition function: $\widetilde{\delta}(q, a)$ is the dual formula of $\delta(q, a)$ for all states q and symbols a.

Frame Graphs. We define the *graph* of a frame $\mathcal{F}$ as $(V_{\mathcal{F}}, E_{\mathcal{F}})$ where $V_{\mathcal{F}} = Q$ and there is an edge in $E_{\mathcal{F}}$ from p to q whenever q is in some minimal model of $\delta(p, a)$ for some symbol a. Since the union of all minimal models of a formula is the same set as the union of all minimal models of its dual formula, the edge relation is the same for the graph of a frame and its specular frame:

Proposition 3 (Frame Graphs). *The graph of a frame and the graph of its specular frame are identical.*

By construction, if $(p, k) \to (q, k + 1)$ is an edge in some run of a given frame, then $p \to q$ is an edge in the graph of the frame. Consequently, the set of traces of runs on a frame correspond to the set of walks in the graph, which in turn is also the set of traces of runs on the specular frame.

Automata. A frame $\mathcal{F} : \langle \Sigma, Q, \delta, I \rangle$ can be enriched into an automaton $\mathcal{A} :$ $\langle \Sigma, Q, \delta, I, F \rangle$ by adding an acceptance condition F. In this paper we use the *parity* acceptance condition $F : Q \rightarrow \{0 \ldots d\}$. Given an infinite sequence of states $\pi : q_0, q_1, q_2 \ldots$ we let $inf(\pi)$ be those states from Q that occur infinitely many times in π. The sequence π is accepting according to F, which we denote $\pi \in acc(F)$, whenever the maximum value that occurs infinitely often (i.e., $max\{F(q) \mid q \in inf(\pi)\}$) is even. A *run* of a word w on an automaton $\mathcal{A}$ is a run on its frame. A run is called accepting whenever all its traces are accepting sequences. We say that a word w is in the language of an automaton $\mathcal{A}$, and we write $w \in \mathcal{L}(\mathcal{A})$ whenever there is an accepting run for w on $\mathcal{A}$.

Definition 1 (Specular Automata). *Two automata $\mathcal{A} : \langle \Sigma, Q, \delta, I, F_A \rangle$ and $\mathcal{B} : \langle \Sigma, Q, \tilde{\delta}, \tilde{I}, F_B \rangle$ with specular frames are specular automata whenever for all paths π in the frame graph, $\pi \in acc(F_A)$ iff $\pi \notin acc(F_B)$.*

The standard construction for complementing an alternating parity automaton proceeds by creating the dual automaton, which is obtained by dualizing the initial condition and transition function, and making $F_B(q) = F_A(q) + 1$ for every q. Observe that dual automata are special cases of specular automata. In fact, in many cases it is possible to exploit the particular structure of $\mathcal{A}$ to define lower values for F_B than those defined by the standard construction.

3.2   Automata and Games

We show now that specular automata accept complementary languages, using game theory. From a given automaton $\mathcal{A}$ and a word w, we create a parity game called a *word game* as a tuple $\mathbf{G}(\mathcal{A}, w) : \langle V_A, V_P, E_A, E_P, f \rangle$ where:

$$V_A = Q \times \omega$$
$$V_P = \{(M, q, i) \mid M \in MOD(\delta(q, w[i]))\} \cup \{(M, \cdot, 0) \mid M \in MOD(I)\}$$
$$E_A = (q, i) \rightarrow (M, q, i) \text{ for each } M \in MOD(\delta(q, w[i]))$$
$$E_P = (M, q, i) \rightarrow (q', i + 1) \text{ for } q' \in M$$

The game is played by two players: *Automaton (A)* and *Pathfinder (P)*. The set of positions $V = V_A \cup V_P$ is partitioned into positions in which A plays and those in which P plays. The game begins by A choosing a model M of I, which determines the initial position $(M, \cdot, 0)$ (here $\cdot$ denotes an irrelevant state). The legal moves of the game are captured by the relation $E = E_A \cup E_P$. From a position $(q, i) \in V_A$, player A chooses a model M of $\delta(q, w[i])$ and moves to $(M, q, i) \in V_E$. Then, player P chooses the next successor q' from M, and moves to $(q', i + 1)$. A *play* is an infinite sequence of positions $\pi : V_0 v_0 V_1 v_1 \ldots$ with V_0 being an initial position, v_i obtained from V_i by a P move, and V_{i+1} obtained from v_i by an A move. The map $f : V \rightarrow \{0 \ldots d\}$ determines the outcome of a play. We define the *trace* of a play $\pi : V_0 v_0 V_1 v_1 \ldots$ as the sequence of states $trace(\pi) : p_0 p_1 \ldots$ obtained by projecting the first component of the V_A positions of the play (i.e., $v_i = (p_i, i)$). The following result holds, directly from the definitions.

Proposition 4. *Every trace of a play of* $G(\mathcal{A}, w)$ *is also a trace of some run of* $\mathcal{A}$ *on* w.

As for parity automata the outcome of a play is determined by the highest color that is seen infinitely often in the play. Player A wins play π whenever: $max\{f(q) \mid q \in inf(trace(\pi))\}$ is even. Otherwise, P wins play π. A strategy for player A is a map $\rho_A : (V^* V_A \cup \epsilon) \to V$, that maps histories of positions into moves. Here, ϵ denotes the empty sequence of positions, to let player A choose an initial state in the game. A memoryless strategy simply takes into account the last position: $\rho_A : V_A \cup \epsilon \to V$. Since parity games are memoryless determined [4] it is enough to consider memoryless strategies. Similarly, a strategy for player P is a map $\rho_P : V_P \to V$. A play $\pi : V_0 v_0 V_1 v_1 \dots$ is played according to strategy ρ_A whenever the initial position is $V_0 = \rho_A(\epsilon)$ and all moves of A are played according to it $V_i = \rho_A(v_i)$. A strategy ρ_A is winning for player A whenever all plays played according to ρ_A are winning for A. Memoryless determinacy of parity games guarantees that either player A has a memoryless winning strategy or player P has a memoryless winning strategy. We say that π is a $G \cdot \rho_A$ play whenever π is played in G according to ρ_A.

We restrict our attention to strategies for A that choose minimal models, and strategies for P that are proper choice functions. This is not a drastic restriction. Clearly, if there is a winning strategy for A that does not choose a minimal model, then any strategy that chooses a smaller minimal model is also winning. This is because the set of plays is reduced, and all plays in the unrestricted set are winning for A. Similarly, if ρ_P is a winning strategy for P, then restricting its moves to a proper choice functions also gives a winning strategy. In both cases, the set of successor moves is restricted but still confined within winning regions. Lemma 1 is similar to Prop. 2 from [15], where complementation of weak alternation automata by dualization is studied.

Lemma 1. $w \in \mathcal{L}(\mathcal{A})$ *if and only if* A *has a winning strategy in* $G(\mathcal{A}, w)$.

3.3 Specular Pairs and Complementation

We show in this section that specular automata accept complementary languages. In the rest of the section we let $\mathcal{A}$ and $\widetilde{\mathcal{A}}$ be a specular automata pair, w be a word and $G : G(\mathcal{A}, w)$ and $\widetilde{G} : G(\widetilde{\mathcal{A}}, w)$ be the corresponding word games. First we need some preliminary definitions.

Definition 2. *We say that strategies* ρ_A *(for A in G) and* $\widetilde{\rho}_P$ *(for P in $\widetilde{G}$) are duals whenever both:*
  - *for every* $G \cdot \rho_A$ *play* π *there is a* $\widetilde{G} \cdot \widetilde{\rho}_P$ *play* $\widetilde{\pi}$ *s.t.* $trace(\widetilde{\pi}) = trace(\pi)$, *and*
  - *for every* $\widetilde{G} \cdot \widetilde{\rho}_P$ *play* $\widetilde{\pi}$ *there is a* $G \cdot \rho_A$ *play* π *s.t.* $trace(\widetilde{\pi}) = trace(\pi)$.

Theorem 1 (Dual Strategies). *The following holds:*
(1) For every strategy ρ_A *for A in G, there is a dual strategy* $\widetilde{\rho}_P$ *for P in $\widetilde{G}$.*
(2) For every ρ_P *for P in G, there is a dual strategy* $\widetilde{\rho}_A$ *for A in $\widetilde{G}$.*

Proof. We prove the two statements separately:

(1) Let ρ_A be a strategy for A in G. This strategy ρ_A is characterized by

$$\rho_A(\epsilon) = (M_0, \cdot, 0) \qquad \text{where } M_0 \in mod(I)$$
$$\rho_A((q, i)) = (M, q, i+1) \quad \text{where } M \in mod(\delta(q, w[i]))$$

By Prop. 2.1 there are choice functions satisfying

$$f_{M_0} : MOD(\widetilde{I}) \to Q \qquad\qquad Img\, f_{M_0} = M_0$$
$$f_{\langle M,q,a\rangle} : MOD(\widetilde{\delta}(q, a)) \to Q \qquad Img\, f_{\langle M,q,a\rangle} = M$$

Moreover, these functions are proper choice functions. We now define the dual strategy $\widetilde{\rho}_P$ for P in $\widetilde{G}$ as follows:

$$\widetilde{\rho}_P((N_0, \cdot, 0)) = (f_{M_0}(N_0), 0)$$
$$\widetilde{\rho}_P((N, q, i+1)) = (f_{\langle M,q,a\rangle}(N), q, i+1)$$

where M is the move of A in G from (q, i): $\rho_A(q, i) = (M, q, i+1)$, and $a = w[i]$. Our choice of choice functions $f_{\langle M,q,a\rangle}$ guarantees that for every move of player P from M, there is a move for player A in $\widetilde{G}$ that, when followed by $f_{\langle M,q,a\rangle}$ results in the same state. The properties of f_{M_0} and $f_{\langle M,q,a\rangle}$ ensure that the strategy $\widetilde{\rho}_P$ is proper.

We are ready to show that for every $G \cdot \rho_A$ play there is a $\widetilde{G} \cdot \widetilde{\rho}_P$ play with the same trace, and vice-versa.

"$\to$" Consider an arbitrary $G \cdot \rho_A$ play $\pi : V_0 v_0 V_1 v_1 \ldots$, and let $\rho_A(\epsilon) = (M_0, \cdot, 0)$ and $\rho_A(v_i) = (M_{i+1}, q_i, i+1)$. We use q_i for $v_i = (q_i, i)$. Note that $q_{i+1} \in M_{i+1}$ because all moves of player P in π are legal moves. We create the $\widetilde{G} \cdot \widetilde{\rho}_P$ play $\widetilde{\pi} : \widetilde{V}_0, \widetilde{v}_0, \widetilde{V}_1, \widetilde{v}_1 \ldots$ as follows:

- $\widetilde{V}_0 = (N_0, \cdot, 0)$ where N_0 is such that $f_{M_0}(N_0) = q_0$. One such N_0 exists since $Img\, f_{M_0} = M_0$ and $q_0 \in M_0$ (recall that $(q_0, 0)$ is the result of a move of P in G from $(M_0, \cdot, 0)$).
- From (q_i, i), player A chooses in $\widetilde{G}$ the position $(N_{i+1}, q_i, i+1)$, where N_{i+1} is chosen such that $f_{\langle M_{i+1}, q, w[i]\rangle} = q_{i+1}$.

By induction, we show that $v_i = \widetilde{v}_i$. First, $\widetilde{v}_0 = \widetilde{\rho}_P((N_0, \cdot, 0)) = (f_{M_0}(N_0), 0) = (q_0, 0) = v_0$. Now, assume that for some i, $v_i = \widetilde{v}_i$. Then, $\widetilde{V}_i = (N_{i+1}, q_i, i+1)$, and $V_i = \rho_A(q_i, i) = (M_{i+1}, q_i, i+1)$. Now,

$$
\begin{aligned}
\widetilde{v}_{i+1} = \widetilde{\rho}_P(\widetilde{V}_i) = \widetilde{\rho}_P((N_{i+1}, q_i, i+1)) &= \\
= (f_{\langle M_{i+1}, q_i, w[i]\rangle}(N_{i+1}), i+1) &= \\
= (q_{i+1}, i+1) &= v_{i+1}.
\end{aligned}
$$

Hence, $trace(\pi) = trace(\widetilde{\pi})$.

"$\leftarrow$" Consider an arbitrary $\widetilde{G} \cdot \widetilde{\rho}_P$ play $\widetilde{\pi} : \widetilde{V}_0 \widetilde{v}_0 \widetilde{V}_1 \widetilde{v}_1 \ldots$, and let q_i and N_i be such that:

$$\widetilde{v}_i = (q_i, i) \qquad \widetilde{V}_0 = (N_0, \cdot, 0) \qquad \widetilde{V}_{i+1} = (N_{i+1}, q_i, i+1)$$

Since $\tilde{\pi}$ is a $\tilde{G} \cdot \tilde{\rho}_P$ play, then $\tilde{v}_{i+1} = \tilde{\rho}_P(\tilde{V}_{i+1}) = (f_{\langle M_{i+1}, q_i, w[i] \rangle}(N_{i+1}), i+1)$ where M_i is obtained from $\rho_A(q_i, i) = (M_{i+1}, i+1)$. Now, we define the play $\pi : V_0 v_0 V_1 v_1 \ldots$ as follows. First the move for A is played according to ρ_A:

$$V_0 = \rho_A(\epsilon) = (M_0, \cdot, 0) \qquad V_{i+1} = \rho_A(v_i)$$

Then, we let the moves of P to be:

$$v_0 = (q_0, 0) \qquad v_{i+1} = (q_{i+1}, i+1)$$

We only need to show that these moves for P are legal. First, $q_0 = f_{M_0}(N_0)$, and since $Img\ f_{M_0} = M_0$ it follows that $q_0 \in M_0$, so moving from V_0 into v_0 is a legal move.

Moreover, $(q_{i+1} = f_{\langle M_{i+1}, q_i, w[i] \rangle}(N_i))$. Since $Img\ f_{\langle M_{i+1}, q_i, w[i] \rangle} = M_{i+1}$ it follows that $q_{i+1} \in M_{i+1}$, so again moving from V_{i+1} into v_{i+1} is a legal move. By construction, $trace(\pi) = trace(\tilde{\pi})$ again.

(2) Assume now that ρ_P is a (proper) strategy for P in G. The strategy ρ_P is characterized by

$$\rho_P((M_0, \cdot, 0)) = (q_0, 0) \qquad \rho_P((M, q, i)) = (q_i, i)$$

Since the strategy is proper there are proper choice functions:

$$g_0 : MOD(I) \to Q \qquad g_{q,i} : MOD(\delta(q, w[i])) \to Q$$

with

$$\begin{array}{ll} g_0 : MOD(I) \to Q & Img\ g_0 \in mod(\tilde{I}) \\ g_{q,i} : MOD(\delta(q, w[i])) \to Q & Img\ g_{q,i} \in mod(\tilde{\delta}(q, w[i])) \end{array} \qquad (1)$$

We define the strategy $\tilde{\rho}_A$ for A in $\tilde{G}$ as follows:

$$\tilde{\rho}_A(\epsilon) = Img\ g_0 \qquad \tilde{\rho}_A((q, i)) = Img\ g_{q,i}$$

By (1), $\tilde{\rho}_A$ is well defined. We show now that $\tilde{\rho}_A$ and ρ_P are dual strategies. First, consider (q, i) an arbitrary state and (M, q, i) a legal move for player A in G. Player P will move to $(q', i+1) = \rho_P((M, q, i))$ with $q' = g_{q,i}((M, q, i))$. In $\tilde{G}$, player A will move from (q, i) into $(Img\ g_{q,i}, q, i)$. We let player P move in $\tilde{G}$ to $(q', i+1)$, which is legal, since $q' \in Img\ g_{q,i}$. Consider now an arbitrary state (p, i) and the move of A in $\tilde{G}$: $\tilde{\rho}_A((p, i)) = (Img\ g_{p,i}, p, i)$, and consider an arbitrary legal move for P, $(p', i+1)$, hence $p' \in Img\ g_{p,i}$. Consequently, there is an $M \in MOD(\delta(p, w[i]))$ such that $g_{p,i}((M, p, i)) = p'$. Let A choose (M, p, i) as the move from (p, i), which is a legal move. Then, playing from (M, p, i) in G according to ρ_P, the resulting state is $(p', i+1)$. This shows that ρ_A and $\tilde{\rho}_P$ are dual strategies.

It is important to note that the moves of the players playing against the strategies are not restricted to follow proper strategies (give minimal models or be proper choice functions). Still, ρ_A is winning precisely whenever $\tilde{\rho}_P$ is. □

The following theorem follows directly from Lemma 1 and Theorem 1. This theorem allows to reason about complementation simply by reasoning about traces of two automata with specular frames. In [15] a similar result is proved the weak acceptance condition.

Theorem 2. *Let $\mathcal{A}$ and $\widetilde{\mathcal{A}}$ be specular automata. Then $\mathcal{L}(\mathcal{A}) = \Sigma^\omega \setminus \mathcal{L}(\widetilde{\mathcal{A}})$.*

4   Temporal Logic to Specular Automata

We show in this section how the results in Section 3 can be used to translate temporal logic expressions into alternating parity automata. Most previous translations fix the logic first, and then show a monolithic translation from the whole expression into automata. Typically, these translations begin with a previous transformation of the expression into negation normal form, by pushing the negation operator to the propositional level. This transformation requires the logics to enjoy duality laws for all operators, or in other words, to admit a negation normal form. With this preprocessing the negation operator need not be considered in the translation into automata.

We follow here a different approach. For each operator we construct a specular automata pair: one automaton is equivalent to the expression, and another equivalent to its complement. The construction for a given operator starts from a specular automata pair for each of the operands. This approach has two advantages. First, negation becomes trivial. Second, adding operands to a logic simply requires defining the translation of the added operands. In this manner, operators from different logics can be easily combined. We present here a few examples of constructs from LTL and some of its extensions.

Linear Temporal Logic: Linear temporal Logic was introduced by Pnueli [13], see also [11]. We consider here the following operators

$$\varphi ::= p \mid \neg\varphi \mid \varphi \vee \varphi \mid \bigcirc\varphi \mid \square\varphi \mid \Diamond\varphi \mid \varphi\,\mathcal{U}\,\varphi \mid \varphi\,\mathcal{R}\,\varphi \mid \varphi\,\mathcal{W}\,\varphi$$

This definition is not minimal but it serves to illustrate how to translate some of the operators into APW. The semantics of LTL expressions are defined using a binary relation $\vDash$ between pointed ω-words and LTL expressions:

- $(w, i) \vDash p$ when $p \in w[j]$.
- $(w, i) \vDash \neg x$ when $(w, i) \nvDash x$.
- $(w, i) \vDash x \vee y$ when $(w, i) \vDash x$ or $(w, i) \vDash y$ or both.
- $(w, i) \vDash \bigcirc x$ when $(w, i+1) \vDash x$.
- $(w, i) \vDash \Diamond x$ when $(w, j) \vDash x$ for some $j \geq i$.
- $(w, i) \vDash \square x$ when $(w, j) \vDash x$ for all $j \geq i$.
- $(w, i) \vDash x\,\mathcal{U}\,y$ when $(w, j) \vDash y$ for some $j \geq i$, and $(w, k) \vDash x$ for all $i \leq k < j$.
- $(w, i) \vDash x\,\mathcal{R}\,y$ when $(w, j) \vDash y$ for all $j \geq i$, or
             for some j, $(w, j) \vDash x$ and for all k in $i \leq k \leq j$, $(w, k) \vDash y$.
- $(w, i) \vDash x\,\mathcal{W}\,y$ when $(w, j) \vDash x$ for all $j \geq i$, or
             $(w, j) \vDash y$ for some $j \geq i$, and $(w, k) \vDash x$ for all $i \leq k < j$.

We now show the translation of each operator. We assume a pair of dual automata $(\mathcal{A}_x, \mathcal{A}_{\overline{x}})$ for each operand x.

- p: The automaton $\mathcal{A}_p$ is $\langle Q, \delta, I, F \rangle$ such that $Q = \{q_0, q_1, q_2\}$, $I = q_0$, $F(q_0) = F(q_1) = 2$ and $F(q_2) = 1$. The transitions function is: $\delta(q_0, p) = q_1$, $\delta(q_0, \neg p) = q_2$, and $\delta(q_1, \cdot) = q_1$ and $\delta(q_2, \cdot) = q_2$ are self loops. The dual automaton $\mathcal{A}_{\overline{p}}$ has, as final condition, $F(q_0) = F(q_1) = 1$, $F(q_2) = 2$. Note how the dualization of the acceptance condition is not performed by incrementing the color of each state.
- $\neg x$: the automaton for $\mathcal{A}_{\neg x}$ is $\mathcal{A}_{\overline{x}}$ and the automaton for $\mathcal{A}_{\overline{\neg x}}$ is $\mathcal{A}_x$.
- $x \vee y$: The automaton $\mathcal{A}_{x \vee y}$ is $\langle Q, \delta, I, F \rangle$ with $Q = Q_x \cup Q_y$, and $I = I_x \vee I_y$. The acceptance condition works as F_x for Q_x and as F_y for Q_y. For $\mathcal{A}_{\overline{x \vee y}}$, the automaton is build similarly, but from $\mathcal{A}_{\overline{x}}$ and $\mathcal{A}_{\overline{y}}$, with $I = I_{\overline{x}} \wedge I_{\overline{y}}$.
- $\Box x$: The automaton $\mathcal{A}_{\Box x}$ has $Q = \{q_0\} \cup Q_x$, where q_0 is a fresh state. The initial condition is $I = \{q_0\}$. The acceptance condition works as F_x in Q_x, and assigns $F(q_0) = 2$. Finally, $\delta(q_0, a) = q_0 \wedge \delta_x(I_x, a)$. The dual automaton $\mathcal{A}_{\overline{\Box x}}$ is built analogously, from $\mathcal{A}_{\overline{x}}$, except: $F(q_0) = 1$ and $\delta(q_0, a) = q_0 \vee \delta_{\overline{x}}(I_{\overline{x}}, a)$.
- $\Diamond x$: The construction is exactly the dual as for $\Box x$. Hence, given $(\mathcal{A}_x, \mathcal{A}_{\overline{x}})$ the automata obtained for $\mathcal{A}_{\Diamond x}$ is identical to $\mathcal{A}_{\overline{\Box \neg x}}$, and $\mathcal{A}_{\overline{\Diamond x}}$ is identical to $\mathcal{A}_{\Box \neg x}$. This construction directly proves the duality of $\Diamond$ and $\Box$.
- $x \, \mathcal{U} \, y$: The automaton $\mathcal{A}_{x \mathcal{U} y}$ has $Q = \{q_0\} \cup Q_x \cup Q_y$ and $I = \{q_0\}$. The acceptance condition is $F(q_0) = 1$, and as F_x for states in Q_x and F_y for states in Q_y. The transition function, maps $\delta(q_0, a) = \delta(I_y, a) \vee (\delta(I_x, a) \wedge q_0)$; for states in Q_x and Q_y, δ is as δ_x and δ_y. The dual automaton is constructed analogously, except that $F(q_0) = 2$ and $\overline{\delta}(q_0, a) = \delta_{\overline{y}}(I_{\overline{y}}, a) \wedge (\delta_{\overline{x}}(I_{\overline{x}}, a) \vee q_0)$. This case illustrates again how colors need not to be increased in the dualization. The only trace to be considered when incrementally proving the correctness (accepting complementary languages) of $\mathcal{A}_{x \mathcal{U} y}$ and $\mathcal{A}_{\overline{x \mathcal{U} y}}$ is the infinite sequence $q_0 q_0 q_0 \dots$, which is rejecting for $\mathcal{A}_{x \mathcal{U} y}$ and accepting for $\mathcal{A}_{\overline{x \mathcal{U} y}}$. The other traces follow from the inductive construction.
- $x \, \mathcal{R} \, y$: The construction is exactly dual as for $x \, \mathcal{U} \, y$, which illustrates the duality between $\mathcal{U}$ and $\mathcal{R}$.
- $x \, \mathcal{W} \, y$: The construction is as for $\mathcal{U}$, except that $F(q_0) = 2$ for $\mathcal{A}_{x \mathcal{W} y}$ and $\textbf{false}(q_0) = 1$ for $\mathcal{A}_{\overline{x \mathcal{W} y}}$.

In all these translations, the APW generated uses only two colors: 1 and 2. Every APW(1,2) automaton is a Büchi automaton: traces will be accepted if at least one 2 state is visited infinitely often. Also, by looking at the automaton graph, we see that all even valued states can be assigned any even value, and all odd states can be assigned any odd value, because every trace will still have the same acceptance outcome. Hence, choosing 0 instead of 2 in all steps of the inductive construction will produce an APW with colors 0 and 1, which is a co-Büchi automaton. Our construction avoids to upfront conversion of the formula into negation normal form.

Regular Linear Temporal Logic. We sketch here an incremental construction for operators of Regular Linear Temporal Logic RLTL [10,14]. RLTL is a logic that fuses regular expressions and temporal operators in a single formalism. RLTL is defined in two stages: the first stage consists of a variation of regular expressions over finite words, using

$$\alpha ::= p \mid \alpha + \alpha \mid \alpha\, ;\, \alpha \mid \alpha^*\alpha$$

where p is a proposition. We will later use a to refer to letters in an the power-set propositional alphabet. We assume that a non-deterministic finite automaton of linear size is constructed from a given regular expression. The second stage defines temporal logic expressions that describe languages over infinite words, using regular expressions as building blocks. Since regular expressions are used to later build temporal expressions, the semantics for regular expressions are defined to accept *segments* of infinite words. Given an infinite word w and two positions i and j, the tuple (w, i, j) is called a segment of the word w (it is worth to note that the letter $w[i]$ is considered as being included in the segment while $w[j]$ is not). The syntax of RLTL expressions is defined by the following grammar:

$$\varphi ::= \varnothing \mid \varphi \vee \varphi \mid \neg\varphi \mid \alpha\, ;\, \varphi \mid \varphi|\alpha\rangle\!\rangle\varphi \mid \varphi|\alpha\rangle\varphi$$

where α ranges over regular expressions. The symbol ; stands for the conventional concatenation of an expression over finite words followed by an expression over infinite words. The operator $\varnothing$ represents the empty language.

The operators $\varphi|\alpha\rangle\!\rangle\varphi$ and its weak version $\varphi|\alpha\rangle\varphi$ are the power operators. The power expressions $x|r\rangle\!\rangle y$ and $x|r\rangle y$ (read x *at* r *until* y, and, respectively, x *at* z *weak-until* y) are built from three elements: y (the *attempt*), x (the *obligation*) and r (the *delay*). Informally, for $x|r\rangle\!\rangle y$ to hold, either the attempt holds, or the obligation is met and the whole expression evaluates successfully after the delay; in particular, for a power expression to hold the obligation must be met after a finite number of delays. On the contrary, $x|r\rangle y$ does not require the obligation to be met after a finite number of delays. These two simple operators allow the construction of many other operators like $x\,\mathcal{U}\,y$ and r^ω, which make RLTL ω-complete. Also, for every LTL operator there is an RLTL operator with the same number of operands, and consequently LTL can be translated linearly into RLTL. The semantics of the new RLTL operands $\varnothing$, $r; x$, $r|x\rangle\!\rangle y$ and $r|x\rangle y$ is:

- $(w, i) \vDash \varnothing$ never holds.
- $(w, i) \vDash r\, ;\, y$ when for some k, $(w, i, k) \vDash_{RE} r$ and $(w, k) \vDash y$
- $(w, i) \vDash x|r\rangle\!\rangle y$ when $(w, i) \vDash y$ or for some $(i_0 = i, i_1, \ldots i_m)$, and for all $k < m$
                   $(w, i_k, i_{k+1}) \vDash_{RE} r$ and $(w, i_k) \vDash x$, and $(w, i_m) \vDash y$
- $(w, i) \vDash x|r\rangle y$ when one of:
  (i) $(w, i) \vDash y$.
  (ii) for some $(i_0 = i, i_1, \ldots i_m)$, $(w, i_m) \vDash y$, and
       $(w, i_k, i_{k+1}) \vDash_{RE} r$ and $(w, i_k) \vDash x$ for all $k < m$.
  (iii) for some inf. seq. $(i_0 = i, i_1, \ldots)$, $(w, i_k, i_{k+1}) \vDash_{RE} r$ and $(w, i_k) \vDash x$

We show now the translations of RLTL into APW. The operators $\vee$ and $\neg$ can be reused from LTL. We assume again that we have the automata pair $(\mathcal{A}_x, \mathcal{A}_{\bar{x}})$ for all operands x, and a non-deterministic automaton N_r for each regular expression r.

- $\varnothing$: The automaton $\mathcal{A}_\varnothing$ consists of a single state $Q = \{q_0\}$ with $I = \{q_0\}$ and a self-loop $\delta(q_0, a) = q_0$. The accepting condition maps $F(q_0) = 1$. The dual automaton $\mathcal{A}_{\overline{\varnothing}}$ is identical except that $F(q_0) = 0$.

- $r; x$: The automaton for $\mathcal{A}_{r;x}$ consists of $Q = Q_r \cup Q_x$, and $I = I_r$. The transition function is as in $\mathcal{A}_x$ for states Q_x; for states q in Q_r:
  - if $\delta_r(q, a) \cap F_r = \emptyset$, then $\delta(q, a) = \bigvee \delta_r(q, a)$.
  - if $\delta_r(q, a) \cap F_r \neq \emptyset$, then $\delta(q, a) = \bigvee \delta_r(q, a) \vee I_x$.

  This allows δ to non-deterministically jump to x when an accepting segment is matched by r. Finally, the acceptance condition is $F(q) = F_x(q)$ for all states in Q_x and $F(q) = 1$ for all states in Q_r. Hence, a trace that remains in Q_r is a non-accepting trace.

  The automaton for $\mathcal{A}_{\overline{r;x}}$ is built from N_r and $\mathcal{A}_{\overline{x}}$: $Q = Q_r \cup Q_{\overline{x}}$. The transition function now interprets the transitions from states in Q_r universally:
  - if $\delta_r(q, a) \cap F_r = \emptyset$, then $\delta(q, a) = \bigwedge \delta_r(q, a)$.
  - if $\delta_r(q, a) \cap F_r \neq \emptyset$, then $\delta(q, a) = \bigwedge \delta_r(q, a) \wedge I_{\overline{x}}$.

  Finally, $F(q) = F_{\overline{x}}(q)$ for q in Q_x and $F(q) = 0$ for q in Q_r. Note how a trace that gets trapped in Q_r is now accepting, and how the frame corresponding to the regular expression r is universal.

- $x|r\rangle\!\rangle y$: The set of states is $Q = Q_x \cup Q_y \cup Q_r \cup \{q_0\}$. The initial condition is $I = \{q_0\}$. The transition function is as δ_x for states in Q_x, as δ_y for states in Q_y. For states q in Q_r:
  - if $\delta_r(q, a) \cap F_r = \emptyset$ then $\delta(q, a) = \bigvee \delta_r(q, a)$.
  - if $\delta_r(q, a) \cap F_r \neq \emptyset$ then $\delta(q, a) = \bigvee \delta_r(q, a) \vee q_0$.

  For q_0:
  - if $\delta_r(I_r, a) \cap F_r = \emptyset$ then $\delta(q_0, a) = \delta_y(I_y, a) \vee (\delta_x(I_x, a) \wedge \delta_r(I_r, a))$.
  - if $\delta_r(q, a) \cap F_r \neq \emptyset$ then $\delta(q_0, a) = \delta_y(I_y, a) \vee (\delta_x(I_x, a) \wedge (\delta_r(I_r, a) \vee q_0))$.

  The acceptance condition is $F(q) = F_x(q)$ for q in Q_x, $F(q) = F_y(q)$ for q in Q_y, and $F(q_0) = F(q) = 1$ for q in Q_r.

  The dual automaton $\mathcal{A}_{\overline{x|r\rangle\!\rangle y}}$ is built analogously. The transition function is dual of $\mathcal{A}_{x|r\rangle\!\rangle y}$. The acceptance condition is $F(q) = F_{\overline{x}}(q)$ for q in $Q_{\overline{x}}$, $F(q) = F_{\overline{y}}(q)$ for q in $Q_{\overline{y}}$, and $F(q_0) = F(q) = 2$ for q in $Q_{\overline{r}}$.

- $x|r\rangle y$: The set of states Q, the initial state I and the transition function δ are like in $x|r\rangle\!\rangle y$. The acceptance condition is $F(q) = F_x(q)$ for q in Q_x, $F(q) = F_y(q)$ for q in Q_y, and $F(q_0) = 2$, $F(q) = 1$ for q in Q_r. This makes traces that visit q_0 infinitely often accepting, but traces that get trapped in r rejecting.

  The dual automaton $\mathcal{A}_{\overline{x|r\rangle\!\rangle y}}$ is built with a dual frame and $F(q_0) = 1$, and $F(q) = 0$ for $q \in Q_r$. Color increasing was once again prevented by reasoning about traces independently.

These translations are depicted graphically in Fig. 2. Note how the obtained automata are APW(0,1,2). Still, the automata obtained have a particular structure: all strongly connected components (SCCs) are either labeled with 0 and 1, or labeled with 1 and 2. This is not a weak but a hesitant acceptance condition [8]. This fact can be used to improved the translation into NBW further, but this optimization is out of the scope of this paper.

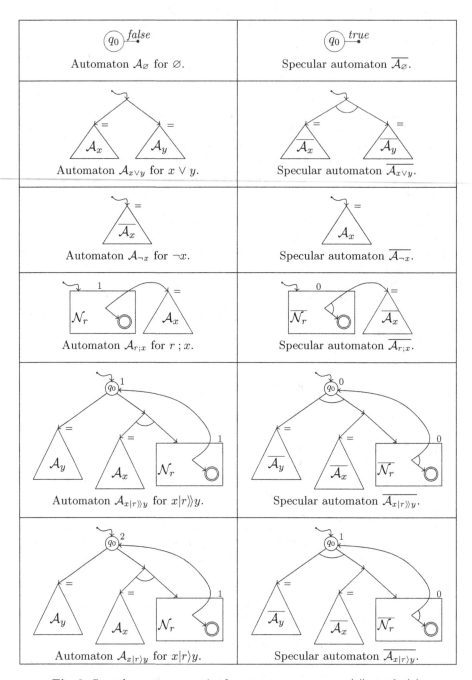

Fig. 2. Specular automata pairs for $\varnothing$, $x \vee y$, $\neg x$, $x \,;\, y$, $x|r\rangle\!\rangle y$ and $x|r\rangle y$

PSL Operators. The logic PSL [5] and its precursors ForSpec [1] and Sugar [2], also combine regular expressions with temporal operators. We illustrate here how to translate the PSL operator $r \mapsto x$ and its dual $r \diamondsuit\!\!\rightarrow x$, assuming that r is a regular expression as defined above. The semantics of $r \mapsto x$ and $r \diamondsuit\!\!\rightarrow x$ is:

- $(w, i) \vDash r \mapsto x$ when there is a j with $(w, i, j+1) \vDash r$ and $(w, j) \vDash x$.
- $(w, i) \vDash r \diamondsuit\!\!\rightarrow x$ when for all j with $(w, i, j+1) \vDash r$, then $(w, j) \vDash x$.

We sketch the translation from $r \mapsto x$ and $r \diamondsuit\!\!\rightarrow x$ into specular APW pairs:

- $r \mapsto x$: The automaton for $\mathcal{A}_{r \mapsto x}$ consists of $Q = Q_r \cup Q_x$, and $I = I_r$. The transition function is as in $\mathcal{A}_x$ for states Q_x. For states q in Q_r:
  - if $\delta_r(q, a) \cap F_r = \emptyset$, then $\delta(q, a) = \bigvee \delta_r(q, a)$.
  - if $\delta_r(q, a) \cap F_r \neq \emptyset$, then $\delta(q, a) = \bigvee \delta_r(q, a) \vee \delta_x(I_x, a)$.

  This allows δ to non-deterministically jump to x when an accepting segment is matched by r, overlapping the last state. Finally, the acceptance condition is $F(q) = F_x(q)$ for all states in Q_x and $F(q) = 1$ for all states in Q_r. Hence, a trace that remains in Q_r is a non-accepting trace.

  The automaton for $\mathcal{A}_{\overline{r \mapsto x}}$ is built dually. For the accepting condition: $F(q) = F_{\overline{x}}(q)$ for q in Q_x and $F(q) = 2$ for q in Q_r. Note how a trace that gets trapped in Q_r is now accepting, and how the frame corresponding to the regular expression r is universal.
- $r \diamondsuit\!\!\rightarrow x$ is dual of $r \mapsto x$.

Dynamic Linear Temporal Logic DLTL. DLTL is defined as a dynamic logic in [7]. DLTL introduces a generalized until operator $x \, \mathcal{U}^r \, y$ that constraints those points at which the attempt y can be evaluated by successful matches of the regular expression r. In order for $x \, \mathcal{U}^r \, y$ to be satisfied, there must be a segment met by regular expression r after which y is satisfied, and x must be satisfied in all the positions until the successful match of r. More formally:

- $(w, i) \vDash x \, \mathcal{U}^r \, y$ when there is a j with $(w, i, j) \vDash r$ and $(w, j) \vDash y$, and for all k within $i \leq k < j$, $(w, k) \vDash x$.

The translation into APW is:

- $x \, \mathcal{U}^r \, y$: The set of states is $Q = Q_x \cup Q_y \cup Q_r \cup \{q_0\}$. The initial state is $I = q_0$. The transition function is like δ_x for states in Q_x and like δ_y for states in Q_y. For q_0:
  - if $\delta_r(I_r, a) \cap F_r = \emptyset$ then $\delta(q_0, a) = \delta_y(I_y, a) \vee (\delta_x(I_x, a) \wedge \delta_r(I_r, a))$.
  - if $\delta_r(I_r, a) \cap F_r \neq \emptyset$ then $\delta(q_0, a) = \delta_y(I_y, a) \vee (\delta_x(I_x, a) \wedge (\delta_r(I_r, a) \vee q_0))$.

  For states $q \in Q_r$:
  - if $\delta_r(q, a) \cap F_r = \emptyset$ then $\delta(q, a) = (\delta_x(I_x, a) \wedge \delta_r(q, a))$.
  - if $\delta_r(q, a) \cap F_r \neq \emptyset$ then $\delta(q, a) = (\delta_x(I_x, a) \wedge (\delta_r(q, a) \vee q_0))$.

  The acceptance condition is $F(q) = F_x(q)$ for q in Q_x, $F(q) = F_y(q)$ for q in Q_y, and $F(q_0) = 1$, $F(q) = 1$ for q in Q_r. The dual automaton $\mathcal{A}_{\overline{x \mathcal{U}^r y}}$ is built analogously, with the dual frame and $F(q_0) = 0$, and $F(q) = 0$ for $q \in Q_r$.

5   Conclusions

In this paper we have presented a finer grain complementation construction for alternating automata with the parity condition. This complementation allows to reason about walks in the graph of the specular automata pair, which are the only potential traces of runs. In turn, we showed how this result can be used to inductively translate temporal logic into APW. The translation of each operator produces a specular automata pair: one for the expression, one for its complement. This construction generates APW with few colors (2 for most expressions, 3 for the most sophisticated), which enables its efficient translation into non-deterministic Büchi Automata for model-checking. Future work includes the design of antichain algorithms directly for the APW generated from temporal logic expressions to alleviate even further the state explosion.

References

1. Armando, A., Ranise, S., Rusinowitch, M.: A rewriting approach to satisfiability procedures. Information and Computation 183(2), 140–164 (2003)
2. Beer, I., Ben-David, S., Eisner, C., Fisman, D., Gringauze, A., Rodeh, Y.: The Temporal Logic Sugar. In: Berry, G., Comon, H., Finkel, A. (eds.) CAV 2001. LNCS, vol. 2102, pp. 363–367. Springer, Heidelberg (2001)
3. Dax, C., Klaedtke, F.: Alternation Elimination by Complementation (Extended Abstract). In: Cervesato, I., Veith, H., Voronkov, A. (eds.) LPAR 2008. LNCS (LNAI), vol. 5330, pp. 214–229. Springer, Heidelberg (2008)
4. Emerson, E.A., Jutla, C.S.: Tree automata, mu-calculus and determinacy. In: FOCS 1991, pp. 368–377. IEEE Computer Society (1991)
5. Fisman, D., Eisner, C., Havlicek, J.: Formal syntax and Semantics of PSL: App. B of Accellera Property Language Ref. Manual, v1.1 (March 2004)
6. Gastin, P., Oddoux, D.: Fast LTL to Büchi Automata Translation. In: Berry, G., Comon, H., Finkel, A. (eds.) CAV 2001. LNCS, vol. 2102, pp. 53–65. Springer, Heidelberg (2001)
7. Henriksen, J.G., Thiagarajan, P.S.: Dynamic linear time temporal logic. Annals of Pure and Applied Logic 96(1-3), 187–207 (1999)
8. Kupferman, O., Piterman, N., Vardi, M.Y.: Extended Temporal Logic Revisited. In: Larsen, K.G., Nielsen, M. (eds.) CONCUR 2001. LNCS, vol. 2154, pp. 519–535. Springer, Heidelberg (2001)
9. Kupferman, O., Vardi, M.Y.: Weak alternating automata are not that weak. ACM Transactions on Computational Logic 2(3), 408–429 (2001)
10. Leucker, M., Sánchez, C.: Regular Linear Temporal Logic. In: Jones, C.B., Liu, Z., Woodcock, J. (eds.) ICTAC 2007. LNCS, vol. 4711, pp. 291–305. Springer, Heidelberg (2007)
11. Manna, Z., Pnueli, A.: Temporal Verification of Reactive Systems. Springer (1995)
12. Muller, D.E., Schupp, P.E.: Altenating automata on infinite trees. TCS 54, 267–276 (1987)
13. Pnueli, A.: The temporal logic of programs. In: FOCS 1977, pp. 46–67 (1977)

14. Sánchez, C., Leucker, M.: Regular Linear Temporal Logic with Past. In: Barthe, G., Hermenegildo, M. (eds.) VMCAI 2010. LNCS, vol. 5944, pp. 295–311. Springer, Heidelberg (2010)
15. Thomas, W.: Complementation of Büchi automata revisited. In: Jewels are Forever, pp. 109–120. Springer (1999)
16. Vardi, M.Y., Wolper, P.: An automata-theoretic approach to automatic program verification. In: LICS 1986, pp. 332–344. IEEE CS Press (1986)
17. Vardi, M.Y., Wolper, P.: Reasoning about infinite computations. Information and Computation 115, 1–37 (1994)

Correctness of Object Oriented Models by Extended Type Inference

Simon Foster[1], Ondřej Rypáček[2], and Georg Struth[2]

Department of Computer Science, University of York
simon.foster@york.ac.uk
Department of Computer Science, University of Sheffield
{g.struth,o.rypacek}@dcs.shef.ac.uk

Abstract. Modelling and analysing data dependencies and consistency between classes and objects is a complex task. We show that dependently typed programming languages can handle this in a particularly simple, convenient and highly automated way. Dependent datatypes are used to implement (meta)models for classes and objects directly and concisely. Data dependencies and similar system constraints are specified within the language's expressive type system. Verification and propagation of these constraints is handled by type inference, which can be enhanced by customised decision procedures or external solvers if needed. The approach thus supports the development of software models that are correct by construction.

1 Introduction

This research is motivated by the Model Driven Architecture[1] (MDA), where software is developed by integrating global platform independent system models with heterogeneous platform specific models. The MDA provides models for object-oriented designs at various meta-levels (MOF), languages for expressing constraints between models (OCL), and various languages and methods for model transformations. The approach depends on the ability to compose platform specific models in a highly automatic fashion, while maintaining global consistency and constraints that have been declared at the abstract level [9]. This is still difficult to achieve in practice.

This work focuses on modelling and analysing data dependencies and consistency between class diagrams, their corresponding object diagrams and meta-level templates that yield constraints for specifying these diagrams.

This work is inspired by and builds on previous work on formalising model transformations in constructive type theory [11]. We propose an approach that uses the dependently typed programming language Agda [2] for modelling system (meta)models for classes and objects, as they arise in MDA. Agda is a functional programming language similar to Haskell but with a much more powerful type system in which intuitionistic higher-order logic can be used for expressing

---

[1] http://www.omg.org/mda

A. Roychoudhury and M. D'Souza (Eds.): ICTAC 2012, LNCS 7521, pp. 46–60, 2012.

type constraints. Since, in this context, type inference is undecidable, the programming language is also an interactive theorem prover (ITP), in which type constraints can be resolved by incrementally filling in holes in proofs. Agda has a similar theory pedigree to the Coq ITP [1].

At the specification side, dependently typed programming is very convenient for MDA because data dependencies between classes and objects can be declared very simply and directly by using dependent datatypes, in particular dependent records. At the verification side, data consistency can often be established fully automatically by type checking and type inference. For more complex type constraints, this can be augmented by customised decision procedures, domain specific solvers or automated theorem provers [4].

Our main contributions are as follows.

- We show how class graphs—a restricted version of the MOF—can be implemented by Agda's dependent records. As an example, we populate the general infrastructure for classes provided by a simple meta-model for classes.
- We demonstrate how object graphs—which are dependent on class graphs— can be implemented in such a way that class-level constraints, for instance range constraints of associations, are automatically maintained. As an example, we derive object diagrams that are correct by type checking with respect to the constraints imposed.
- To illustrate the use of more advanced constraints, we show how bidirectional associations can be declared and verified automatically.

These results show that, with Agda, modelling, verification and implementation of our approach can be achieved in one and the same language. This is in contrast to other approaches where external formal methods like B or verification approaches like model checking are used [13,7].

Agda, as a functional language without side-effects, is also ideally suited for compositional system development. Compositionality is particularly important for integrating heterogeneous models in MDA.

While this paper focuses on the proof of concept that dependently typed programming has much to offer for MDA, and therefore shows and discusses the Agda implementation in detail, these technicalities should be hidden as far as possible to software engineers. A UML-style graphical toolkit providing templates for class and object diagrams could use our implementation as a backend, providing mechanisms for validating inputs and resolving system constraints behind the scenes in a highly sophisticated way.

The complete code featured in this paper can be found at our website[2].

2   Agda Preliminaries

This section contains a basic introduction to the features of Agda needed for this work. A more complete tutorial can be found on the Agda Wiki[3]. Agda is

---

[2] http://www-users.cs.york.ac.uk/~simonf/MDA/

[3] http://wiki.portal.chalmers.se/agda

a dependently typed functional programming language and proof assistant. Its syntax is inspired by Haskell, although Agda has support for both unicode and mixfix (e.g. ternary) operators. Agda is space sensitive – if a string has no spaces it is treated as a single name (or name part for a mixfix operator), for instance "x≤y" is a single name whilst "x ≤ y" consists of three names.

Agda is set apart as a programming language by its support for developing programs or systems that are *correct by construction*. Its type system is expressive enough to capture correctness properties concisely and sufficiently. These properties are verified within the development process by type checking. Whereas in simple cases this can be achieved fully automatically, more advanced tasks require interactive theorem proving within Agda. Agda also supports incremental development of programs and proofs by the technique of meta-variable refinement, which we illustrate below.

There are three main programming concepts which we here highlight:

- Algebraic Datatypes, which may be (co)inductive and can be used to define both data and propositions (e.g. proof datatypes);
- Functions, which can be recursive and contain proofs;
- Dependent records, a special form of datatype with field projections.

Datatypes are specified using a type constructor declaration, followed by a list of constructors with their respective types.

```
data N : Set where
  zero : N
  suc  : N → N
data Vec (A : Set) : N → Set where
  []   : Vec A zero
  _::_ : {n : N} → (x : A) → (xs : Vec A n) → Vec A (suc n)
```

Set is the type of all types. The natural numbers datatype declares the two usual constructors. The vector type Vec is a *dependent* datatype, because it is parameterised by its length, a property that depends on the particular data. The type constructor has two parameters. The first parameter, A, is an arbitrary element of Set which is fixed for all constructors. This is indicated by its position before the colon. The second parameter is a natural number which specifies the vector's length, and varies depending on the constructor. The first constructor [] constructs a Vec over A with zero length. The second infix constructor ::, given a value of type A and a vector of length n, constructs a vector of length suc n. Parameter n is hidden by the presence of braces. This means that the type system will try to infer its value via the other parameters and thus it need not be explicitly given. Parameter types in general can often also be inferred by insertion of a ∀ quantifier. Hidden arguments are useful to reduce verbosity of declarations. So 1 :: 2 :: 3 :: [] is a vector of length three over N.

Functions in Agda are total; a coverage checker ensures that all possible inputs have associated outputs. Partial functions can be specified by a partiality type, akin to Haskell's Maybe. Functions are specified using a type-signature followed by a sequence of equations. We define function ++ and map below.

$$\_+\!\!+\_ \ : \ \{A \ : \ \text{Set}\} \ \{m \ n \ : \ \mathbb{N}\} \to \text{Vec A m} \to \text{Vec A n} \to \text{Vec A } (m + n)$$

```
[] ++ ys       = ys
(x :: xs) ++ ys = x :: (xs ++ ys)
```

$$\text{map} \ : \ \{A \ B \ : \ \text{Set}\} \ \{m \ : \ \mathbb{N}\} \to (A \to B) \to \text{Vec A m} \to \text{Vec B m}$$

```
map f []       = []
map f (x :: xs) = f x :: map f xs
```

Concatenation, ++, is a binary operation on vectors defined, as usual, by recursion. It takes two vectors of element type A with lengths m and n and produces a vector of length m + n. This last property is beyond the expressivity of most traditional type systems. The map function takes a vector of A's and a function from A to B and produces a vector of B's by applying the function to every element. It is defined in the usual way.

Functions can also be used to represent lemmas and proofs; here the property that ++ distributes over map. We prove it by meta-variable refinement:

$$\text{map-}+\!\!+ \ : \forall \{m \ n\} \ \{A \ B \ : \ \text{Set}\} \ (f \ : \ A \to B) \ (xs \ : \ \text{Vec A m}) \ (ys \ : \ \text{Vec A n})$$
$$\to \text{map f xs} +\!\!+ \text{map f ys} \equiv \text{map f } (xs +\!\!+ ys)$$

```
map-++ f xs ys = { } 0
```

We begin with a type declaration, which encodes the proof goal for a function f and arbitrary vectors xs and ys, all supplied as parameters. In the type declaration, $\equiv$ represents propositional equality, that is equality of normal forms in all contexts. The function equation is populated with a meta-variable hole, { } 0, which we incrementally fill in using a divide and conquer strategy. To proceed with the inductive proof we have Agda split xs into its two possible cases.

```
map-++ f [] ys       = { } 0
map-++ f (x :: xs) ys = { } 1
```

We can then fill in both of these proof obligations as below.

```
map-++ f [] ys       = refl
map-++ f (x :: xs) ys = cong (_::_ (f x)) (map-++ f xs ys)
```

The first case has type map f [] ++ map f ys $\equiv$ map f ([] ++ ys), after substitution, which normalises to map f ys $\equiv$ map f ys. Therefore the two terms are propositionally equal by application of the reflexivity constructor refl. The second case is obtained by application of the induction hypothesis and the congruence rule cong under the context $C[X] = (f \ x) :: X$.

Records are specified in the usual way by listing fields with their types.

```
record Person : Set where
  field
    name       : String
    age        : ℕ
    ageInRange : age < 200
```

This is a *dependent* record because fields can depend on predecessors. Here the field called ageInRange, which is a proof of the proposition age < 200, depends on age. Thus fields can be used to encode both data and data constraints. We make much use of this for our MDA datatypes.

3   Overview of the Encoding

The fundamental MDA datatypes are UML class diagrams and object diagrams. To deal with them uniformly, MDA provides the meta-object facility (MOF) in which templates for objects are provided as class diagrams. Here we do not attempt an accurate portrayal of the MOF, but rather a simplified interpretation in terms of directed graphs (digraphs).

We model digraphs as labelled transition systems, using a transition function to map vertices and edges onto vertices. Recall that given a set $\mathcal{V}$ of vertices and $\mathcal{E}$ of edges, a digraph is a function $\delta : \mathcal{V} \times \mathcal{E} \rightarrow \mathcal{V}$.

- In Section 4 we introduce a set of class graphs, ClassGraph : Set_1 in Agda. A ClassGraph can be regarded as a digraph where the set of vertices is Class and the transition function is $\Delta : \forall \{c : Class\} \rightarrow Assoc\ c \rightarrow Class$.
- In Section 6 we define ObjGraph : ClassGraph $\rightarrow$ Set, assigning to each class graph c : ClassGraph a set of all object graphs validating c. ObjGraph is a digraph indexed by Class and the transition function is δ followed by a projection out of the object vector.
- In Section 8 we add bidirectionality constraints to class and object graphs.

The intermediate sections illustrate these implementations with simple examples.

4   Class Graphs in Agda

In Agda we represent class graphs as a dependent record.

```
record ClassGraph (Types : Set) : Set₁ where
    field
        Class        : Set
        Attr         : Class → Set
        Assoc        : Class → Set
        attrType     : {c : Class} → Attr c → Types
        assocRange   : {c : Class} → Assoc c → Interval
        Δ            : {c : Class} → Assoc c → Class
```

A class graph is parameterised over a set Types of primitive types, which we use in class attributes. Class is the set of class names. Attr and Assoc are parametric types, indicated by their definition as functions from Class into Set. They give the attribute and association names for each class. Field attrType gives a type to each attribute, and assocRange a target multiplicity for each association. Finally, Δ gives the target class of each association. This record is dependent because, for instance, assocRange depends on the definition given for Assoc. Constraints imposed on Assoc are therefore automatically inherited by assocRange.

Specifications like this would be difficult to formulate as concisely in languages without dependent types. We strongly use dependent records for the implementation of MDA concepts in this paper.

The parameter Interval in the definition of assocRange is defined as follows.

```
record Interval : Set where
  constructor _−_
  field
    lb : ℕ
    ub : Maybe ℕ
  IsInRange : ℕ → Set
  IsInRange n = lb ℕ≤ n × n ≤ⁱ ub
```

Interval ranges over the natural numbers. It consists of a lower bound lb and an upper bound ub, with just n representing upper bound n and nothing an unbounded range *. The predicate IsInRange over ℕ defines whether the given number is in range by means of a pair of inequalities, which are customised for the respective types. In constructive logic × performs the function of ∧. We also define a simple binary constructor so that we can write ranges like 0 − just 1.

5   A Class Graph Example

To exemplify the use of class graphs, we populate a simple meta-model for a class diagram as shown in Figure 1. We first declare some datatypes to act as names for classes, associations and attributes.

```
data CDClass : Set where
  NamedElt Classifier Class Attribute DataType : CDClass
data CDAssoc : CDClass → Set where
  att super   : CDAssoc Class
  type owner  : CDAssoc Attribute
  *super      : ∀ {c} → CDAssoc c
data CDAttr : CDClass → Set where
  name        : CDAttr NamedElt
  isAbstract  : CDAttr Class
  multivalued : CDAttr Attribute
```

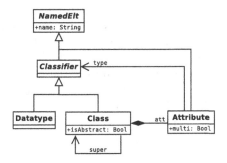

Fig. 1. Basic metamodel class diagram

The classes in this diagram are the labels of the nodes in the class graph. In our case these are precisely the elements NamedElt, Classifier, Class, Attribute and DataType of the datatype CDClass. The elements CDAssoc and CDAttr represent the names of associations and attributes in the class graph. They are parameterised by the name of the class from which they are drawn.

CDAssoc has elements att—the attributes of each class, type—the attribute type, owner—the owner class of an attribute, super—the superclass of a class, and *super—a polymorphic association which we use to model inheritance at the meta-level. We could automatically instrument the representation of inheritance through a preorder on the classes, but for this simple example it will be encoded manually. CDAttr has elements name, isAbstract and multivalued, as depicted in the example diagram.

To assign types to each attribute we also need a set Prim of primitive types. The types $\mathbb{N}$, Bool and String are all drawn from Agda's standard library[4].

```
data Prim  :  Set where Nat Bl Str  :  Prim
 [[ _ ]]  :  Prim → Set
 [[ Nat ]]  =  ℕ
 [[ Bl ]]   =  Bool
 [[ Str ]]  =  String
```

We now define the functions for attrType, assocRange and Δ for the remaining fields of our instance of ClassGraph.

```
cd-attrType  :  ∀ {c} → CDAttr c → Prim        cd-Δ  :  ∀ {c} → CDAssoc c → CDClass
cd-attrType name        = Str                   cd-Δ {NamedElt} *super = NamedElt
cd-attrType isAbstract  = Bl                    cd-Δ {Class} att       = Attribute
cd-attrType multivalued = Bl                    cd-Δ {Class} super     = Class
                                                cd-Δ {Class} *super    = Classifier
cd-asrn  :  ∀ {c} → CDAssoc c → Interval        cd-Δ {Attribute} type  = Classifier
cd-asrn {NamedElt} *super = none                cd-Δ {Attribute} owner = Class
cd-asrn {_} *super        = one                 cd-Δ {Attribute} *super = NamedElt
cd-asrn {Class} att       = many                cd-Δ {DataType} *super = Classifier
cd-asrn {Class} super     = optional            cd-Δ {Classifier} *super = NamedElt
cd-asrn {Attribute} type  = one
cd-asrn {Attribute} owner = one
```

The definition of cd-attrType assigns to each attribute in the class graph a type symbol from Prim. The function cd-asrn associates a range to each association, where none is empty, many is $0 - *$, optional is $0 - 1$ and one is $1 - 1$. The implementation of these functions is not shown. We must pattern match on both the class name and association name because of the polymorphic *super which has a different arity for each type. In particular for NamedElt it is empty as there is no superclass. The code for Δ essentially programs the transition function of the graph, that is, it gives a target class to each association. In particular *super targets the direct superclass of each class.

Using these functions we can complete the definition of our class graph.

---

[4] http://wiki.portal.chalmers.se/agda/agda.php?n=Libraries.StandardLibrary

```
classGraph : ClassGraph Prim
classGraph = record
  { Class       = CDClass  ; Attr     = CDAttr
  ; Assoc       = CDAssoc   ; attrType = cd-attrType
  ; assocRange  = cd-asrn   ; Δ        = cd-Δ }
```

6 Object Graphs in Agda

We can now define object graphs. At this level we need to provide an infrastructure for mapping the fields in an object graph, which represent the object instance data, to fields in a class graph, which represent their meta information.

```
record ObjGraph {T} (G : ClassGraph T) (⟦_⟧ : T → Set) : Set₁ where
  open ClassGraph G
  field
    Obj         : Class → Set
    attrVals    : ∀ {c} (o : Obj c) (a : Attr c) → ⟦ attrType a ⟧
    assocIndices : ∀ {c} (o : Obj c) (a : Assoc c)
                    → InRange (assocRange a)
    δ           : ∀ {c} (o : Obj c) (a : Assoc c)
                    → Vec (Obj (Δ a)) (value (assocIndices o a))
```

An object graph is parametrised by a class graph G, from which its structure is drawn, and a primitive type interpretation function ⟦_⟧, which assigns an Agda type to each abstract type. Within the record we first open the class graph G, thus bringing its fields into scope. Obj defines the set of all objects for each class, thus an Obj c is an object of class c. Field attrVals assigns, for each object and attribute name, a value for the attribute, using ⟦_⟧ to give a concrete type. Field assocIndices gives a cardinality for each association of each object, which naturally must satisfy the constraint of being in the range of the association's interval, as specified in G. Finally, δ gives, for each object and association, a vector of target objects of the association's target class (Δ a) and given size.

ObjGraph is again heavily dependent, so for example all fields depend on the definition of the underlying class graph, and, in addition, attrVals, assocIndices and δ depend on the definition of Obj. From the object oriented point of view this is, of course, obvious, but being able to encode this directly in a specification language is certainly unusual (without dependent types).

Values within intervals are provided by the type InRange.

```
record InRange (i : Interval) : Set where
  constructor #ʳ_
  open Interval i
  field
    value : ℕ
    {ni} : True (decIsInRange i value)
```

InRange uses a decision procedure to check whether a number is in the range of a given interval. This is, again, declared at the type level. It shows how Agda's type system can be effectively augmented with customised decision procedures. The InRange record consists of a number value and a proof that this value is in the correct range. The proof is automatically provided by the decision procedure

$$\mathsf{decIsInRange} \; : \; (\mathsf{i} \; : \; \mathsf{Interval}) \; (\mathsf{n} \; : \; \mathbb{N}) \to \mathsf{Dec} \; (\mathsf{IsInRange} \; \mathsf{i} \; \mathsf{n})$$

which makes direct use of the Agda standard library decision procedure for $\leqslant$.

The type Dec P represents a decision of the proposition P, containing either yes P or no ¬P. True is a function which returns type $\top$ if the parameterised value is yes and otherwise $\bot$. In the context of Agda, $\bot$ is a vacuous (unsatisfiable) type. $\top$ is a single element type which can also be automatically populated by the type checker. This means that field ni can be automatically inferred if value is populated with a number in the given range, whilst an out-of-range value will not yield a proof and invalidate InRange. We can therefore write $\#^r$ 1 : InRange (0 − just 1), which is certified to be correct automatically by the type checker. Conversely, $\#^r$ 6 : InRange (1 − just 5) will not type check as there is no proof of $6 \leqslant^i$ just 5. An IsInRange proof witness can then be extracted from a valid InRange and used in other proofs.

This simple example illustrates how constraints on objects and classes can effectively be captured by extended type checking in Agda, based on decision procedures, automated theorem provers or other solvers.

7   Populating Correct Object Graphs

This section shows how the class and object graph infrastructure developed in the previous sections can be used for populating concrete object graphs while checking the constraints imposed on classes and objects at the type level. This process can be seen in analogy to completing a template or filling in a web form while type checking is used behind the scenes to guarantee that the data is correct. However, while usually only simple properties can be verified, for instance that some input string consists of numbers, much more powerful properties and system constraints can be captured by Agda's expressive type system.

As an example, we construct the object graph of Figure 2. Agda supports type-safe incremental construction of data through meta-variable refinement, which we use to define the object graph. We first create datatypes to represent our objects.

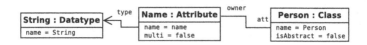

Fig. 2. Basic model object diagram

```
data PersonObj  :  CDClass → Set where
   Person    :  PersonObj Class
   Person'   :  PersonObj Classifier
   Person''  :  PersonObj NamedElt
   Name      :  PersonObj Attribute
   Name'     :  PersonObj NamedElt
   Str       :  PersonObj DataType
   Str'      :  PersonObj Classifier
   Str''     :  PersonObj NamedElt
```

Each object requires identifiers for each of the superclasses so that the respective *super associations can be populated. In real applications, such names would be allocated automatically; they are here shown explicitly for the sake of presentation. Using the object type we can then go ahead to construct the three functions attrVals, assocIndices and δ, each by meta-variable refinement. We now show this step-by-step. First we create the template for our object graph.

```
personOG  :  ObjGraph classGraph ⟦_⟧
personOG  =  record
   { Obj           =  PersonObj
   ; attrVals      =  og-attrVals
   ; assocIndices  =  og-assocIndices
   ; δ             =  og-δ }
og-attrVals  :  ∀ {c} → PersonObj c → (a  :  CDAttr c) → ⟦ attrType a ⟧
og-attrVals o a  =  { } 0
og-assocIndices  :  ∀ {c} → PersonObj c → (a  :  CDAssoc c)
                    → InRange (assocRange a)
og-assocIndices o a  =  { } 1
og-δ  :  ∀ {c  :  CDClass} (o  :  PersonObj c) (a  :  CDAssoc c)
         → Vec (PersonObj (Δ a)) (value (og-assocIndices o a))
og-δ o a  =  { } 2
```

The types of these three functions can be inferred automatically, but we write them explicitly for the sake of explanation. The body of each function is populated by a meta-variable hole. To fill in og-attrVals we case split on first the o parameter, the type of objects, and then the a parameter, the attribute type. This gives us the following holes to fill in (with corresponding types).

```
og-attrVals Person isAbstract  =  { } 0  -- Bool
og-attrVals Person'' name       =  { } 1  -- String
og-attrVals Name multivalued    =  { } 2  -- Bool
og-attrVals Name' name          =  { } 3  -- String
og-attrVals Str'' name          =  { } 4  -- String
```

Agda infers the type of each meta-variable and presents this information to the user. We have added comments that indicate these types. These meta-variables can all be filled in with correct values, and the type checker prevents us from substituting an incorrectly typed value.

```
og-attrVals Person isAbstract  = false
og-attrVals Person" name       = "Person"
og-attrVals Name multivalued   = false
og-attrVals Name' name         = "name"
og-attrVals Str" name          = "String"
```

We follow a similar procedure for og-assocIndices, each case of which needs to be populated by a suitable InRange for the corresponding association. For instance the case for association owner of Name has range one $(1-1)$, meaning the only possible value is 1.

```
og-assocIndices Name owner  =  #ʳ 1
```

If we try and insert any other value, for instance

```
og-assocIndices Name owner  =  #ʳ 2
```

the type checker will fail to resolve the internal constraint proof (ni) of the InRange, since it resolves to $\bot$. In this way the type system acts as a static checker for the multiplicities whilst we build the diagram.

Finally we construct the object assocation function og-δ, each element of which is a vector of suitably typed object, with length drawn from the corresponding association index.

```
og-δ Person att        = { } 0   -- Vec (PersonObj Attribute) 1
og-δ Person super      = { } 1   -- Vec (PersonObj Class) 0
og-δ Person *super     = { } 2   -- Vec (PersonObj Classifier) 1
og-δ Person' *super    = { } 3   -- Vec (PersonObj NamedElt) 1
og-δ Person" *super    = { } 4   -- Vec (PersonObj NamedElt) 0
...
```

We then fill in each meta-variable with associations from Figure 2.

```
og-δ Person att       = [Name]        og-δ Name owner     = [Person]
og-δ Person super     = []            og-δ Name *super    = [Name']
og-δ Person *super    = [Person']     og-δ Name' *super   = []
og-δ Person' *super   = [Person"]     og-δ Str *super     = [Str']
og-δ Person" *super   = []            og-δ Str' *super    = [Str"]
og-δ Name type        = [Str']        og-δ Str" *super    = []
```

This simple example shows how class and object graphs can be generated that are correct by construction. We are using the type system to check quite complicated constraints about the structures, rather than simple set-style constraints. Already simple object graphs can capture rather complex data dependencies that even involve the corresponding class. In a dependently type language, resolving these dependencies does not require any external proof engines or solvers. The entire process in this section is completely automatic as far as type inference is concerned. For instance, it is inferred that object Person has type Obj Class, class Class has association att, and association att in the class graph has range many and it must point to objects of type Attribute from the definition of Δ. It therefore follows that the Person case of function δ must consist of a vector of Obj Attribute, of a length within the many interval.

Although the constraints in our small examples are relatively simple, more complex constraints can be encoded at the type level if they can be expressed in intuitionistic higher-order logic.

8   Type Checking Bidirectionality Constraints

This section gives an example of how the verification of more complex constraints can be based on type checking. Many associations in class diagrams are bidirectional, for instance in Figure 1 att and owner are bidirectional. In our class graph model we encode a bidirectional association as a pair of unidirectional associations, but so far cannot explicitly declare and verify the constraint that a given association is bidirectional. We encode bidirectionality of associations with the following record.

> **record** Bidirect $\{$ T $\}$ (G : ClassGraph T) : Set$_1$ **where**
>   constructor [_ $\longleftrightarrow$ _] _
> **open** ClassGraph G
> **field**
> $\{$ class $\}$: Class
>   assoc   : Assoc class
>   assoc'   : Assoc (Δ assoc)
>   converse : Δ assoc' $\equiv$ class

Bidirect consists of a pair of associations, the first of which has its source in class and its target in the associated class, whereas for the second association source and target class are swapped, which is ensured by the converse constraint. We then use this new record to extend class graphs to class diagrams with bidirectional associations.

> **record** ClassDiagram (Types : Set) : Set$_1$ **where**
>   **field**
>   classGraph : ClassGraph Types
>   bidirects   : Σ [n : $\mathbb{N}$] (Vec (Bidirect classGraph) n)

A class diagram simply adds a vector of associations which are bidirectional. These can then be used in object diagrams, which constrain bidirectionality of concrete associations. First we define the interpretation function for bidirectional constraints with the function IsBidirect.

> Assoclx : $\forall$ $\{$ c $\}$ (o : Obj c) (a : Assoc c) $\rightarrow$ Set
> Assoclx o a = Fin (value (assocIndices o a))
>
> IsBidirect : Bidirect G $\rightarrow$ Set
> IsBidirect b = **let open** Bidirect b **in**
> $\forall$ (o : Obj class) (i : Assoclx o assoc) $\rightarrow$
>   **let** o' = lookup i (δ o assoc) **in**
> Σ [i' : Assoclx o' assoc'] (lookup i' (δ o' assoc') $\cong$ o)

A bidirectional relation is encoded between associations assoc and assoc' as a logical formula that satisfies the following condition. For every object o of the source class of assoc, and each of its indices i, targeting object o', there exists an index i' of assoc' targeting object o. To satisfy this constraint for a given object graph we have to supply a lambda term of the correct type. In certain circumstances such a lambda term can be generated automatically.

We can then enforce this constraint when building object diagrams.

```
record ObjDiagram { T } (G  :  ClassDiagram T)  :  Set₁ where
    open ClassDiagram G
    field
        objGraph : ObjGraph classGraph
    open ObjGraph objGraph
    field
        isBidirects : ∀ (i : Fin (proj₁ bidirects)) → IsBidirect (lookup i (proj₂ bidirects))
```

An object diagram consists of an object graph and a function mapping each bidirectional association to a proof that bidirectionality holds.

9   A Bidirectionality Example

We can extend our examples from the previous sections, making att and owner converses of each other. This will turn our type into an accurate representation of the class diagram in Figure 1, ensuring that only valid object diagrams are elements.

```
classDiagram  :  ClassDiagram Prim
classDiagram  =  record
    { classGraph  =  classGraph
    ; bidirects  =  (2, [att ⟷ owner] PropEq.refl :: [owner ⟷ att] PropEq.refl :: []) }
```

Both directions must be stated. Each constraint also uses the simple proof PropEq.refl that following att and then owner returns to Class, and vice versa. We can then extend our object graph to an object diagram.

```
personOD  :  ObjDiagram classDiagram
personOD  =  record
    { objGraph  =  personOG
    ; isBidirects  =  isBidirects }
    where open ObjGraph personOG
        isBidirects : (i : Fin (proj₁ bidirects)) → IsBidirect (lookup i (proj₂ bidirects))
        isBidirects zero Person zero  =  zero, HetEq.refl
        isBidirects (suc zero) Name zero  =  zero, HetEq.refl
```

The function isBidirects satisfies both of the bidirectional constraints (vacuous cases are omitted). The first requires a proof of

$$\Sigma \, [i \, : \, \text{Fin } 1] \, (\text{lookup i (Person :: [])}) \cong \text{Person})$$

where i is an index of owner under object Name, which is reached by following att from Person. This is trivially satisfied by index zero, with Person ≅ Person satisfied by HetEq.refl. The second case is similarly satisfied, but with att and owner reversed. Both of these proofs can be automatically discharged by Agda's auto tactic. This completes the definition of the object diagram.

10   Related Work

The area of formal semantics for UML is vast and space restricts their full consideration, though we note that both Object-Z and VDM have class diagram mappings. Specific to our work is the use of graphs to represent class diagrams, for which a comprehensive discussion exists in [8]. We use a fairly standard graph encoding, though with the addition of dependent types.

Works with similar aims using different ITPs exist. For instance, HOL-OCL [3] is a well-developed Isabelle/HOL library for verifying OCL expressions on UML class diagrams. Similarly, Object-Z has been mechanised [12]. The key difference in our work is the intimate relationship between data and proof, provided by dependent type theory. Nevertheless, Agda lacks the automated proof support which more mature ITPs (like Isabelle) enjoy, though similar results could potentially be achieved [4]. Moreover, we do not currently support OCL, but since we do have well-typed navigation an elegant implementation is possible.

11   Conclusion and Future Work

We have implemented basic MDA concepts and shown how Agda can be used for inferring system constraints. With dependent types, system dependencies and constraints can be modelled succinctly and directly; they can be resolved, often automatically, by extended type inference.

Additional work focuses on the implementation of a library for representing valid models and transformations between them. In general a model transformation can be represented as a function.

$$\_ \Rightarrow \_ \; : \; \forall \, \{\, T \,\} \to \mathsf{ClassDiagram}\; T \to \mathsf{ClassDiagram}\; T \to \mathsf{Set}$$
$$\mathsf{P} \Rightarrow \mathsf{Q} \; = \; \mathsf{ObjDiagram}\; \mathsf{P} \to \mathsf{ObjDiagram}\; \mathsf{Q}$$

Such a function must, for each valid instance of the class diagram P, provide a valid instance of the class diagram Q. We can use the type system to aid with construction of such a transformation by having it exhaustively supply all possibilities for the input, thus ensuring that a model transformation is complete.

Refinement and implementation of transformations can proceed in several ways. We are currently collaborating on extending an Agda based graph transformation library [6] for this purpose. Graph transformations are one of the standard approaches to model transformations. Alternatively we are designing a state-based embedded language in Agda for graph traversals and manipulation, inspired by languages such as ATL [5] and Kermeta [10]. The type system can be used during program construction to inform programmers about data and constraints relevant to a particular object. Also, integration of automated theorem provers in Agda beyond the current prototype [4] would be of great benefit to the semi-automatic composition and development of model transformations.

In conclusion, we believe that Agda provides many benefits to the integration of formal methods, for instance by both ensuring that code is correct with respect to a suitable model and supplying useful information during code construction. In applicable formal methods the Agda layer needs to be hidden as much as possible behind an interface, for which a high degree of automation is a prerequisite. In the future we would therefore like to see an Eclipse frontend, which would interface to a suitable Agda domain-specific language and convert Agda error messages and information into a format readable by a software engineer.

Acknowledgements. The authors acknowledge support for this project by the EPSRC (grants EP/G031711/1 and EP/G031711/1).

References

1. Bertot, Y., Castéran, P.: Interactive Theorem Proving and Program Development. Texts in Theoretical Computer Science. Springer (2004)
2. Bove, A., Dybjer, P., Norell, U.: A Brief Overview of Agda – A Functional Language with Dependent Types. In: Berghofer, S., Nipkow, T., Urban, C., Wenzel, M. (eds.) TPHOLs 2009. LNCS, vol. 5674, pp. 73–78. Springer, Heidelberg (2009)
3. Brucker, A.D., Wolff, B.: HOL-OCL: Experiences, Consequences and Design Choices. In: Jézéquel, J.-M., Hussmann, H., Cook, S. (eds.) UML 2002. LNCS, vol. 2460, pp. 196–211. Springer, Heidelberg (2002)
4. Foster, S., Struth, G.: Integrating an Automated Theorem Prover into Agda. In: Bobaru, M., Havelund, K., Holzmann, G.J., Joshi, R. (eds.) NFM 2011. LNCS, vol. 6617, pp. 116–130. Springer, Heidelberg (2011)
5. Jouault, F., Allilaire, F., Bézivin, J., Kurtev, I.: ATL: A model transformation tool. Sci. Comput. Program. 72(1-2), 31–39 (2008)
6. Kahl, W.: Dependently-typed formalisation of typed term graphs. In: Echahed, R. (ed.) TERMGRAPH 2011. EPTCS, pp. 38–53 (2011)
7. Knapp, A., Merz, S.: Model checking and code generation for UML state machines and collaborations. Tech. Rep. 2002-11, Institut für Informatik, Universität Augsburg (2002); in Proc. FM-TOOLS 2002
8. Kuske, S., Gogolla, M., Kreowski, H., Ziemann, P.: Towards an integrated graph-based semantics for UML. Software and Systems Modeling 8, 403–422 (2009)
9. Lano, K.: Constraint-driven development. Information & Software Technology 50(5), 406–423 (2008)
10. Muller, P.-A., Fleurey, F., Jézéquel, J.-M.: Weaving Executability into Object-Oriented Meta-languages. In: Briand, L.C., Williams, C. (eds.) MoDELS 2005. LNCS, vol. 3713, pp. 264–278. Springer, Heidelberg (2005)
11. Poernomo, I.: Proofs-as-Model-Transformations. In: Vallecillo, A., Gray, J., Pierantonio, A. (eds.) ICMT 2008. LNCS, vol. 5063, pp. 214–228. Springer, Heidelberg (2008)
12. Smith, G.P., Kammüller, F., Santen, T.: Encoding Object-Z in Isabelle/HOL. In: Bert, D., P. Bowen, J., C. Henson, M., Robinson, K. (eds.) ZB 2002. LNCS, vol. 2272, pp. 82–99. Springer, Heidelberg (2002)
13. Snook, C.F., Butler, M.J.: UML-B: Formal modeling and design aided by UML. ACM Trans. Softw. Eng. Methodol. 15(1), 92–122 (2006)

Non-termination Sets of Simple Linear Loops

Liyun Dai and Bican Xia*

LMAM & School of Mathematical Sciences, Peking University
dailiyun@pku.edu.cn, xbc@math.pku.edu.cn

Abstract. A simple linear loop is a simple while loop with linear assignments and linear loop guards. If a simple linear loop has only two program variables, we give a complete algorithm for computing the set of all the inputs on which the loop does not terminate. For the case of more program variables, we show that the non-termination set cannot be described by Tarski formulae in general.

Keywords: Simple linear loop, termination, non-termination set, eigenvalue, Tarski formula.

1 Introduction

Termination of programs is an important property of programs and one of the main research topics in the field of program verification. It is well known that the following so-called "uniform halting problem" is undecidable in general.

Using only a finite amount of time, determine whether a given program will always finish running or could execute forever.

However, there are some well known techniques for deciding termination of some special kinds of programs. A popular technique is to use ranking functions. A ranking function for a loop maps the values of the loop variables to a well-founded domain; further, the values of the map decrease on each iteration. A linear ranking function is a ranking function that is a linear combination of the loop variables and constants. Some methods for the synthesis of ranking functions and some heuristics concerning how to automatically generate linear ranking functions for linear programs have been proposed, for example, in Colón and Sipma [3], Dams et al. [4] and Podelski and Rybalchenko [6]. Podelski and Rybalchenko [6] provided an efficient and complete synthesis method based on linear programming to construct linear ranking functions. Chen et al. [2] proposed a method to generate nonlinear ranking functions based on semi-algebraic system solving. The existence of ranking function is only a sufficient condition on the termination of a program. There are programs, which terminate, but do not have ranking functions. Another popular technique based on well-orders, presented in Lee et al. [5], is size-change principle. The well-founded data can ensure that there are no infinitely descents, which guarantees termination of programs.

---

* Corresponding author.

A. Roychoudhury and M. D'Souza (Eds.): ICTAC 2012, LNCS 7521, pp. 61–73, 2012.

For linear loops, some other methods based on calculating eigenvectors of matrices have been proposed. Tiwari [7] proved that the termination problem of a class of linear programs (simple loops with linear loop conditions and updates) over the reals is decidable through Jordan form and eigenvector computation. Braverman [1] proved that it is also decidable over the integers. Xia et al. [8] considered the termination problems of simple loops with linear updates and polynomial loop conditions, and proved that the termination problem of such loops over the integers is undecidable. In [9], Xia et al. provided a novel symbolic decision procedure for termination of simple linear loops, which is as efficient as the numerical one given in [7].

A counter-example to termination is an infinite program execution. In program verification, the search for counter-examples to termination is as important as the search for proofs of termination. In fact, these are the two folds of termination analysis of programs. Gupta et al. [10] proposed a method for searching counter-examples to termination, which first enumerates lasso-shaped candidate paths for counter-examples and proves the feasibility of a given lasso by solving the existence of a recurrent set as a template-based constraint satisfaction problem. Gulwani et al. [11] proposed a constraint-based approach to a wide class of program analyses and weakest precondition and strongest postcondition inference. The approach can be applied to generating most-general counter-examples to termination.

In this paper, we consider the set of all inputs on which a given program does not terminate. The set is called NT throughout the paper. For simple linear loops, we are interested in whether the NT is decidable and how to compute it if it is decidable. Similar problems was also considered in [12]. One possible application of computing NT (and thus termination sets) is to construct preconditions and/or postconditions for loops. Our contributions in this paper are as follows. First, for homogeneous linear loops (see Section 2 for the definition) with only two program variables, we give a complete algorithm for computing the NT. For the case of more program variables, we show that the NT cannot be described by Tarski formulae in general.

The rest of this paper is organized as follows. Section 2 introduces some notations and basic results on simple linear loops. Section 3 presents an algorithm for computing the NT of homogeneous linear loops with only two program variables. The correctness of the algorithm is proved by a series of lemmas. For linear loops with more than two program variables, it is proved in Section 4 that the NT is not a semi-algebraic set in general, i.e., it cannot be described by Tarski formulae in general. The paper is concluded in Section 5.

2   Preliminaries

In this paper, the domain of inputs of programs is $\mathbb{R}$, the field of real numbers. A *simple linear loop* in general form over $\mathbb{R}$ can be formulated as

$$\texttt{P1}: \quad \text{while } (B\boldsymbol{x} > \boldsymbol{b}) \ \{\boldsymbol{x} := A\boldsymbol{x} + \boldsymbol{c}\}$$

where b, c are real vectors, $A_{n \times n}, B_{m \times n}$ are real matrices. $Bx > b$ is a conjunction of m linear inequalities in x and $x := Ax + c$ is a linear assignment on the program variables x.

Definition 1. [7] *The non-termination set of a program is the set of all inputs on which the program does not terminate. It is denoted by* NT *in this paper.*

In particular, $\mathrm{NT}(\texttt{P1}) = \{x \in \mathbb{R}^n | \texttt{P1} \text{ does not terminate on } x\}$.
We list some related results in [7].

Proposition 1. [7] *For a simple linear loop* P1, *the following is true.*

- *The termination of* P1 *is decidable.*
- *If* A *has no positive eigenvalues, the* NT *is empty.*
- *The* NT *is convex.*

In this paper, only the following *homogeneous case* is considered.

$$\texttt{P2}: \quad \text{while } (Bx > 0) \ \{x := Ax\} \ .$$

Let $B_1, \ldots, B_m$ be the rows of B. Consider the following loops

$$L_i: \quad \text{while } (B_i x > 0) \ \{x := Ax\} \ .$$

Obviously, $\mathrm{NT}(\texttt{P2}) = \bigcap_{i=1}^m \mathrm{NT}(L_i)$. Therefore, without loss of generality, we assume throughout this paper that $m = 1$, *i.e.*, there is only one inequality as the loop guard. The following is a simple example of such loops.

$$\text{while } (4x_1 + x_2 > 0) \quad \left\{ \begin{pmatrix} x_1 \\ x_2 \end{pmatrix} := \begin{pmatrix} -2 & 4 \\ 4 & 0 \end{pmatrix} \begin{pmatrix} x_1 \\ x_2 \end{pmatrix} \right\} \ .$$

That is $B = (4, 1), A = \begin{pmatrix} -2 & 4 \\ 4 & 0 \end{pmatrix}$.

3 Two-Variable Case

To make things clear, we restate the problem for this two-variable case as follows.
For a given homogeneous linear loop P2 *with exactly two program variables and only one inequality as the loop guard, compute* $\mathrm{NT}(\texttt{P2})$.

For simplicity, we denote the program variables by x_1, x_2 and use NT instead of $\mathrm{NT}(\texttt{P2})$ in this section. If α is a non-zero point in the plane, we denote by $\overrightarrow{\alpha}$ a ray starting from the origin of plane and going through the point α.

Proposition 2. NT *must be one of the following:*
(1) an empty set;
(2) a single ray starting from the origin;
(3) a sector between two rays starting from the origin.

Proof. We view an input (x_1, x_2) as a point in the real plane with origin O. If there exists a point $M(x_1, x_2) \in \text{NT}$, any point $\boldsymbol{P}$ on the ray $\overrightarrow{OM}$ can be written as $\boldsymbol{P} = kM = (kx_1, kx_2)$ for a positive number k. So $BA^n(kx_1, kx_2)^T = kBA^n(x_1, x_2)^T > 0$ for any $n \in \mathbb{N}$. That means $\boldsymbol{P} \in \text{NT}$. Therefore, it is clear from the item 3 of Proposition 1 that the conclusion is true.

By the above proposition, the key point for computing the NT is to compute the ray(s) which is (are) the boundary of NT. We give the following algorithm to compute the ray(s) (and thus the NT) for P2 if the NT is not empty. The algorithm, as can be expected, is mainly based on the computation of eigenvalues and eigenvectors of A. The correctness of our algorithm will be proved by a series of lemmas following the algorithm.

Algorithm 1. NonTermination

   Input: Matrices $A_{2\times2}$ and $B_{1\times2}$.
   Output: The NT of P2 with A and B.
1 if $A = \mathbf{0}$ *or* $B = \mathbf{0}$ then
2 | return $\emptyset$;
3 Compute the eigenvalues of A and denote them by λ_1, λ_2;
4 if $\lambda_1 \not> 0 \wedge \lambda_2 \not> 0$ then
5 | return $\emptyset$;   // Proposition 1
6 Take $\boldsymbol{\alpha_0} \in \mathbb{R}^2 \setminus \{\mathbf{0}\}$ such that $B\boldsymbol{\alpha_0} = 0$ and $BA\boldsymbol{\alpha_0} \geq 0$;
7 if $BA\boldsymbol{\alpha_0} = 0$ then
8 | choose $\boldsymbol{\xi}$ such that $B\boldsymbol{\xi} > 0$
9 | if $B(A\boldsymbol{\xi}) > 0$ then
10 | | return $\{\boldsymbol{x} | \boldsymbol{x} \in \mathbb{R}^2, B\boldsymbol{x} > 0\}$ // Lemma 4
11 | else
12 | | return $\emptyset$ // Lemma 5
13 if $\lambda_1 = 0 \vee \lambda_2 = 0$ then
14 | return $\{\boldsymbol{x} | \boldsymbol{x} \in \mathbb{R}^2, B\boldsymbol{x} > 0, BA\boldsymbol{x} > 0\}$;   // Lemma 6
15 Suppose $\lambda_1 \geq \lambda_2$
16 if $\lambda_1 \geq \lambda_2 > 0$ then
17 | choose an eigenvector $\boldsymbol{\beta_2}$ related to λ_2 such that $B\boldsymbol{\beta_2} > 0$;
18 | return $\{\boldsymbol{x} | \boldsymbol{x} = k_1\boldsymbol{\alpha_0} + k_2\boldsymbol{\beta_2}, k_1 \geq 0, k_2 > 0\}$;   // Lemmas 7 and 8
19 if $\lambda_1 > 0 \wedge \lambda_2 < 0$ then
20 | if $\lambda_1 \geq |\lambda_2|$ then
21 | | let $\boldsymbol{\alpha_{-1}} = A^{-1}\boldsymbol{\alpha_0}$ and return $\{\boldsymbol{x} | \boldsymbol{x} = k_1\boldsymbol{\alpha_0} + k_2\boldsymbol{\alpha_{-1}}, k_1 > 0, k_2 > 0\}$;
22 | if $\lambda_1 < |\lambda_2|$ then
23 | | choose an eigenvector $\boldsymbol{\beta}$ related to λ_1 such that $B\boldsymbol{\beta} > 0$ and
24 | | return $\{\boldsymbol{x} | \boldsymbol{x} = k\boldsymbol{\beta}, k > 0\}$ // Lemma 10

To better understand the idea of the following lemmas, it would be helpful to remember an obvious fact that NT $\subseteq \{\boldsymbol{x} | B\boldsymbol{x} > 0\}$. Actually, in Lemma 3, we

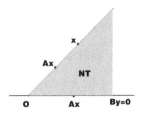

Fig. 1. Lemma 1

will prove that, if the boundary of NT consists of two rays (see Proposition 2), one of the two rays must lie on the line $B\boldsymbol{x} = 0$.

Lemma 1. *Suppose* NT *is not empty and* ∂NT *is the boundary of* NT. *If* $\boldsymbol{x} \in \partial$NT *and* $B\boldsymbol{x} \neq 0$, *then* $A\boldsymbol{x} \in \partial$NT.

Proof. Obviously, B is a linear map from $\mathbb{R}^2$ to $\mathbb{R}$. Because $B\boldsymbol{y} > 0$ for all $\boldsymbol{y} \in$ NT, we have $B\boldsymbol{x} \geq 0$. And thus $B\boldsymbol{x} > 0$ by the assumption that $B\boldsymbol{x} \neq 0$. Hence, there exists an open ball $o_1(\boldsymbol{x}, r_1)$ such that $B\boldsymbol{y} > 0$ for all $\boldsymbol{y} \in o_1(\boldsymbol{x}, r_1)$.

Let F be the linear map from $\mathbb{R}^2$ to $\mathbb{R}^2$ that $F(\boldsymbol{y}) = A\boldsymbol{y}$ for any $\boldsymbol{y} \in \mathbb{R}^2$ and hence F is continuous. So for any neighborhood $o(A\boldsymbol{x}, r)$ of $A\boldsymbol{x}$, there exists a positive real number r_2 such that $o_2(\boldsymbol{x}, r_2) \subseteq o_1(\boldsymbol{x}, r_1)$ and $F(o_2(\boldsymbol{x}, r_2)) \subseteq o(A\boldsymbol{x}, r)$. Because $\boldsymbol{x} \in \partial$NT, there exist $\boldsymbol{y}, \boldsymbol{z} \in o_2(\boldsymbol{x}, r_2)$ such that $\boldsymbol{y} \in$ NT and $\boldsymbol{z} \notin$ NT. Then $A(\boldsymbol{y}), A(\boldsymbol{z}) \in o(A\boldsymbol{x}, r)$, $A(\boldsymbol{y}) \in$ NT and $A(\boldsymbol{z}) \notin$ NT since $B\boldsymbol{z} > 0$. It is followed that there are both terminating and non-terminating inputs in any neighborhood of $A\boldsymbol{x}$. Therefore, $A\boldsymbol{x} \in \partial$NT.

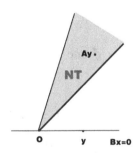

Fig. 2. Lemma 2

To prove Lemma 3, we first prove Lemma 2 which will be used in the proof of Lemma 3 to construct a contradiction.

Lemma 2. *Suppose* ∂NT *is composed of two rays* l_1 *and* l_2 *and neither* l_1 *nor* l_2 *is on* $B\boldsymbol{x} = 0$. *If* $B\boldsymbol{y} = 0$ *and* $BA\boldsymbol{y} > 0$, *then* $A\boldsymbol{y} \in$ NT.

Proof. Since neither l_1 nor l_2 is on $Bx = 0$, l_1 and l_2 are not collinear. So we can choose two points $z \in l_1$ and $v \in l_2$ such that $Bz > 0$, $Bv > 0$ and $y = t_1 z + t_2 v$ for some $t_1 \in \mathbb{R}, t_2 \in \mathbb{R}$. By Lemma 1, Az and Av must be on the boundary of NT, i.e., l_1 or l_2. Thus, we have at most four possible cases as follows.

(1) $Az = k_1 z, Av = k_2 v$, (i.e., $Az \in l_1, Av \in l_2$)
(2) $Az = k_1 z, Av = k_2 z$, (i.e., $Az \in l_1, Av \in l_1$)
(3) $Az = k_1 v, Av = k_2 v$, (i.e., $Az \in l_2, Av \in l_2$)
(4) $Az = k_1 v, Av = k_2 z$, (i.e., $Az \in l_2, Av \in l_1$)

where $k_1 > 0, k_2 > 0$.

Case (1). Because $By = t_1 Bz + t_2 Bv = 0$ and

$$BAy = BA(t_1 z + t_2 v) = t_1 k_1 Bz + t_2 k_2 Bv > 0,$$

we have $t_1 t_2 < 0$. Without loss of generality, assume that $t_1 > 0$ and $t_2 < 0$. We denote $t_1 Bz$ by P. Note that $P > 0$ and $t_2 Bv = -P$. Since $BAy = (k_1 - k_2)P > 0$, we have $k_1 > k_2 > 0$ and

$$BA^n(Ay) = k_1^{n+1} t_1 Bz + k_2^{n+1} t_2 Bv = k_1^{n+1} P - k_2^{n+1} P > 0$$

for any $n \in \mathbb{N}$. By the definition of NT, $Ay \in$ NT.

Case (2). Because $BAy = (t_1 k_1 + t_2 k_2)Bz > 0$, we have

$$BA^n(Ay) = k_1^n (t_1 k_1 + t_2 k_2)Bz > 0$$

for any $n \in \mathbb{N}$. By the definition of NT, we have $Ay \in$ NT.

Case (3). Similarly as Case (2), we can prove $Ay \in$ NT.

Case (4). We shall show that this case cannot happen. Let

$$S = \{x | x = r_1 y + r_2 Ay, r_1 > 0, r_2 > 0\}$$

be the sector between the two rays $\overrightarrow{y}$ and $\overrightarrow{Ay}$. For any $w \in S$, we have $Bw = r_1 By + r_2 BAy = r_2 BAy > 0$.

Because

$$A^2 y = A(t_1 k_1 v + t_2 k_2 z) = t_1 k_1 k_2 z + t_2 k_1 k_2 v = k_1 k_2 y,$$

we have $Aw = r_1 Ay + r_2 A^2 y = r_1 Ay + r_2 k_1 k_2 y \in S$. Therefore, $w \in$ NT and $S \subseteq$ NT. As $\overrightarrow{y}$ is a boundary of S and $By = 0$, $\overrightarrow{y}$ is contained in ∂NT, which contradicts with the assumption of the lemma. So (4) cannot happen.

In summary, $Ay \in$ NT.

Lemma 3. *If ∂NT is composed of two rays l_1 and l_2, then either l_1 or l_2 is on $Bx = 0$.*

Proof. Assume neither l_1 nor l_2 is on $Bx = 0$. Choose a point y such that $y \neq 0$, $By = 0$ and $BAy \geq 0$.

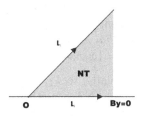

Fig. 3. Lemma 3

Suppose $BA\boldsymbol{y} = 0$. As NT is not empty, there exists $\boldsymbol{z} \in$ NT. Hence $A\boldsymbol{y}$ can be rewritten as $A\boldsymbol{y} = h_1\boldsymbol{z} + h_2\boldsymbol{y}$ for some $h_1 \in \mathbb{R}, h_2 \in \mathbb{R}$. As a result of $BA\boldsymbol{y} = h_1B\boldsymbol{z} + h_2B\boldsymbol{y} = h_1B\boldsymbol{z} = 0$, $h_1 = 0$. Note that

$$A^n\boldsymbol{y} = h_2^n\boldsymbol{y}, BA^n\boldsymbol{y} = h_2^nB\boldsymbol{y} = 0 \ . \tag{1}$$

According to Eq.(1) and $\boldsymbol{z} \in$ NT, we have $BA^n(k_1\boldsymbol{z} + k_2\boldsymbol{y}) = k_1BA^n\boldsymbol{z} + k_2BA^n\boldsymbol{y} = k_1BA^n\boldsymbol{z} > 0$ for any $k_1 > 0, n \in \mathbb{N}$. Hence $\{\boldsymbol{x}|\boldsymbol{x} = k_1\boldsymbol{z} + k_2\boldsymbol{y}, k_1 > 0\} \subseteq$ NT. Therefore, $\{\boldsymbol{x}|B\boldsymbol{x} = 0\} = \partial$NT, which contradicts with the assumption.

If $BA\boldsymbol{y} > 0$, $A\boldsymbol{y} \in$ NT follows from Lemma 2. Let $S = \{\boldsymbol{x}|k_1\boldsymbol{y} + k_2A\boldsymbol{y}, k_1 > 0, k_2 > 0\}$. And we have $BA^n\boldsymbol{z} = k_1BA^n\boldsymbol{y} + k_2BA^{n+1}\boldsymbol{y} > 0$ for any $n \in \mathbb{N}$, $\boldsymbol{z} \in S$. Thus $\boldsymbol{z} \in$ NT and $S \subseteq$ NT. By the method of choosing $\boldsymbol{y}$, $\overrightarrow{\boldsymbol{y}} \subseteq \partial$NT. That means $\overrightarrow{\boldsymbol{y}}$ is l_1 or l_2, which contradicts with the assumption.

Lemma 4. *Suppose A has an eigenvector $\boldsymbol{\alpha}$ satisfying $B\boldsymbol{\alpha} = 0$. If there is a vector $\boldsymbol{\xi}$ such that $B\boldsymbol{\xi} > 0$ and $BA\boldsymbol{\xi} > 0$, then NT $= \{\boldsymbol{x}|B\boldsymbol{x} > 0\}$.*

Proof. For any $\boldsymbol{y} \in \{\boldsymbol{x}|B\boldsymbol{x} > 0\}$, it can be written as $\boldsymbol{y} = k_1\boldsymbol{\xi} + k_2\boldsymbol{\alpha}$ for some $k_1 \in \mathbb{R}, k_2 \in \mathbb{R}$. As $B\boldsymbol{y} = k_1B\boldsymbol{\xi} + k_2B\boldsymbol{\alpha} = k_1B\boldsymbol{\xi} > 0$, we have $k_1 > 0$. Thus $BA\boldsymbol{y} = k_1BA\boldsymbol{\xi} + k_2BA\boldsymbol{\alpha} = k_1BA\boldsymbol{\xi} > 0$ and $A\boldsymbol{y} \in \{\boldsymbol{x}|B\boldsymbol{x} > 0\}$. By the definition of NT, we have $\{\boldsymbol{x}|B\boldsymbol{x} > 0\} \subseteq$ NT and hence NT $= \{\boldsymbol{x}|B\boldsymbol{x} > 0\}$.

Lemma 5. *Suppose A has an eigenvector $\boldsymbol{\alpha}$ satisfying $B\boldsymbol{\alpha} = 0$. If there is a vector $\boldsymbol{\xi}$ such that $B\boldsymbol{\xi} > 0$ and $BA\boldsymbol{\xi} \leq 0$, then NT $= \emptyset$.*

Proof. For any $\boldsymbol{y} \in \{\boldsymbol{x}|B\boldsymbol{x} > 0\}$, it can be written as $\boldsymbol{y} = k_1\boldsymbol{\alpha} + k_2\boldsymbol{\xi}$ for some $k_1 \in \mathbb{R}, k_2 \in \mathbb{R}$. Since $B\boldsymbol{y} = k_2B\boldsymbol{\xi} > 0$, we have $k_2 > 0$. And because $BA\boldsymbol{y} = k_2BA\boldsymbol{\xi} \leq 0$, NT $= \emptyset$.

Lemma 6. *Suppose A has a positive eigenvalue and a zero eigenvalue and the eigenvector related to the positive eigenvalue is not on the line $B\boldsymbol{x} = 0$. Then NT $= \{\boldsymbol{x}|B\boldsymbol{x} > 0, BA\boldsymbol{x} > 0\}$.*

Proof. Let $\boldsymbol{\beta}$ be an eigenvector with respect to eigenvalue 0 and λ be the positive eigenvalue. Select an eigenvector $\boldsymbol{\gamma}$ related to the positive eigenvalue such that $B\boldsymbol{\gamma} > 0$. Let S be the set $\{\boldsymbol{x}|B\boldsymbol{x} > 0, BA\boldsymbol{x} > 0\}$. For any $\boldsymbol{y} \in S$, it can be written as $k_1\boldsymbol{\beta} + k_2\boldsymbol{\gamma}$ for some $k_1 \in \mathbb{R}, k_2 \in \mathbb{R}$. We have $BA\boldsymbol{y} = k_2\lambda B\boldsymbol{\gamma} > 0$, thus $k_2 > 0$. Note that $BA^n\boldsymbol{y} = k_2\lambda^n B\boldsymbol{\gamma} > 0$ for any $n \in \mathbb{N}$, hence $S \subseteq$ NT. Because $\{\boldsymbol{x}|B\boldsymbol{x} \leq 0 \vee BA\boldsymbol{x} \leq 0\} \cap$ NT $= \emptyset$, NT $= \{\boldsymbol{x}|B\boldsymbol{x} > 0, BA\boldsymbol{x} > 0\}$.

Lemma 7. *Suppose A has two positive eigenvalues $\lambda_1 \geq \lambda_2 > 0$ and the eigenvectors related to the positive eigenvalues are not on the line $Bx = 0$. If β_2 is an eigenvector related to λ_2 such that $B\beta_2 > 0$ and there is a vector α such that $B\alpha = 0$ and $BA\alpha > 0$, then $NT = \{x | x = k_1\alpha + k_2\beta_2, k_1 \geq 0, k_2 > 0\}$.*

Proof. Select an eigenvector β_1 related to λ_1, respectively, such that $B\beta_1 > 0$. It is easy to know $\beta_1, \beta_2 \in NT$, thus NT is neither empty nor a ray. By Lemma 3 there is a $\overrightarrow{y} \subseteq \partial NT$ and y satisfies $By = 0$. Since for any $z \in \partial NT$, we have $BAz \geq 0$. So $BAy \geq 0$ and hence $\overrightarrow{\alpha} = \overrightarrow{y}$. In other word, $\overrightarrow{\alpha}$ is one ray of ∂NT. Let the other ray of ∂NT be l. As $-BA\alpha < 0$, $\overrightarrow{-\alpha}$ is not l. By Lemma 1, we have $Al \in \partial NT$. So l is one of $\overrightarrow{\beta_1}, \overrightarrow{\beta_2}$ and $\overrightarrow{A^{-1}\alpha}$. By directly checking, we know $\overrightarrow{\beta_2}$ is l and so $NT = \{x | x = k_1\alpha + k_2\beta_2, k_1 \geq 0, k_2 > 0\}$.

Lemma 8. *Assume that A has one positive eigenvalue λ with multiplicity 2 and only one eigenvector β satisfying $B\beta > 0$. If α is a vector such that $B\alpha = 0$ and $BA\alpha > 0$, then $NT = \{x | x = k_1\alpha + k_2\beta, k_1 \geq 0, k_2 > 0\}$.*

Proof. By the theory of Jordan normal form in linear algebra, there exists a vector β_1 such that $A\beta_1 = \beta + \lambda\beta_1$ and β and β_1 are linearly independent.

Let $\alpha_1 = A\alpha$. We claim that

$$\forall n \in \mathbb{N}.(BA^n\alpha_1 > 0 \wedge \exists h_2 > 0.(A^n\alpha_1 = h_1\beta + h_2\beta_1)). \tag{2}$$

To prove this claim we use induction on the value of n.

Suppose $\alpha = h_1\beta + h_2\beta_1$. If $n = 0$, then $\alpha_1 = A\alpha = (h_1\lambda + h_2)\beta + h_2\lambda\beta_1$. Because $B\alpha_1 = \lambda B\alpha + h_2 B\beta = h_2 B\beta > 0$, we have $h_2 > 0$.

Now assume that the claim is true for $n - 1$. Let $A^{n-1}\alpha_1 = h_1\beta + h_2\beta_1$ where $h_2 > 0$. Because $A^n\alpha_1 = A(A^{n-1}\alpha_1) = (\lambda h_1 + h_2)\beta + \lambda h_2\beta_1$, we have $\lambda h_2 > 0$ and $BA^n\alpha_1 = \lambda BA^{n-1}\alpha_1 + h_2 B\beta > 0$. So the claim is true for any $n \in \mathbb{N}$ and we have $\alpha_1 \in NT$.

Obviously, $\beta \in NT$ and β and α_1 are linearly independent, so NT is not a ray. By Lemma 3, $\overrightarrow{\alpha} \subseteq \partial NT$.

Let the other ray of ∂NT be l. As $-BA\alpha < 0$, $\overrightarrow{-\alpha}$ is not l. By Lemma 1, $Al = l$ or $Al = \overrightarrow{\alpha}$. So l must be $\overrightarrow{\beta}$ or $\overrightarrow{A^{-1}\alpha}$. By directly checking, we know l is $\overrightarrow{\beta}$ and thus $NT = \{x | x = k_1\alpha + k_2\beta, k_1 \geq 0, k_2 > 0\}$.

Lemma 9. *Suppose A has a positive eigenvalue λ_1 and a negative eigenvalue λ_2 with $\lambda_1 \geq |\lambda_2|$ and the eigenvectors related to the eigenvalues are not on the line $Bx = 0$. Suppose α is a vector such that $B\alpha = 0$ and $BA\alpha > 0$. Let $\alpha_{-1} = A^{-1}\alpha$. Then $NT = \{k_1\alpha + k_2\alpha_{-1}, k_1 > 0, k_2 > 0\}$.*

Proof. Select two eigenvectors β_1 and β_2 related to λ_1 and λ_2, respectively, such that $B\beta_1 > 0$ and $B\beta_2 > 0$. Let $\alpha_{-1} = h_1\beta_1 + h_2\beta_2$. So $\alpha = A\alpha_{-1} = h_1\lambda_1\beta_1 + h_2\lambda_2\beta_2$ and $\alpha_1 = A\alpha = h_1\lambda_1^2\beta_1 + h_2\lambda_2^2\beta_2$. Because $B\alpha = 0$ and $B\alpha_1 > 0$, h_1, h_2 and $A\alpha_{-1}$ are all positive.

Note that $\alpha_1 = (-\lambda_1\lambda_2)\alpha_{-1} + (\lambda_1 + \lambda_2)\alpha$ where $-\lambda_1\lambda_2 > 0$ and $\lambda_1 + \lambda_2 \geq 0$. Let $S = \{x | x = k_1\alpha + k_2\alpha_{-1}, k_1 > 0, k_2 > 0\}$. Since $By = k_2 B\alpha_{-1} > 0$ and $Ay = (k_2 + k_1(\lambda_1 + \lambda_2))\alpha - k_1\lambda_1\lambda_2\alpha_{-1} \in S$ for any $y \in S$, we have $NT \supseteq S$.

Let $y = k_1\alpha + k_2\alpha_{-1}$. Because $By = k_2B\alpha_{-1} \leq 0$ for any $k_2 \leq 0$ and $BAy = k_1B\alpha_1 \leq 0$ for any $k_1 \leq 0$, we have NT $= S$.

Lemma 10. *Suppose A has a positive eigenvalue λ_1 and a negative eigenvalue λ_2 such that $\lambda_1 < |\lambda_2|$ and the eigenvectors related to the eigenvalues are not on the line $Bx = 0$. Let β_1 be an eigenvector related to λ_1 such that $B\beta_1 > 0$, then* NT $= \{x|x = k\beta_1, k > 0\}$.

Proof. Select an eigenvector β_2 related to λ_2 such that $B\beta_2 > 0$. Consider any $\beta = k_1\beta_1 + k_2\beta_2 \in \mathbb{R}^2$.

If $k_2 \neq 0$, because $A^n(k_1\beta_1 + k_2\beta_2) = k_1\lambda_1^n\beta_1 + k_2\lambda_2^n\beta_2$ and

$$BA^n(k_1\beta_1 + k_2\beta_2)BA^{n+1}(k_1\beta_1 + k_2\beta_2) < 0$$

when n is large enough, $k_1\beta_1 + k_2\beta_2 \notin$ NT.

If $k_2 = 0$, obviously, NT $\supseteq \{x|x = k\beta_1, k > 0\}$ and $Bk\beta_1 \notin$ NT for any $k \leq 0$.

So NT $= \{x|x = k\beta_1, k > 0\}$.

Now, the correctness of our algorithm NonTermination can be easily obtained as follows.

Theorem 1. *The algorithm* NonTermination *is correct.*

Proof. First, the termination of NonTermination is obvious because there are no loops and no iterations in it. Second, it is also clear that the algorithm discusses all the cases of eigenvalues of A, respectively. we will show that the output of the algorithm in each case is correct.

Obviously, the outputs of Lines 2 and 5 are correct. If the algorithm goes to Line 6, A must have at least one positive eigenvalue.

If the algorithm goes to Line 8, α_0 must be an eigenvector of A because $A\alpha_0$ and α_0 are both on the same line $Bx = 0$. So, by Lemmas 4 and 5, the outputs of Line 10 and Line 12 are correct.

If the algorithm goes to Line 13, A must have at least one positive eigenvalue and the eigenvectors of A do not lie on the line $Bx = 0$. So, for a nonzero eigenvalue, we can choose a related eigenvector γ such that $B\gamma > 0$. That is to say, the assumptions of Lemmas 6-10 can be satisfied in each of the following cases, respectively. Therefore, the outputs of Lines 14, 18, 21 and 24 are correct.

Example 1. Compute the NT of the following loop.

$$\text{while } (4x_1 + x_2 > 0) \quad \left\{ \begin{pmatrix} x_1 \\ x_2 \end{pmatrix} = \begin{pmatrix} -2 & 4 \\ 4 & 0 \end{pmatrix} \begin{pmatrix} x_1 \\ x_2 \end{pmatrix} \right\}$$

Herein, $B = (4, 1), A = \begin{pmatrix} -2 & 4 \\ 4 & 0 \end{pmatrix}$.

The computation of NonTermination on the loop is:

Line 1. $B \neq 0$ and $A \neq 0$.

Line 4. A has a positive eigenvalue $-1 + \sqrt{17}$.

Line 6. Let $\alpha_0 = (-1, 4)^T, \alpha_1 = A\alpha_0 = (18, -4)^T$.

Line 7. $B\alpha_1 = 68 \neq 0$.

Line 13. The two eigenvalues of A are $-1 + \sqrt{17}, -1 - \sqrt{17}$, respectively. Neither of them is 0.

Line 19. A has two eigenvalues, of which one is positive and the other negative.

Line 20. The absolute value of the negative eigenvalue is greater than the positive eigenvalue.

Line 22. The eigenvector with respect to the positive eigenvalue is $\beta = (1, \frac{\sqrt{17}+1}{4})^T$ and $B\beta > 0$. Return $\{x | x = k\beta, k > 0\}$.

4 More Variables

Theorem 2. *In general,* NT *is not a semi-algebraic set.*

Remark 1. All Tarski formulae are in the form of conjunctions or/and disjunctions of polynomial equalities and/or inequalities, so, in other words, semi-algebraic sets are exactly the sets defined by Tarski formulae. By Theorem 2, we can conclude that the non-termination sets of linear loops with more than two variables cannot be defined by Tarski formulae in general.

Remark 2. It should be noticed that all polynomial invariants are semi-algebraic sets.

In order to prove the above theorem, we give an example to demonstrate its NT is not a semi-algebraic set.

Proposition 3. *Let a linear loop with three program variables be as follows.*

$$\text{P3} : \text{while } (x_1 + 2x_2 + x_3 \geq 0) \quad \left\{ \begin{pmatrix} x_1 \\ x_2 \\ x_3 \end{pmatrix} = \begin{pmatrix} 2 & 0 & 0 \\ 0 & 3 & 0 \\ 0 & 0 & 5 \end{pmatrix} \begin{pmatrix} x_1 \\ x_2 \\ x_3 \end{pmatrix} \right\}.$$

Then NT(P3) *is not a semi-algebraic set.*

The conclusion can be proved by using the following lemmas. For simplicity, NT(P3) is denoted by NT in this section.

Lemma 11. *Denote by τ the following set*

$$\{9(x_1^2 + x_2^2) - x_3^2 < 0, x_3 > 0\},$$

then $\tau \subseteq$ NT.

Proof. For any $(x_1, x_2, x_3) \in \tau$, we have $x_3 > 3|x_1|, x_3 > 3|x_2|$ and thus $x_1 + 2x_2 + x_3 > 0$. Because $A(x_1, x_2, x_3)^T = (2x_1, 3x_2, 5x_3)^T$ and $9(4x_1^2 + 9x_2^2) - 25x_3^2 < 0$, $A(x_1, x_2, x_3)^T \in \tau$. Therefore $\tau \subseteq$ NT.

Lemma 12. $\partial \mathrm{NT} \subseteq \mathrm{NT}$.

Proof. Because the loop guard is of the form $B(x_1, x_2, x_3)^T \geq 0$, NT is a closed set. So the conclusion is correct. Furthermore, for any $(x_1, x_2, x_3) \in \partial \mathrm{NT}, x_1 + 2x_2 + x_3 \geq 0$.

Lemma 13. *If* $(x_1, x_2, x_3) \in \mathrm{NT}$ *and* $A(x_1, x_2, x_3)^T \in \partial \mathrm{NT}$, *then* $(x_1, x_2, x_3) \in \partial \mathrm{NT}$.

Proof. Let $\boldsymbol{x} = (x_1, x_2, x_3)$. If the conclusion is not true, there exists a ball $o(\boldsymbol{x}, r) \subseteq \mathrm{NT}$. Because $A\boldsymbol{x}^T \in \partial \mathrm{NT}$, there exists $\boldsymbol{x}'$ such that $|A\boldsymbol{x} - \boldsymbol{x}'| < r$ and $\boldsymbol{x}'$ is not in NT.

Since $|A^{-1}\boldsymbol{x}' - \boldsymbol{x}| < |\boldsymbol{x}' - A\boldsymbol{x}| < r$, $A^{-1}\boldsymbol{x}' \in o(\boldsymbol{x}, r)$. So $A^{-1}\boldsymbol{x}' \in \mathrm{NT}$ and thus $\boldsymbol{x}' \in \mathrm{NT}$, which is a contradiction.

Lemma 14. $\{(\frac{1}{2^n}, -\frac{1}{3^n}, \frac{1}{5^n})\}_{n=0}^{\infty} \subseteq \partial \mathrm{NT}$.

Proof. Let $\boldsymbol{p}_n = (\frac{1}{2^n}, -\frac{1}{3^n}, \frac{1}{5^n}), n \geq 0$. We use induction on the value of n.

When $n = 0$, because $B\boldsymbol{p}_0 = B(1, -1, 1)^T = 0$ and

$$BA^k \boldsymbol{p}_0 = 2^k - 2 \times 3^k + 5^k > 0 \quad \text{for any } k \in \mathbb{N}^+,$$

we have $\boldsymbol{p}_0 \in \partial \mathrm{NT}$.

Now assume that the conclusion holds for $n-1$. So, $A\boldsymbol{p}_n = \boldsymbol{p}_{n-1} \in \partial \mathrm{NT} \subseteq \mathrm{NT}$. By Lemma 13, $\boldsymbol{p}_n \in \partial \mathrm{NT}$.

Lemma 15. *For any non-zero polynomial* $f(x_1, x_2, x_3) \in \mathbb{R}[x_1, x_2, x_3]$, *there exists an* N *such that* $f(\frac{1}{2^n}, -\frac{1}{3^n}, \frac{1}{5^n}) \neq 0$ *for all* $n > N$.

Proof. Assume that the conclusion does not hold. Then there exists a subsequence $\{((\frac{1}{2})^{n_k}, -(\frac{1}{3})^{n_k}, (\frac{1}{5})^{n_k})\}_{k=1}^{\infty}$ such that f vanishes on each point of it.

Let $f = b_1 x_1^{\alpha_1} x_2^{\beta_1} x_3^{\gamma_1} + ... + b_s x_1^{\alpha_s} x_2^{\beta_s} x_3^{\gamma_s}$ where $b_i \in \mathbb{R}, b_i \neq 0, \alpha_i \in \mathbb{N}, \beta_i \in \mathbb{N}, \gamma_i \in \mathbb{N}$, and $(\alpha_i, \beta_i, \gamma_i) \neq (\alpha_j, \beta_j, \gamma_j)$ for $i \neq j$.

Obviously $s \geq 1$ because $f \neq 0$. Let $t_i = (\frac{1}{2})^{\alpha_i} (\frac{1}{3})^{\beta_i} (\frac{1}{5})^{\gamma_i}$.

It is an obvious fact that $2^{\alpha_j} 3^{\beta_j} 5^{\gamma_j} \neq 2^{\alpha_i} 3^{\beta_i} 5^{\gamma_i}$ for $i \neq j$. Hence $t_1, t_2, ..., t_s$ are pairwise distinct. Without loss of generality, let $t_1 > t_2 > ... > t_s$.

For every $j > 1$, we have $\lim\limits_{k \to \infty} (\frac{t_j}{t_1})^{n_k} = 0$. Thus

$$\lim_{k \to \infty} \left| \frac{f((\frac{1}{2})^{n_k}, -(\frac{1}{3})^{n_k}, (\frac{1}{5})^{n_k})}{((\frac{1}{2})^{\alpha_1} (\frac{1}{3})^{\beta_1} (\frac{1}{5})^{\gamma_1})^{n_k}} \right| = |b_1| \neq 0 .$$

This contradicts with $f((\frac{1}{2})^{n_k}, -(\frac{1}{3})^{n_k}, (\frac{1}{5})^{n_k}) = 0$. Therefore the conclusion follows.

Using the above lemmas, we can now prove Theorem 2.

Proof. Denote by S the sequence $\{(\frac{1}{2})^n, -(\frac{1}{3})^n, (\frac{1}{5})^n)\}$. By Lemma 14, $S \subseteq \partial\mathrm{NT}$.

Assume NT is a semi-algebraic set. Then there exist finite many polynomials $f_{i,j} \in \mathbb{R}[x_1, x_2, x_3]$ and $\lhd_{i,j} \in \{<, =\}$ for $i = 1, ..., s$ and $j = 1, ..., r_i$ such that

$$\mathrm{NT} = \bigcup_{i=1}^{s} \bigcap_{j=1}^{r_i} \{(x_1, x_2, x_3) \in \mathbb{R}^3 | f_{i,j} \lhd_{i,j} 0\}. \tag{3}$$

Because $S \subseteq \partial\mathrm{NT} \subseteq \{f_{i,j} = 0\}_{i,j}$, for any $x \in S$, there exists a polynomial $f_{i,j}$ such that $f_{i,j}(x) = 0$. By pigeonhole principle there exists an $f_{i,j}$ and a subsequence S_1 of S such that $f_{i,j}$ vanishes on S_1, which contradicts with Lemma 15.

5   Conclusion

In this paper, we consider whether the NT of a simple linear loop is decidable and how to compute it if it is decidable. For homogeneous linear loops with only two program variables, we give a complete algorithm for computing the NT. For the case of more program variables, we show that the NT cannot be described by Tarski formulae in general.

Acknowledgements. The work is partly supported by the EXACTA project (NNSFC 91018012) and the project SYSKF1207 from State Key Laboratory of Computer Science, Institute of Software, Chinese Academy of Sciences. The authors thank the reviewers for their valuable comments and suggestion.

References

1. Braverman, M.: Termination of Integer Linear Programs. In: Ball, T., Jones, R.B. (eds.) CAV 2006. LNCS, vol. 4144, pp. 372–385. Springer, Heidelberg (2006)
2. Chen, Y., Xia, B., Yang, L., Zhan, N., Zhou, C.: Discovering Non-linear Ranking Functions by Solving Semi-algebraic Systems. In: Jones, C.B., Liu, Z., Woodcock, J. (eds.) ICTAC 2007. LNCS, vol. 4711, pp. 34–49. Springer, Heidelberg (2007)
3. Colón, M.A., Sipma, H.B.: Synthesis of Linear Ranking Functions. In: Margaria, T., Yi, W. (eds.) TACAS 2001. LNCS, vol. 2031, pp. 67–81. Springer, Heidelberg (2001)
4. Dams, D., Gerth, R., Grumberg, O.: A heuristic for the automatic generation of ranking functions. In: Workshop on Advances in Verification (WAVe 2000), pp. 1–8 (2000)
5. Lee, C.S., Jones, N.D., Ben-Amram, A.M.: The size-change principle for program termination. In: POPL, pp. 81–92 (2001)
6. Podelski, A., Rybalchenko, A.: A Complete Method for the Synthesis of Linear Ranking Functions. In: Steffen, B., Levi, G. (eds.) VMCAI 2004. LNCS, vol. 2937, pp. 239–251. Springer, Heidelberg (2004)
7. Tiwari, A.: Termination of Linear Programs. In: Alur, R., Peled, D.A. (eds.) CAV 2004. LNCS, vol. 3114, pp. 70–82. Springer, Heidelberg (2004)

8. Xia, B., Zhang, Z.: Termination of linear programs with nonlinear constraints. Journal of Symbolic Computation 45, 1234–1249 (2010)
9. Xia, B., Yang, L., Zhan, N., Zhang, Z.: Symbolic decision procedure for termination of linear programs. Formal Aspects of Computing 23, 171–190 (2011)
10. Gupta, A., Henzinger, T., Majumdar, R., Rybalchenko, A., Xu, R.G.: Proving non-termination. In: POPL, pp. 147–158 (2008)
11. Gulwani, S., Srivastava, S., Venkatesan, R.: Program analysis as constraint solving. In: POPL, pp. 281–292 (2008)
12. Zhao, S., Chen, D.: Decidability Analysis on Termination Set of Loop Programs. In: The International Conference on Computer Science and Service System(CSSS), pp. 3124–3127 (2011)

Definite Expression Aliasing Analysis for Java Bytecode

Đurica Nikolić[1,2] and Fausto Spoto[1]

[1] Dipartimento di Informatica, University of Verona
[2] The Microsoft Research - University of Trento Center for Computational and Systems Biology
{durica.nikolic,fausto.spoto}@univr.it

Abstract. We define a novel static analysis for Java bytecode, called *definite expression aliasing*. It infers, for each variable v at each program point p, a set of expressions whose value at p is equal to the value of v at p, for every possible execution of the program. Namely, it determines which expressions *must* be aliased to local variables and stack elements of the Java Virtual Machine. This is a useful piece of information for a static analyzer, such as Julia, since it can be used to refine other analyses at conditional statements or assignments. We formalize and implement a *constraint-based* analysis, defined and proved correct in the abstract interpretation framework. Moreover, we show the benefits of our definite expression aliasing analysis for nullness and termination analysis with Julia.

1 Introduction

Static analyses infer properties of computer programs and prove those programs secure for some classes of bugs. Modern programming languages are, however, very complex. Static analysis must cope with that complexity and remain precise enough to be of practical interest. This is particularly true for low-level languages such as Java bytecode [9], whose instructions operate on stack or local variables, which are typically aliased to expressions. Consider, for instance, the method onOptionsItemSelected in Fig. 1, taken from the Google's HoneycombGallery Android application. The statement if (mCamera!=null) at line 4 is compiled into the following bytecode instructions:

```
aload_0
getfield mCamera:Landroid/hardware/Camera;
ifnull [go to the else branch]
[then branch]
```

Bytecode ifnull checks whether the topmost variable of the stack, *top*, is null and passes control to the opportune branch. A static analysis that infers non-null variables can, therefore, conclude that *top* is non-null at the [then branch]. But this information is irrelevant: *top* gets consumed by the ifnull and disappears from the stack. It is, instead, much more important to know that *top* was a definite alias of the field mCamera of local 0, i.e., of this.mCamera, because of the previous two bytecodes (local 0 stands for this). That observation is important at the subsequent call to mCamera.stopPreview() at line 5, since it allows us to conclude that this.mCamera is still non-null there: line 5 is part of the then branch starting at line 4 and we proved that *top* (definitely aliased to this.mCamera) is non-null at that point.

A. Roychoudhury and M. D'Souza (Eds.): ICTAC 2012, LNCS 7521, pp. 74–89, 2012.

```
1  public boolean onOptionsItemSelected(MenuItem item) {
2    switch (item.getItemId()) {
3    case R.id.menu_switch_cam:
4      if (mCamera != null) {
5        mCamera.stopPreview();
6        mPreview.setCamera(null);
7        mCamera.release();
8        mCamera = null;
9      }
10     mCurrentCamera = (mCameraCurrentlyLocked+1)%mNumberOfCameras;
11     mCamera = Camera.open(mCurrentCamera);
12     mCameraCurrentlyLocked = mCurrentCamera;
13     mCamera.startPreview();
14     return true;
15   case ....
16   ....
17 }
```

Fig. 1. A method of the CameraFragment class by Google

As another example of the importance of definite aliasing for static analysis, suppose that we statically determined that the value returned by the method open and written in this.mCamera at line 11 is non-null. The compilation of that assignment is:

```
aload_0
aload_0
getfield mCurrentCamera:I
invokestatic android/hardware/Camera.open:(I)Landroid/hardware/Camera;
putfield mCamera:Landroid/hardware/Camera;
```

and the putfield bytecode writes the top of the stack (open's returned value) into the field mCamera of the underlying stack element s. Hence s.mCamera becomes non-null, but this information is irrelevant, since s disappears from the stack after the putfield is executed. The actual useful piece of information at this point is that s was a definite alias of expression this (local variable 0) at the putfield, which is guaranteed by the first aload_0 bytecode. Hence, this.mCamera becomes non-null there, which is much more interesting for the analysis of the subsequent statements.

The previous examples show the importance of definite expression aliasing analysis for nullness analysis. However, the former is useful for other analyses as well. For instance, consider the termination analysis of a loop whose upper bound is the return value of a function call: for (i = 0; i < max(a, b); i++) {body}. In order to prove its termination, a static analyzer needs to prove that the upper bound max(a, b) remains constant during the loop. However, in Java bytecode, that upper bound is just a stack element and the static analyzer must rather know that the latter is a definite alias of the return value of the call max(a, b).

These examples show that it is important to know which expressions are *definitely* aliased to stack and local variables of the Java Virtual Machine (JVM) at a given program point. Moreover, when a bytecode instruction affects a variable, this modification is propagated to all the expressions containing that variable. This way we can determine different properties about the aliased expressions. In this article, we introduce a static analysis called *definite expression aliasing analysis*, which provides, for each program point p and each variable v, a set of expressions E such that the values of E and v at point p coincide, for every possible execution path. We call these expressions *definite expression aliasing information*. In general, we want to deal with relatively complex expressions (e.g., a field of a field of a variable, the return value of a method call, possibly non-pure, and so on). We show, experimentally, that this analysis supports nullness and termination analyses of our tool Julia, but this paper is only concerned with the expression aliasing analysis itself. Our analysis has been proven sound, but due to space limitations, proofs can only be found in an extended version of this paper [10].

We opt for a semantical analysis rather than simple syntactical checks. For instance, in Fig. 1, the result of the analysis must not change if we introduce a temporary variable temp = this.mCamera and then check whether temp != null: it is still this.mCamera that is compared to null there. Moreover, since we analyze Java bytecode, a semantical approach is important in order to be independent from the specific compilation style of high-level expressions and be able to analyze obfuscated code (for instance, malware) or code not decompilable into Java (for instance, not organized into scopes).

Our definite expression aliasing analysis is constraint-based: a large constraint is built from the program, whose solution is a sound approximation of the expressions aliased to each variable at each program point. The correctness of our analysis is proved in the abstract interpretation framework [5] and follows from a correct treatment of the potential side-effects of statements.

Related Work. Alias analysis belongs to the large group of pointer analyses [7], and its task is to determine whether a memory location can be accessed in more than one way. There exist two types of alias analyses: possible (may) and definite (must). The former detects those pairs of variables that might point to the same memory location. There are very few tools performing this analysis on Java programs (e.g., WALA [2], soot [1], JAAT [12]). On the other hand, definite alias analysis under-approximates the actual aliasing information and, to the best of our knowledge, the analysis introduced in this article is the first of this type dealing with Java bytecode programs and providing expressions aliased to variables. Similarly, the authors of [6] deal with definite aliasing, but their *must-aliasing* information is used for other goals and they do not deal with aliasing expressions. The idea of a constraint-based analysis is not new: we have already used it to formalize possible analyses [14,11]. However, the construction of the constraint and the definition of the propagation rules are different there. A static analysis that over-approximates the set of fields that might be null at some point has been introduced in [13]. More complex expressions than fields are not considered there, though. Our analysis is also related to the well-known *available expression analysis* [3] where, however, only variables of primitive type are considered, hence it is much easier to deal with side-effects. Fields can be sometimes transformed into local variables before a static analysis is performed [4], but this requires a preliminary modification of the code and we want to deal with more general expressions than just fields.

2 Operational Semantics

This section introduces a formal operational semantics of our target, Java bytecode-like language, used also in [14,11] and inspired by the standard informal semantics [8].

The target language contains the following instructions: const x, dup, load, store, inc, ifeq, ifne, new, getfield, putfield, throw and call. They abstract whole classes of Java bytecode instructions such as iconst_x, ldc, bipush, dup, iload, aload, istore, astore, iinc, ifeq, ifne, if_null, if_nonnull, new, getfield, putfield, athrow, invokevirtual, and invokespecial. In addition, we introduce an instruction op corresponding to the arithmetic bytecode instructions such as iadd, isub, imul, idiv and irem, and an instruction catch starting the exception handlers. An informal semantics of this language is provided at the end of this section. We analyze programs at bytecode level for several reasons: there is a small number of bytecode instructions, compared to varieties of source statements; bytecode lacks complexities such as inner classes; our implementation of definite expression aliasing is at bytecode level as well, which brings formalism, implementation and correctness proofs closer.

For simplicity, we assume that the only primitive type is int and that reference types are *classes* containing *instance fields* and *instant methods* only. Our implementation handles all Java types and bytecodes, as well as classes with static fields and methods.

Definition 1 (Classes). *We let $\mathbb{K}$ denote the set of* classes *and we define* $\mathbb{T} = \{\text{int}\} \cup \mathbb{K}$, *the set of all possible* types. *Every class* $\kappa \in \mathbb{K}$ *might have* instance fields *$\kappa.f: t$ (field f of type $t \in \mathbb{T}$ defined in class κ) and* instance methods *$\kappa.m(\vec{t}): t$ (method m, defined in class κ, with arguments of type $\vec{t}$ taken from $\mathbb{T}$, returning a value of type $t \in \mathbb{T} \cup \{\text{void}\}$), where $\kappa, \vec{t},$ and t are often omitted. We let $\mathbb{F}(\kappa)$ denote the set of all fields contained in κ.*

We analyze bytecode preprocessed into a control flow graph (CFG), i.e., a directed graph of *basic blocks*, with no jumps inside them.
$$\boxed{\begin{array}{l} \text{ins} \\ \hline \text{rest} \end{array}}\begin{array}{l} \to b_1 \\ \cdots \\ \to b_m \end{array}$$
denotes a block of code starting at instruction ins, possibly followed by a sequence of instructions *rest* and linked to m subsequent blocks $b_1, \ldots, b_m$.

Example 1. Consider the Java method delayMinBy and its corresponding graph of basic blocks of bytecode instructions given in Fig. 2. The latter contains a branch since the getfield min might throw a NullPointerException which would be temporarily caught and then re-thrown to the caller of the method. Otherwise, the execution continues with a block that reads the other parameter (load 1), adds it to the value read from the field min and returns the result. Every bytecode instruction except return and throw always has one or more immediate successors. The latter are placed at the end of a method or constructor and typically have no successors. ∎

Bytecode instructions operate on *variables*, which encompass both stack elements and local variables. A standard algorithm [8] infers their static types.

Definition 2 (Type environment). *Let V be the set of* variables *from $L = \{l_0, \ldots, l_{i-1}\}$ (i local* variables*) and $S = \{s_0, \ldots, s_{j-1}\}$ (j stack* elements*). A* type environment *is a function $\tau : V \to \mathbb{T}$, and its domain is written as $\mathsf{dom}(\tau)$. The set of all type environments is $\mathcal{T}$. For simplicity, we write $\mathsf{dom}(\tau) = \{v_0, \ldots, v_{i+j-1}\}$, where $v_r = l_r$ if $0 \leq r < i$ and $v_r = s_{r-i}$ if $i \leq r < i + j$. Moreover, we let $|\tau|$ denote $|\mathsf{dom}(\tau)| = i + j$.*

Definition 3 (State). *A* value *is an element of $\mathbb{V} = \mathbb{Z} \cup \mathbb{L} \cup \{\text{null}\}$, where $\mathbb{L}$ is an infinite set of* memory locations. *A* state *over a type environment τ is $\langle \rho, \mu \rangle$, where*

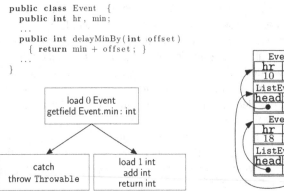

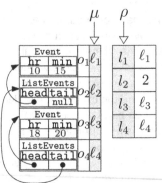

Fig. 2. Our running example   **Fig. 3.** A JVM state $\sigma = \langle \rho, \mu \rangle$

$\rho \in \mathsf{dom}(\tau) \to \mathbb{V}$ *is called* environment *and assigns a value to each variable from* $\mathsf{dom}(\tau)$, *while* $\mu \in \mathbb{M}$ *is called* memory *and binds locations to objects. Every object* o *has class* $o.\kappa$ *and an internal state* $o.\phi$ *mapping each field* f *of* o *into its value* $(o.\phi)(f)$. *The set of all states over* τ *is* Ξ_τ. *We assume that states are well-typed, i.e., variables hold values consistent with their static types.*

The JVM supports exceptions and we distinguish between *normal* and *exceptional* states. These latter arise *immediately after* a bytecode throwing an exception and in that case there is only one element on the stack: a location bound to the thrown exception.

Example 2. Let $\tau = [l_1 \mapsto \mathtt{ListEvents}; l_2 \mapsto \mathtt{int}; l_3 \mapsto \mathtt{Event}; l_4 \mapsto \mathtt{ListEvents}] \in \mathcal{T}$, where class $\mathtt{ListEvents}$ defines two fields: $\mathtt{head}$ of type $\mathtt{Event}$ and $\mathtt{tail}$ of type $\mathtt{ListEvents}$. Fig. 3 shows a state $\sigma = \langle \rho, \mu \rangle \in \Sigma_\tau$. Environment ρ maps variables l_1, l_2, l_3 and l_4 to values ℓ_2, 2, ℓ_3 and ℓ_4, respectively. Memory μ maps locations ℓ_2 and ℓ_4 to objects o_2 and o_4 of class $\mathtt{ListEvents}$, and ℓ_3 to o_3 of class $\mathtt{Event}$. Objects are shown as boxes in μ with a class tag and a local environment mapping fields to integers, locations or $\mathtt{null}$. For instance, fields $\mathtt{head}$ and $\mathtt{tail}$ of o_4 contain locations ℓ_3 and ℓ_2, respectively.   ∎

The semantics of an instruction ins of our target language is a partial map $ins : \Sigma_\tau \to \Sigma_{\tau'}$ from *initial* to *final* states. Number of local variables and stack elements at its start, as well as their static types, are specified by $\tau \in \mathcal{T}$. In the following we assume that $\mathsf{dom}(\tau)$ contains i local variables and j stack elements. Moreover, we suppose that the semantics is undefined for input states of wrong sizes or types, as is required in [8]. The formal semantics is given in [14] and we discuss it informally below.

Basic Instructions. const x pushes $x \in \mathbb{Z}$ on top of the stack. Like any other instruction except catch, it is defined only when the JVM is in a normal state. catch starts instead the exceptional handlers from an exceptional state and is, therefore, undefined on a normal state. dup t duplicates the top of the stack, of type t. load k t pushes on the stack the value of local variable number k, l_k, which must exist and have type t. Conversely, store k t pops the top of the stack of type t and writes it in local variable l_k; it might potentially enlarge the set of local variables. In our formalization, conditional bytecodes are used in complementary pairs (such as ifne t and ifeq t), at a conditional branch. For instance, ifeq t checks whether the top of the stack, of type t, is 0 when t = int or null when t ∈ K. Otherwise, its semantics is undefined. Bytecode inc k x increments the integer held in local variable l_k by a constant x. Bytecode op pops two integers from the operand stack, performs a suitable binary algebraic operation on them, and pushes the integer result back onto the stack. op may be add, sub, mul, div and rem, and the corresponding algebraic operations are $+, -, \times, \div$ and $\%$.

Object-Manipulating Instructions. These create or access objects in memory. new κ pushes on the stack a reference to a new object o of class κ, whose fields are initialized to a default value: null for reference fields, and 0 for integer fields [8]. getfield f reads field f of a receiver object r popped from the stack. putfield f writes the top of the stack inside field f of the object pointed to by the underlying value r.

Exception-Handling Instructions. throw κ throws the top of the stack, whose type κ is a subclass of Throwable. catch starts an exception handler: it takes an exceptional state and transforms it into a normal state at the beginning of the handler. After catch, an appropriate handler dependent on the run-time class of the exception is selected.

Method Call and Return. We use an activation stack of states. Methods can be re-defined in object-oriented code, so a call instruction has the form call $m_1 \ldots m_k$, enumerating an over-approximation of the set of its possible run-time targets. See [14] for details.

3   Alias Expressions

In this section, we define our expressions of interest (Definition 4), their *non-standard evaluation* (Definition 6), which might modify the content of some memory locations and we introduce the notion of *alias expression* (Definition 7). Moreover, we specify in which cases *a bytecode instruction might affect the value of an expression* (Definition 8), and when *the evaluation of an expression might modify a field* (Definition 9).

Definition 4 (Expressions). *Given* $\tau \in \mathcal{T}$, *let* $\mathcal{F}_\tau$ *and* $\mathcal{M}_\tau$ *respectively denote the sets of the names of all possible fields and methods of all the objects available in* Σ_τ. *We define the set of expressions over* $\mathsf{dom}(\tau)$: $\mathbb{E}_\tau \ni \mathsf{E} ::= n \mid v \mid \mathsf{E} \oplus \mathsf{E} \mid \mathsf{E}.f \mid \mathsf{E}.m(\mathsf{E}, \ldots)$, *where* $n \in \mathbb{Z}$, $v \in \mathsf{dom}(\tau)$, $\oplus \in \{+, -, \times, \div, \%\}$, $f \in \mathcal{F}_\tau$ *and* $m \in \mathcal{M}_\tau$.

Definition 5. *We define a map* vars : $\mathbb{E}_\tau \to \wp(\mathsf{dom}(\tau))$ *yielding the variables occurring in an expression and a map* flds : $\mathbb{E}_\tau \to \wp(\mathcal{F}_\tau)$ *yielding the fields that might be read during the evaluation of an expression, for a given* $\tau \in \mathcal{T}$ *as:*

E	vars(E)	flds(E)
$n \in \mathbb{Z}$	$\varnothing$	$\varnothing$
$v \in \mathsf{dom}(\tau)$	$\{v\}$	$\varnothing$
$\mathsf{E}_1 \oplus \mathsf{E}_2$	$\mathsf{vars}(\mathsf{E}_1) \cup \mathsf{vars}(\mathsf{E}_2)$	$\mathsf{flds}(\mathsf{E}_1) \cup \mathsf{flds}(\mathsf{E}_2)$
$\mathsf{E}.f$	$\mathsf{vars}(\mathsf{E})$	$\mathsf{flds}(\mathsf{E}) \cup \{f\}$
$\mathsf{E}_0.m(\mathsf{E}_1, \ldots, \mathsf{E}_\pi)$	$\bigcup_{i=0}^{\pi} \mathsf{vars}(\mathsf{E}_i)$	$\bigcup_{i=0}^{\pi} \mathsf{flds}(\mathsf{E}_i) \cup \{f \mid m \text{ might read } f\}$

Note that the definition of flds requires a preliminary computation of the fields possibly read by a method m, which might just be a transitive closure of the field f for which a getfield occurs in m or in at least one method invoked by m. For instance, if the static type of the local variable l_2 is Event, then expression $E = l_2$.delayMinBy(15) satisfies the following equalities: vars(E_2) = {l_2}, and flds(E_2) = {min}. The latter follows from the fact that delayMinBy contains only one getfield and no call instruction (Ex. 1). There exist some more precise approximations of this useful piece of information, e.g., the one determined by our Julia tool. Anyway, in the absence of this approximation, we can always assume the least precise sound hypothesis: every method can read every field.

Some of the expressions defined above represent the result of a method invocation. Their evaluation, in general, might modify the memory, so we must be aware of the side-effects of the methods appearing in these expressions. We define the non-standard evaluation of an expression e in a state $\langle \rho, \mu \rangle$ as a pair $\langle w, \mu' \rangle$, where w is the computed value of e, while μ' is the updated memory obtained from μ after the evaluation of e.

Definition 6 (Non-standard evaluation of expressions). *A* non-standard evaluation of expressions *in a state* $\sigma = \langle \rho, \mu \rangle \in \Sigma_\tau$ *is a partial map* $[\![\cdot]\!]^* : \mathbb{E}_\tau \to \mathbb{V} \times \mathbb{M}$ *defined as:*

- *for every* $n \in \mathbb{Z}$, $[\![n]\!]^* \sigma = \langle n, \mu \rangle$, *while for every* $v \in \mathrm{dom}(\tau)$, $[\![v]\!]^* \sigma = \langle \rho(v), \mu \rangle$;
- $[\![E_1 \oplus E_2]\!]^* \sigma$ *is defined only if* $[\![E_1]\!]^* \sigma = \langle w_1, \mu_1 \rangle$, $[\![E_2]\!]^* \langle \rho, \mu_1 \rangle = \langle w_2, \mu_2 \rangle$ *and* $w_1, w_2 \in \mathbb{Z}$. *In that case* $[\![E_1 \oplus E_2]\!]^* \sigma = \langle w_1 \oplus w_2, \mu_2 \rangle$, *otherwise it is undefined;*
- $[\![E.f]\!]^* \sigma$ *is defined only if* $[\![E]\!]^* \sigma = \langle \ell, \mu_1 \rangle$, $\ell \in \mathbb{L}$ *and* $f \in \mathbb{F}(\mu_1(\ell).\kappa)$. *In that case* $[\![E.f]\!]^* \sigma = \langle (\mu_1(\ell).\phi)(f), \mu_1 \rangle$;
- *in order to compute* $[\![E_0.m(E_1, \ldots, E_\pi)]\!]^* \sigma$, *we determine* $[\![E_0]\!]^* \langle \rho, \mu \rangle = \langle w_0, \mu_0 \rangle$, *and for each* $1 \leq i < \pi$, *we evaluate* E_{i+1} *in the state* $\langle \rho, \mu_i \rangle$: $[\![E_{i+1}]\!]^* \langle \rho, \mu_i \rangle = \langle w_{i+1}, \mu_{i+1} \rangle$. *If* $w_0 \in \mathbb{L}$, *we run* m *on the object* $\mu_\pi(w_0)$ *with parameters* $w_1, \ldots, w_\pi$ *and if it terminates with no exception, the result of the evaluation is the pair of* m's *return value* w *and the memory* μ' *obtained from* μ_π *as a side-effect of* m.

We write $[\![E]\!] \sigma$ *for the value of* E, *without the updated memory.*

Definition 7 (Alias Expression). *We say that an expression* $E \in \mathbb{E}_\tau$ *is an* alias expression *of a variable* $v \in \mathrm{dom}(\tau)$ *in a state* $\sigma = \langle \rho, \mu \rangle \in \Sigma_\tau$ *if and only if* $[\![E]\!] \sigma = \rho(v)$.

We specify when the value of an expression might be affected by an instruction's execution. An information about the fields that might be modified during the execution of the methods is required. Without that information, the analysis would be less precise.

Definition 8 (canBeAffected). *Let* τ *and* τ' *be the static type information at and immediately after an instruction* ins. *We define a map* canBeAffected$(\cdot, \text{ins}) : \mathbb{E}_\tau \to \{$true, false$\}$ *which, for every expression* $E \in \mathbb{E}_\tau$ *determines whether* E *might be affected by* ins:

E	canBeAffected(E, ins)
$n \in \mathbb{V}$	*false*
$v \in \mathrm{dom}(\tau)$	$(v \notin \mathrm{dom}(\tau')) \vee (\text{ins} \in \{\text{inc } k\ x, \text{store } k\ t\} \wedge v = l_k)$ $\vee(\text{ins} = \text{getfield } f \wedge v = s_{j-1}) \vee (\text{ins} = \text{op} \wedge v = s_{j-2})$
$E_1 \oplus E_2$	canBeAffected$(E_1, \text{ins}) \vee$ canBeAffected(E_2, ins)
$E.g$	canBeAffected$(E, \text{ins}) \vee (\text{ins} = \text{putfield } f \wedge f = g)$ $\vee (\text{ins} = \text{call } m \wedge \text{execution of } m \text{ might modify } g)$
$E_0.p(E_1, \ldots, E_\pi)$	$\bigvee_{i=0}^{\pi}$ canBeAffected$(E_i, \text{ins}) \vee (\text{ins} = \text{putfield } f \wedge f \in \text{flds}(E))$ $\vee (\text{ins} = \text{call } m \wedge \text{the execution of } m \text{ might modify a field in flds}(E))$

That is, instructions that remove some variables from the stack (putfield, op, ifne, ifeq and store) affect the evaluation of all the expressions in which these variables appear; instructions that write into one particular variable (inc, store, getfield and op) might affect the evaluation of the expressions containing that variable; putfield f might modify the evaluation of all the expressions that might read f; call $m_1 \ldots m_k$ might modify the evaluation of all expressions that might read a field f possibly modified by an m_i.

On the other hand, the evaluation of an expression in a state, might update the memory component of that state by modifying the value of some fields.

Definition 9 (mightMdf). *Function* mightMdf *specifies whether a field belonging to a set of fields* $F \subseteq \mathcal{F}_\tau$ *might be modified during the evaluation of an expression* E:

- mightMdf(n, F) = mightMdf(v, F) = *false, for every* $n \in \mathbb{Z}$ *and every* $v \in \text{dom}(\tau)$;
- mightMdf$(\mathsf{E}_1 \oplus \mathsf{E}_2, F)$ = mightMdf$(\mathsf{E}_1, F) \lor$ mightMdf(E_2, F);
- mightMdf$(\mathsf{E}.g, F)$ = mightMdf(E, F);
- mightMdf$(\mathsf{E}_0.p(\mathsf{E}_1, \ldots, \mathsf{E}_\pi), F)$ = *true if there exists* $0 \le i \le \pi$, *s.t.* mightMdf(E_i, F) = *true or if the execution of* p *might write a field from* F.

4 Definite Expression Aliasing Analysis

The concrete semantics works over concrete states, that our abstract interpretation abstracts into tuples of sets of expressions.

Definition 10 (Concrete and Abstract Domain). *The concrete domain over* $\tau \in \mathcal{T}$ *is* $\mathbf{C}_\tau = \langle \wp(\Sigma_\tau), \subseteq, \cup, \cap \rangle$ *and the abstract domain over* τ *is* $\mathbf{A}_\tau = \langle (\wp(\mathbb{E}_\tau))^{|\tau|}, \sqsubseteq, \sqcup, \sqcap \rangle$, *where for every* $A^1 = \langle \mathsf{A}_0^1, \ldots, \mathsf{A}_{|\tau|-1}^1 \rangle$ *and* $A^2 = \langle \mathsf{A}_0^2, \ldots, \mathsf{A}_{|\tau|-1}^2 \rangle$, $A^1 \sqsubseteq A^2$ *if and only if for each* $0 \le i < |\tau|$, $\mathsf{A}_i^1 \supseteq \mathsf{A}_i^2$. *Moreover, the join operator* $\sqcup$ *is defined as* $A^1 \sqcup A^2 = \langle \mathsf{A}_0^1 \cap \mathsf{A}_0^2, \ldots, \mathsf{A}_{|\tau|-1}^1 \cap \mathsf{A}_{|\tau|-1}^2 \rangle$. *The meet operator* $\sqcap$ *is dually defined.*

Concrete states σ corresponding to an abstract element $\langle \mathsf{A}_0, \ldots, \mathsf{A}_{|\tau|-1} \rangle$ must satisfy the aliasing information represented by the latter, i.e., for each $0 \le r < |\tau|$, the value of all the expressions from A_r in σ must coincide with the value of v_r in σ (*definite* aliasing).

Definition 11 (Concretization map). *Let* $\tau \in \mathcal{T}$ *and* $A = \langle \mathsf{A}_0, \ldots, \mathsf{A}_{|\tau|-1} \rangle \in \mathbf{A}_\tau$. *We define* $\gamma_\tau : \mathbf{A}_\tau \to \mathbf{C}_\tau$ *as follows:* $\gamma(A) = \{\sigma = \langle \rho, \mu \rangle \in \Sigma_\tau \mid \forall 0 \le r < |\tau|. \forall \mathsf{E} \in \mathsf{A}_r. \llbracket \mathsf{E} \rrbracket \sigma = \rho(v_r)\}$.

Both $\mathbf{C}_\tau$ and $\mathbf{A}_\tau$ are complete lattices. Moreover, we proved γ_τ co-additive, and therefore it is the concretization map of a Galois connection [5] and $\mathbf{A}_\tau$ is actually an abstract domain, in the sense of abstract interpretation.

4.1 The Abstract Constraint Graph

Our analysis is constraint-based: we construct an *abstract constraint graph* from the program under analysis and then we solve these constraints. For each bytecode of the program there is a node containing an approximation of the actual aliasing information at that point. Arcs of the graph propagate these approximations, reflecting, in abstract terms, the effects of the concrete semantics on the aliasing information. In other words, an arc between the nodes corresponding to two bytecodes b_1 and b_2 propagates the aliasing information at b_1 into that at b_2. The exact meaning of *propagates* depends here on b_1, since each bytecode has different effects on the abstract information.

	ins	A'_r
#1	dup t	$A'_r = \begin{cases} A_r \cup A_r[s_j/s_{j-1}] & \text{if } r < |\tau|-1 \\ A_{|\tau|-1} \cup \{s_j\} & \text{if } r = |\tau|-1 \\ A_{|\tau|-1} \cup \{s_{j-1}\} & \text{if } r = |\tau| \end{cases}$
#2	new κ	$A'_r = \begin{cases} A_r & \text{if } r \neq |\tau| \\ \varnothing & \text{if } r = |\tau| \end{cases}$
#3	load k t	$A'_r = \begin{cases} A_r \cup A_r[s_j/l_k] & \text{if } r \notin \{k,|\tau|\} \\ A_k \cup \{s_j\} & \text{if } r = k \\ A_k \cup \{l_k\} & \text{if } r = |\tau| \end{cases}$
#4	store k t	$A'_r = \begin{cases} \{E \in A_r \mid \neg\text{canBeAffected}(E, \text{ins})\} & \text{if } r \neq k \\ \{E \in A_{|\tau|-1} \mid \neg\text{canBeAffected}(E, \text{ins})\} & \text{if } r = k \end{cases}$
#5	getfield f	$A'_r = \begin{cases} \{E \in A_r \mid \neg\text{canBeAffected}(E, \text{ins})\} & \text{if } r \neq |\tau|-1 \\ \{E.f \mid E \in A_{|\tau|-1} \wedge \neg\text{canBeAffected}(E, \text{ins}) \\ \quad \wedge \neg\text{mightMdf}(E, \{f\})\} & \text{if } r = |\tau|-1 \end{cases}$
#6 #7	putfield f catch, ifne t, ifeq t	$A'_r = \{E \in A_r \mid \neg\text{canBeAffected}(E, \text{ins})\}$
#8	const v	$A'_r = \begin{cases} A_r & \text{if } r \neq |\tau| \\ \{x\} & \text{if } r = |\tau| \end{cases}$
#9	inc k x	$A'_r = \begin{cases} \{E[l_k - x/l_k] \mid E \in A_r\} & \text{if } r \neq k \\ \varnothing & \text{if } r = k \end{cases}$
#10	op	$A'_r = \begin{cases} \{E \in A_r \mid \neg\text{canBeAffected}(E, \text{ins})\} & \text{if } r \neq |\tau|-2 \\ \{E_1 \oplus E_2 \mid E_1 \in A_{|\tau|-2} \wedge E_2 \in A_{|\tau|-1} \\ \quad \wedge \neg\text{canBeAffected}(E_1 \oplus E_2, \text{ins})\} & \text{if } r = |\tau|-2 \end{cases}$
#11	return void	$A'_r = \{E \in A_r \mid \text{noStackElements}(E)\}$
#12	return t	$A'_r = \begin{cases} \{E \in A_r \mid \text{noStackElements}(E)\} & \text{if } r \neq i \\ \{E \in A_{|\tau|-1} \mid \text{noStackElements}(E)\} & \text{if } r = i \end{cases}$
#13	throw κ	
#14	call $m_1 \ldots m_k$	$A'_r = \begin{cases} \{E \in A_r \mid \text{noStackElements}(E)\} & \text{if } r \neq i \\ \varnothing & \text{if } r = i \end{cases}$
#15	new κ, throw κ getfield f, putfield f	

Fig. 4. Propagation rules of $1-1$ arcs

Definition 12 (ACG). *Let P be the program under analysis, already in the form of a CFG of basic blocks for each method or constructor (Section 2). The* abstract constraint graph *(ACG) for P is a directed graph $\langle V, E \rangle$ (nodes, arcs) where:*

- *V contains a node $\boxed{\text{ins}}$ for each bytecode ins in P;*
- *for each method or constructor m in P, V contains nodes $\boxed{\text{exit@}m}$ and $\boxed{\text{exception@}m}$, representing the normal and the exceptional final states of m;*
- *each node contains an abstract element $A \in \mathbf{A}$ representing an approximation of the actual aliasing information at that point;*
- *E contains directed arcs with one $(1-1)$ or two $(2-1)$ sources and always one sink. Each arc has a* propagation rule *i.e., a function over $\mathbf{A}$, from the aliasing information at its source(s) to the aliasing information at its sink.*

The arcs in E are built from P as follows. We assume for all $1-1$ arcs that τ and τ' are the static type information at and immediately after the execution of a bytecode

A'_r

$$\#17 \quad A'_r = \begin{cases} A_r & \text{if } r \neq |\tau_C| - \pi \\ \{E = R[E_0, \ldots, E_{\pi-1}/l_0, \ldots, l_{\pi-1}] \mid R \in R_{|\tau_E|-1} \wedge \mathsf{safeReturn}(R, m_w) \wedge \mathsf{safeAlias}(E, \mathsf{ins}_C)\} & \\ \quad \cup \{E = E_0.m(E_1, \ldots, E_{\pi-1}) \mid \mathsf{safeAlias}(E, \mathsf{ins}_C)\} & \text{if } r = |\tau_C| - \pi \end{cases}$$

$$\#18 \quad A'_r = \begin{cases} \{E \mid \mathsf{safeExecution}(E, A_r, \mathsf{ins}_C)\} & \text{if } r \neq |\tau_C| - \pi \\ \mathbb{E}_{\tau_N} & \text{if } r = |\tau_C| - \pi \end{cases}$$

$\mathsf{safeExecution}(E, A, \mathsf{ins}_C)$	$=$	$E \in A \wedge \mathsf{noParameters}(E) \wedge \neg\mathsf{canBeAffected}(E, \mathsf{ins}_C)$
$\mathsf{safeAlias}(E, \mathsf{ins}_C)$	$=$	$\bigwedge_{k=0}^{\pi-1} \mathsf{safeExecution}(E_k, A_{|\tau_C|-\pi+k}, \mathsf{ins}_C) \wedge \neg\mathsf{mightMdf}(E, \mathsf{flds}(E))$
$\mathsf{safeReturn}(R, m_w)$	$=$	$\forall l_k \in \mathsf{vars}(R) \subseteq \{l_0, \ldots, l_{\pi-1}\}.l_k \text{ is not modified by } m_w$
$\mathsf{noParameters}(E)$	$=$	$\mathsf{vars}(E) \cap \{v_{|\tau_C|-\pi}, \ldots, v_{|\tau_C|-1}\} = \varnothing$

Fig. 5. Propagation rules of $2-1$ arcs

ins, *respectively. Moreover, we assume that τ contains j stack elements and i local variables and, for every expression E, we write* noStackElements(E) *to denote that no stack element appears in E, i.e.,* vars(E) $\cap \{s_0, \ldots, s_{j-1}\} = \varnothing$.

Sequential arcs. *If* ins *is a bytecode in P, distinct from* call, *immediately followed by a bytecode* ins', *distinct from* catch, *then an $1-1$ arc is built from* ins *to* ins' , *with a propagation rule $\lambda\langle A_0, \ldots, A_{|\tau|-1}\rangle.\langle A'_0, \ldots, A'_{|\tau'|-1}\rangle$ where, for each $0 \leq r < |\tau'|$, A'_r is defined by one of the rules #1 – #10 in Fig. 4.*

Final arcs. *For each* return t *and* throw κ *occurring in a method or constructor m of P, there are $1-1$ arcs from* return t *to* exit@m *and from* throw κ *to* exception@m , *respectively, with a propagation rule $\lambda\langle A_0, \ldots, A_{|\tau|-1}\rangle.\langle A'_0, \ldots, A'_{|\tau'|-1}\rangle$ where, for each $0 \leq r < |\tau'|$, A'_r is defined by one of the rules #11 – #13 in Fig. 4.*

Exceptional arcs. *For each* ins *throwing an exception, immediately followed by a* catch, *an arc is built from* ins *to* catch , *with a prop. rule $\lambda\langle A_0, \ldots, A_{|\tau|-1}\rangle.\langle A'_0, \ldots, A'_{|\tau'|-1}\rangle$ where, for each $0 \leq r < |\tau'|$, A'_r is defined by rules #14 or #15 in Fig. 4.*

Parameter passing arcs. *For each* call $m_1 \ldots m_q$ *occurring in P with π parameters (including the implicit parameter* this*), for each $1 \leq i \leq q$ we build an $1-1$ arc from* call $m_1 \ldots m_q$ *to the node corresponding to the first bytecode of m_i, with a propagation rule #16: $\lambda\langle A_0, \ldots, A_{|\tau|-1}\rangle.\langle A'_0, \ldots, A'_{\pi-1}\rangle$ where, for each $0 \leq r < \pi$, $A'_r = \varnothing$.*

Return value arcs. *For each* ins$_C$ = call $m_1 \ldots m_q$ *to a method with π parameters (including the implicit parameter* this*) returning a value of type $t \neq$ void, and each subsequent bytecode* ins$_N$ *distinct from* catch, *we build, for each $1 \leq w \leq q$, a $2-1$ arc from* ins$_C$ *and* exit@m_w *(2 sources, in that order) to* ins$_N$. *Suppose that the static type information at* ins$_C$, exit@m_w *and* ins$_N$ *are τ_C, τ_E and τ_N, respectively. We define a propagation rule $\lambda\langle A_0, \ldots, A_p, \ldots, A_{|\tau_C|-1}\rangle, \langle R_0, \ldots, R_{|\tau_E|-1}\rangle.\langle A'_0, \ldots, A'_{|\tau_C|-1}\rangle$, where for each $0 \leq r \leq |\tau_C| - \pi$, A'_r is defined by the rule #17 in Fig. 5.*

Side-effects arcs. *For each* ins$_C$ = call $m_1 \ldots m_q$ *to a method with π parameters (including the implicit parameter* this*), and each subsequent bytecode* ins$_N$, *we build, for each $1 \leq w \leq q$, a $2-1$ arc from* ins$_C$ *and* exit@m_w *(2 sources, in that order) to* ins$_N$, *if* ins$_N$ *is not a* catch *and a $2-1$ arc from* ins$_C$ *and* exception@m_w *(2 sources, in that order) to* catch . *Suppose that the static type information at* ins$_C$, exit@m_w *(or* exception@m_w *) and* ins$_C$ *are τ_C, τ_E and τ_N respectively. We define a propagation rule*

$\lambda\langle A_0, \ldots, A_{|\tau_C|-\pi}, \ldots, A_{|\tau_C|-1}\rangle, \langle R_0, \ldots, R_{|\tau_E|-1}\rangle.\langle A'_0, \ldots, A'_{|\tau_N|-1}\rangle$, where for each $0 \le r < |\tau_N|$, A'_r is defined by the rule #18 in Fig. 5.

Example 3. In Fig. 6 we give the ACG of the method `delayMinBy` from Fig. 2. Nodes **a**, **b** and **c** belong to the caller of this method and exemplify the arcs related to the call and return bytecodes. Arcs are decorated with the number of their associated propagation rules. In the following examples, for each node x, we let $A^x = \langle A^x_0, \ldots, A^x_{n_x-1}\rangle$ be the aliasing information at x, where n_x is the number of variables at x and, for each r, we let A^x_r be an approximation of the definite aliasing expressions of variable v_r. ∎

The **sequential arcs** link an instruction ins to its immediate successor ins' propagating, for every variable v at ins', all those expressions E aliased to v at ins that cannot be affected by ins itself, i.e., such that ¬canBeAffected(E, ins) holds. However, some new alias expressions might be added to the initial approximation as well. For instance, in the case of ins = dup t (rule #1), the new added variable $v_n = s_j$ is a copy of $v_{n-1} = s_{j-1}$, hence they are trivially aliased to each other, and all definite alias expressions of v_{n-1} at ins become definite alias expressions of v_n at ins' (i.e., $A'_{n-1} = A_{n-1} \cup \{s_j\}$, $A'_n = A_{n-1} \cup \{s_{j-1}\}$). Approximations related to the rest of the variables are enriched with the same expressions where occurrences of s_{j-1} are replaced by s_j ($A'_r = A_r \cup A_r[s_j/s_{j-1}]$). Rule #5 is more interesting: ins = getfield f inserts an expression E.f among alias expressions of v_{n-1} at ins' if E is aliased to v_{n-1} (holding the receiver) at ins, it cannot be modified by ins (¬canBeAffected(E, ins)) and the evaluation of E cannot modify the field f (¬mightMdf(E, $\{f\}$)). For instance, suppose that in Ex. 3 we have $n_2 = 3$ and $A^2_2 = \{v_0\}$, i.e., v_2, the top of the stack and the receiver of the getfield at **2**, is aliased to v_0. There is an arc with rule #5 connecting nodes **2** and **3**. According to that rule, since the getfield cannot affect v_0, but only v_2, and since no evaluation of v_0 can modify any field (in particular min), we conclude that $A^3_2 = \{v_0.\text{min}\}$, i.e., the new top of the stack is aliased to the field min of the only alias of the old top of the stack.

The **final arcs** feed nodes $\boxed{\text{exit@}m}$ and $\boxed{\text{exception@}m}$ for each method m. They propagate, for each local variable l_k at ins', all those expressions aliased to l_k at ins where no stack variable occurs. In the case of ins = return t, with t ≠ void, the alias expressions of $v_i = s_0$ at ins' are alias expressions of $v_{n-1} = s_{j-1}$ at ins with no stack elements.

The **exceptional arcs** link every instruction that might throw an exception to the catch at the beginning of their exception handler(s). They propagate alias expressions of local variables analogously to the final arcs. For the only stack element ($v_i = s_0$), holding the thrown exception, there is no alias expression ($A_i = \emptyset$).

Let us explain the auxiliary functions introduced in Fig. 5. An *execution of* ins = call $m_1 \ldots m_t$ *is safe for an expression* E ∈ A (safeExecution(E, A, ins) holds), if the fields possibly read during the evaluation of E must not be modified by the invoked method (¬canBeAffected(E, ins)) and if no actual parameter of that method appears in E (noParameters(E)), since they disappear from the stack after the call. An *alias expression* E *in which* $E_0, \ldots, E_{\pi-1}$ *appear is safe* (safeAlias(E, ins) holds) if ins is safe for each E_r and if no field might be both read and modified during all possible evaluations of E (¬mightMdf(E, flds(E))). An *alias expression* R *of a return value at the exit from a method* m_w *is safe*, i.e., safeReturn(R, m_w) holds, if only local variables corresponding to the formal parameters of m_w ($l_0, \ldots, l_{\pi-1}$) appear in R and none of them is modified by m_w (for every $l_k \in$ vars(R), no store k t nor inc k x occurs in m_w).

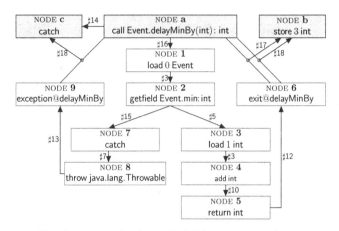

Fig. 6. The ACG for the method `delayMinBy` in Fig. 2

There exists a **return value 2−1 arc** for each target m_w of a call returning a value. Rule #17 considers $\langle A_0, \ldots, A_{|\tau_C|-1} \rangle$ and $\langle R_0, \ldots, R_{|\tau_E|-1} \rangle$, approximations at $\boxed{\text{ins}_C}$ and $\boxed{\text{exit@}m_w}$, and builds the alias expressions related to the returned value $s_{|\tau_C|-\pi}$ at $\boxed{\text{ins}_N}$. An alias expression $R \in R_{|\tau_E|-1}$ of the computed value s_0 at $\boxed{\text{exit@}m_w}$ can be turned into an alias expression of $s_{|\tau_C|-\pi}$ at $\boxed{\text{ins}_N}$ if (i) R is safe; (ii) every occurrence of a formal parameter l_k in R is replaced by an alias expression $E_k \in A_{|\tau_C|-\pi+k}$ of the corresponding actual parameter $s_{|\tau_C|-\pi+k}$ at $\boxed{\text{ins}_C}$, which is safe w.r.t. ins_C. Moreover, $E = E_0.m_w(E_1, \ldots, E_{\pi-1})$ can be an alias of $s_{|\tau_C|-\pi}$ at $\boxed{\text{ins}_N}$ if it is safe w.r.t. ins_C. For instance, suppose that in Ex. 3 the actual parameters of the call at node **a** (which become the local variables v_0 and v_1 inside `delayMinBy`) are aliased to v_1 and 15, and that at the exit node **6** the return value is aliased to v_0.min + v_1. Since this expression is composed of local variables corresponding to the formal parameters of `delayMinBy` and the latter does not modify any variable (it contains no **store** nor **inc**), we conclude that v_0.min + v_1 is safe. v_0 and v_1 at **6** correspond to the actual parameters at **a**, thus the aliases v_1 and 15 of these latter can substitute these former obtaining the alias expression $E = v_1$.min + 15 at **b**. Indeed, no evaluation of E can modify any field (Definition 9), so ¬mightMdf(E, flds(E)) trivially holds. Moreover, v_1 and 15 contain no actual parameter at **a**, and no execution of the method can modify a local variable or a constant of the caller, hence E is safe and can be an alias expression of the returned value at node **b**.

The **side-effects 2−1 arcs** consider the alias expressions E of the variables v_r different from the actual parameters $(s_{|\tau_C|-\pi}, \ldots, s_{|\tau_C|-1})$ of the method at $\boxed{\text{ins}_C}$ and insert them among the alias expressions of v_r also at $\boxed{\text{ins}_N}$ if they are safe w.r.t. ins_C.

Definition 13 (Alias Expression Analysis). *A solution of an ACG is an assignment of an abstract element A_n to each node n of the ACG such that the propagation rules of the arcs are satisfied, i.e., for every arc from nodes $n_1 \ldots n_k$ to n with propagation rule $\lambda A_1, \ldots, \lambda A_k . \Pi(A_1, \ldots, A_k)$, the condition $A_n \sqsubseteq \Pi(A_{n_1}, \ldots, A_{n_k})$ holds. The alias expression analysis of the program is the minimal solution of its ACG w.r.t. $\sqsubseteq$.*

Definition 13 entails that if k arcs reach the same node n, bringing to it k approximations, i.e., k sets of alias expressions for each variable at n, then the approximation of

NODE n	A_0^n	A_1^n	A_2^n	A_3^n	i_n	j_n
a	∅	$\{v_0.\texttt{getHead}(), s_0\}$	$\{v_0.\texttt{getHead}(), v_1\}$	$\{15\}$	2	2
1	∅	∅	−	−	2	0
2	$\{s_0\}$	∅	$\{v_0\}$	−	2	1
3	∅	∅	$\{v_0.\texttt{min}\}$	−		
4	∅	$\{s_1\}$	$\{v_0.\texttt{min}\}$	$\{v_1\}$	2	2
5, 6	∅	∅	$\{v_0.\texttt{min} + v_1\}$	−		
7, 8, 9	∅	∅	∅	−		
b	∅	$\{v_0.\texttt{getHead}()\}$	$\{v_1.\texttt{delayMinBy}(15), v_0.\texttt{getHead}().\texttt{min}+15,$ $v_1.\texttt{min}+15, v_0.\texttt{getHead}().\texttt{delayMinBy}(15)\}$	−	2	1
c	∅	$\{v_1.\texttt{getHead}()\}$	∅	−		

Fig. 7. The solution of the ACG from Fig. 6

the actual aliasing information for each variable v at n is the intersection of the k sets related to v. The minimal solution w.r.t. $\sqsubseteq$ corresponds to the greatest sets of expressions for each variable (Definition 10). In order to guarantee its existence, we fix an upper bounds on the height of the alias expressions (e.g., a maximal number of field accesses and method invocations) which makes the abstract domain A_τ finite. The solution of the constraint can, hence, be computed by starting with the bottom approximation for every node: the set of all possible alias expressions; and then applying the propagation of the arcs and computing the intersection at each node entry, until stabilization.

Example 4. Fig. 7 shows the solution of the ACG from Fig. 6. For each node n, the values shown in columns i_n, j_n and A_r^n are respectively the number of local variables, stack elements and the final approximation of the aliasing information related to the variable v_r at that point. When the latter is −, it means that v_r is not available there. It is worth noting that the variable v_0 at nodes **a**, **b** and **c** is of type ListEvents (Ex. 2) and that getHead only returns the field head of that class. ∎

The following theorem states that our analysis is sound.

Theorem 1 (Soundness). *Suppose that an execution of a program leads to a state* $\sigma \in \Sigma_\tau$. *Let* $A^{\text{ins}} \in A_\tau$ *be the approximation of the definite expression aliasing information at the node* **ins** *corresponding to ins, computed by our static analysis. Then,* $\sigma \in \gamma_\tau(A^{\text{ins}})$.

5 Experiments

We have implemented our definite expression aliasing analysis inside the Julia analyzer for Java bytecode (http://www.juliasoft.com) and we have analyzed some real-life benchmark programs. We provide the names of these latter together with their identification numbers used in Fig. 8 and 9. The majority of our benchmarks are Android applications: Mileage (15), OpenSudoku (19), Solitaire (26) and TiltMazes[1] (29); Chime-Timer (4), Dazzle (7), OnWatch (18) and Tricorder[2] (31); TxWthr[3] (32). There are also some Java programs: JFlex (12) is a lexical analyzers generator[4]; Plume is a library by

---

[1] http://f-droid.org/repository/browse/
[2] http://moonblink.googlecode.com/svn/trunk/
[3] http://typoweather.googlecode.com/svn/trunk/
[4] http://jflex.de

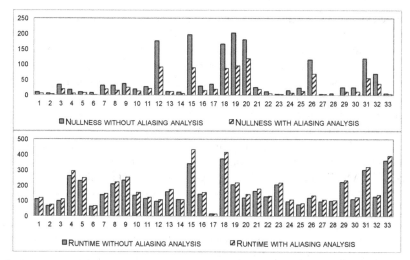

Fig. 8. Comparison of the number of warnings (possible dereference of null, possibly passing null to a library method) produced by the nullness tool of Julia (top) and of the run-times (in seconds) of that tool (bottom) when our definite aliasing analysis is present and absent

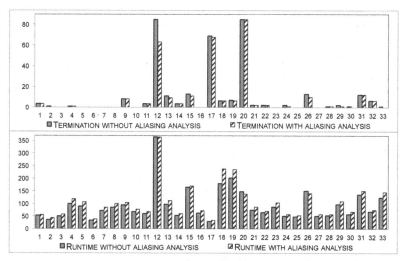

Fig. 9. Comparison between number of warnings (possible divergence of constructors or methods) produced by the termination tool of Julia (top) and between run-times (in seconds) of that tool (bottom) when our definite aliasing analysis is present and absent

Michael D. Ernst[5]; Nti (17) is a non-termination analyzer by Étienne Payet[6]; Lisimplex (13) is a numerical simplex implementation by Ricardo Gobbo[7]. The others are sample programs from the Android 3.1 distribution by Google.

---

[5] http://code.google.com/p/plume-lib
[6] http://personnel.univ-reunion.fr/epayet/Research/NTI/NTI.html
[7] http://sourceforge.net/projects/lisimplex

Definite expression aliasing analysis is used to support Julia's nullness and termination analyses. In particular, we use our analysis at the then branch of each comparisson `if (v!=null)` to infer that the definite aliases of `v` are non-`null` there, and at each assignment `w.f=exp` to infer that expressions `E.f` are non-`null` when `exp` is non-`null` and when `E` is a definite alias of `w` whose evaluation does not read nor write `f`. Moreover, we use it to infer symbolic upper or lower bounds of variables whenever we have a comparison such as `x < y`: all definite alias expressions of `y` (resp. `x`) are upper (resp. lower) bounds for `x` (resp. `y`). This is important for termination analysis.

Figures 8 and 9 report the precision and the run-time of our nullness and termination analyses on a Linux quad-core Intel Xeon machine running at 2.66GHz, with 8 gigabytes of RAM. We performed these analyses first without and then with the help of our definite expression aliasing analysis. This way, we notice how the tools' precision changes. A clear difference between the two runs is that the run-time of the nullness and termination analyses increased by 9.88% and 12.57% respectively, when the definite expression aliasing analysis is activated. On the other hand, the precision of both analyses is improved in the presence of the definite expression aliasing analysis: 45.98% and 11.44% less warnings are produced by the nullness and termination analyses, respectively. These improvements are well worth the extra time required for the analyses.

6   Conclusion

Our expression aliasing analysis is a *constraint-based definite* analysis for Java bytecode. To the best of our knowledge, it is the first definite aliasing analysis dealing with Java bytecode programs and with aliases to expressions. Our experimental evaluation shows the benefits of our new analysis for the nullness and termination analyses of Julia.

References

1. Soot: A Java Optimization Framework, http://www.sable.mcgill.ca/soot/
2. WALA: T.J. Watson Libraries for Analysis, http://wala.sourceforge.net/
3. Aho, A.V., Sethi, R., Ullman, J.D.: Compilers: Principles, Techniques and Tools. Addison-Wesley (1986)
4. Albert, E., Arenas, P., Genaim, S., Puebla, G., Ramírez Deantes, D.V.: From Object Fields to Local Variables: A Practical Approach to Field-Sensitive Analysis. In: Cousot, R., Martel, M. (eds.) SAS 2010. LNCS, vol. 6337, pp. 100–116. Springer, Heidelberg (2010)
5. Cousot, P., Cousot, R.: Abstract Interpretation: A Unified Lattice Model for Static Analysis of Programs by Construction or Approximation of Fixpoints. In: Proc. of the 4th Symp. on Principles of Programming Languages (POPL), pp. 238–252. ACM (1977)
6. Fink, S., Yahav, E., Dor, N., Ramalingam, G., Geay, E.: Effective Typestate Verification in the Presence of Aliasing. In: Proc. of the International Symposium on Software Testing and Analysis (ISSTA), pp. 133–144. ACM (2006)
7. Hind, M.: Pointer Analysis: Haven't We Solved This Problem Yet? In: Proc. of the Workshop on Prog. Analysis for Software Tools and Engineering (PASTE), pp. 54–61. ACM (2001)
8. Lindholm, T., Yellin, F.: The Java^{TM} Virtual Machine Specification, 2nd edn. Addison-Wesley (1999)

9. Logozzo, F., Fähndrich, M.: On the Relative Completeness of Bytecode Analysis Versus Source Code Analysis. In: Hendren, L. (ed.) CC 2008. LNCS, vol. 4959, pp. 197–212. Springer, Heidelberg (2008)
10. Nikolić, Đ., Spoto, F.: Definite Expression Aliasing Analysis for Java Bytecode, http://profs.sci.univr.it/~nikolic/download/ICTAC2012/ICTAC2012Ext.pdf
11. Nikolić, Đ., Spoto, F.: Reachability Analysis of Program Variables. In: Gramlich, B., Miller, D., Sattler, U. (eds.) IJCAR 2012. LNCS (LNAI), vol. 7364, pp. 423–438. Springer, Heidelberg (2012)
12. Ohata, F., Inoue, K.: JAAT: Java Alias Analysis Tool for Program Maintenance Activities. In: Proc. of the 9th International Symposium on Object-Oriented Real-Time Distributed Computing (ISORC), pp. 232–244. IEEE (2006)
13. Spoto, F.: Precise Null-pointer Analysis. Software and Syst. Modeling 10(2), 219–252 (2011)
14. Spoto, F., Ernst, M.D.: Inference of Field Initialization. In: Proc. of the 33rd International Conference on Software Engineering (ICSE), pp. 231–240. ACM (2011)

Using Semantics Specified
in Maude to Generate Test Cases[*]

Adrián Riesco

Facultad de Informática, Universidad Complutense de Madrid, Spain

Abstract. Testing is one of the most important and most time-consuming tasks in the software developing process and thus techniques and systems to generate and check test cases have become crucial. For these reasons, when specifying a prototype of a programming language it may be very useful to have a tool that, beyond testing the semantics of the program, generates test cases for the programs written in the specified language. In this way, we could use the test cases generated in the prototyping stage to check the implementation. To build these prototypes we can use rewriting logic, which has been proposed as a logical framework where other logics can be represented, and as a semantic framework for the specification of languages and systems.

   In this paper we propose a technique to generate test cases for programs written in programming languages specified in Maude, although it can be generalized to similar languages. In this way Maude becomes an even more powerful prototyping language providing a test-case generator (in addition to an interpreter of the language). The test cases can be generated in two ways: computing a set of test cases using all the instructions required by a given coverage criterion or trying to disprove a property over the program. This methodology has been implemented in a Maude prototype and its use is described by means of an example.

Keywords: testing, semantics, Maude, coverage, property-based, narrowing.

1   Introduction

Testing is a technique for checking the correctness of programs by means of executing several inputs and studying the obtained results. Testing is one of the most important stages of the software-development process, but it also is a very time-consuming and tedious task, and for this reason several efforts have been devoted to automate it [12,3]. Basically, we can distinguish two different approaches to testing: white-box testing [9,17], that uses the specific statements of the system to generate the most appropriate test cases, and black-box testing [26,10,3], that considers the system as a black box with an unknown structure and where a specification of the system is used to generate the test cases and check their correctness. When using white-box testing we can also distinguish between generating ground test cases that are later executed and using test cases with variables that must be refined by using the program. From the programming-languages prototyping point of view, it would be interesting to generate test cases for

---

* Research supported by MICINN Spanish project *DESAFIOS10* (TIN2009-14599-C03-01) and Comunidad de Madrid program *PROMETIDOS* (S2009/TIC-1465).

A. Roychoudhury and M. D'Souza (Eds.): ICTAC 2012, LNCS 7521, pp. 90–104, 2012.

programs written in the programming language being prototyped, instead of the standard approach which generates test cases for the semantics of the language. That is, if we define, for example, the semantics of Java in a programming language providing a test-case generator, we could use it for testing that the semantics are defined in the appropriate way (e.g., the while loop works properly in general), but we could not use it for testing a program written in Java and executed used this semantics (e.g., does my sorting method work?). The advantages of having this kind of tool are that (i) test cases can be obtained in the prototyping stage, executed, and used again once the real system is implemented, and (ii) since several well-known languages have been already represented in Maude [15], we can generate test cases for them. The technique presented here—which can be adapted to any programming language providing features similar to reflection and narrowing—is, to the best of our knowledge, the first one applying this "meta-level" approach.

We are especially interested in prototypes of programming languages specified in Maude [5], a high-level language and high-performance system supporting both equational and rewriting logic computation. Maude modules correspond to specifications in rewriting logic [14], a simple and expressive logic which allows the representation of many models of concurrent and distributed systems. This logic is an extension of equational logic; in particular, Maude functional modules correspond to specifications in membership equational logic [2], which, in addition to equations, allows the statement of membership axioms characterizing the elements of a sort. Rewriting logic extends membership equational logic by adding rewrite rules, that represent transitions in a concurrent system. Maude system modules are used to define specifications in this logic. The current version of Maude supports a limited version of narrowing [25], a generalization of term rewriting that allows to execute terms with variables by replacing pattern matching by unification, for some unconditional rewriting logic theories without memberships. As a semantical framework, Maude has been used to specify the semantics of several languages, such as LOTOS [27], CCS [27], or C [7]. These researches, as well as several other efforts to describe a methodology to represent the semantics of programming languages in Maude, led to the *rewriting logic semantics project* [15], which presents a comprehensive compilation of these works, and to the development of K [24], a programming language built upon a continuation-based technique that provides mechanisms (i) to ease language definitions and (ii) to translate these definitions into Maude, allowing the programmer to uses its analysis tools.

In previous works we have presented a tool to generate test cases for Maude modules [19,20]. This kind of tool generates test cases in different ways: they can try to use all the equations, membership axioms, and rules required by a given *coverage criterion*; they can try to falsify a given property; or they can check whether a given Maude system module, the implementation, performs the same actions as another Maude system module, the specification, which has been previously tested and debugged. However, when specifying other programming languages the user could test the Maude specification but not the programs written in that programming language. In this paper we present a methodology for generating test cases for the programming languages specified in Maude. In this way, one of the main features of Maude, providing an interpreter of the language being described for free (obtained because Maude specifications are executable) is now extended with a test-case generator for the language being specified. This tool computes test cases (i) trying to cover all the statements of the sort indicated by the user (as we will explain later, this is known as *global branch coverage*), what means that he can e.g. try to cover all the assignments in imperative languages or all the equations in functional languages; and (ii) trying to disprove a property over the program. As an extra feature obtained from the coverage approach, we can perform static analysis in the programs written in these languages and check whether all the statements are reachable, that is, if the program contains dead code.

The rest of the paper is organized as follows: Section 2 presents the related work and the differences with our approach. Section 3 introduces Maude and narrowing, while Section 4 describes the methodology followed to test programs whose semantics has been previously specified in Maude. Section 5 shows how this approach has been implemented in a Maude prototype by means of an example. Finally, Section 6 concludes and outlines the future work. The source code of the tool, examples, related papers, and much more information is available at http://maude.sip.ucm.es/testing/.

2   Related Work

Different approaches to testing have been proposed in the literature. We present in this section the most similar approaches to ours: testing of imperative languages following a declarative approach (in the sense that they use a methodology initially designed for declarative languages) and testing using symbolic execution approaches (like narrowing). We thus rule out from the picture other interesting approaches like conformance testing [26], which checks that an implementation performs the same actions as a given specification, because it is very different from the ideas presented here, although we consider it an interesting subject of future work. Correspondingly, we do not include the verification of security protocols [13], that symbolically explore the state space trying to find a flaw in the protocol, because they focus on a very specific problem.

An important example of test-case generator initially developed for a functional language that has been extended to imperative languages is Quickcheck [4], a tool developed for Haskell specifications where the programmer writes assertions about logical properties that a function should fulfill; test cases are randomly generated by using the constructors of the data type to test and attempt to falsify these assertions. Note that these test cases are just ground terms used to check whether the properties stated by the user hold. The project, started in 2000, has been extended to generate test cases for several languages such as Java, C++, Erlang, and several others following the same approach. Quickcheck has also inspired other tools like PropEr [18], a test case generator for Erlang, although we will focus our comparison on Quickcheck.

An interesting symbolic approach is applied by Lazy Smallcheck [23] (an improvement of a previous system called SparseCheck), a library for Haskell to test partially-defined values that uses a mechanism similar to narrowing to test whether the system fulfills some requirements. Another way of achieving symbolic execution in a generic way is by considering that the statements in the program under test introduce constraints on the variables, an approach followed by PET (Partial Evaluation-based Test Case Generation) [11], that uses Constraint Logic Programming to generate test cases satisfying some coverages on object-oriented languages (focusing on Java bytecode).

Table 1. Comparison of different test-case generators

	Quickcheck	Lazy Smallcheck	PET	MSTCG
Tested language	Haskell, C++, Java, Erlang, and others	Haskell	Java bytecode	Languages specified in Maude
Type of testing	Property-based	Property-based	Code coverage	Property-based and code coverage
Technique	Random testing	Narrowing	Constraints	Narrowing
Other remarks	Shrinking Best performance (industrial tool)	Shrinking Research tool	Breakpoints GUI More coverages	Shrinking Generic approach Research tool

The comparison between these tools and ours (called MSTCG, from Maude Semantical Test-Case Generator) is outlined in Table 1. Note that we do not include our own test-case generator for Maude specifications [19], because it would share part of the features of Quickcheck and Lazy Smallcheck, and thus it would not add any new information. The table presents the tested language, the focus of the test cases generated (property-based or code coverage), the mechanism used to generate them, and some interesting remarks about them; we discuss in the following the main points of this comparison. Quickcheck is applied to several different languages; however, the tool for testing each language is implemented specifically and thus it is not generic. From the features point of view, it provides property-based testing and, since it is an industrial tool with several heuristics, it presents a better performance than our tool. On the other hand, an advantage of our tool is the computation of test cases fulfilling a coverage criterion, allowing the user to test the specification by checking test cases "by hand" (that is, against his intended interpretation) even when no properties over the specification are stated. Finally, Quickcheck implements a mechanism called shrinking that computes, for a test-case disproving the property, the smaller one (in terms of constructors) that also disproves it. Test cases obtained by using symbolic execution provide a similar result (for both code coverage and property-based testing in our case), due to the fact that they perform the smallest amount of modifications to the initial terms in order to execute the given program; in this way, we are sure that the test cases are the smallest ones. Lazy Smallcheck is very similar to our tool in the sense that both are narrowing-based experimental tools that focus on research rather than in efficiency, and thus they present a similar performance; however, this tool is not generic and only applies property-based testing. Finally, PET is not generic and does not allow the user to state properties over the program. However, it is more mature than MSTCG and presents many advantages: its provides a graphical user interface, which allows the user to see which commands are covered with each test case, put breakpoints in the code that are later used for the tool, and many other options; and offers more coverage strategies than our approach.

Summarizing, an important point of our approach is that it is *generic*, in the sense that any user can define the semantics of a programming language and then generating test cases for its programs; our tool is to the best of our knowledge the first one of this kind. It is also important to note that we provide two different techniques: code coverage and property-based testing, while most tools only provide one of them. The strong point of our tool reveals its main weaknesses: (i) it is necessary to specify in Maude the semantics of the language and (ii) the performance of the tool is low due to the intensive use of metalevel computation, which takes a great amount of time.

3 Preliminaries

We present in this section the Maude system and its narrowing mechanisms [6].

3.1 Maude

Maude modules are executable rewriting logic specifications. Maude functional modules [5, Chap. 4], introduced with syntax fmod ... endfm, are executable membership equational specifications that allow the definition of sorts (by means of keyword sort(s)); subsort relations between sorts (subsort); operators (op) for building values of these sorts, giving the sorts of their arguments and result, and which may have attributes such as being associative (assoc) or commutative (comm), for example; memberships (mb) asserting that a term has a sort; and equations (eq) identifying terms. Both memberships and equations can be conditional (cmb and ceq). Maude system modules [5, Chap. 6], introduced with syntax mod ... endm, are executable rewrite theories. A system module can contain all the declarations of a functional module and, in addition, declarations for rules (rl) and conditional rules (crl).

We introduce Maude modules with an example showing how to define the evaluation semantics of a simple imperative language; the complete specification of this language is presented in [27]. In the following, we will call this programming language the *object language* to distinguish it from Maude; we will also use this name in general to refer to any programming language specified in Maude. Assume we have defined in a module called EVALUATION-EXP-EVAL the syntax of a language with the empty instruction skip, assignment, If statement, While loop, and composition of instructions, all of them of sort Com; some simple operations over expressions and Boolean expressions such as addition and equality; and a state, of sort ST, mapping variables to values. Using this module we specify the evaluation semantics of this language in EVALUATION-SEMANTICS, that first defines a Program as a pair of a term of sort Com and a state:

```
(mod EVALUATION-SEMANTICS is
  pr EVALUATION-EXP-EVAL .
  op <_,_> : Com ST -> Program .
```

The semantics for the assignment are described by the rule AsR, that computes the value of the expression in the condition and then updates the state of the variables by substituting the value in the variable with the one computed in the condition:

```
crl [AsR] : < X := e, st > => < skip, st[v / X] >
  if < e, st > => v .
```

The rules IfR1 and IfR2 describe the behavior of the If statement. If the boolean condition be reaches the value T (which stands for true) then we execute the Then branch and return the reached state st'; otherwise, the Else part is executed:

```
crl [IfR1] : < If be Then C Else C', st > => < skip, st' >
  if < be, st > => T /\
     < C, st > => < skip, st' > .
crl [IfR2] : < If be Then C Else C', st > => < skip, st' >
  if < be, st > => F /\
     < C', st > => < skip, st' > .
```

Analogously, WhileR1 and WhileR2 describe the behavior of the while loop:

```
crl [WhileR1] : < While be Do C, st > => < skip, st >
  if < be, st > => F .
crl [WhileR2] : < While be Do C, st > => < skip, st' >
  if < be, st > => T /\
     < C ; (While be Do C), st > => < skip, st' > .
```

Finally, the rule ComR combines two different computations, using the state reached in the first one to continue with the second one:

```
crl [ComR] : < C ; C', st > => < skip, st'' >
  if < C, st > => < skip, st' > /\
     < C', st' > => < skip, st'' > .
endm)
```

Given this semantics, we can now write and execute programs of the form:

```
< If Equal(x, 0) Then y := 0
                 Else y := 1 ;
  If Equal(w, 0) Then z := 0
                 Else z := 1, st:ST >
```

where st is a free variable of sort ST (the state) that will be instantiated by the testing process. We can see now the differences between testing the Maude specification and testing the imperative program executed by Maude.[1] Assuming that in both Maude and our imperative language the coverage criteria is *global branch coverage* [9], which requires that all the reachable statements (membership, equations, and rules in the Maude case; assignments, If, and While statements otherwise) are executed, we would obtain the following results: the state x = 0, w = 1 would cover all the possible Maude rules (AsR, IfR1, IfR2, and ComR rules, the rest of the rules are not reachable) but only covers two assignments y := 0 and z := 1 (and, obviously, the two If statements), that is, we would need another state (e.g. x = 1, w = 0) to meet the criterion. It is easy to see that, although the techniques for covering Maude specifications and for programs written in another language previously specified in Maude are similar, the rules that must be applied are different, and thus it is necessary to specify the kind of statements we want to cover, manipulate the object program to "mark" these statements,[2] and indicate for each Maude rule the statements that are executed. We will see the details in Section 4.

---

[1] In fact, test case generation is even more different between Maude and any other program written in the given object language, because in Maude we would start with a term containing only variables, that is, the initial term would be < prog:Com, st:ST >. However, we present the differences over this partially instantiated term to show that even setting the program the required coverage is different.

[2] In this specific example we want to cover assignments, but note that this methodology also works for other languages and even other paradigms. For example, in Haskell-like programs we would want to cover all the cases for all the reachable functions.

3.2 Narrowing

Narrowing [25,8,16] is a generalization of term rewriting that allows free variables in terms and replaces pattern matching by unification in order to reduce these terms. It was first used for solving equational unification problems [22] and then generalized to deal with problems of symbolic reachability. Similarly to rewriting, where at each rewriting step one must choose which subterm of the subject term and which rule of the specification are going to be considered, at each narrowing step one must choose which subterm of the subject term, which rule of the specification, and which instantiation of the variables of the subject term and the rule's lefthand side are going to be considered. The difference between a rewriting step and a narrowing step is that in both cases we use a rewrite rule $l \Rightarrow r$ to rewrite t at a position p, but narrowing unifies the lefthand side l and the chosen subject term t before actually performing the rewriting step, while in rewriting this term must be an instance of l (i.e., only matching is required). Using this narrowing approach, we can obtain a substitution that, applied to an initial term that contains variables, generates the most general term that can apply the traversed rules.

We denote by $t \rightsquigarrow_\theta^\sigma t'$, with $\sigma = q_1; \dots; q_n$ a sequence of labels, the succession of narrowing steps applying (in the given order) the statements $q_1; \dots; q_n$ that leads from the initial term t (possibly with variables) to the term t', and where θ is the substitution used by this sequence, which results from the composition of the substitutions obtained in each narrowing step. The latest version of Maude includes an implementation of narrowing for unconditional free, C, AC, or ACU theories in Full Maude [6]. We have improved this implementation by using the techniques described in [20] to use membership axioms and conditional statements.

4 Using Semantics to Generate Test Cases

We describe in this section the methodology to test programs whose semantics has been previously specified in Maude. It consists of three steps: identifying the appropriate sort of statements that must be covered, manipulating the program to mark these statements, and modifying the Maude rules to indicate the statements applied by each of them. It is important to state first that the coverage criterion applied to all the programs is global branch coverage, that tries to apply all the reachable statements, as illustrated above. Also note that some of the steps explained in this section will be later performed automatically, as shown in Section 5. Note that this approach is only required for coverage strategies, and hence property checking will be explained later.

The first step relies on the user to indicate the sort of statements that he wants to cover. In our example, the user should mark Com, the sort for all the possible instructions (skip, assignment, If conditional, and While loop) as this sort. The second step is automatically performed by the tool, and consists of "marking" the given program and each Maude rule with a unique identifier distinguishing the different statements. For example, the program presented at the end of Section 3.1 would be marked as follows:[3]

---

[3] In fact, an extra label for the whole program, which will be executed by an application of the extraInfo-ComR rule, would also be computed. We do not show it here for the sake of readability.

```
< ¹If Equal(x, 0)
  Then ²y := 0
  Else ³y := 1 ;
  ⁴If Equal(w, 0)
  Then ⁵z := 0
  Else ⁶z := 1, st:ST >
```

where the two conditional statements and the four assignments have been labeled with natural numbers indicating that they are statements of the sort given by the user. The test-case generator will look for states executing all of these commands. In the same way, rules have to be modified to deal with this kind of terms by adding variables of sort Nat (the predefined sort for natural numbers) to each statement of the given sort. In this way, the rule IfR1 is extended as follows:

```
crl [extraInfo-IfR1] : <ⁿIf be Then ⁿ'C Else ⁿ"C', st> => <skip, st'>
  if < be, st > => T /\
     < ⁿ'C, st > => < skip, st' > .
```

Note that extended rules are renamed by using the prefix extraInfo. We can see now in the extraInfo-IfR1 rule above that it contains several labeled statements, but not all of them are executed by the rule: the Else branch is never executed, the Then branch is executed in the conditions (and thus the execution of this statement is in charge of the the assignment rule, which will indicate that this statement has been used), and finally the whole If statement *is* executed. As we will show in the next section, we provide a semi-automatic approach to relate rules and executed statements: the tool computes a mapping following a fixed strategy, that the user can check and edit it if required. Finally, note that the initial term must also be provided by the user. It must contain at least one variable, indicating the values of the variables through the execution of the program, which is instantiated to generate the test cases.

We can use now narrowing to our labeled initial term. Assuming that initial is the labeled term shown above, we can apply the following narrowing step:

$$\text{initial} \rightsquigarrow^{\text{extraInfo-ComR}} < \text{skip, } x = 0 \ y = 0 \ w = 0 \ z = 0 >$$

after applying the statements 1, 2, 4, and 5, where extraInfo-ComR is a rule that defines the composition of statements by execution them in the conditions and then putting the result in the righthand side of the rule. However, this step does not clarify the process due to the fact that all the important steps are applied in the rewrite conditions. For this reason, let's see how the first If statement is executed (note here the importance of transmitting the label information to the conditions, which requires a careful rule transformation) by using a narrowing step with the rule extraInfo-IfR1 shown above:

```
< ¹If Equal(x, 0) Then ²y := 0 Else ³y := 1, st > ⇝IfR1
< skip, x = 0 st' >
```

It is important to see that the mapping between rules and applied statements computed by the tool indicates that extraInfo-IfR1 applies (covers) the statement labeled with n in the transformed rule above, which refers to the complete If statement. In this case n is bound to 1, and thus this rule is executing the first If statement. Again, most of the information is developed in the rewrite conditions. Although we have not shown the rule for the equality, it is easy to see that it requires both values in Equal to be equal to return T. Hence, in this step we really see how narrowing works, since thus far all the rules have been applied by using matching instead of unification. In this case, unification requires the state to contain the variable x mapped to the value 0, while another state st' remains:

$$< \text{Equal}(\text{x, 0}), \text{ st } > \leadsto_{\text{st} \mapsto \text{x = 0 st'}}^{\text{EqR1}} < \text{T, x = 0 st'} >$$

where EqR1 is the rule in charge of the positive case of Equal; note that this rule has not been modified with respect to the original module because it does not contain statements of sort Com, and thus its label does not use the extraInfo prefix. Once this first rewrite condition of extraInfo-IfR1 holds, we try to fulfill to second one, that contains the statement labeled with 2 in the initial term. Before using narrowing, the substitution obtained in the previous step is applied:

$$< {}^{2}\text{y := 0, x = 0 st' } > \leadsto^{\text{AsR}} < \text{skip, x = 0 y = 0 st'' } >$$

where the new state requires a simple application of narrowing to update the state that we can omit. The main points in this step, which concludes the execution of the first If statement, is that the statement labeled with 2 is executed and y = 0 added to the state. The second If statement can be executed in a similar way to obtain the final state x = 0 y = 0 w = 0 z = 0. Note that this is the *final* state reached after executing the statements 1, 2, 4, and 5, and thus we need now to compute the *initial* one. For this reason, our tool also returns the initial states, which consists of the term introduced by the user with the variables instantiated with the substitution computed during the narrowing process, in this case it would be st ↦ x = 0 y = 0 w = 0 z = 0.

Given the explanation above for the variables, it may seem strange to have the variables y and z with value 0, since these variables may contain any value and it does not affect the executed statements, and thus it deserves a careful explanation. In fact, the rule in charge of updating the state checks whether the variable is already there. If it is not in the state, what would force the state to be empty, then it is added and it would not appear in the initial state, but in this case the next statements cannot be applied because the state does not contain y and the process cannot continue. For this reason, we (as well as the tool in the next section) have used the rule that forces the state to contain the variable. Thus, at the end of the process, the term representing the initial state will contain a value of the form y = N:Nat, with N:Nat a fresh variable. This variable is instantiated, to ease the readability, with the smaller term of the appropriate sort, which is the constant 0. The same happens with the remaining variable of sort ST, that would be named st'''', which is substituted with the identity element for states, empty, and thus disappears.

5 Maude Prototype

We briefly present in this section the Maude prototype and its main commands by using the example in the previous sections. Much more information about the prototype can be found at http://maude.sip.ucm.es/testing/.

5.1   Code Coverage

Once all the modules have been introduced in Full Maude and the tool has been started, we can indicate the module where testing must take place and the sort of the statements that we want to cover with the following commands:

```
Maude> (semantics module EVALUATION-SEMANTICS .)
Module EVALUATION-SEMANTICS selected for semantics testing.
Maude> (set sort statements Com .)
Sort Com selected as sort of statements.
```

Once these commands are introduced the tool manipulates the rules in the (flattened) EVALUATION-SEMANTICS module as described in the previous section. We can display these modified rules with the command (show semantics rules .), but it is worth seeing the map between the rules and the executed statements. The tool follows a simple strategy to generate this map that consists of selecting as executed statement the first term of the given sort found (i) in the lefthand side of the rule, traversed following a breadth-first search in the tree representing the term; or (ii) in the conditions if the lefthand side does not contain a term of this sort. Note that, although this strategy is quite simple, it works very well in practice because, when several statements appear in a term, the outermost is the one usually applied (e.g. to direct the execution of the inner ones). The command in charge of showing this information is:

```
Maude> (show applied statements .)
The rule extraInfo-AsR :
 crl < stmntIndx(X:Var := e:Exp,V$#0:Nat),st:ST >
  => < skip,st:ST[v:Num / X:Var]>
  if < e:Exp,st:ST > => v:Num .
  applies the statement
  X:Var := e:Exp identified by the variable V$#0
...
```

which shows for each rule the associated statement, as in the extraInfo-AsR shown above, where the new variables have the form V$# to avoid clashes with other variables in the rule and the operator stmntIndx generates pairs of the given sort and variables. When the tool fails to associate the appropriate information to a rule, the following commands can be used:

```
Maude> (rule Q is not associated to any statement .)
The mapping for rule Q has been updated.
Maude> (rule Q is associated to VL .)
The mapping for rule Q has been updated.
```

where Q is a rule label and VL is the list of variables identifying the applied statements. We can now introduce the program we want to test with the following command:

```
Maude> (object program init .)
Object program introduced.
```

where init has the form indicated in the previous section (a term with variables instead of state). It will be reduced by using equations before labeling to allow the user to use constants instead of big terms in the command line. Assuming that init is the program described at the end of Section 3.1 and it is labeled as shown in Section 4 (which can be checked with the command (show object program .)), the tool can start the test generation process. However, we may be interested in only covering some of the statements of the initial coverage (e.g., because we want to know whether a specific one, such as an exception, is reached). The user can modify the statements in the coverage with:

```
Maude> (statements in coverage NL .)
The required coverage has been updated.
```

where NL is a list of natural numbers indicating the statements to be covered. When all the options have been set, we can start the testing process. The current version of the tool only supports, as explained in the previous section, the global branch coverage strategy, and thus the following result is obtained:

```
Maude> (start semantics testing .)
2 test cases must be checked by the user:
  The program reaches the state < skip, x = 0 y = 0 w = 0 z = 0 >
starting with the substitution st:ST |-> x = 0 y = 0 w = 0 z = 0
and covers the statements 1, 2, 4, 5
  The program reaches the state < skip, x = 1 y = 1 w = 1 z = 1 >
starting with the substitution st:ST |-> x = 1 y = 0 w = 1 z = 0
and covers the statements 1, 3, 4, 6
All the statements were covered
```

Where the variables y and z appear in the initial state for the reasons given in the previous section. The user would be now in charge of checking whether the reached states are the expected ones. Remember that an important idea behind this tool is to use the generated test cases during the prototyping stage to test programs written in the programming language prototyped in Maude once it is implemented in other language. In this case, we can introduce the values for the variables in the "real" language and then check that the results obtained in both cases are equivalent.

5.2   Property-Driven Test-Case Generation

Another very useful way of testing a program is by defining a property and then trying to find a state where the *negation* of the property holds, that is, where the property does not hold. This generic scheme has been studied in [5, Chapter 12] when using the Maude search command to check invariants; we apply the same idea here with *symbolic* search. Note that, since we are just trying to check if the property holds in all the reachable states we are not concerned about coverages, and thus the module transformations presented above are not required, although the underlying narrowing mechanism remains unchanged. It is also important to note that, as explained below, we take conditions into account when performing this search, thus making this approach much more powerful than the current narrowing search available in Maude.

The current command is an improvement of a previous command used in [20], where we provided a command to check whether a property holds in a Maude specification providing the name of the function we wanted to test, when dealing with functional modules, or the sort under test, when working with system modules. We have modified this command to accept terms partially instantiated that, as we have seen above, stand in our case for programs written in some programming language specified in Maude. For the sake of example, we can state a very simple property over the program described in the previous sections. We can define a function allEq that checks whether all the variables in a state contain the same values. Since we use the negation of the property, what we are really checking is that all the reachable states contain at least two different values, which is incorrect, as we have seen in Section 4. The command for this kind of testing is:

```
Maude> (semantics property reaches < skip, st':ST > s.t. allEq(st':ST) .)
  The property does not hold.
  The program reaches the state < skip, x = 0 y = 0 w = 0 z = 0 >
starting with the substitution st:ST |-> x = 0 y = 0 w = 0 z = 0
```

where the command mimics the standard search command available in Maude and thus requires a pattern to wrap the reached state and a condition over that pattern;[4] note that the initial state is introduced with the command described above for the object program and thus it is not necessary. An interesting approach using this pattern would consist of trying to match part of the program, for example related to loops, and then check that some properties hold before and after the loop. In our case, the pattern is < skip, st':ST >, indicating that the program has finished, while the condition is allEq(st':ST). As expected, the tool has found a counterexample proving that the property does not hold, showing the initial and final states.

Observe that, in this kind of analysis it is not necessary to extend the test case (if it exists) to the implementation. We have proved the program is erroneous and must be modified; once it is fixed and the property holds, we could use global branch coverage to test all its possible branches. It is also important to note that, as the rest of testing approaches, the ones used by our tool are not complete, in the sense that the program may contain a bug and it cannot be found. To palliate this problem the tool uses a bound in the number of steps that can be modified by the user with (set narrowing depth N .), with N a natural number, in order to traverse a bigger search space.

5.3 Implementation Notes

Exploiting the fact that rewriting logic is reflective, a key distinguishing feature of Maude is its systematic and efficient use of reflection through its predefined META-LEVEL module [5, Chap. 14], a feature that makes Maude remarkably extensible and that allows many advanced metaprogramming and metalanguage applications. This powerful feature allows access to metalevel entities such as specifications or computations as usual data. In this way, we can manipulate the modules introduced by the user, direct the narrowing process, and implement the input/output interactions in Maude itself. More specifically, we are interested in the metaNarrowSearchPath function that, given a term and a bound on the number of narrowing steps, returns all the possible paths starting from this term, the used substitutions, and the applied rules. We use this command to perform a breadth-first search of the state space. Moreover, the test-case generator is implemented on top of Full Maude [5, Chap. 18], a tool completely written in Maude which includes features for parsing, storing modules, and pretty-printing

---

[4] Obviously, if the pattern contains enough information about the reached state the condition can be nil.

terms, improving the input/output interaction. Although conceptually our tool uses two levels of reflection (the meta-represented Maude module standing for the semantics of a programming language and the program written in this language, which is used to generate the test cases; this second level is the novelty of our approach), at the implementation level one reflection level is enough.

It is worth mentioning some important implementation issues. First, and following the module transformation described in [20], we consider that equations are oriented from left to right and thus can be transformed into rules (analogously transforming equational conditions into rewrite conditions with fresh variables), allowing the narrowing process to use equations to refine the variables. Moreover, the current narrowing commands available in Maude only work with unconditional rules, which prevents us from using this kind of rules. Since this constraint would exclude most of the language specifications developed in Maude thus far, we use a mechanism [20] that checks by using narrowing, for each narrowing step, the rewrite conditions (remember that, as said above, equational conditions become rewrite conditions), and adds the obtained substitution to the one obtained with the body of the rule. In this way we can extend the substitution obtained for the rule with the extra variables that appear in rewrite conditions and may appear, as shown in the example at the end of Section 4, in the righthand side of the rule. This extension makes the search command used in the previous section more powerful than the current narrowing search available in Maude. Finally, we provide a rule-based definition for some predefined functions, such as _<_ for natural numbers. They follow the standard definitions distinguishing the different constructors (0 and successor) of these functions and allow us to apply our technique to a much wider range of programming languages, that use most of these functions in conditions.

6   Concluding Remarks and Ongoing Work

We have presented a methodology to test programs written in any programming language whose semantics has been previously defined. In this way we propose a novel way to generate test-cases using a meta-level approach, instead of just testing the given semantics. We use this approach to improve the Maude features as prototyping language because it provides now, in addition to an interpreter of the language being specified, a test-case generator for programs written in that language. These test cases can be also used after prototyping to check that the implementation follows the specification or to detect dead code. The process to accomplish this generic coverage is semi-automatic: the user is in charge of indicating the sort of statements he wants to cover and of checking that the rules execute the statements inferred by the tool, modifying them if needed; the rest of module manipulations is automatically performed by the tool. Finally, we also allow the user to check whether a property holds in the program.

The work presented in this paper offers a good basis for potential extensions and enrichment that can improve its usability and generality. We are currently working on a generic way to modify the output generated by the tool; our goal is to generate JUnit-like [1] output for each programming language, i.e., an executable program with assertions written in the object language that allows the user to really test its program in the original language. This idea would be an important step to perform testing against the specification [10] in a natural and automatic way. Similarly, it is interesting to study how to combine conformance testing [26] with our approach, that is, how to check that transitions used in the specification are replicated in the implementation. Moreover, expanding our approach to deal with program definitions specified in the K framework [24] would also be very useful. This option is not available in the current version of the tool due to the internal transformations of K, which modifies the form of the rewrite rules. We also want to provide more coverage criteria in addition to the global branch coverage criterion presented in this work. However, we require generic criteria, that is, criteria that can be applied independently of the paradigm of the object language, which makes the implementation of these criteria far more complicated than for specific programming languages. It would also be interesting to see how the random testing approach, successfully followed in other tools like Quickcheck [4], works here. Furthermore, we plan to extend our declarative debugger [21], that currently presents the same problem as the previous version of the test-case generator: it can only debug Maude specifications, but not the object language. Our aim is to develop a universal declarative debugger that takes as input a program in any object language specified in Maude, applies the test-case generator presented in this work and, if any of the test cases reveal an error, debug it with this new debugger. Finally, we want to study how the test-case generator works for languages with parallelism and synchronization. We expect the narrowing mechanism to traverse all the possible paths and check, following the ideas of property-based testing, whether the program fulfills some requirements.

References

1. Beck, K., Gamma, E.: Test-infected: programmers love writing tests, pp. 357–376. Cambridge University Press (2000)
2. Bouhoula, A., Jouannaud, J.-P., Meseguer, J.: Specification and proof in membership equational logic. Theoretical Computer Science 236, 35–132 (2000)
3. Cartaxo, E.G., Neto, F.G.O., Machado, P.D.L.: Test case generation by means of UML sequence diagrams and labeled transition systems. In: Proceedings of the IEEE International Conference on Systems, Man and Cybernetics, SMC 2007, pp. 1292–1297. IEEE (2007)
4. Claessen, K., Hughes, J.: Quickcheck: A lightweight tool for random testing of Haskell programs. In: ACM SIGPLAN Notices, pp. 268–279. ACM Press (2000)
5. Clavel, M., Durán, F., Eker, S., Lincoln, P., Martí-Oliet, N., Meseguer, J., Talcott, C. (eds.): All About Maude - A High-Performance Logical Framework. LNCS, vol. 4350. Springer, Heidelberg (2007)
6. Clavel, M., Durán, F., Eker, S., Lincoln, P., Martí-Oliet, N., Meseguer, J., Talcott, C.: Maude Manual (Version 2.6) (January 2011), http://maude.cs.uiuc.edu/maude2-manual
7. Ellison, C., Roşu, G.: An executable formal semantics of C with applications. In: Proceedings of the 39th Symposium on Principles of Programming Languages, POPL 2012, pp. 533–544. ACM (2012)
8. Fay, M.J.: First-order unification in an equational theory. In: Joyner, W.H. (ed.) Proceedings of the 4th Workshop on Automated Deduction, pp. 161–167. Academic Press (1979)
9. Fischer, S., Kuchen, H.: Systematic generation of glass-box test cases for functional logic programs. In: Proceedings of the 9th ACM SIGPLAN International Conference on Principles and Practice of Declarative Programming, PPDP 2007, pp. 63–74. ACM Press (2007)

10. Gaudel, M.-C.: Software Testing Based on Formal Specification. In: Borba, P., Cavalcanti, A., Sampaio, A., Woodcook, J. (eds.) PSSE 2007. LNCS, vol. 6153, pp. 215–242. Springer, Heidelberg (2010)
11. Gomez-Zamalloa, M., Albert, E., Puebla, G.: Test case generation for object-oriented imperative languages in CLP. Theory and Practice of Logic Programming 10, 659–674 (2010)
12. Hierons, R.M., Bogdanov, K., Bowen, J.P., Rance Cleaveland, J.D., Dick, J., Gheorghe, M., Harman, M., Kapoor, K., Krause, P., Lüttgen, G., Simons, A.J.H., Vilkomir, S., Woodward, M.R., Zedan, H.: Using formal specifications to support testing. ACM Computing Surveys 41(2), 1–76 (2009)
13. Meadows, C.: Applying formal methods to the analysis of a key management protocol. Journal of Computer Security 1 (1992)
14. Meseguer, J.: Conditional rewriting logic as a unified model of concurrency. Theoretical Computer Science 96(1), 73–155 (1992)
15. Meseguer, J., Roşu, G.: The rewriting logic semantics project. Theoretical Computer Science 373(3), 213–237 (2007)
16. Middeldorp, A., Hamoen, E.: Counterexamples to Completeness Results for Basic Narrowing. In: Kirchner, H., Levi, G. (eds.) ALP 1992. LNCS, vol. 632, pp. 244–258. Springer, Heidelberg (1992)
17. Müller, R.A., Lembeck, C., Kuchen, H.: A symbolic Java virtual machine for test case generation. In: IASTED Conf. on Software Engineering, pp. 365–371 (2004)
18. Papadakis, M., Sagonas, K.: A PropEr integration of types and function specifications with property-based testing. In: Proceedings of the 2011 ACM SIGPLAN Erlang Workshop, pp. 39–50. ACM Press (2011)
19. Riesco, A.: Test-Case Generation for Maude Functional Modules. In: Mossakowski, T., Kreowski, H.-J. (eds.) WADT 2010. LNCS, vol. 7137, pp. 287–301. Springer, Heidelberg (2012)
20. Riesco, A.: Using Narrowing to Test Maude Specifications. In: Durán, F. (ed.) Proceedings of the 9th International Workshop on Rewriting Logic and its Applications, WRLA 2012. LNCS. Springer (to appear, 2012)
21. Riesco, A., Verdejo, A., Martí-Oliet, N., Caballero, R.: Declarative debugging of rewriting logic specifications. Journal of Logic and Algebraic Programming (to appear, 2012)
22. Robinson, J.A.: A machine-oriented logic based on the resolution principle. Journal of the ACM 12(1), 23–41 (1965)
23. Runciman, C., Naylor, M., Lindblad, F.: Smallcheck and Lazy Smallcheck: automatic exhaustive testing for small values. In: Gill, A. (ed.) Proceedings of the 1st ACM SIGPLAN Symposium on Haskell, Haskell 2008, pp. 37–48. ACM (2008)
24. Şerbănuţă, T., Ştefănescu, G., Roşu, G.: Defining and Executing P Systems with Structured Data in K. In: Corne, D.W., Frisco, P., Păun, G., Rozenberg, G., Salomaa, A. (eds.) WMC 2008. LNCS, vol. 5391, pp. 374–393. Springer, Heidelberg (2009)
25. Slagle, J.R.: Automated theorem-proving for theories with simplifiers, commutativity and associativity. Journal of the ACM 21(4), 622–642 (1974)
26. Tretmans, J.: Conformance testing with labelled transition systems: Implementation relations and test generation. Computer Networks and ISDN Systems 29(1), 49–79 (1996)
27. Verdejo, A., Martí-Oliet, N.: Executable structural operational semantics in Maude. Journal of Logic and Algebraic Programming 67, 226–293 (2006)

A Locally Nameless Representation
for a Natural Semantics for Lazy Evaluation

Lidia Sánchez-Gil[1], Mercedes Hidalgo-Herrero[2], and Yolanda Ortega-Mallén[1]

[1] Dpto. Sistemas Informáticos y Computación, Facultad de CC. Matemáticas,
Universidad Complutense de Madrid, Spain
[2] Dpto. Didáctica de las Matemáticas, Facultad de Educación,
Universidad Complutense de Madrid, Spain

Abstract. We propose a locally nameless representation for Launchbury's natural semantics for lazy evaluation. Names are reserved for free
variables, while bound variable names are replaced by indices. This avoids
the use of α-conversion and Barendregt's variable convention, and facilitates proof formalization. Our definition includes the management of
multi-binders to represent simultaneous recursive local declarations. We
use cofinite quantification to express the semantic rules that require the
introduction of fresh names, but we show that existential rules are admissible too. Moreover, we prove that the choice of names during the
evaluation of a term is irrelevant as long as they are fresh enough.

1 Motivation

Call-by-need evaluation, which avoids repeated computations, is the semantic
foundation for lazy functional programming languages like Haskell or Clean.
Launchbury defines in [7] a natural semantics for lazy evaluation where the set
of *bindings*, i.e., (variable, expression) pairs, is explicitly managed to make possible their sharing. In order to prove that this lazy semantics is *correct* and
computationally adequate with respect to a standard denotational semantics,
Launchbury introduces some variations in his natural semantics. On the one
hand, functional application is modeled denotationally by extending the environment with a variable bound to a value. This new variable represents the
formal parameter of the function, while the value corresponds to the actual ar-
gument. For a closer approach of this mechanism, applications are carried out in
the alternative semantics by introducing indirections instead of by performing
the β-reduction through substitution. On the other hand, the update of bindings
with their computed values is an operational notion without counterpart in the
standard denotational semantics, so that the alternative natural semantics does
no longer update bindings and becomes a *call-by-name* semantics.

Unfortunately, the proof of the equivalence between the lazy natural semantics
and its alternative version with indirections and nonupdate is detailed nowhere,
and a simple induction turns out to be insufficient. Intuitively, both reduction
systems should produce the same results. However, this cannot be directly established since final values may contain free variables which are dependent on the

A. Roychoudhury and M. D'Souza (Eds.): ICTAC 2012, LNCS 7521, pp. 105–119, 2012.

context of evaluation, which is represented by the heap of bindings. The changes introduced by the alternative semantics do deeply affect the heaps. Although indirections and "duplicated" bindings (a consequence of no updating) do not add relevant information to the context, it is awkward to prove this fact.

In the usual representation of the lambda-calculus, i.e., with variable names for free and bound variables, terms are identifed up to α-conversion. Dealing with α-equated terms usually implies the use of Barendregt's variable convention [3] to avoid the renaming of bound variables. However, the use of the variable convention in rule inductions is sometimes dubious and may lead to *faulty* results (as it is shown by Urban et al. in [15]). Looking for a system of binding more amenable to formalization, we have chosen a *locally nameless* representation (as presented by Charguéraud in [5]). This is a mixed notation where bound variable names are replaced by de Bruijn indices [6], while free variables preserve their names. Hence, α-conversion is no longer needed and variable substitution is easily defined because there is no danger of name capture. Moreover, this representation is suitable for working with proof assistants like Coq [4] or Isabelle [9].

The present work is the first step to prove formally the equivalence between Launchbury's semantics and its alternative version. We start by defining a locally nameless representation of the λ-calculus extended with recursive local declarations. Then we express Launchbury's rules in the new style and present several properties of the reduction system that are useful for the equivalence proof.

Our concern for reproducing and formalizing the proof of this equivalence is not arbitrary. Launchbury's semantics has been cited frequently and has inspired many further works as well as several extensions [2,8,13,17], where the corresponding adequacy proofs have been obtained by just adapting Launchbury's proof scheme. We have extended ourselves the λ-calculus with a new expression that introduces parallelism when performing functional applications [11]. This *parallel application* creates new processes to distribute the computation; these processes exchange values through communication channels. The corresponding adequacy property relies on the adequacy of Launchbury's natural semantics.

The paper is structured as follows: In Section 2 we present the locally nameless representation of the lambda calculus extended with recursive local declarations. In Section 3 we describe a locally nameless translation of Launchbury's natural semantics for lazy evaluation [7], together with the corresponding regularity, introduction and renaming lemmas. The proofs (by hand) of these lemmas and other auxiliary results are detailed in [12]. In Section 4 we comment on some related work. The last two sections are devoted to conclusions and future work.

2   The Locally Nameless Representation

The language described by Launchbury in [7] is a normalized lambda calculus extended with recursive local declarations. We reproduce the restricted syntax in Figure 1. Normalization is achieved in two steps. First an α-conversion is carried out so that all bound variables have distinct names. In a second phase, arguments for applications are enforced to be variables. These static transformations simplify the definition of the reduction rules.

$$x \in Id \qquad i,j \in \mathbb{N}$$

$$x \in Var$$

$$v \in Var \quad ::= \text{bvar } i\ j \mid \text{fvar } x$$

$$e \in Exp ::= x \mid \lambda x.e \mid (e\ x) \mid$$

$$t \in LNExp ::= v \mid \text{abs } t \mid \text{app } t\ v \mid$$

$$\text{let } \{x_i = e_i\}_{i=1}^{n} \text{ in } e$$

$$\text{let } \{t_i\}_{i=1}^{n} \text{ in } t$$

Fig. 1. Restricted *named* syntax   **Fig. 2.** Locally nameless syntax

We give the corresponding locally nameless representation by following the methodology summarized in [5]:

1. Define the syntax of the extended λ-calculus in the locally nameless style.
2. Define the variable opening and variable closing operations.
3. Define the free variables and substitution functions, as well as the local closure predicate.
4. State and prove the properties of the operations on terms that are needed in the development to be carried out.

2.1   Locally Nameless Syntax

The locally nameless (restricted) syntax is shown in Figure 2. *Var* stands now for the set of *variables*, where *bound variables* and *free variables* are distinguished. The calculus includes two binding constructions: λ-abstraction and let-declaration. Being the latter a *multi-binder*, we follow Charguéraud [5] and represent bound variables with two natural numbers: The first number is a de Bruijn index that counts how many binders (abstraction or let) one needs to cross to the left to reach the corresponding binder for the variable, while the second refers to the position of the variable inside that binder. Abstractions are seen as multi-binders that bind one variable; thus, the second number should be zero. In the following, a list like $\{t_i\}_{i=1}^{n}$ is represented as $\bar{t}$, with length $|\bar{t}| = n$.

Example 1. Let $e \in Exp$ an expression in the named representation:

$$e \equiv \lambda z.\text{let } x_1 = \lambda y_1.y_1, x_2 = \lambda y_2.y_2, x_3 = x \text{ in } (z\ x_2).$$

The corresponding locally nameless term $t \in LNExp$ is:

$$t \equiv \text{abs (let abs (bvar 0 0), abs (bvar 0 0), fvar } x \text{ in app (bvar 1 0) (bvar 0 1)).}$$

Notice that x_1 and x_2 denote α-equivalent expressions in e. This is more clearly seen in t, where both expressions are represented with syntactically equal terms.   □

As bound variables are nameless, the first phase of Launchbury's normalization is unneeded. However, application arguments are still restricted to variables.

$$\{k \to \overline{x}\}(\texttt{bvar } i\ j) \quad = \begin{cases} \texttt{fvar (List.nth } j\ \overline{x}) & \text{if } i = k \land j < |\overline{x}| \\ \texttt{bvar } i\ j & \text{otherwise} \end{cases}$$

$$\{k \to \overline{x}\}(\texttt{fvar } x) \quad = \texttt{fvar } x$$
$$\{k \to \overline{x}\}(\texttt{abs } t) \quad = \texttt{abs } (\{k+1 \to \overline{x}\}\ t)$$
$$\{k \to \overline{x}\}(\texttt{app } t\ v) \quad = \texttt{app } (\{k \to \overline{x}\}\ t)\ (\{k \to \overline{x}\}\ v)$$
$$\{k \to \overline{x}\}(\texttt{let } \overline{t} \texttt{ in } t) = \texttt{let } (\{k+1 \to \overline{x}\}\ \overline{t}) \texttt{ in } (\{k+1 \to \overline{x}\}\ t)$$

where $\{k \to \overline{x}\}\ \overline{t} = \texttt{List.map } (\{k \to \overline{x}\}\cdot)\ \overline{t}.$

Fig. 3. Variable opening

2.2 Variable Opening and Variable Closing

Variable opening and *closing* are the main operations to manipulate locally nameless terms. We extend to `let` the definitions given by Charguéraud in [5].[1]

To explore the body of a binder (abstraction or `let`), one needs to replace the corresponding bound variables by fresh names. In the case of an abstraction `abs` t the *variable opening operation* replaces in t with a (fresh) name every bound variable which refers to the outermost abstraction. Analogously, to open `let` $\overline{t}$ `in` t we provide a list of $|\overline{t}|$ distinct fresh names to replace the bound variables that occur in $\overline{t}$ and in the body t which refer to this particular declaration.

Variable opening is defined by means of a more general function $\{k \to \overline{x}\}t$ (Figure 3), where the number k represents the nesting level of the binder to be opened, and $\overline{x}$ is a list of pairwise-distinct identifiers in Id. Since the level of the outermost binder is 0, variable opening is defined as: $t^{\overline{x}} = \{0 \to \overline{x}\}t$. We extend this operation to lists of terms: $\overline{t}^{\overline{x}} = \texttt{List.map } (\cdot^{\overline{x}})\ \overline{t}$.

The last definition and those in Figure 3 include some operations on lists. We use an ML-like notation. For instance, `List.nth` $j\ \overline{x}$ represents the $(j+1)^{th}$ element of $\overline{x}$,[2] and `List.map` $f\ \overline{t}$ indicates that the function f is applied to every term in the list $\overline{t}$. In the rest of definitions we will use similar list operations.

Example 2. Let $t \equiv \texttt{abs (let bvar } 0\ 1, \texttt{bvar } 1\ 0 \texttt{ in app (abs bvar } 2\ 0)\ (\texttt{bvar } 0\ 1))$. Hence, the body of the abstraction is:

$u \equiv \texttt{let bvar } 0\ 1, \boxed{\texttt{bvar } 1\ 0}\ \texttt{in app (abs } \boxed{\texttt{bvar } 2\ 0})\ (\texttt{bvar } 0\ 1).$

But then in u the bound variables referring to the outermost abstraction (shown squared) point to nowhere. Therefore, we consider $u^{[x]}$ instead of u, where

$u^{[x]} = \{0 \to x\}(\texttt{let bvar } 0\ 1, \texttt{bvar } 1\ 0 \texttt{ in app (abs bvar } 2\ 0)\ (\texttt{bvar } 0\ 1))$
$\quad = \texttt{let}\{1 \to x\}(\texttt{bvar } 0\ 1, \texttt{bvar } 1\ 0) \texttt{ in }\{1 \to x\}(\texttt{app (abs bvar } 2\ 0)(\texttt{bvar } 0\ 1))$
$\quad = \texttt{let bvar } 0\ 1, \texttt{fvar } x \texttt{ in app (abs }\{2 \to x\}(\texttt{bvar } 2\ 0))\ (\texttt{bvar } 0\ 1)$
$\quad = \texttt{let bvar } 0\ 1, \texttt{fvar } x \texttt{ in app (abs fvar } x)\ (\texttt{bvar } 0\ 1)$

□

---

[1] Multiple binders are defined in [5]. Two constructions are given: One for non-recursive local declarations, and another for mutually recursive expressions. Yet both extensions are not completely developed.

[2] Elements in lists are numbered starting with 0 to match bound variables indices.

$$\{k \leftarrow \overline{x}\}(\texttt{bvar}\ i\ j)\ = \texttt{bvar}\ i\ j$$
$$\{k \leftarrow \overline{x}\}(\texttt{fvar}\ x)\ = \begin{cases} \texttt{bvar}\ k\ j & \text{if } \exists j : 0 \le j < |\overline{x}|.x = \texttt{List.nth}\ j\ \overline{x} \\ \texttt{fvar}\ x & \text{otherwise} \end{cases}$$

$$\{k \leftarrow \overline{x}\}(\texttt{abs}\ t)\ = \texttt{abs}\ (\{k+1 \leftarrow \overline{x}\}\ t)$$
$$\{k \leftarrow \overline{x}\}(\texttt{app}\ t\ v)\ = \texttt{app}\ (\{k \leftarrow \overline{x}\}\ t)\ (\{k \leftarrow \overline{x}\}\ v)$$
$$\{k \leftarrow \overline{x}\}(\texttt{let}\ \overline{t}\ \texttt{in}\ t)\ = \texttt{let}\ (\{k+1 \leftarrow \overline{x}\}\ \overline{t})\ \texttt{in}\ (\{k+1 \leftarrow \overline{x}\}\ t)$$

where $\{k \leftarrow \overline{x}\}\ \overline{t} = \texttt{List.map}\ (\{k \leftarrow \overline{x}\}\ \cdot)\ \overline{t}.$

Fig. 4. Variable closing

Inversely to variable opening, there is an operation to transform free names into bound variables. The *variable closing* of a term is represented by $^{\backslash\overline{x}}t$, where $\overline{x}$ is the list of names to be bound (recall that the names in $\overline{x}$ are distinct). The definition of variable closing is based on a more general function $\{k \leftarrow \overline{x}\}t$ (Figure 4), where k indicates the level of nesting of binders. Whenever a free variable $\texttt{fvar}\ x$ is encountered, x is looked up in $\overline{x}$. If x occurs in position j, then the free variable is replaced by the bound variable $\texttt{bvar}\ k\ j$, otherwise it is left unchanged. Variable closing is then defined as $^{\backslash\overline{x}}t = \{0 \leftarrow \overline{x}\}t$. And its extension to lists is: $^{\backslash\overline{x}}\overline{t} = \texttt{List.map}\ (^{\backslash\overline{x}}\cdot)\ \overline{t}.$

Example 3. Now we close the term obtained by opening u in Example 2. Let $t \equiv \texttt{let bvar}\ 0\ 1, \texttt{fvar}\ x\ \texttt{in app (abs fvar}\ x)\ (\texttt{bvar}\ 0\ 1).$

$^{\backslash x}t = \{0 \leftarrow x\}(\texttt{let}\ \{\texttt{bvar}\ 0\ 1, \texttt{fvar}\ x\}\ \texttt{in app (abs (fvar}\ x))\ (\texttt{bvar}\ 0\ 1))$
$\quad = \texttt{let}\ \{1 \leftarrow x\}(\texttt{bvar}\ 0\ 1, \texttt{fvar}\ x)$
$\quad\quad \texttt{in}\ \{1 \leftarrow x\}(\texttt{app (abs fvar}\ x)\ (\texttt{bvar}\ 0\ 1))$
$\quad = \texttt{let bvar}\ 0\ 1, \texttt{bvar}\ 1\ 0\ \texttt{in app (abs}\ \{2 \leftarrow x\}(\texttt{fvar}\ x))\ (\texttt{bvar}\ 0\ 1)$
$\quad = \texttt{let bvar}\ 0\ 1, \texttt{bvar}\ 1\ 0\ \texttt{in app (abs bvar}\ 2\ 0)\ (\texttt{bvar}\ 0\ 1)$

Notice that the closed term coincides with u, the body of the abstraction in Example 2, although this is not always the case. □

2.3 Local Closure, Free Variables and Substitution

The locally nameless syntax in Figure 2 allows to build terms that have no corresponding expression in *Exp* (Figure 1). For instance, in $\texttt{abs (bvar}\ 1\ 5)$ index 1 does not refer to a binder in the term. Well-formed terms, i.e., those matching expressions in *Exp*, are called *locally closed*. To determine if a term is locally closed one should check that every bound variable has valid indices, i.e., that they refer to binders in the term. An easier method is to open with fresh names every abstraction and $\texttt{let}$-declaration in the term to be checked, and verify that no bound variable is reached. This checking is implemented with the *local closure* predicate $\texttt{lc}$ given in Figure 5.

Observe that we use cofinite quantification (as introduced by Aydemir et al. in [1]) in the rules for the binders, i.e., abstraction and $\texttt{let}$. Cofinite quantification is an elegant alternative to exist-fresh conditions and provides stronger induction

$$\text{LC\_VAR} \quad \frac{}{\text{lc (fvar } x)} \qquad\qquad \text{LC\_ABS} \quad \frac{\forall x \notin L \subseteq Id \quad \text{lc } t^{[x]}}{\text{lc (abs } t)}$$

$$\text{LC\_APP} \quad \frac{\text{lc } t \quad \text{lc } v}{\text{lc (app } t\ v)} \qquad\qquad \text{LC\_LET} \quad \frac{\forall \overline{x}^{|\overline{t}|} \notin L \subseteq Id \quad \text{lc } [t : \overline{t}]^{\overline{x}}}{\text{lc (let } \overline{t} \text{ in } t)}$$

$$\text{LC\_LIST} \quad \frac{\text{List.forall (lc } \cdot)\ \overline{t}}{\text{lc } \overline{t}}$$

Fig. 5. Local closure

$$\text{LCK-BVAR} \quad \frac{i < k \wedge j < \text{List.nth } i\ \overline{n}}{\text{lc\_at } k\ \overline{n}\ (\text{bvar } i\ j)} \qquad \text{LCK-APP} \quad \frac{\text{lc\_at } k\ \overline{n}\ t \quad \text{lc\_at } k\ \overline{n}\ v}{\text{lc\_at } k\ \overline{n}\ (\text{app } t\ v)}$$

$$\text{LCK-FVAR} \quad \frac{}{\text{lc\_at } k\ \overline{n}\ (\text{fvar } x)} \qquad \text{LCK-LET} \quad \frac{\text{lc\_at } (k+1)\ [|\overline{t}| : \overline{n}]\ [t : \overline{t}]}{\text{lc\_at } k\ \overline{n}\ (\text{let } \overline{t} \text{ in } t)}$$

$$\text{LCK-ABS} \quad \frac{\text{lc\_at } (k+1)\ [1 : \overline{n}]\ t}{\text{lc\_at } k\ \overline{n}\ (\text{abs } t)} \qquad \text{LCK-LIST} \quad \frac{\text{List.forall (lc\_at } k\ \overline{n}\ \cdot)\ \overline{t}}{\text{lc\_at } k\ \overline{n}\ \overline{t}}$$

Fig. 6. Local closure at level k

and inversion principles. Proofs are simplified, because it is not required to define exactly the set of fresh names (several examples of this are given in [5]). The rule LC-ABS establishes that an abstraction is locally closed if there exists a finite set of names L such that, for any name x not in L, the term $t^{[x]}$ is locally closed. Similarly, in the rule LC-LET we write $\overline{x}^{|\overline{t}|} \notin L$ to indicate that the list of distinct names $\overline{x}$ of length $|\overline{t}|$ are not in the finite set L. For any list $\overline{x}$ satisfying this condition, the opening of each term in the list of local declarations, $\overline{t}^{\overline{x}}$, and of the term affected by these declarations, $t^{\overline{x}}$, are locally closed. Notice that we have overloaded the predicate lc to work both on terms and list of terms. In the following we will overload other predicates and functions similarly. We write $[t : \overline{t}]$ for the list with head t and tail $\overline{t}$. In the following, $[\ ]$ represents the empty list, $[t]$ is a unitary list, and $+\!\!+$ is the concatenation of lists.

We define a new predicate that checks if indices in bound variables are valid from a given level: t *is closed at level* k, written lc_at $k\ \overline{n}\ t$ (Figure 6). As usual, k indicates the current depth, that is, how many binders have been passed by. Since binders can be either abstractions or local declarations, we need to keep the size of each binder (1 in the case of an abstraction, n for a let with n local declarations). These sizes are collected in the list $\overline{n}$, thus $|\overline{n}|$ should be at least k. A bound variable bvar $i\ j$ is closed at level k if i is smaller than k and j is smaller than List.nth $i\ \overline{n}$. The list $\overline{n}$ is new with respect to [5] because there the predicate lc_at is not defined for multiple binders.

It can be proved that if t is locally closed at level k for a given list of numbers $\overline{n}$, then it is also locally closed at level k for any list of numbers greater than $\overline{n}$.

Lemma 1. LC_AT_M_FROM_N   lc_at $k\ \overline{n}\ t \Rightarrow \forall \overline{m} \geq \overline{n}.\,$lc_at $k\ \overline{m}\ t$

Where $\overline{m} \geq \overline{n}$ is the pointwise lifting to lists of the usual ordering on naturals.

$$
\begin{array}{ll}
\texttt{fv(bvar } i\ j) & = \emptyset \\
\texttt{fv(fvar } x) & = \{x\} \\
\\
\texttt{fv(abs } t) & = \texttt{fv}(t) \\
\texttt{fv(app } t\ v) & = \texttt{fv}(t) \cup \texttt{fv}(v) \\
\texttt{fv(let } \bar{t} \texttt{ in } t) & = \texttt{fv}(\bar{t}) \cup \texttt{fv}(t)
\end{array}
$$

$$
\begin{array}{ll}
(\texttt{bvar } i\ j)[z/y] & = \texttt{bvar } i\ j \\
(\texttt{fvar } x)[z/y] & = \begin{cases} \texttt{fvar } z & \text{if } x = y \\ \texttt{fvar } x & \text{if } x \neq y \end{cases} \\
(\texttt{abs } t)[z/y] & = \texttt{abs } t[z/y] \\
(\texttt{app } t\ v)[z/y] & = \texttt{app } t[z/y]\ v[z/y] \\
(\texttt{let } \bar{t} \texttt{ in } t)[z/y] & = \texttt{let } \bar{t}[z/y] \texttt{ in } t[z/y]
\end{array}
$$

where $\texttt{fv}(\bar{t}) = \texttt{List.foldright } (\cdot \cup \cdot)\ \emptyset\ (\texttt{List.map fv } \bar{t})$
$\bar{t}[z/y] = \texttt{List.map } ([z/y]\cdot)\ \bar{t}.$

Fig. 7. Free variables and substitution

The two approaches for local closure are equivalent, so that it can be proved that a term is locally closed if and only if it is closed at level 0.

Lemma 2. LC_IIF_LC_AT $\texttt{lc } t \Leftrightarrow \texttt{lc\_at } 0\ [\,]\ t$

If the opening of a term is locally closed then the opening of the term with a different variable is locally closed too.

Lemma 3. LC_OP $\texttt{lc } t^{[x]} \Rightarrow \texttt{lc } t^{[y]}$

Computing the *free variables* of a term t is very easy in the locally nameless representation, since bound and free variables are syntactically different. The set of free variables of $t \in LNExp$ is denoted as $\texttt{fv}(t)$, and it is defined in Figure 7.

A name x is said to be *fresh for a term* t, written $\texttt{fresh } x \texttt{ in } t$, if x does not belong to the set of free variables of t. Similarly for a list of distict names $\bar{x}$:

$$
\frac{x \notin \texttt{fv}(t)}{\texttt{fresh } x \texttt{ in } t} \qquad\qquad \frac{\bar{x} \notin \texttt{fv}(t)}{\texttt{fresh } \bar{x} \texttt{ in } t}
$$

A term t is *closed* if it has no free variables at all:

$$
\frac{\texttt{fv}(t) = \emptyset}{\texttt{closed } t}
$$

Substitution replaces a variable name by another. For $t \in LNExp$ and $z, y \in Id$, $t[z/y]$ is the term where z substitutes any occurrence of y in t (see Figure 7).

Under some conditions variable closing and variable opening are inverse operations. More precisely, opening a term with fresh names and closing it with the same names, produces the original term. Symmetrically, closing a locally closed term and then opening it with the same names gives back the initial term.

Lemma 4.
CLOSE_OPEN_VAR $\texttt{fresh } \bar{x} \texttt{ in } t \Rightarrow {}^{\backslash \bar{x}}(t^{\bar{x}}) = t$
OPEN_CLOSE_VAR $\texttt{lc } t \Rightarrow ({}^{\backslash \bar{x}}t)^{\bar{x}} = t$

$$\text{LAM} \quad \Gamma : \lambda x.e \Downarrow \Gamma : \lambda x.e \qquad \text{APP} \quad \frac{\Gamma : e \Downarrow \Theta : \lambda y.e' \quad \Theta : e'[x/y] \Downarrow \Delta : w}{\Gamma : (e\ x) \Downarrow \Delta : w}$$

$$\text{VAR} \quad \frac{\Gamma : e \Downarrow \Delta : w}{(\Gamma, x \mapsto e) : x \Downarrow (\Delta, x \mapsto w) : \hat{w}} \qquad \text{LET} \quad \frac{(\Gamma, \{x_i \mapsto e_i\}_{i=1}^n) : e \Downarrow \Delta : w}{\Gamma : \text{let } \{x_i = e_i\}_{i=1}^n \text{ in } e \Downarrow \Delta : w}$$

Fig. 8. Natural semantics

3 Natural Semantics for Lazy λ-Calculus

The semantics defined by Launchbury in [7] follows a lazy strategy. Judgements are of the form $\Gamma : e \Downarrow \Delta : w$, that is, the expression $e \in Exp$ in the context of the heap Γ reduces to the value w in the context of the heap Δ. Values ($w \in Val$) are expressions in weak-head-normal-form (*whnf*). *Heaps* are partial functions from variables into expressions. Each pair (variable, expression) is called a *binding*, and it is represented by $x \mapsto e$. During evaluation, new bindings may be added to the heap, and bindings may be updated to their corresponding computed values. The rules of this natural semantics are shown in Figure 8. The normalization of the λ-calculus, that has been mentioned in Section 2, simplifies the definition of the operational rules, although a renaming is still needed ($\hat{w}$ in VAR) to avoid name clashing. This renaming is justified by Barendregt's variable convention [3].

Example 4. Without the renaming in rule VAR heaps may end up binding a same name more than once. Take for instance the evaluation of the expression $e \equiv \text{let } x_1 = \lambda y.(\text{let } z = \lambda v.y \text{ in } y), x_2 = (x_1\ x_3), x_3 = (x_1\ x_4), x_4 = \lambda s.s \text{ in } x_2$ in the context of the empty heap. The evaluation of e implies the evaluation of x_2, and then the evaluation of $(x_1 x_3)$. This application leads to the addition of z to the heap bound to $\lambda v.x_3$. Subsequently, the evaluation of x_3 implies the evaluation of $(x_1 x_4)$. Without a renaming of values, variable z is added again to the heap, now bound to $\lambda v.x_4$.   □

Theorem 1 in [7] states that "every heap/term pair occurring in the proof of a reduction is *distinctly named*", but we have found that the renaming fails to ensure this property. At least, it depends on how much fresh is this renaming.

Example 5. Let us evaluate in the context of the empty heap the expression

$e \equiv \text{let } x_1 = (x_2\ x_3), x_2 = \lambda z.\text{let } y = \lambda t.t \text{ in } y, x_3 = \lambda s.s \text{ in } x_1$

$\{\,\} : e$

LET $\quad \{x_1 \mapsto (x_2\ x_3), x_2 \mapsto \lambda z.\text{let } y = \lambda t.t \text{ in } y, x_3 \mapsto \lambda s.s\} : x_1$

VAR $\quad \{x_2 \mapsto \lambda z.\text{let } y = \lambda t.t \text{ in } y, x_3 \mapsto \lambda s.s\} : (x_2\ x_3)$

APP $\quad \{x_2 \mapsto \lambda z.\text{let } y = \lambda t.t \text{ in } y, x_3 \mapsto \lambda s.s\} : x_2$

VAR $\quad \{x_3 \mapsto \lambda s.s\} : \lambda z.\text{let } y = \lambda t.t \text{ in } y$

LAM

$\quad \{x_3 \mapsto \lambda s.s\} : \boxed{\lambda z.\text{let } y = \lambda t.t \text{ in } y}$

At this point the rule VAR requires to rename the value highlighted in the square. Notice that x_1 is fresh in the actual heap/term pair, and hence can be chosen to rename y. This would lead later in the derivation to introduce twice x_1 in the heap. The solution is to consider the condition of freshness in the whole derivation. This notion has not been formally defined by Launchbury.   □

3.1 Locally Nameless Heaps

Before translating the semantic rules in Figure 8 to the locally nameless representation defined in Section 2, we have to establish how *bindings* and *heaps* are represented in this notation.

Recall that bindings associate expressions to free variables, therefore bindings are now pairs (fvar x, t) with $x \in Id$ and $t \in LNExp$. To simplify, we will just write $x \mapsto t$. In the following, we will represent a heap $\{x_i \mapsto t_i\}_{i=1}^n$ as $(\overline{x} \mapsto \overline{t})$, with $|\overline{x}| = |\overline{t}| = n$. The set of the locally-nameless-heaps is denoted as *LNHeap*.

The *domain* of a heap Γ, written $\mathtt{dom}(\Gamma)$, collects the set of names that are bound in the heap.

$$\mathtt{dom}(\emptyset) = \emptyset \qquad \mathtt{dom}(\Gamma, x \mapsto t) = \mathtt{dom}(\Gamma) \cup \{x\}$$

In a well-formed heap names are defined at most once and terms are locally closed. The predicate ok expresses that a heap is well-formed:

$$\text{OK-EMPTY} \;\frac{}{\mathtt{ok}\ \emptyset} \qquad\qquad \text{OK-CONS} \;\frac{\mathtt{ok}\ \Gamma \quad x \notin \mathtt{dom}(\Gamma) \quad \mathtt{lc}\ t}{\mathtt{ok}\ (\Gamma, x \mapsto t)}$$

The function **names** returns the set of names that appear in a heap, i.e., the names occurring in the domain or in the right-hand side terms:

$$\mathtt{names}(\emptyset) = \emptyset \qquad \mathtt{names}(\Gamma, x \mapsto t) = \mathtt{names}(\Gamma) \cup \{x\} \cup \mathtt{fv}(t)$$

This definition can be extended to (heap: term) pairs:

$$\mathtt{names}(\Gamma : t) = \mathtt{names}(\Gamma) \cup \mathtt{fv}(t)$$

Next we define the freshness predicate of a list of names in a (heap:term) pair:

$$\frac{\overline{x} \notin \mathtt{names}(\Gamma : t)}{\mathtt{fresh}\ \overline{x}\ \mathtt{in}\ (\Gamma : t)}$$

Substitution of variable names is extended to heaps as follows:

$$\emptyset[z/y] = \emptyset \qquad (\Gamma, x \mapsto t)[z/y] = (\Gamma[z/y], x[z/y] \mapsto t[z/y])$$
$$\textit{where}\ x[z/y] = \begin{cases} z & \text{if } x = y \\ x & \text{otherwise} \end{cases}$$

The following property is verified:

Lemma 5. OK_SUBS_OK   ok $\Gamma \wedge y \notin \mathtt{dom}(\Gamma) \Rightarrow$ ok $\Gamma[y/x]$

$$\text{LNL{\scriptsize AM}} \qquad \frac{\{\text{ok } \Gamma\} \qquad \{\text{lc (abs } t)\}}{\Gamma : \text{abs } t \Downarrow \Gamma : \text{abs } t}$$

$$\text{LNV{\scriptsize AR}} \qquad \frac{\Gamma : t \Downarrow \Delta : w \qquad \{x \notin \text{dom}(\Gamma) \cup \text{dom}(\Delta)\}}{(\Gamma, x \mapsto t) : (\text{fvar } x) \Downarrow (\Delta, x \mapsto w) : w}$$

$$\text{LNA{\scriptsize PP}} \qquad \frac{\Gamma : t \Downarrow \Theta : \text{abs } u \qquad \Theta : u^{[x]} \Downarrow \Delta : w \qquad \{x \notin \text{dom}(\Gamma) \Rightarrow x \notin \text{dom}(\Delta)\}}{\Gamma : \text{app } t \ (\text{fvar } x) \Downarrow \Delta : w}$$

$$\text{LNL{\scriptsize ET}} \qquad \frac{\forall \overline{x}^{|t|} \notin L \subseteq Id \ (\Gamma, \overline{x} \mapsto \overline{t}^{\overline{x}}) : t^{\overline{x}} \Downarrow (\overline{x} + \!\!\!+ \, \overline{z} \mapsto \overline{u}^{\overline{x}}) : w^{\overline{x}} \qquad \{\overline{y}^{|t|} \notin L \subseteq Id\}}{\Gamma : \text{let } \overline{t} \text{ in } t \Downarrow (\overline{y} + \!\!\!+ \, \overline{z} \mapsto \overline{u}^{\overline{y}}) : w^{\overline{y}}}$$

Fig. 9. Locally nameless natural semantics

3.2 Locally Nameless Semantics

Once the locally nameless syntax and the corresponding operations, functions and predicates have been defined, three steps are sufficient to translate an inductive definition on λ-terms from the named representation into the locally nameless notation (as it is explained in [5]):

1. Replace the named binders, i.e., abstractions and let-constructions, with nameless binders by opening the bodies.
2. Cofinitely quantify the names introduced for variable opening.
3. Add premises to inductive rules in order to ensure that inductive judgements are restricted to locally closed terms.

We apply these steps to the inductive rules for the lazy natural semantics given in Figure 8. These rules produce judgements involving λ-terms as well as heaps. Hence, we also add premises that ensure that inductive judgements are restricted to well-formed heaps. The rules using the locally nameless representation are shown in Figure 9. For clarity, in the rules we put in braces the side-conditions to distinguish them better from the judgements.

The main difference with the rules in Figure 8 is the rule LNL{\scriptsize ET}. To evaluate let $\overline{t}$ in t the local terms in $\overline{t}$ have to be introduced in the heap, so that the body t is evaluated in this new context. To this purpose fresh names $\overline{x}$ are needed to open the local terms and the body. The evaluation of $t^{\overline{x}}$ produces a final heap and a value. Both are dependent on the names chosen for the local variables. The domain of the final heap consists of the local names $\overline{x}$ and the rest of names, say $\overline{z}$. The rule LNL{\scriptsize ET} is cofinite quantified. As it is explained in [5], the advantage of the cofinite rules over existential and universal ones is that the freshness side-conditions are not explicit. In our case, the freshness condition for $\overline{x}$ is *hidden* in the finite set L, which includes the names that should be avoided during the reduction. The novelty of our cofinite rule, compared with the ones appearing in [1] and [5] (that are similar to the cofinite rules for the predicate lc in Figure 5), is that the names introduced in the (infinite) premises do appear in the conclusion too. Therefore, in the conclusion of the rule LNL{\scriptsize ET} we can replace the names $\overline{x}$ by any list $\overline{y}$ not in L.

The problem with explicit freshness conditions is that they are associated just to rule instances, while they should apply to the whole reduction proof. Take for instance the rule LNVar. In the premise the binding $x \mapsto t$ does no longer belong to the heap. Hence, a valid reduction for this premise may chose x as fresh (this corresponds to the problem shown in Example 5). We avoid this situation by requiring that x remains undefined in the final heap too. By contrast to the rule Var in Figure 8, no renaming of the final value w is needed.

The side-condition of rule LNApp deserves an explanation too. Let us suppose that x is undefined in the initial heap Γ. We must avoid that x is chosen as a fresh name during the evaluation of t. For this reason we require that x is defined in the final heap Δ only if x was already defined in Γ. Notice how the body of the abstraction, that is u, is open with the name x. This is equivalent to the substitution of x for y in the body of the abstraction $\lambda y.e'$ (see rule App in Figure 8).

A *regularity* lemma ensures that the judgements produced by this reduction system involve only well-formed heaps and locally closed terms.

Lemma 6.

REGULARITY $\Gamma : t \Downarrow \Delta : w \Rightarrow \texttt{ok } \Gamma \wedge \texttt{lc } t \wedge \texttt{ok } \Delta \wedge \texttt{lc } w$

Similarly, Theorem 1 in [7] ensures that the property of being *distinctly named* is preserved by the rules in Figure 8. However, as shown in Example 5, the correctness of this result requires that freshness is relative to whole reduction proofs instead to the scope of rules.

The next lemma states that names defined in a context heap remain defined after the evaluation of any term in that context.

Lemma 7.

DEF_NOT_LOST $\Gamma : t \Downarrow \Delta : w \Rightarrow \texttt{dom}(\Gamma) \subseteq \texttt{dom}(\Delta)$

Furthermore, fresh names are introduced only by the rule LNLet and, by the previous lemma, they remain bound in the final (heap: value) pair. Hence, any free variable appearing in a final (heap: value) pair is undefined only if the variable already occurs in the initial (heap: term) pair.

Lemma 8.

ADD_VARS $\Gamma : t \Downarrow \Delta : w$
$\Rightarrow (x \in \texttt{names}(\Delta : w) \Rightarrow (x \in \texttt{dom}(\Delta) \vee x \in \texttt{names}(\Gamma : t)))$

A *renaming* lemma ensures that the evaluation of a term is independent of the fresh names chosen in the reduction process. Moreover, any name in the context can be replaced by a fresh one without changing the meaning of the terms evaluated in that context. In fact, reduction proofs for (heap: term) pairs are unique up to renaming of the variables defined in the context heap.

Lemma 9.

RENAMING $\Gamma : t \Downarrow \Delta : w \wedge \texttt{fresh } y \texttt{ in } (\Gamma : t) \wedge \texttt{fresh } y \texttt{ in } (\Delta : w)$
$\Rightarrow \Gamma[y/x] : t[y/x] \Downarrow \Delta[y/x] : w[y/x]$

In addition, the renaming lemma permits to prove an *introduction* lemma for the cofinite rule LNLET which establishes that the corresponding existential rule is admissible too.

Lemma 10.
LET_INTRO $(\Gamma, \overline{x} \mapsto \overline{t}^{\overline{x}}) : t^{\overline{x}} \Downarrow (\overline{x} +\!\!+ \overline{z} \mapsto \overline{u}^{\overline{x}}) : w^{\overline{x}} \wedge \texttt{fresh } \overline{x} \texttt{ in } (\Gamma : \texttt{let } \overline{t} \texttt{ in } t)$
    $\Rightarrow \Gamma : \texttt{let } \overline{t} \texttt{ in } t \Downarrow (\overline{x} +\!\!+ \overline{z} \mapsto \overline{u}^{\overline{x}}) : w^{\overline{x}}$

This result, together with the renaming lemma, justifies that our rule LNLET is equivalent to Launchbury's rule LET used with normalized terms.

4   Related Work

In order to avoid α-conversion, we first considered a nameless representation like the de Bruijn notation [6], where variable names are removed and replaced by natural numbers. But this notation has several drawbacks. First of all, the de Bruijn representation is hard to read for humans. Even if we intend to check our results with some proof assistant like Coq [4], human readability helps intuition. At a more technical level, the de Bruijn notation does not have a good way to handle free variables, which are represented by indices, alike to bound variables. This is a serious weakness for our application. Recall that Launchbury's semantics uses contexts heaps that collect the bindings for the free variables that may occur in the term under evaluation. Any change in the domain of a heap, i.e., adding or deleting a binding, would lead to a shifting of the indices, thus complicating the statement and proof of results. Therefore, we prefer the more manageable locally nameless representation, where bound variable names are replaced by indices but free variables keep their names. This mixed notation combines the advantages of both named and nameless representations. On the one hand, α-conversion is avoided all the same. On the other hand, terms stay readable and easy to manipulate.

There exists in the literature different proposals for a locally nameless representation, and many works using these representations. Charguéraud offers in [5] a brief survey on these works, that we recommend to the interested reader.

Launchbury (implicitly) assumes Barendregt's variable convention [3] twice in [7]. First when he defines his operational semantics only for normalized λ-terms (i.e. every binder in a term binds a distinct name, which is also distinct from any free variable); and second, when he requires a (fresh) renaming of the values in the rule VAR (see Figure 8). Urban, Berghofer and Norrish propose in [15] a method to strengthen an induction principle (corresponding to some inductive relation), so that Barendregt's variable convention comes already built in the principle. Unfortunately, we cannot apply these ideas to Launchbury's semantics, because the semantic rules (shown in Figure 8) do not satisfy the conditions that guarantee the *variable convention compatibility*, as described in [15]. In fact, as we have already pointed out, Launchbury's Theorem 1 (in [7]) is only correct if the renaming required in each application of the rule VAR is fresh in the whole reduction proof. Therefore, we cannot use directly Urban's nominal package for

Isabelle/HOL [14] (including its recent extensions for general bindings described in [16]).

Nevertheless, Urban et al. achieve the "inclusion" of the variable convention in an induction principle by adding to each induction rule a side condition which expresses that the set of *bound* variables (i.e., those that appear in a binding position in the rule) are fresh in some *induction context* ([15]). Furthermore, this context is required to be finitely supported. This is closely related to the cofinite quantification that we have used for the rule LNLET in Figure 9. Besides, one important condition to ensure the variable convention compatibility is the *equivariance* of the functions and predicates occurring in the induction rules. Equivariance is a notion from nominal logic [10]. A relation is equivariant if it is preserved by permutation of names. Although we have not proven that the reduction relation defined by the rules in Figure 9 is equivariant, our *renaming lemma* (Lemma 9) establishes a similar result, that is, the reduction relation is preserved by (fresh) renaming.

5 Conclusions

We have used a more modern approach to binding, i.e., a locally nameless representation for the λ-calculus extended with mutually recursive local declarations. With this representation the reduction rule for local declarations implies the introduction of fresh names. We have used neither an existential nor a universal rule for this case. Instead, we have opted for a cofinite rule as introduced by Aydemir et al. in [1]. Freshness conditions are usually considered in each rule individually. Nevertheless, this technique produces name clashing when considering whole reduction proofs. A solution might be to decorate judgements with the set of forbidden names and indicate how to modify this set during the reduction process (this approach has been taken by Sestoft in [13]). However, this could be too restrictive in many occasions. Besides, existential rules are not easy to deal with because each reduction is obtained just for one specific list of names. If any of the names in this list causes a name clashing with other reduction proofs, then it is cumbersome to demonstrate that an alternative reduction for a fresh list does exist. Cofinite quantification has allowed us to solve this problem because in a single step reductions are guaranteed for an infinite number of lists of names. Nonetheless, our introduction lemma (Lemma 10) guarantees that a more conventional exists-fresh rule is correct in our reduction system too.

The cofinite quantification that we have used in our semantic rules is more complex than those in [1] and [5]. Our cofinite rule LNLET in Figure 9 introduces quantified variables in the conclusion as well, as the latter depends on the chosen names.

Compared to Launchbury's original semantic rules, our locally nameless rules include several extra side-conditions. Some of these conditions require that heaps and terms are well-formed (like in rule LNLAM). The rest of side-conditions express restrictions on the choice of fresh names. These restrictions, together with the cofinite quantification, fix the problem with the renaming in rule VAR that we have shown in Example 5.

For our locally nameless semantics we have shown a *regularity lemma* (Lemma 6) which ensures that every term and heap involved in a reduction proof is well-formed, and with a *renaming lemma* (Lemma 9) which indicates that the choice of names (free variables) is irrelevant as long as they are fresh enough. A heap may be seen as a multiple binder. Actually, the names defined (bound) in a heap can be replaced by other names, provided that terms keep their meaning in the context represented by the heap. Our renaming lemma ensures that whenever a heap is renamed with fresh names, reduction proofs are preserved. This renaming lemma is essential in rule induction proofs for some properties of the reduction system. More concretely, when one combines several reduction proofs coming from two or more premises in a reduction rule (for instance, in rule LNApp in Figure 9).

In summary, the contributions of this paper are:

1. A locally nameless representation of the λ-calculus extended with recursive local declarations;
2. A locally nameless version of the inductive rules of Launchbury's natural semantics for lazy evaluation;
3. A new version of cofinite rules where the variables quantified in the premises do appear in the conclusion too;
4. A set of interesting properties of our reduction system, including the regularity, the introduction and the renaming lemmas; and
5. A way to guarantee Barendregt's variable convention by redefining Launchbury's semantic rules with cofinite quantification and extra side-conditions.

6   Future Work

Our future tasks include the implementation in the proof assistant Coq [4] of the natural semantics redefined in this paper, and the formalization of the proofs for the lemmas given (regularity, renaming, introduction, etc.), which at present are just paper-and-pencil proofs. We will use this implementation to prove formally the equivalence of Launchbury's natural semantics with the alternative version given also in [7]. As we mentioned in Section 1, this alternative version differs from the original one in the introduction of indirections during β-reduction and the elimination of updates. At present we are working on the definition (using the locally nameless representation) of two intermediate semantics, one introducing indirections and the other without updates. Then, we will establish equivalence relations between the heaps obtained by each semantics, which makes able to prove the equivalence of the original natural semantics and the alternative one through the intermediate semantics.

Acknowledgments. This work is partially supported by the projects: TIN2009-14599-C03-01 and S2009/TIC-1465.

References

1. Aydemir, B.E., Charguéraud, A., Pierce, B.C., Pollack, R., Weirich, S.: Engineering formal metatheory. In: ACM Symposium on Principles of Programming Languages, POPL 2008, pp. 3–15. ACM Press (2008)
2. Baker-Finch, C., King, D., Trinder, P.W.: An operational semantics for parallel lazy evaluation. In: ACM-SIGPLAN International Conference on Functional Programming (ICFP 2000), pp. 162–173. ACM Press (2000)
3. Barendregt, H.P.: The Lambda Calculus: Its Syntax and Semantics. Studies in Logic and the Foundations of Mathematics, vol. 103. North-Holland (1984)
4. Bertot, Y.: Coq in a hurry. CoRR, abs/cs/0603118 (2006)
5. Charguéraud, A.: The locally nameless representation. Journal of Automated Reasoning, 1–46 (2011)
6. de Bruijn, N.G.: Lambda calculus notation with nameless dummies, a tool for automatic formula manipulation, with application to the Church-Rosser theorem. Indagationes Mathematicae 75(5), 381–392 (1972)
7. Launchbury, J.: A natural semantics for lazy evaluation. In: ACM Symposium on Principles of Programming Languages, POPL 1993, pp. 144–154. ACM Press (1993)
8. Nakata, K., Hasegawa, M.: Small-step and big-step semantics for call-by-need. CoRR, abs/0907.4640 (2009)
9. Nipkow, T., Paulson, L.C., Wenzel, M.T.: Isabelle/HOL — A Proof Assistant for Higher-Order Logic. LNCS, vol. 2283. Springer, Heidelberg (2002)
10. Pitts, A.M.: Nominal logic, a first order theory of names and binding. Information and Computation 186(2), 165–193 (2003)
11. Sánchez-Gil, L., Hidalgo-Herrero, M., Ortega-Mallén, Y.: An Operational Semantics for Distributed Lazy Evaluation. In: Trends in Functional Programming, vol. 10, pp. 65–80. Intellect (2010)
12. Sánchez-Gil, L., Hidalgo-Herrero, M., Ortega-Mallén, Y.: A locally nameless representation for a natural semantics for lazy evaluation. Technical Report 01/12, Dpt. Sistemas Informáticos y Computación. Universidad Complutense de Madrid (2012), http://maude.sip.ucm.es/eden-semantics/
13. Sestoft, P.: Deriving a lazy abstract machine. Journal of Functional Programming 7(3), 231–264 (1997)
14. Urban, C.: Nominal techniques in Isabelle/HOL. Journal of Automatic Reasoning 40(4), 327–356 (2008)
15. Urban, C., Berghofer, S., Norrish, M.: Barendregt's Variable Convention in Rule Inductions. In: Pfenning, F. (ed.) CADE 2007. LNCS (LNAI), vol. 4603, pp. 35–50. Springer, Heidelberg (2007)
16. Urban, C., Kaliszyk, C.: General Bindings and Alpha-Equivalence in Nominal Isabelle. In: Barthe, G. (ed.) ESOP 2011. LNCS, vol. 6602, pp. 480–500. Springer, Heidelberg (2011)
17. van Eekelen, M., de Mol, M.: Reflections on Type Theory, λ-calculus, and the Mind. Essays dedicated to Henk Barendregt on the Occasion of his 60th Birthday, chapter Proving Lazy Folklore with Mixed Lazy/Strict Semantics, pp. 87–101. Radboud University Nijmegen (2007)

Modal Process Rewrite Systems

Nikola Beneš[1],* and Jan Křetínský[1,2],**

[1] Faculty of Informatics, Masaryk University, Brno, Czech Republic
[2] Institut für Informatik, Technische Universität München, Germany
{xbenes3,jan.kretinsky}@fi.muni.cz

Abstract. We consider modal transition systems with infinite state space generated by finite sets of rules. In particular, we extend process rewrite systems to the modal setting and investigate decidability of the modal refinement relation between systems from various subclasses. Since already simulation is undecidable for most of the cases, we focus on the case where either the refined or the refining process is finite. Namely, we show decidability for pushdown automata extending the non-modal case and surprising undecidability for basic parallel processes. Further, we prove decidability when both systems are visibly pushdown automata. For the decidable cases, we also provide complexities. Finally, we discuss a notion of bisimulation over MTS.

1 Introduction

The ever increasing complexity of software systems together with their reuse call for efficient *component-based* design and verification. One of the major theoretically well founded frameworks that answer this call are *modal transition systems* (MTS) [LT88]. Their success resides in natural combination of two features. Firstly, it is the simplicity of labelled transition systems, which have proved appropriate for behavioural description of systems as well as their compositions; MTS as their extension inherit this appropriateness. Secondly, as opposed to temporal logic specifications, MTS can be easily *gradually refined* into implementations while preserving the desired behavioural properties.

MTS consist of a set of states and two transition relations. The *must* transitions prescribe which behaviour has to be present in every refinement of the system; the *may* transitions describe the behaviour that is allowed, but need not be realized in the refinements. This allows for underspecification of non-critical behaviour in the early stage of design, focusing on the main properties, verifying them and sorting out the details of the yet unimplemented non-critical behaviour later.

The formalism of MTS has proven to be useful in practice. Industrial applications are as old as [Bru97] where MTS have been used for an air-traffic system at Heathrow airport. Besides, MTS are advocated as an appropriate base for interface theories in [RBB+09] and for product line theories in [Nym08]. Further,

---

* The author has been supported by the Czech Science Foundation, grant No. GAP202/11/0312.
** The author is a holder of Brno PhD Talent Financial Aid and is supported by the Czech Science Foundation, grant No. P202/12/G061.

A. Roychoudhury and M. D'Souza (Eds.): ICTAC 2012, LNCS 7521, pp. 120–135, 2012.

MTS based software engineering methodology for design via merging partial descriptions of behaviour has been established in [UC04]. Moreover, the tool support is quite extensive, e.g. [BLS95, DFFU07, BML11, BČK11].

Over the years, many extensions of MTS have been proposed. While MTS can only specify whether or not a particular transition is required, some extensions equip MTS with more general abilities to describe what *combinations* of transitions are possible [LX90, FS08, BK10, BKL+11]. Further, MTS framework has also been lifted to *quantitative settings*. This includes probabilistic [CDL+10] and timed systems [ČGL93, JLS11, BFJ+11, BKL+12, DLL+10, BLPR11] with clear applications in the embedded systems design. As far as the infinite state systems are concerned, only a few more or less ad hoc extensions have been proposed, such as systems with asynchronous communication based on FIFO [BHJ10] or Petri nets [EBHH10]. In this paper, we introduce modalities into a general framework for infinite-state systems, where we study modal extensions of well-established classes of infinite-state systems.

Such a convenient unifying framework for infinite-state systems is provided by *Process rewrite systems* (PRS) [May00]. They encompass many standard models such as pushdown automata (PDA) or Petri nets (PN) as syntactic subclasses. A PRS consists of a set of rewriting rules that model computation. These rules may contain sequential and parallel composition. For example, a transition t of a Petri net with input places I_1, I_2 and output places O_1, O_2 can be described by the rule $I_1 \parallel I_2 \xrightarrow{t} O_1 \parallel O_2$. A transition of a pushdown automaton in a state s with a top stack symbol X reading a letter a resulting in changing the state to q and pushing Y to the stack can be written as $sX \xrightarrow{a} qYX$. Limiting the occurrences of parallel and sequential composition on the left and right sides of the rules yields the most common automata theoretic models. For these syntactic subclasses of PRS, see Figure 1 and a more detailed description in Section 2.

Motivation. One can naturally lift PRS to the modal world by having two sets of rules, may and must rules. What is then the use of such *modal process rewrite systems* (mPRS)? Firstly, potentially infinite-state systems such as Petri nets are very popular for modelling whenever communication or synchronization between processes occurs. This is true even when they are actually bounded and thus with a finite state space.

Example 1. Consider the following may rule (we use dashed arrows to denote may rules) generating a small Petri net.

$$\text{resource} \parallel \text{customer} \xdashrightarrow{\text{consume}} \text{trash}$$

This rewrite rule implies that e.g. a process resource $\parallel$ customer $\parallel$ customer may be changed into trash $\parallel$ customer. Therefore, if there is no other rule with trash on the right side a safety property is guaranteed for all implementations of this system, namely that trash can only arise if there is at least one resource and one customer. On the other hand, it is not guaranteed that trash can indeed be produced in such a situation. This is very useful as during the design process new requirements can arise, such as necessity of adding more participants to perform this transition. For instance,

$$\text{resource} \parallel \text{customer} \parallel \text{permit} \overset{\text{consume}}{\dashrightarrow} \text{trash}$$

expresses an auxiliary condition required to produce trash, namely that permit is available. Replacing the old rule with the new one is equivalent to adding an input place permit to the Petri net. In the modal transition system view, the new system *refines* the old one. Indeed, the new system is only more specific about the allowed behaviour than the old one and does not permit any previously forbidden behaviour. One can further refine the system by the one given by

$$\text{resource} \parallel \text{customer} \parallel \text{permit} \parallel \text{bribe} \overset{\text{consume}}{\longrightarrow} \text{trash}$$

where additional condition is imposed and now the trash-producing transition has to be available (denoted by an unbroken arrow) whenever the left hand side condition is satisfied.

Secondly, even if an original specification is finite its refinements and the final implementation might be infinite. For instance, consider a specification where permit needs to be available but is not consumed or there is an unlimited amount of permits. In an implementation, the number of permits could be limited and thus this number with no known bounds needs to be remembered in the state of the system. Similarly, consider a finite safety specification of a browser together with its implementation that due to the presence of back button requires the use of stack, and is thus a pushdown system. Further, sometimes both the specification and the implementation are infinite such as a stateless BPA specification of a stateful component implemented by a PDA.

Example 2. Consider a basic process algebra (BPA) given by rules $X \overset{(}{\longrightarrow} XX$ and $X \overset{)}{\dashrightarrow} \varepsilon$ for correctly parenthesized expressions with $X \overset{a}{\dashrightarrow} X$ for all other symbols a, i.e. with no restriction on the syntax of expressions. One can easily refine this system into a PDA that accepts correct arithmetic expressions by remembering in the state whether the last symbol read was an operand or an operator.

Further, opposite to the design of correct software where an abstract verified MTS is transformed into a concrete implementation, one can consider checking correctness of software through abstracting a concrete implementation into a coarser system. The use of MTS as abstractions has been advocated e.g. in [GHJ01]. While usually overapproximations (or underapproximations) of systems are constructed and thus only purely universal (or existential) properties can be checked, [GHJ01] shows that using MTS one can check mixed formulae (arbitrarily combining universal and existential properties) and, moreover, at the same cost as checking universal properties using traditional conservative abstractions. This advantage has been investigated also in the context of systems equivalent or closely related to MTS [HJS01, DGG97, Nam03, DN04, CGLT09, GNRT10]. Although one is usually interested in generating finite abstractions of infinite systems, it might be interesting to consider situations where the abstract system is infinite. For instance,

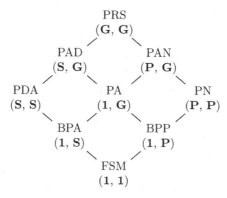

Fig. 1. PRS hierarchy

if one is interested in a property that is inherently non-regular such as correct parenthesizing in the previous example, the abstraction has to capture this feature. One could thus abstract the PDA from the previous example into the smaller BPA above and prove the property here using algorithms for BPA. Moreover, if one is interested in mixed properties the abstract system has to be modal. It would be useful to extend the verification algorithms for systems such as PDA to their modal versions along the lines of the generalized model checking approach [BG00, BČK11]. This is, however, beyond the scope of this paper.

Our Contribution. In this paper, we focus on modal infinite-state systems and decidability of the most fundamental problem here, namely deciding the refinement relation, for most common classes of systems. Since simulation is undecidable already on basic parallel processes (BPP) [Hüt94] and basic process algebras (BPA) [GH94], cf. Figure 1, the refinement as a generalization of simulation is undecidable in general. However, one can consider the case where either the refined or the refining system is finite (a finite state machine, FSM). This case is still very interesting, e.g. in the context of finite abstractions or implementations with bounded resources. [KM99] shows that while simulation remains undecidable between process algebras (PA) and FSM, it is decidable between PDA and FSM. We extend this result using methods of [KM02b] to the modal setting. Further, although simulation is decidable between PN and FSM [JM95] (in both directions), we show that surprisingly this result cannot be extended and the refinement is undecidable even for BPP and FSM in the modal setting. Although the decidability of the refinement seems quite limited now, we show that refinement is sometimes decidable even between two infinite-state systems, namely between modal extensions of visibly pushdown automata [AM04], cf. Example 2; for this, we use the methods of [Srb06]. To summarize:

- We introduce a general framework for studying modal infinite-state system, namely we lift process rewrite systems to the modal setting. This definition comes along with the appropriate notion of refinement.

- We prove un/decidability of the refinement problem for modal extensions of standard classes of infinite-state systems. Apart from trivial corollaries due to the undecidability of simulation, this amount to proving undecidability of refinement between Petri nets and FSM (on either side) and decidability between pushdown systems and FSM (again on either side). Moreover, we prove decidability for visibly PDA. For the decidable cases, we show that the complexity is the same as for checking the respective simulation in the non-modal setting. Finally, we discuss a notion of bisimulation over MTS, which we name birefinement.

Related Work. There are various other approaches to deal with component refinements. They range from subtyping [LW94] over Java modelling language [JP01] to interface theories close to MTS such as interface automata [dAH01]. Similarly to MTS, interface automata are behavioural interfaces for components. However, their composition works very differently. Furthermore, its notion of refinement is based on alternating simulation [AHKV98], which has been proved strictly less expressive than MTS refinement—actually coinciding on a subclass of MTS—in a paper [LNW07] that combines MTS and interface automata based on I/O automata [Lyn88]. The compositionality of this combination is further investigated in [RBB+11].

MTS can also be viewed as a fragment of mu-calculus that is "graphically representable" [BL90]. The graphical representability of a variant of alternating simulation called covariant-contravariant simulation has been recently studied in [AFdFE+11].

The PRS framework has been introduced in [May00]. Simulation on classes of PRS tends to be computationally harder than bisimilarity [KM02b]. While e.g. bisimulation between any PRS and FSM is decidable [KŘS05], simulation with FSM is undecidable already for PA (see above). Therefore, the decidability is limited to PDA and PN, and we show that refinement is even harder (undecidability for BPP). Another aspect that could help to extend the decidability is determinism. For instance, simulation between FSM and deterministic PA is decidable [KM99]. It is also the case with the abovementioned [EBHH10] where refinement over "weakly deterministic" modal Petri nets is shown decidable.

Outline of the Paper. In Section 2, we introduce modal process rewrite systems formally and recall the refinement preorder. In Section 3 and 4, we show undecidability and decidability results for the refinement. Section 5 concludes.

2   Refinement Problems

In this section, we introduce modal transition systems generated by process rewrite systems and define the notion of modal refinement. We start with the usual definition of MTS.

2.1 Modal Transition Systems

Definition 1 (Modal transition system). *A* modal transition system (MTS) *over an action alphabet Act is a triple* $(\mathcal{P}, \dashrightarrow, \longrightarrow)$, *where* $\mathcal{P}$ *is a set of* processes *and* $\longrightarrow \subseteq \dashrightarrow \subseteq \mathcal{P} \times Act \times \mathcal{P}$ *are* must *and* may *transition relations, respectively.*

Observe that $\mathcal{P}$ is not required to be finite. We often use letters $s, t, \ldots$ for processes of MTS. Whenever clear from the context, we refer to processes without explicitly mentioning their underlying MTS.

We proceed with the standard definition of (modal) refinement.

Definition 2 (Refinement). *Let* $(\mathcal{P}_1, \dashrightarrow_1, \longrightarrow_1), (\mathcal{P}_2, \dashrightarrow_2, \longrightarrow_2)$ *be MTS over the same action alphabet and* $s \in \mathcal{P}_1$, $t \in \mathcal{P}_2$ *be processes. We say that s refines t, written* $s \leq_m t$, *if there is a relation* $\mathcal{R} \subseteq \mathcal{P}_1 \times \mathcal{P}_2$ *such that* $(s, t) \in \mathcal{R}$ *and for every* $(p, q) \in \mathcal{R}$ *and every* $a \in Act$:

1. *if* $p \overset{a}{\dashrightarrow}_1 p'$ *then there is a transition* $q \overset{a}{\dashrightarrow}_2 q'$ *s.t.* $(p', q') \in \mathcal{R}$, *and*
2. *if* $q \overset{a}{\longrightarrow}_2 q'$ *then there is a transition* $p \overset{a}{\longrightarrow}_1 p'$ *s.t.* $(p', q') \in \mathcal{R}$.

The ultimate goal of the refinement process is to obtain an *implementation*, i.e. an MTS with $\dashrightarrow = \longrightarrow$. Implementations can be considered as the standard labelled transition systems (LTS). Note that on implementations refinement coincides with strong bisimilarity, and on modal transition systems without any must transitions it corresponds to the simulation preorder, denoted by $\leq_{\mathrm{sim}}$. Further, refinement has a game characterization [BKLS09] similar to (bi)simulation games, which we often use in the proofs.

2.2 Modal Process Rewrite Systems

We now move our attention to infinite-state MTS generated by finite sets of rules. Let *Const* be a set of *process constants*. We define the set of process expressions $\mathcal{E}$ by the following abstract syntax:

$$E ::= \varepsilon \mid X \mid E \parallel E \mid E; E$$

where X ranges over *Const*. We often use Greek letters $\alpha, \beta, \ldots$ for elements of $\mathcal{E}$. The process expressions are considered modulo the usual structural congruence, i.e. the smallest congruence such that the operator ; is associative, $\parallel$ is associative and commutative and ε is a unit for both ; and $\parallel$. We often omit the ; operator.

Definition 3 (Modal process rewrite system). *A* process rewrite system (PRS) *is a finite relation* $\Delta \subseteq (\mathcal{E} \setminus \{\varepsilon\}) \times Act \times \mathcal{E}$, *elements of which are called* rewrite rules. *A* modal process rewrite system (mPRS) *is a tuple* $(\Delta_{\mathrm{may}}, \Delta_{\mathrm{must}})$ *where* Δ_{may}, Δ_{must} *are process rewrite systems such that* $\Delta_{\mathrm{must}} \subseteq \Delta_{\mathrm{may}}$.

An mPRS $\Delta = (\Delta_{\mathrm{may}}, \Delta_{\mathrm{must}})$ *induces an MTS* $\mathrm{MTS}(\Delta) = (\mathcal{E}, \dashrightarrow, \longrightarrow)$ *as follows:*

$$\frac{(E, a, E') \in \Delta_{\mathrm{may}}}{E \overset{a}{\dashrightarrow} E'} \qquad \frac{E \overset{a}{\dashrightarrow} E'}{E; F \overset{a}{\dashrightarrow} E'; F} \qquad \frac{E \overset{a}{\dashrightarrow} E'}{E \parallel F \overset{a}{\dashrightarrow} E' \parallel F}$$

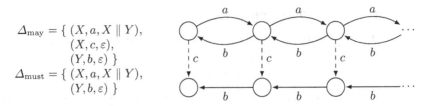

$$\Delta_{\text{may}} = \{\ (X, a, X \parallel Y),$$
$$(X, c, \varepsilon),$$
$$(Y, b, \varepsilon)\ \}$$
$$\Delta_{\text{must}} = \{\ (X, a, X \parallel Y),$$
$$(Y, b, \varepsilon)\ \}$$

Fig. 2. An example of a mBPP and its corresponding (infinite) MTS; the dashed arrows represent *may* transitions, the unbroken arrows represent *must* transitions; as $s \xrightarrow{a} t$ implies $s \dashrightarrow t$ we omit the may transitions where must transitions are also present

$$\frac{(E, a, E') \in \Delta_{\text{must}}}{E \xrightarrow{a} E'} \qquad \frac{E \xrightarrow{a} E'}{E; F \xrightarrow{a} E'; F} \qquad \frac{E \xrightarrow{a} E'}{E \parallel F \xrightarrow{a} E' \parallel F}$$

We consider four distinguished classes of process expressions. Class **S** stands for expressions with no $\parallel$ (purely sequential expressions) and class **P** stands for expressions with no ; (purely parallel expressions). Further, we use **G** for the whole $\mathcal{E}$ (general expressions) and **1** for *Const* (one process constant and no operators). Now restricting the left and right sides of rules of PRS to these classes yields subclasses of PRS as depicted in Figure 1 using the standard shortcuts also introduced in Section 1. Each subclass $\mathcal{C}$ has a corresponding modal extension m$\mathcal{C}$ containing all mPRS ($\Delta_{\text{may}}, \Delta_{\text{must}}$) with both Δ_{may} and Δ_{must} in $\mathcal{C}$. For instance, mFSM correspond to the standard finite MTS and mPN are modal Petri nets as introduced in [EBHH10]. An example of an mBPP and the resulting MTS are depicted in Figure 2.

For any classes $\mathcal{C}$, $\mathcal{D}$, we define the following decision problem m$\mathcal{C} \leq_{\text{m}}$ m$\mathcal{D}$.

> Given mPRS $\Delta_1 \in$ m$\mathcal{C}$, $\Delta_2 \in$ m$\mathcal{D}$ and process terms δ_1, δ_2 conforming to. left-hand side restrictions of $\mathcal{C}, \mathcal{D}$, respectively, does $\delta_1 \leq_{\text{m}} \delta_2$ hold considering δ_1, δ_2 as processes of $\text{MTS}(\Delta_1), \text{MTS}(\Delta_2)$?

3   Undecidability Results

In this section, we present all the negative results. As already discussed in Section 1, simulation—and thus refinement—is undecidable already on BPP [Hüt94] and BPA [GH94]. When considering the case where one of the two classes is mFSM, the undecidability holds for mPA [KM99]. Thus we are left with the problems mFSM$\leq_{\text{m}}$mPDA, mPDA$\leq_{\text{m}}$mFSM and mFSM$\leq_{\text{m}}$mPN, mPN$\leq_{\text{m}}$mFSM. On the one hand, the two former are shown decidable in Section 4 using non-modal methods for simulation of [KM02b]. On the other hand, the non-modal methods for simulation of [JM95] cannot be extended to the latter two problems. In this section, we show that (surprisingly) they are both undecidable and, moreover, even for mBPP.

Theorem 1. *The problem mBPP$\leq_{\text{m}}$mFSM is undecidable.*

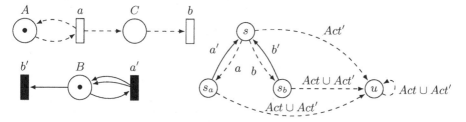

Fig. 3. $A \parallel B \leq_m s$ where the original two BPPs are given by $A \xrightarrow{a} A \parallel C$, $C \xrightarrow{b} \varepsilon$, $B \xrightarrow{a} B \parallel B$, $B \xrightarrow{b} \varepsilon$

Proof. We reduce the undecidable problem of simulation between two BPPs (even normed ones) to the problem mBPP$\leq_m$mFSM.

Let A, B be two BPP processes with underlying PRS Δ_A and Δ_B; w.l.o.g. $\Delta_A \cap \Delta_B = \emptyset$. We transform them as follows. We rename all actions of the underlying PRS of B from a to a'. Let Act' be the set of these renamed actions and let Δ_B' be the modification of Δ_B by renaming the actions. The mBPP is defined as $(\Delta_A \cup \Delta_B', \Delta_B')$, i.e. the transitions of A are just may, the (modified) transitions of B are both must and may.

We then build a finite mPRS as follows. The states are $\{s, u\} \cup \{s_a \mid a \in Act\}$.

- $s \dashrightarrow{a} s_a$ and $s \dashrightarrow{a'} u$ for all $a \in Act$
- $s_a \xrightarrow{a'} s$ for all $a \in Act$ (with the corresponding may transition)
- $s_a \dashrightarrow{x} u$ for all $a \in Act$ and $x \in Act \cup Act'$
- $u \dashrightarrow{x} u$ for all $x \in Act \cup Act'$

Clearly $q \leq_m u$ for any process q. The construction is illustrated in Figure 3.

We now show that $A \leq_{sim} B$ iff $A \parallel B \leq_m s$. In the following, α always denotes a process of Δ_A, while β denotes a process of Δ_B. Furthermore, we use the notation $\mathbb{LTS}(\Delta_A)$ to denote the LTS induced by Δ_A (similarly for Δ_B). We use the refinement game argumentation, see [BKLS09].

$\Rightarrow$: Let $\mathcal{R} = \{(\alpha \parallel \beta, s) \mid \alpha \leq_{sim} \beta\}$. We show that $\mathcal{R}$ can be extended to be a modal refinement relation. Let $(\alpha \parallel \beta, s) \in \mathcal{R}$:

- If the attacker plays $\alpha \parallel \beta \dashrightarrow{a'} \alpha \parallel \beta'$ (where $a' \in Act'$), the defender can play $s \dashrightarrow{a'} u$ and obviously wins.
- If the attacker plays $\alpha \parallel \beta \dashrightarrow{a} \alpha' \parallel \beta$ (where $a \in Act$), the defender has to play $s \dashrightarrow{a} s_a$. There are two possibilities then:
  - if the attacker plays $\alpha' \parallel \beta \dashrightarrow{x}$, the defender can play $s_a \dashrightarrow{x} u$ and obviously wins;
  - if the attacker plays $s_a \xrightarrow{a'} s$, the defender can play $\alpha' \parallel \beta \xrightarrow{a'} \alpha' \parallel \beta'$ where β' is a process such that $\beta \xrightarrow{a} \beta'$ in $\mathbb{LTS}(\Delta_B)$ and $\alpha' \leq_{sim} \beta'$. Such β' obviously exists due to $\alpha \leq_{sim} \beta$. Thus $(\alpha' \parallel \beta', s) \in \mathcal{R}$.

$\Leftarrow$: We show that $\mathcal{R} := \{(\alpha, \beta) \mid \alpha \parallel \beta \leq_m s\}$ is a simulation. Let $(\alpha, \beta) \in \mathcal{R}$:

- If $\alpha \xrightarrow{a} \alpha'$ in $\mathbb{LTS}(\Delta_A)$ then $\alpha \parallel \beta \dashrightarrow^{a} \alpha' \parallel \beta$. This has to be matched by $s \dashrightarrow^{a} s_a$. Furthermore, $s_a \xrightarrow{a'} s$ has to be matched by $\alpha' \parallel \beta \xrightarrow{a'} \alpha' \parallel \beta'$. This means that $\beta \xrightarrow{a} \beta'$ in $\mathbb{LTS}(\Delta_B)$ and that $(\alpha', \beta') \in \mathcal{R}$.   □

Theorem 2. *The problem mFSM$\leq_m$mBPP is undecidable.*

Proof. We reduce the undecidable problem of simulation between two BPPs to the problem mFSM$\leq_m$mBPP. The proof is similar to the previous one. However, as the situation is not entirely symmetric (the requirement that $\Delta_{must} \subseteq \Delta_{may}$ introduces asymmetry), we need to modify the construction somewhat.

Let again A, B be two BPP processes with underlying PRS Δ_A and Δ_B; w.l.o.g. $\Delta_A \cap \Delta_B = \emptyset$. We rename all actions of Δ_B from a to a'. Let Act' be the set of these renamed actions and let Δ'_B be the modification of Δ_B. We further create a new PRS as follows:

$$\Delta_X = \{(X, a, Y) \mid a \in Act\} \cup \{(Y, x, X) \mid x \in Act \cup Act'\}$$

The mBPP is defined as $(\Delta_A \cup \Delta'_B \cup \Delta_X, \Delta_A)$, i.e. the (modified) transitions of B are just may, the transitions of A are both must and may, and the new transitions of Δ_X are may.

We then build a finite mPRS as follows. The states are $\{s, v\} \cup \{s_a \mid a \in Act\}$.

- $s \xrightarrow{a} s_a$ for all $a \in Act$ (with the corresponding may transitions)
- $s_a \dashrightarrow^{a'} s$ for all $a \in Act$
- $s_a \xrightarrow{a} v$ for all $a \in Act$ (with the corresponding may transitions)
- $v \xrightarrow{a} v$ for all $a \in Act$ (with the corresponding may transitions)

The construction is illustrated in Figure 4.

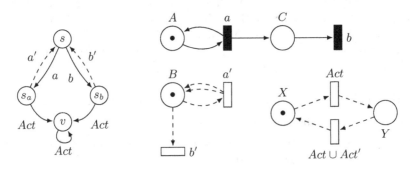

Fig. 4. $s \leq_m A \parallel B \parallel X$ where the original two BPPs are again given by $A \xrightarrow{a} A \parallel C$, $C \xrightarrow{b} \varepsilon$, $B \xrightarrow{a} B \parallel B$, $B \xrightarrow{b} \varepsilon$

We now show that $A \leq_{sim} B$ iff $s \leq_m A \parallel B \parallel X$. As in the previous proof, α denotes a process of Δ_A while β denotes a process of Δ_B.

We first show that $v \leq_m \alpha \parallel \beta \parallel V$ for all $V \in \{X, Y\}$ and all processes α, β. Whenever the attacker plays a must transition of α, it is matched by $v \xrightarrow{a} v$. Whenever the attacker plays a may transition of v, it is matched either by $X \dashrightarrow{a} Y$ or by $Y \dashrightarrow{a} X$ (α and β are unaffected).

$\Rightarrow$: Let $\mathcal{R} = \{(s, \alpha \parallel \beta \parallel X) \mid \alpha \leq_{sim} \beta\}$. We show that $\mathcal{R}$ can be extended to be a modal refinement relation. Let $(s, \alpha \parallel \beta \parallel X) \in \mathcal{R}$:

- If the attacker plays $s \dashrightarrow{a} s_a$ then the defender can play $\alpha \parallel \beta \parallel X \dashrightarrow{a} \alpha \parallel \beta \parallel Y$. The attacker then has two possibilities:
  - if the attacker plays $s_a \dashrightarrow{a'} s$ then the defender can play $\alpha \parallel \beta \parallel Y \dashrightarrow{a'} \alpha \parallel \beta \parallel X$ and the game is back in $\mathcal{R}$;
  - if the attacker plays $\alpha \parallel \beta \parallel Y \xrightarrow{a} \alpha' \parallel \beta \parallel Y$ then the defender can play $s_a \xrightarrow{a} v$ and win due to the fact above.
- If the attacker plays $\alpha \parallel \beta \parallel X \xrightarrow{a} \alpha' \parallel \beta \parallel X$ then the defender has to play $s \xrightarrow{a} s_a$. The attacker then has three possibilities:
  - if the attacker plays $\alpha' \parallel \beta \parallel X \xrightarrow{b} \alpha'' \parallel \beta \parallel X$ then the defender can play $s_a \xrightarrow{b} v$ and win due to the fact above.
  - if the attacker plays $s_a \dashrightarrow{b} v$ then the defender can play $\alpha' \parallel \beta \parallel X \dashrightarrow{b} \alpha' \parallel \beta \parallel Y$ and win due to the fact above.
  - if the attacker plays $s_a \dashrightarrow{a'} s$ then the defender plays $\alpha' \parallel \beta \parallel X \dashrightarrow{a'} \alpha' \parallel \beta' \parallel X$ where β' is a process such that $\beta \xrightarrow{a} \beta'$ in $\mathrm{LTS}(\Delta_B)$ and $\alpha' \leq_{sim} \beta'$. Such process has to exist due to $\alpha \leq_{sim} \beta$. Therefore, $(s, \alpha' \parallel \beta' \parallel X) \in \mathcal{R}$.

$\Leftarrow$: Let $\mathcal{R} = \{(\alpha, \beta) \mid s \leq_m \alpha \parallel \beta \parallel X\}$. We show that $\mathcal{R}$ is a simulation. Let $(\alpha, \beta) \in \mathcal{R}$.

- If $\alpha \xrightarrow{a} \alpha'$ then $\alpha \parallel \beta \parallel X \xrightarrow{a} \alpha' \parallel \beta \parallel X$. This has to be matched by $s \xrightarrow{a} s_a$. Furthermore, $s_a \dashrightarrow{a'} s$ has to be matched by $\alpha' \parallel \beta \parallel X \dashrightarrow{a'} \alpha' \parallel \beta' \parallel X$ (note that neither α' nor X can make an a'-transition). This means that $\beta \xrightarrow{a} \beta'$ in $\mathrm{LTS}(\Delta_B)$ and that $(\alpha', \beta') \in \mathcal{R}$. $\qquad \square$

4 Decidability Results

We prove that the problems mFSM$\leq_m$mPDA and mPDA$\leq_m$mFSM are decidable and EXPTIME-complete like the corresponding simulation problems.

We modify the result of [KM02b] and show that, in certain classes of mPRS, refinement can be reduced to simulation. The original method introduces two translations, A and D, that transform two processes s and t into A(s) and D(t) in such a way that s and t are bisimilar iff A(s) $\leq_{sim}$ D(t). This approach can be modified in a straightforward way to work with modal refinement instead of bisimulation. The idea of the modification is that the part of the construction that simulates the attacker's possibility to play on the right-hand side is only done for must transitions. The modified A and D translations are then functions from MTS to LTS such that if we have two MTS processes s and t, it holds that $s \leq_m t$ iff $A(s) \leq_{sim} D(t)$. As these translations are only slightly changed from the original ones, we omit their definition here and refer to [BK12].

The applicability of this method is the same (modulo the modal extension) as the applicability of the original method. Both the A-translation and the D-translation preserve the following subclasses of PRS: PDA, BPA, FSM, nPDA, nBPA and OC. Here, nPDA and nBPA are the normed variants (every process may be rewritten to ε in finite number of steps) of PDA and BPA, respectively. OC is the subclass of one-counter automata, i.e. PDA with only one stack symbol. Furthermore, the A-translation also preserves determinism.

As a direct corollary of the previous remark and the results of [KM02a], we obtain the following.

Theorem 3. *The problem $mPDA \leq_m mFSM$ is EXPTIME-complete in both ways, even if the mFSM is of a fixed size. The problem $mBPA \leq_m mFSM$ is EXPTIME-complete in both ways, but if the mFSM is of a fixed size, it is PTIME-complete.*

4.1 Visibly PDA

We have seen that the refinement relation is undecidable between any two infinite classes of the hierarchy depicted in Figure 1. However, there are other subclasses where the refinement is decidable. In this section, we show that the refinement between two modal visibly PDA is decidable.

Definition 4. *A PDA is a* visibly PDA (vPDA) *if there is a partitioning $Act = Act_c \uplus Act_r \uplus Act_i$ such that every rule $pX \xrightarrow{a} q\alpha$ satisfies the following:*

- *if $a \in Act_c$ then $|\alpha| = 2$ (call),*
- *if $a \in Act_r$ then $|\alpha| = 0$ (return),*
- *if $a \in Act_i$ then $|\alpha| = 1$ (internal).*

The modal extension (mvPDA) is straightforward; its subclass mvBPA can be defined similarly.

In order to prove decidability, we make use of the idea of [Srb06] for showing that simulation between two vPDA is decidable. We modify and simplify the method somehow, as the original method is used to prove decidability of various kinds of equivalences and preorders, while we are only considering the modal refinement.

Theorem 4. *The problem $mvPDA \leq_m mvPDA$ is decidable.*

Proof. Let $(\Delta_{may}, \Delta_{must})$ be a mvPDA with a stack alphabet Γ and a set of control states Q. Let sA and tB be two processes of the mvPDA. Note that for simplicity we consider two processes of a single mvPDA. However, as a disjoint union of two mPRS is a mPRS, this also solves the case of two distinct mvPDA. Our goal is to transform the mvPDA into a PDA with a distinguished process such that this process satisfies certain μ-calculus formula if and only if $sA \leq_m tB$.

We create a PDA Δ' with actions $Act' = \{att, def\}$, stack alphabet $\Gamma' = \mathcal{G} \times \mathcal{G}$ where $\mathcal{G} = \Gamma \cup (\Gamma \times \Gamma) \cup (\Gamma \times Act) \cup \{\varepsilon\}$, and control states $\mathcal{Q}' = \mathcal{Q} \times \mathcal{Q}$. We write Y_a instead of (Y, a) as an element of $\mathcal{G}$.

We use a (stack merging) partial mapping $[X\alpha, Y\beta] = (X, Y)[\alpha, \beta]$, $[\varepsilon, \varepsilon] = \varepsilon$. In the following, we abuse the notation of the rules, as we did in the introduction, and write e.g. $pX \dashrightarrow^{a} p'\alpha$ instead of $(pX, a, p'\alpha) \in \Delta_{\mathrm{may}}$.

The set of rules of Δ' is as follows:

- Whenever $pX \dashrightarrow^{a} p'\alpha$ then
  - $(p, q)(X, Y) \xrightarrow{att} (p', q)(\alpha, Y_a)$ for every $q \in \mathcal{Q}$ and $Y \in \Gamma$
  - $(q, p)(\beta, X_a) \xrightarrow{def} (q, p')[\beta, \alpha]$ for every $q \in \mathcal{Q}$ and $\beta \in \Gamma \times \Gamma \cup \Gamma \cup \{\varepsilon\}$
- Whenever $pX \xrightarrow{a} p'\alpha$ then
  - $(q, p)(Y, X) \xrightarrow{att} (q, p')(Y_a, \alpha)$ for every $q \in \mathcal{Q}$ and $Y \in \Gamma$
  - $(p, q)(X_a, \beta) \xrightarrow{def} (p', q)[\alpha, \beta]$ for every $q \in \mathcal{Q}$ and $\beta \in \Gamma \times \Gamma \cup \Gamma \cup \{\varepsilon\}$

Note that $[\alpha, \beta]$ and $[\beta, \alpha]$ is always well defined as $|\alpha| = |\beta|$ is guaranteed (the transition that created β has to have the same label as the transition that creates α – this is guaranteed via X_a). We conclude by the following claim whose proof can be found in [BK12].

Claim. Let φ denote an alternation-free μ-calculus formula $\nu Z.[att]\langle def\rangle Z$. Then $sA \leq_{\mathrm{m}} tB$ iff $(s, t)(A, B) \models \varphi$ □

The following theorem can be proved using complexity bounds for μ-calculus model checking, as in [Srb06].

Theorem 5. *The problem $mvPDA \leq_{\mathrm{m}} mvPDA$ is EXPTIME-complete, the problem $mvBPA \leq_{\mathrm{m}} mvBPA$ is PTIME-complete.*

4.2 Birefinement

Since the refinement is often undecidable, the same holds for refinement equivalence ($\leq_{\mathrm{m}} \cap \geq_{\mathrm{m}}$). Nevertheless, one can consider an even stronger relation that is still useful. We define the notion of birefinement as the modification of refinement where we require both conditions of Definition 2 to be satisfied in both directions, similarly as bisimulation can be defined as a symmetric simulation.

Definition 5 (Birefinement). *A birefinement is a symmetric refinement. We say that α birefines β ($\alpha \sim_{\mathrm{m}} \beta$) if there exists a birefinement containing (α, β).*

This notion then naturally captures the bisimilarity of modal transition systems. Furthermore, the birefinement problem on MTS can be reduced to bisimulation on LTS in the following straightforward way. Let $(\Delta_{\mathrm{may}}, \Delta_{\mathrm{must}})$ and $(\Gamma_{\mathrm{may}}, \Gamma_{\mathrm{must}})$ be two mPRS over the same action alphabet Act. We create a new action $\bar{a}$ for every $a \in Act$. We then translate the mPRS into ordinary PRS as follows. Let $\Delta = \Delta_{\mathrm{may}} \cup \{(\alpha, \bar{a}, \beta) \mid (\alpha, a, \beta) \in \Delta_{\mathrm{must}}\}$ and similarly for Γ. It is then clear that if we take two processes δ of $(\Delta_{\mathrm{may}}, \Delta_{\mathrm{must}})$ and γ of $(\Gamma_{\mathrm{may}}, \Gamma_{\mathrm{must}})$

Table 1. Summary of the decidability results

decidable	mFSM $\lesssim_m$ mPDA, mvPDA $\lesssim_m$ mvPDA, mFSM $\sim_m$ mPRS
undecidable	mFSM $\lesssim_m$ mBPP, mBPA $\lesssim_m$ mBPA

then the following holds: δ birefines γ if and only if δ and γ are bisimilar when taken as processes of Δ and Γ, respectively.

The decidability and complexity of birefinement is thus identical to that of bisimulation in the non-modal case. Therefore, we may apply the powerful result that bisimilarity between any PRS and FSM is decidable [KŘS05] to get the following theorem.

Theorem 6. *Birefinement between an mFSM and any mPRS is decidable.*

This is an important result since it allows us to check whether we can replace an infinite MTS with a particular finite one, which in turn may allow for checking further refinements.

5   Conclusions

We have defined a generic framework for infinite-state modal transition systems generated by finite descriptions. We investigated the corresponding notion of modal refinement on important subclasses and determined the decidability border, see Table 1. Although in some classes it is possible to extend the decidability of simulation to decidability of refinement, it is not possible always. We have shown that somewhat surprisingly the parallelism is a great obstacle for deciding the refinement relation. Therefore, the future work will concentrate on identifying conditions leading to decidability. One of the best candidates is imposing determinism, which has a remarkable effect on the complexity of the problem in the finite case [BKLS09] as well as in the only infinite case considered so far, namely modal Petri nets [EBHH10]. Further, we leave the question whether the problem becomes decidable in some cases when the refining system is an implementation open, too. Finally, it remains open to what extent can verification results on finite MTS, such as [BČK11], be extended to infinite-state MTS.

References

[AFdFE+11] Aceto, L., Fábregas, I., de Frutos-Escrig, D., Ingólfsdóttir, A., Palomino, M.: Graphical representation of covariant-contravariant modal formulae. In: EXPRESS, pp. 1–15 (2011)

[AHKV98]   Alur, R., Henzinger, T.A., Kupferman, O., Vardi, M.Y.: Alternating Refinement Relations. In: Sangiorgi, D., de Simone, R. (eds.) CONCUR 1998. LNCS, vol. 1466, pp. 163–178. Springer, Heidelberg (1998)

[AM04]   Alur, R., Madhusudan, P.: Visibly pushdown languages. In: STOC, pp.
            202–211 (2004)
[BČK11]   Beneš, N., Černá, I., Křetínský, J.: Modal Transition Systems: Composi-
            tion and LTL Model Checking. In: Bultan, T., Hsiung, P.-A. (eds.) ATVA
            2011. LNCS, vol. 6996, pp. 228–242. Springer, Heidelberg (2011)
[BFJ$^+$11] Bauer, S.S., Fahrenberg, U., Juhl, L., Larsen, K.G., Legay, A., Thrane,
            C.R.: Quantitative Refinement for Weighted Modal Transition Systems.
            In: Murlak, F., Sankowski, P. (eds.) MFCS 2011. LNCS, vol. 6907, pp.
            60–71. Springer, Heidelberg (2011)
[BG00]   Bruns, G., Godefroid, P.: Generalized Model Checking: Reasoning about
            Partial State Spaces. In: Palamidessi, C. (ed.) CONCUR 2000. LNCS,
            vol. 1877, pp. 168–182. Springer, Heidelberg (2000)
[BHJ10]   Bauer, S.S., Hennicker, R., Janisch, S.: Interface theories for
            (a)synchronously communicating modal I/O-transition systems. In: FIT,
            pp. 1–8 (2010)
[BK10]   Beneš, N., Křetínský, J.: Process algebra for modal transition systemses.
            In: MEMICS, pp. 9–18 (2010)
[BK12]   Beneš, N., Křetínský, J.: Modal process rewrite systems. Technical report
            FIMU-RS-2012-02, Faculty of Informatics, Masaryk University, Brno
            (2012)
[BKL$^+$11] Beneš, N., Křetínský, J., Larsen, K.G., Møller, M.H., Srba, J.: Parametric
            Modal Transition Systems. In: Bultan, T., Hsiung, P.-A. (eds.) ATVA
            2011. LNCS, vol. 6996, pp. 275–289. Springer, Heidelberg (2011)
[BKL$^+$12] Beneš, N., Křetínský, J., Larsen, K.G., Møller, M.H., Srba, J.: Dual-
            Priced Modal Transition Systems with Time Durations. In: Bjørner,
            N., Voronkov, A. (eds.) LPAR-18 2012. LNCS, vol. 7180, pp. 122–137.
            Springer, Heidelberg (2012)
[BKLS09]   Beneš, N., Křetínský, J., Larsen, K.G., Srba, J.: On determinism in modal
            transition systems. Theor. Comput. Sci. 410(41), 4026–4043 (2009)
[BL90]   Boudol, G., Larsen, K.G.: Graphical versus Logical Specifications. In:
            Arnold, A. (ed.) CAAP 1990. LNCS, vol. 431, pp. 57–71. Springer, Hei-
            delberg (1990)
[BLPR11]   Bertrand, N., Legay, A., Pinchinat, S., Raclet, J.-B.: Modal event-clock
            specifications for timed component-based design. Science of Computer
            Programming (2011) (to appear)
[BLS95]   Børjesson, A., Larsen, K.G., Skou, A.: Generality in design and compo-
            sitional verification using TAV. Formal Methods in System Design 6(3),
            239–258 (1995)
[BML11]   Bauer, S.S., Mayer, P., Legay, A.: MIO Workbench: A Tool for Com-
            positional Design with Modal Input/Output Interfaces. In: Bultan, T.,
            Hsiung, P.-A. (eds.) ATVA 2011. LNCS, vol. 6996, pp. 418–421. Springer,
            Heidelberg (2011)
[Bru97]   Bruns, G.: An industrial application of modal process logic. Sci. Comput.
            Program. 29(1-2), 3–22 (1997)
[CDL$^+$10] Caillaud, B., Delahaye, B., Larsen, K.G., Legay, A., Pedersen, M.L., Wa-
            sowski, A.: Compositional design methodology with constraint markov
            chains. In: QEST, pp. 123–132 (2010)
[ČGL93]   Čerāns, K., Godskesen, J.C., Larsen, K.G.: Timed Modal Specification -
            Theory and Tools. In: Courcoubetis, C. (ed.) CAV 1993. LNCS, vol. 697,
            pp. 253–267. Springer, Heidelberg (1993)

[CGLT09]   Campetelli, A., Gruler, A., Leucker, M., Thoma, D.: *Don't Know* for Multi-valued Systems. In: Liu, Z., Ravn, A.P. (eds.) ATVA 2009. LNCS, vol. 5799, pp. 289–305. Springer, Heidelberg (2009)

[dAH01]   de Alfaro, L., Henzinger, T.A.: Interface automata. In: ESEC / SIGSOFT FSE, pp. 109–120 (2001)

[DFFU07]   D'Ippolito, N., Fischbein, D., Foster, H., Uchitel, S.: MTSA: Eclipse support for modal transition systems construction, analysis and elaboration. In: ETX, pp. 6–10 (2007)

[DGG97]   Dams, D., Gerth, R., Grumberg, O.: Abstract interpretation of reactive systems. ACM Trans. Program. Lang. Syst. 19(2), 253–291 (1997)

[DLL+10]   David, A., Larsen, K.G., Legay, A., Nyman, U., Wąsowski, A.: ECDAR: An Environment for Compositional Design and Analysis of Real Time Systems. In: Bouajjani, A., Chin, W.-N. (eds.) ATVA 2010. LNCS, vol. 6252, pp. 365–370. Springer, Heidelberg (2010)

[DN04]   Dams, D., Namjoshi, K.S.: The existence of finite abstractions for branching time model checking. In: LICS, pp. 335–344 (2004)

[EBHH10]   Elhog-Benzina, D., Haddad, S., Hennicker, R.: Process refinement and asynchronous composition with modalities. In: ACSD/Petri Nets Workshops, pp. 385–401 (2010)

[FS08]   Fecher, H., Schmidt, H.: Comparing disjunctive modal transition systems with an one-selecting variant. J. Log. Algebr. Program. 77(1-2), 20–39 (2008)

[GH94]   Groote, J.F., Hüttel, H.: Undecidable equivalences for basic process algebra. Inf. Comput. 115(2), 354–371 (1994)

[GHJ01]   Godefroid, P., Huth, M., Jagadeesan, R.: Abstraction-Based Model Checking Using Modal Transition Systems. In: Larsen, K.G., Nielsen, M. (eds.) CONCUR 2001. LNCS, vol. 2154, pp. 426–440. Springer, Heidelberg (2001)

[GNRT10]   Godefroid, P., Nori, A.V., Rajamani, S.K., Tetali, S.: Compositional may-must program analysis: unleashing the power of alternation. In: POPL, pp. 43–56 (2010)

[HJS01]   Huth, M., Jagadeesan, R., Schmidt, D.A.: Modal Transition Systems: A Foundation for Three-Valued Program Analysis. In: Sands, D. (ed.) ESOP 2001. LNCS, vol. 2028, pp. 155–169. Springer, Heidelberg (2001)

[Hüt94]   Hüttel, H.: Undecidable Equivalences for Basic Parallel Processes. In: Hagiya, M., Mitchell, J.C. (eds.) TACS 1994. LNCS, vol. 789, pp. 454–464. Springer, Heidelberg (1994)

[JLS11]   Juhl, L., Larsen, K.G., Srba, J.: Modal transition systems with weight intervals. Journal of Logic and Algebraic programming (2011) (to appear)

[JM95]   Jancar, P., Moller, F.: Checking Regular Properties of Petri Nets. In: Lee, I., Smolka, S.A. (eds.) CONCUR 1995. LNCS, vol. 962, pp. 348–362. Springer, Heidelberg (1995)

[JP01]   Jacobs, B., Poll, E.: A Logic for the Java Modeling Language JML. In: Hussmann, H. (ed.) FASE 2001. LNCS, vol. 2029, pp. 284–299. Springer, Heidelberg (2001)

[KM99]   Kučera, A., Mayr, R.: Simulation Preorder on Simple Process Algebras. In: Wiedermann, J., Van Emde Boas, P., Nielsen, M. (eds.) ICALP 1999. LNCS, vol. 1644, pp. 503–512. Springer, Heidelberg (1999)

[KM02a]   Kučera, A., Mayr, R.: On the Complexity of Semantic Equivalences for Pushdown Automata and BPA. In: Diks, K., Rytter, W. (eds.) MFCS 2002. LNCS, vol. 2420, pp. 433–445. Springer, Heidelberg (2002)

[KM02b]   Kučera, A., Mayr, R.: Why Is Simulation Harder than Bisimulation? In:
            Brim, L., Jančar, P., Křetínský, M., Kučera, A. (eds.) CONCUR 2002.
            LNCS, vol. 2421, pp. 594–610. Springer, Heidelberg (2002)
[KŘS05]   Křetínský, M., Řehák, V., Strejček, J.: Reachability of Hennessy-Milner
            Properties for Weakly Extended PRS. In: Sarukkai, S., Sen, S. (eds.)
            FSTTCS 2005. LNCS, vol. 3821, pp. 213–224. Springer, Heidelberg
            (2005)
[LNW07]   Larsen, K.G., Nyman, U., Wąsowski, A.: Modal I/O Automata for In-
            terface and Product Line Theories. In: De Nicola, R. (ed.) ESOP 2007.
            LNCS, vol. 4421, pp. 64–79. Springer, Heidelberg (2007)
[LT88]   Larsen, K.G., Thomsen, B.: A modal process logic. In: LICS, pp. 203–210
            (1988)
[LW94]   Liskov, B., Wing, J.M.: A behavioral notion of subtyping. ACM Trans.
            Program. Lang. Syst. 16(6), 1811–1841 (1994)
[LX90]   Larsen, K.G., Xinxin, L.: Equation solving using modal transition sys-
            tems. In: LICS, pp. 108–117 (1990)
[Lyn88]   Lynch, N.: I/O automata: A model for discrete event systems. In: 22nd
            Annual Conference on Information Sciences and Systems, pp. 29–38.
            Princeton University (1988)
[May00]   Mayr, R.: Process rewrite systems. Inf. Comput. 156(1-2), 264–286 (2000)
[Nam03]   Namjoshi, K.S.: Abstraction for Branching Time Properties. In: Hunt
            Jr., W.A., Somenzi, F. (eds.) CAV 2003. LNCS, vol. 2725, pp. 288–300.
            Springer, Heidelberg (2003)
[Nym08]   Nyman, U.: Modal Transition Systems as the Basis for Interface Theories
            and Product Lines. PhD thesis, Institut for Datalogi, Aalborg Universitet
            (2008)
[RBB+09]   Raclet, J.-B., Badouel, E., Benveniste, A., Caillaud, B., Passerone, R.:
            Why are modalities good for interface theories? In: ACSD. IEEE Com-
            puter Society Press (2009)
[RBB+11]   Raclet, J.-B., Badouel, E., Benveniste, A., Caillaud, B., Legay, A.,
            Passerone, R.: A modal interface theory for component-based design.
            Fundamenta Informaticae 108(1-2), 119–149 (2011)
[Srb06]   Srba, J.: Visibly Pushdown Automata: From Language Equivalence
            to Simulation and Bisimulation. In: Ésik, Z. (ed.) CSL 2006. LNCS,
            vol. 4207, pp. 89–103. Springer, Heidelberg (2006)
[UC04]   Uchitel, S., Chechik, M.: Merging partial behavioural models. In:
            SIGSOFT FSE, pp. 43–52 (2004)

S-Narrowing for Constructor Systems*

Adrián Riesco and Juan Rodríguez-Hortalá

Departamento de Sistemas Informáticos y Computación
Universidad Complutense de Madrid, Spain
{ariesco,juanrh}@fdi.ucm.es

Abstract. Narrowing is a procedure that was conceived in the context of equational E-unification, and that has also been used in a wide range of applications. The classic completeness result due to Hullot states that any term rewriting derivation starting from an instance of an expression that has been obtained by using a normalized substitution can be 'lifted' to a narrowing derivation. Since then, several variants and extensions of narrowing have been developed in order to improve that result under certain assumptions or for particular classes of term rewriting systems.

In this work we propose a new narrowing notion for constructor systems that is based on the novel notion of s-unifier, that essentially allows a variable to be bound to several expressions at the same time. A Maude-based implementation for this narrowing relation, using an adaptation of natural narrowing as on-demand evaluation strategy, is presented, and its use for symbolic reachability analysis applied to the verification of cryptographic protocols is also outlined.

Keywords: narrowing, unification, constructor systems, Maude.

1 Introduction

Narrowing [3] is a procedure that was originally conceived in the context of equational E-unification, and that has also been used in a wide range of applications like for example symbolic reachability analysis [15], test-case generation [20], or as the basic operational mechanism of functional-logic languages [2]. Narrowing can be described as a modification of term rewriting in which matching is replaced by unification. By doing so, in a narrowing derivation from a starting goal expression, the narrowing procedure is able to deduce the instantiation of the variables of the goal expression that is needed for the computation to progress. This idea is reflected in *Hullot's lifting lemma* [11], the key result for the completeness of narrowing w.r.t. term rewriting, which states that given an expression e_1 if we instantiate it with a substitution θ and we perform a term rewriting derivation $e_1\theta \to^* e_2$, then we can *lift* it into a narrowing derivation $e_1 \leadsto_\sigma^* e_3$ such that e_3 and σ are more general than e_2 and θ—w.r.t. to the usual instantiation preorder [4], and for the variables involved in the derivations—, provided that the starting substitution θ is normalized. This latter condition is essential: a

* Research partially supported by the Spanish projects *DESAFIOS10* (TIN2009-14599-C03-01), *FAST-STAMP* (TIN2008-06622-C03-01/TIN), *PROMETIDOS-CM* (S2009/TIC-1465), and *GPD-UCM* (UCM-BSCH-GR58/08-910502).

A. Roychoudhury and M. D'Souza (Eds.): ICTAC 2012, LNCS 7521, pp. 136–150, 2012.

normalized substitution only contains expressions in normal form in its range, which are expressions which cannot be reduced by term rewriting. It is fairly easy to break Hullot's lifting lemma by dropping that condition, for example under the term rewriting system (TRS) $\{f(0,1) \to 2, coin \to 0, coin \to 1\}$, using the expression $f(X,X)$ and the non-normalized substitution $[X/coin]$ we can perform the term rewriting derivation $f(X,X)[X/coin] = f(coin,coin) \to f(0,coin) \to f(0,1) \to 2$, which cannot be lifted by any narrowing derivation. Several variants and extensions of narrowing have been developed in order to improve that result under certain assumptions or for particular classes of term rewriting systems [16,21,15,8].

In this paper we propose a new narrowing relation that tries to improve the completeness results for classic general narrowing, for the class of left-linear constructor-based term rewriting systems or just constructor systems (CS's). In particular we focus on dropping the normalization condition over the starting substitution that is required by Hullot's lifting lemma. In order to test the feasibility of the approach, we have implemented it in Maude [6]. The resulting prototype can be used to evaluate expressions with free variables under any given constructor system with extra variables.

Our starting point is a previous work [12], where a sound and complete compositional semantics for CS's was presented. CS's are characterized by having the signature partitioned in two disjoint sets of function symbols and constructor symbols, so any left-hand side of a rule has a function symbol in its root with constructed terms or just c-terms (expressions built using only constructor symbols and variables) as arguments, and no variable appears more than once in a left-hand side. CS's are usually used to represent programs in declarative languages, therefore we will use 'program' as a synonym for CS from now on. The semantics from [12] gives a characterization of the set of c-terms (an outer constructed part of any expression) reachable by term rewriting from expressions.[1] The key for getting compositionality in that semantics was using a suitable notion of semantic value. Instead of using c-terms, which may seem the obvious choice at a first look, a structured representation of the alternatives between c-terms in a term rewriting derivation is used so the constructor symbols have sets of values as arguments. For example, using a constructor symbol c with arity one and under the program $\{X ? Y \to X, X ? Y \to Y\}$ then $c(\{0,1\})$ is a value for the expression $c(0 ? 1)$ but not for the expression $c(0) ? c(1)$, which reflects the different behavior of these expressions: if we add the rule $g(c(X)) \to d(X,X)$ to the program then it is easy to check that $g(c(0 ? 1)) \to^* d(0,1)$ while $g(c(0) ? c(1)) \not\to^* d(0,1)$, even though the set of c-terms reachable by $c(0 ? 1)$ and $c(0) ? c(1)$ is the same. These structured values are called s-cterms, so an s-csubstitution or just s-csubst is any substitution with s-cterms in its range. And as that semantics is compositional—in fact it is also fully abstract w.r.t. reachability of c-terms [12]—then any pair of expressions with the same set of s-cterms are interchangeable in any context, as long as we are only concerned about the set of reacheable c-terms. This is also reflected at the level of substitutions in an intermediate result of [12], that roughly states that if we can compute a value—i.e., reach that value/c-term by a term rewriting derivation—for an expression instantiated with an arbitrary substitution (for which normalization is not required), then we can

---

[1] We use the terminology *expression* instead of the more usual *term*—in the term rewriting community—in order to stress their difference with the more restricted notion of c-term.

compute the same value instantiating the same expression with an s-csubst such that every s-cterm in its range is a value for the corresponding expression in the range of the starting substitution. This makes sense because although an arbitrary substitution may implicitly contain an infinite amount of information in its range—as it may contain calls to functions with unbounded recursion—any finite term rewriting derivation is a finite computation process that therefore can only consume a finite amount of information in the form of values from the expressions in the range of that substitution. Note that in a sense we should consider that s-csubst are not normalized because they contain alternatives between expressions, so we could evaluate any s-csubst to several c-subst by choosing an element in each of the sets that appear in the s-cterms in the range of the s-csubst.

But what it is important for our purpose here is that this result shows that, for reachability of c-tems in CS's, s-csubstitutions have the same power as arbitrary substitutions. And that is good because narrowing derivations use the left-hand sides of program rules to deduce the instantiation of variables in the goal expression needed for the computation to progress, by syntactic unification in the case of classic narrowing. But we have seen that, in order to have the same power as arbitrary substitutions, what we need to deduce from those left-hand sides is an s-csubst, instead of a normalized substitution. To do that we propose a modification of a classical syntactic unification algorithm that now allows a variable to be bound to several expressions at the same time. We use this novel *s-unification* algorithm as the basis to define a new narrowing relation called *s-narrowing*, that gathers up all the c-terms to which a variable has been bound during the computation. Doing so for every variable in the starting goal expression, and also for the variables in the expressions it has been bound to, we end up building the s-csubst that solves the goal. Applying these ideas to lift the derivation from the example above we get the following s-narrowing derivation:

$$f(X,X) \mid 0 \leadsto 2 \mid \{X \mapsto \{0,1\}\}$$

where the following successful s-unification derivation is used in the application of the rule for f.

$$\{f(0,1) \overset{?}{=} f(X,X)\}; 0 \Rightarrow \{0 \overset{?}{=} X, 1 \overset{?}{=} X\}; 0 \Rightarrow \{X \overset{?}{=} 0, 1 \overset{?}{=} X\}; 0$$
$$\Rightarrow \{1 \overset{?}{=} X\}; \{X \mapsto \{0\}\} \Rightarrow \{X \overset{?}{=} 1\}; \{X \mapsto \{0\}\} \Rightarrow 0; \{X \mapsto \{0,1\}\}$$

Regarding the prototype, s-narrowing is implemented by using an adaptation of the natural narrowing on-demand strategy [9], which indicates the positions that must be reduced in each step. As a proof-of-concept we have tested the prototype with several examples, including a sketch of the verification of cryptographic protocols.

The rest of the paper is organized as follows. In Section 2 we explain the aforementioned semantics for constructor systems, and use it to formalize the intuitions presented in the introduction. In Section 3 we present the notions of s-unification and s-narrowing and some interesting results about them. Then in Section 4 we outline the implementation and commands of our prototype using examples. Finally, Section 5 concludes and outlines some lines of future work. More information and detailed proofs of the results shown here are presented in [18].

2   Prelimininaries and Formal Setting

2.1   Basic Syntax

We consider a first order signature $\Sigma = CS \uplus FS$, where CS and FS are two disjoint set of *constructor* and defined *function* symbols respectively, all them with associated arity. We write CS^n (FS^n resp.) for the set of constructor (function) symbols of arity n. We write $c,d,\ldots$ for constructors, $f,g,\ldots$ for functions and $X,Y,\ldots$ for variables of a numerable set $\mathcal{V}$. The notation $\overline{o}$ stands for tuples of any kind of syntactic objects.

The set *Exp* of *expressions* is defined as $Exp \ni e ::= X \mid h(e_1,\ldots,e_n)$, where $X \in \mathcal{V}$, $h \in CS^n \cup FS^n$ and $e_1,\ldots,e_n \in Exp$. The set *CTerm* of *constructed terms* (or *c-terms*) is defined like *Exp*, but with h restricted to CS^n (so $CTerm \subseteq Exp$). We will write $e,e',\ldots$ for expressions and $t,s,\ldots$ for c-terms. The set of variables occurring in an expression e will be denoted as $var(e)$. We say that an expression e is *ground* iff $var(e) = \emptyset$. We will frequently use *one-hole contexts*, defined as $Cntxt \ni C ::= [\,] \mid h(e_1,\ldots,C,\ldots,e_n)$, with $h \in CS^n \cup FS^n$. The application of a context C to an expression e, written by $C[e]$, is defined inductively as $[\,][e] = e$ and $h(e_1,\ldots,C,\ldots,e_n)[e] = h(e_1,\ldots,C[e],\ldots,e_n)$.

We also consider the extended signature $\Sigma_\perp = \Sigma \cup \{\perp\}$, where $\perp$ is a new 0-arity constructor symbol that does not appear in programs, and that stands for the undefined value. Over this signature we define the sets $Exp_\perp$ and $CTerm_\perp$ of *partial* expressions and c-terms resp. The intended meaning is that *Exp* and $Exp_\perp$ stand for evaluable expressions, i.e., expressions that can contain function symbols, while *CTerm* and $CTerm_\perp$ stand for data terms representing total and partial values resp. Partial expressions are ordered by the *approximation* ordering $\sqsubseteq$ defined as the least partial ordering satisfying $\perp \sqsubseteq e$ and $e \sqsubseteq e' \Rightarrow C[e] \sqsubseteq C[e']$ for all $e,e' \in Exp_\perp, C \in Cntxt$. The *shell* $|e|$ of an expression e represents the outer constructed part of e and is defined as: $|X| = X$; $|c(e_1,\ldots,e_n)| = c(|e_1|,\ldots,|e_n|)$; $|f(e_1,\ldots,e_n)| = \perp$. It is trivial to check that for any expression e we have $|e| \in CTerm_\perp$, that any total expression is maximal w.r.t. $\sqsubseteq$, and that as consequence if t is total then $t \sqsubseteq |e|$ implies $t = e$.

Substitutions $\theta \in Subst$ are finite mappings $\theta : \mathcal{V} \longrightarrow Exp$, extending naturally to $\theta : Exp \longrightarrow Exp$. We write ε for the identity (or empty) substitution. We write $e\theta$ for the application of θ to e, and $\theta\theta'$ for the composition, defined by $X(\theta\theta') = (X\theta)\theta'$. The domain and range of θ are defined as $dom(\theta) = \{X \in \mathcal{V} \mid X\theta \neq X\}$ and $vran(\theta) = \bigcup_{X \in dom(\theta)} var(X\theta)$. By $[X_1/e_1,\ldots,X_n/e_n]$ we denote a substitution σ such that $dom(\sigma) = \{X_1,\ldots,X_n\}$ and $\forall i.\sigma(X_i) = e_i$. Similarly the notation $[X/e \mid P(X,e)]$ where P is some predicate over X and e is used to define substitutions using a set-like notation, so $([X/e \mid P(X,e)])(Y) = e'$ if $P(Y,e')$, and $([X/e \mid P(X,e)])(Y) = Y$ otherwise. If $dom(\theta_0) \cap dom(\theta_1) = \emptyset$, their disjoint union $\theta_0 \uplus \theta_1$ is defined by $(\theta_0 \uplus \theta_1)(X) = \theta_i(X)$, if $X \in dom(\theta_i)$ for some θ_i; $(\theta_0 \uplus \theta_1)(X) = X$ otherwise. Given $W \subseteq \mathcal{V}$ we write $\theta|_W$ for the restriction of θ to W, i.e. $(\theta|_W)(X) = \theta(X)$ if $X \in W$, and $(\theta|_W)(X) = X$ otherwise; we use $\theta|_{\backslash D}$ as a shortcut for $\theta|_{(\mathcal{V} \backslash D)}$. *C-substitutions* $\theta \in CSubst$ verify that $X\theta \in CTerm$ for all $X \in dom(\theta)$. We say a substitution σ is ground iff $vran(\sigma) = \emptyset$, i.e. $\forall X \in dom(\sigma)$ we have that $\sigma(X)$ is ground. The sets $Subst_\perp$ and $CSubst_\perp$ of partial substitutions and partial c-substitutions are the sets of finite mappings from variables to partial expressions and partial c-terms, respectively.

A constructor-based term rewriting system or just *constructor system* or *program* $\mathcal{P}$ (*CS*) is a set of c-rewrite rules of the form $f(\bar{t}) \to r$ where $f \in FS^n$, $r \in Exp$ and $\bar{t}$ is a linear n-tuple of c-terms, where linearity means that variables occur only once in $\bar{t}$. Notice that we allow r to contain so called *extra variables*, i.e., variables not occurring in $f(\bar{t})$. To be precise, we say that $X \in \mathcal{V}$ is an extra variable in the rule $l \to r$ iff $X \in var(r) \setminus var(l)$. the set of extra variables in a program rule R. A fresh variant of a program rule is the result of taking a program rule and applying to it a substitution that replaces each variable of the rule by a fresh variable. We assume that every CS contains the rules $Q = \{X \; ? \; Y \to X, X \; ? \; Y \to Y\}$, defining the behavior of $\_?\_ \in FS^2$, used infix mode, and that those are the only rules for ?. Besides, ? is right-associative so $e_1 \; ? \; e_2 \; ? \; e_3$ is equivalent to $e_1 \; ? \; (e_2 \; ? \; e_3)$. For the sake of conciseness we will often omit these rules when presenting a CS. A consequence of this is that we only consider non-confluent programs.

Given a TRS $\mathcal{P}$, its associated *term rewriting relation* $\to_{\mathcal{P}}$ is defined as: $C[l\sigma] \to_{\mathcal{P}} C[r\sigma]$ for any context C, rule $l \to r \in \mathcal{P}$ and $\sigma \in Subst$. We write $\xrightarrow{*}_{\mathcal{P}}$ for the reflexive and transitive closure of the relation $\to_{\mathcal{P}}$. In the following, we will usually omit the reference to $\mathcal{P}$ or denote it by $\mathcal{P} \vdash e \to e'$ and $\mathcal{P} \vdash e \to^* e'$. By $\mathcal{P} \vdash e_1 \downarrow e_2$ we denote that e_1 and e_2 are *joinable* under $\mathcal{P}$, i.e., it exists some expression e_3 such that $\mathcal{P} \vdash e_1 \to^* e_3 \;^*\!\!\leftarrow e_2$, where $\leftarrow$ denotes the inverse of $\to$, and $^*\!\!\leftarrow$ the reflexive-transitive closure of $\leftarrow$.

2.2 A Proof Calculus for Constructor Systems with Extra Variables

In [12] an adequate semantics for reachability of c-terms by term rewriting in CS's was presented. As we mentioned in Section 1, the key idea in that semantics is using a suitable notion of value, in this case the notion of s-cterm, which is a structured representation of alternative between c-terms in a term rewriting derivation. An s-cterm is a *finite* set of elemental s-cterms, that are variables or constructors applied to s-cterms, so *SCTerm* is an alias for the set of finite sets of elemental s-cterms and the set *ESCTerm* of elemental s-cterms is defined as $ESCTerm \ni est ::= X \mid c(st_1, \ldots, st_n)$ for $X \in \mathcal{V}$, $c \in DC^n$, $st_1, \ldots, st_n \in SCTerm$. We extend this idea to expressions obtaining the sets *SExp* of s-expressions or just s-exp, and *ESExp* of elemental s-expressions, which are defined the same but now using any symbol in Σ in applications instead of just constructor symbols. Note that for s-expressions $\emptyset$ corresponds to $\bot$, so s-exps are partial by default. The approximation preorder $\sqsubseteq$ is defined for s-exps as the least preorder such that $se \sqsubseteq se'$ iff $\forall ese \in se.\exists ese' \in se'$ such that $ese \sqsubseteq ese'$, $X \sqsubseteq X$ for any $X \in \mathcal{V}$, and $h(se_1, \ldots, se_n) \sqsubseteq h(se'_1, \ldots, se'_n)$ iff $\forall i.se_i \sqsubseteq se'_i$.

The sets *SSubst* and *SCSubst* of s-substitutions and s-csubstitutions (or just s-csubst) consist of finite mappings from variables to s-exps or s-cterms, respectively. Some care must be taken when extending s-substs to be applied to *ESExp* and *SExp*, so for any $\sigma \in SSubst$ we define $\sigma : ESExp \to SExp$ as $X\sigma = \sigma(X)$, $h(\overline{se})\sigma = \{h(\overline{se\sigma})\}$; and $\sigma : SExp \to SExp$ as $se\sigma = \bigcup_{ese \in se} ese\sigma$. The approximation preorder $\sqsubseteq$ is defined for s-substs as $\sigma \sqsubseteq \theta$ iff $\forall X \in \mathcal{V}.\sigma(X) \sqsubseteq \theta(X)$.

In this semantics the denotation of an expression is obtained as the denotation of its associated s-expression, assigned by the operator $\widetilde{\cdot} : Exp_{\bot} \to SExp$, which is defined as

E	$se \twoheadrightarrow \emptyset$	
RR	$\{X\} \twoheadrightarrow \{X\}$	if $X \in \mathcal{V}$
DC	$\dfrac{se_1 \twoheadrightarrow st_1 \ \ldots \ se_n \twoheadrightarrow st_n}{\{c(se_1,\ldots,se_n)\} \twoheadrightarrow \{c(st_1,\ldots,st_n)\}}$	if $c \in CS$
MORE	$\dfrac{se \twoheadrightarrow st_1 \ \ldots se \twoheadrightarrow st_n}{se \twoheadrightarrow st_1 \cup \ldots \cup st_n}$	
LESS	$\dfrac{\{esa_1\} \twoheadrightarrow st_1 \ \ldots \ \{esa_m\} \twoheadrightarrow st_m}{\{ese_1,\ldots,ese_n\} \twoheadrightarrow st_1 \cup \ldots \cup st_m}$	if $n \geq 2, m > 0$, for any $\{esa_1,\ldots,esa_m\} \subseteq \{ese_1,\ldots,ese_n\}$
ROR	$\dfrac{se_1 \twoheadrightarrow \widetilde{p_1}\theta \ \ldots \ se_n \twoheadrightarrow \widetilde{p_n}\theta \ \widetilde{r}\theta \twoheadrightarrow st}{\{f(se_1,\ldots,se_n)\} \twoheadrightarrow st}$	if $\dfrac{(f(p_1,\ldots,p_n) \to r) \in \mathcal{P}}{\theta \in SCSubst}$

Fig. 1. A proof calculus for constructor systems

$\widetilde{\perp} = \emptyset; \widetilde{X} = \{X\}$ for any $X \in \mathcal{V}; \widetilde{h(e_1,\ldots,e_n)} = \{h(\widetilde{e_1},\ldots,\widetilde{e_n})\}$ for any $h \in \Sigma^n$. The operator $\widetilde{\ }$ is extended to s-substitutions as $\widetilde{\sigma}(X) = \widetilde{\sigma(X)}$, for $\sigma \in Subst_\perp$. Is is easy to check that $\widetilde{e\sigma} = \widetilde{e}\widetilde{\sigma}$ (see [12]). Conversely, we can flatten an s-expression se to obtain the set $flat(e)$ of expressions "contained" in it, so $flat(\emptyset) = \{\perp\}$ and $flat(se) = \bigcup_{ese \in se} flat(ese)$ if $se \neq \emptyset$, where the flattening of elemental s-exps is defined as $flat(X) = \{X\}; flat(h(se_1, \ldots, se_n)) = \{h(e_1,\ldots,e_n) \mid e_i \in flat(se_i)$ for $i = 1..n\}$.

In Figure 1 we can find the proof calculus that defines the semantics of s-expressions. Our proof calculus proves reduction statements of the form $se \twoheadrightarrow st$ with $se \in SExp$ and $st \in SCTerm$, expressing that st represents an approximation to one of the possible structured sets of values for se. We refer the interested reader to [12] for a detailed explanation of the intuitions behind the rules of the calculus. We write $\mathcal{P} \vdash se \twoheadrightarrow st$ to express that $se \twoheadrightarrow st$ is derivable in our calculus under the CS $\mathcal{P}$. The *denotation* of an s-expression se under a CS $\mathcal{P}$ is defined as $[\![se]\!]^{\mathcal{P}} = \{st \in SCTerm \mid \mathcal{P} \vdash se \twoheadrightarrow st\}$. In the following we will usually omit the reference to $\mathcal{P}$. The denotation of an s-substitution σ is defined as $[\![\sigma]\!] = \{\theta \in SCSubst \mid \forall X \in \mathcal{V}, \sigma(X) \twoheadrightarrow \theta(X)\}$.

The setting originally presented in [12] was not able to deal with extra variables, but in [17] we extended it to deal with them, which is just needed for the present work, as extra variables are very common when using narrowing. To do that we were not required to change the rules of the calculus, but only the proof for the adequacy, as the rule **ROR** from Figure 1 already allows to instantiate extra variables freely with s-cterms. Nevertheless, as a consequence of that freely instantiation of extra variables, every program with extra variables turns into non-deterministic. For example consider a program $\{f \to (X,X)\}$ for which the constructors $0, 1 \in CS^0$ are available, then we can prove $\widetilde{f} = \{f\} \twoheadrightarrow \{(\{0\},\{1\})\} = \widetilde{(0,1)}$. But in fact this is not very surprising, and it has to do with the relation between non-determinism and extra variables [1], but adapted to the run-time choice semantics [19] induced by term rewriting. As a consequence of this—as seen in Section 2.1—we assume that all the programs contains the function ? defined by the rules $Q = \{X ? Y \to X, X ? Y \to Y\}$, so we only consider non-confluent TRS's. We admit that this is a limitation of our setting, but we also conjecture that for confluent TRS's a simpler semantics could be used, for which the packing of alternatives of c-terms would not be needed. Anyway, the point is that having ? at one's disposal is enough to express the non-determinism of any program [10], so we can use it to define the transformation $\widehat{}$ from s-exp and elemental s-exp to partial expressions that, contrary to *flat*, now takes care of keeping the nested set structure by means of uses of the ? function. Then $\widehat{} : ESExp \to Exp_\perp$ is defined by $\widehat{X} = X$, $\widehat{h(se_1, \ldots, se_n)} = h(\widehat{se_1}, \ldots, \widehat{se_n})$; and $\widehat{} : SExp \to Exp_\perp$ is defined by $\widehat{\emptyset} = \perp$, $\widehat{\{ese_1, \ldots, ese_n\}} = \widehat{ese_1} \ ? \ \ldots \ ? \ \widehat{ese_n}$ for $n > 0$, where in the case for $\{ese_1, \ldots, ese_n\}$ we use some fixed arbitrary order on terms for arranging the arguments of ?. This operator is also overloaded for substitutions as $\widehat{} : SSubst \to Subst_\perp$ as $(\widehat{\sigma})(X) = \widehat{\sigma(X)}$. Thanks to the power of ? to express non-determinism, that transformation preserves the semantics from Figure 1, so the following result can be proved—see [12] for details about the proof.

Theorem 1 (Adequacy of $[\![\_]\!]$). *For all $e, e' \in Exp, t \in CTerm_\perp, st \in SCTerm$:*
Soundness *$st \in [\![\widehat{e}]\!]$ and $t \in flat(st)$ implies $e \to^* e'$ for some $e' \in Exp$ such that $t \sqsubseteq |e'|$. Therefore, $\widetilde{t} \in [\![\widehat{e}]\!]$ implies $e \to^* e'$ for some $e' \in Exp$ such that $t \sqsubseteq |e'|$. Besides, in any of the previous cases, if t is total then $e \to^* t$.*
Completeness *$e \to^* e'$ implies $\widetilde{|e'|} \in [\![\widehat{e}]\!]$. Hence, if t is total then $e \to^* t$ implies $\widetilde{t} \in [\![\widehat{e}]\!]$.*

We conclude this section with the following result, that formalizes the intuitions we gave in Section 1 stating that we only need to compute an s-csubst in order to lift any term rewriting derivation starting from an expression instatiated with an arbitrary substitution, if we only care about reachability of c-terms—or its outer constructed part, expressed by the notion of shell.

Proposition 1. *For all $e, e' \in Exp$, $\sigma \in Subst$, $e\sigma \to^* e'$ implies $\exists \theta \in [\![\sigma]\!]$. $e\theta \to^* e''$ such that $|e'| \sqsubseteq |e''|$. Note that $\theta \in [\![\sigma]\!]$ implies $\theta \in SCSubst$. Besides, if $e' = t \in CTerm$ then $e\theta \to^* t$.*

3 S-Narrowing and S-Unification

In this section we will present our proposal for the novel s-narrowing relation—where 's' stands for "set," as in s-cterm—in which we realize the ideas about a new narrowing relation discussed in Section 1. As suggested by Proposition 1, in s-narrowing we use the information contained in the left-hand sides of program rules to compute an s-csubst, in order to lift any term rewriting derivation starting from the instantiation of an expression with an arbitrary substitution. To do that we rely on the notion of s-unification, a modification of syntactic unification that basically allows a variable to be bound to several expressions at the same time.

For the sake of conciseness of the notation, in the rest of the paper we will often omit the braces in singleton sets, so the context determines wheter e refers to $\{e\}$—as $\{0\}$ in $c(0) \in SExp$—or just to e—as 0 in $c(0) \in Exp$.

3.1 S-Unification

The main difference between s-unification and syntactic unification is that, instead of finding a substitution that makes two expressions equal, in s-unification we look for an

VTRIV	$\{X \overset{?}{=} X\} \uplus P; S \Rightarrow P; S$	if $X \in \mathcal{V}$
DEC	$\{h(e_1,\ldots,e_n) \overset{?}{=} h(e'_1,\ldots,e'_n)\} \uplus P; S \Rightarrow \{e_1 \overset{?}{=} e'_1,\ldots,e_n \overset{?}{=} e'_n\} \uplus P; S$	
CLASH	$\{h_1(\overline{e_1}) \overset{?}{=} h_2(\overline{e_2})\} \uplus P; S \Rightarrow fail$	if $h_1 \neq h_2$
TURN	$\{e \overset{?}{=} X\} \uplus P; S \Rightarrow \{X \overset{?}{=} e\} \uplus P; S$	if $e \notin \mathcal{V}$
ADDBIND	$\{X \overset{?}{=} e\} \uplus P; S \Rightarrow P; S \oplus \{X \mapsto e\}$	

Fig. 2. S-Unification algorithm $\mathcal{S}$

s-subst that makes the intersection of two expressions a nonempty set. From the term rewriting point of view this means that an s-unifier of two expressions makes them joinable. Formally, $\sigma \in SSubst$ is an s-unifier of $e_1, e_2 \in Exp$ iff $\mathcal{Q} \vdash e_1 \widehat{\sigma} \downarrow e_2 \widehat{\sigma}$. A particularity of s-unification is that occurs check is not needed: for example we can instantiate the expressions X and $c(X)$ so they have a nonempty intersection by using $[X/\{X, c(X)\}]$, as $\mathcal{Q} \vdash X[X/\{X, c(X)\}] = X ? c(X) \to c(X) \leftarrow c(X ? c(X)) = c(X)[X/\{X, c(X)\}]$.

In Figure 2 we formulate our rule-based s-unification algorithm $\mathcal{S}$, following the style of the rule-based algorithm $\mathcal{U}$ from [4] for computing the most general syntactic unifier. Hence, in $\mathcal{S}$ we rewrite configurations of the shape $P; S$ where P is the problem, i.e., a finite set of equations of the shape $e_1 \overset{?}{=} e_2$ between the expressions to unify, and S is the solution computed so far, represented as a finite set of bindings of the shape $X \mapsto \{e_1,\ldots,e_n\}$ for $X \in \mathcal{V}$ and $e_1,\ldots,e_n \in Exp$. The special configuration $fail$ is used to indicate a failure in the s-unification process. Given a solution S, its domain $dom(S)$ is the set of variables for which a binding is defined in S. By $S[X]$ we denote the binding corresponding to X in S, and by $S[X \mapsto s]$ we denote the solution S' such that $S'[X] = s$ and $S'[Y] = S[Y]$ for each $Y \in dom(S) \setminus \{X\}$. The operator $\oplus$ is used to add a new element to the binding for a variable in a solution, and it is defined as $S \oplus \{X \mapsto e\} = S[X \mapsto \{e\}]$ if $X \notin dom(S)$; $S[X \mapsto c] \oplus \{X \mapsto e\} = S[X \mapsto c \cup \{e\}]$ otherwise. Given some $\mathcal{W} \subseteq \mathcal{V}$ by $S|_{\mathcal{W}}$ we denote the restriction of S to $\mathcal{W}$, i.e., the result of dropping from S the bindings for variables which are not contained in $\mathcal{W}$; and by $S|_{\backslash \mathcal{W}}$ we denote $S|_{(\mathcal{V} \backslash \mathcal{W})}$.

In order to s-unify two given expressions $e_1, e_2 \in Exp$ we start with $\{e_1 \overset{?}{=} e_2\}; \emptyset$ as the initial configuration and apply the rules of $\mathcal{S}$ in a don't care non-deterministic fashion until reaching $fail$ or a configuration of the shape $\emptyset; S$, which is a configuration in solved form. By $\Rightarrow^*$ we denote the reflexive-transitive closure of $\Rightarrow$, therefore $\{e_1 \overset{?}{=} e_2\}; \emptyset \Rightarrow^* \emptyset; S$ indicates that the s-unification procedure for e_1 and e_2 has ended with success computing the solution S. The rules VTRIV, DEC, CLASH and TURN are standard in unification algorithms. The novelty in $\mathcal{S}$ compared to $\mathcal{U}$ is the rule ADDBIND that, together with the absence of a rule for occurs check, tries to reflect the intended meaning of an s-unifier discussed above. Maybe the reader could expect a special case for occurs check where a binding $X \mapsto \{X, e\}$ would be added to the solution, but that case is not needed because of the way we interpret the solutions computed by $\mathcal{S}$, as we will see below.

We conjecture that the set of pairs of expressions that are s-unifiable is bigger than the set of pairs of expressions that are unifiable. However, the algorithm $\mathcal{S}$ only grants the absence of cycles in the computed solutions when unifiying pairs of expression e_1 and e_2 such that $var(e_1) \cap var(e_2) = \emptyset$ and e_1 is linear, which is enough for its uses in s-narrowing. Otherwise the computed solution may contain cyclic bindings: consider for example the problem $h(X, Z, Y) \stackrel{?}{=} h(Z, Y, X)$ which is unifiable with $[Z/Y, X/Y]$, and for which S computes the cyclic solution $[X/Z, Z/Y, Y/X]$; or the problem $d(X, c(X)) \stackrel{?}{=} d(Y, Y)$ which is not unifiable but for which S computes the cyclic solution $[X/Y, Y/c(X)]$, even though $d(X, c(X))$ and $d(Y, Y)$ do not share variables. The absence in S of a rule for variable elimination, that would propagate the binding computed for one variable to the rest of the problem, allows us for example to s-unify $d(X, X)$ and $d(0, 1)$ with $[X/\{0, 1\}]$. But, at the same time, it implies that sometimes S will not compute the most general unifier for two unifiable expressions, so it is not a conservative extension of a unification algorithm. For example $f(c(U), c(V)) \stackrel{?}{=} f(X, X); \emptyset \Rightarrow^* \emptyset; \{X \mapsto \{c(U), c(V)\}\}$, while $[X/c(U), V/U]$ is the most general unifier of $f(c(U), c(V))$ and $f(X, X)$. In order to be more conservative, we could have opted for an alternative definition of the rule ADDBIND in which the bindings computed so far would be reused. But, as we will see in Section 3.2, that would entail computing an s-narrowing solution that would be more concrete that what is needed to lift the term rewriting derivations, so we use ADDBIND as defined above. The algorithm S is terminating as shown in the following result, in the line of [4].

Proposition 2. *For any problem P, every sequence $P; \emptyset \Rightarrow P_1; S_1 \Rightarrow P_2; S_2 \Rightarrow \ldots$ terminates either with fail or with a configuration of the shape $\emptyset; S$*

By $S^*[X]$ we denote the binding corresponding to X in S after resolving the indirections caused by variables in $S[X]$ that are also in the domain of S, which is defined as $S^*[X] = (S[X])[\overline{Y}/S^*[\overline{Y}]]$ for $\overline{Y} = var(S[X]) \cap dom(S)$. Hence in general $S^*[X] \in SExp$. Note that $S^*[X]$ is only well defined for solutions S without cyclic bindings, but that is enough for us as we will only deal with solutions with acyclic bindings. Using this notion we define the *SSubst corresponding to a solution S*, denoted by σ_S, as $\sigma_S = [X/S^*[X] \mid X \in dom(S)]$. Although we do not provide a formal proof, we conjecture that if $var(e_1) \cap var(e_2) = \emptyset$ and e_1 is linear then $\{e_1 \stackrel{?}{=} e_2\}; \emptyset \Rightarrow^* \emptyset; S$ implies that σ_S° is an s-unifier of e_1 and e_2, where the opening σ° of an s-subst σ is defined as $(\sigma^\circ)(X) = \{X\} \cup \sigma(X)$. In fact, in s-unification and s-narrowing we treat any substitution and its opening as if they were indistinguishable, which reflects a view of variables as ever fruitful sources of c-terms. In s-narrowing free variables are never really instantiated, but different alternative binding for the variables are collected, hence a variable can always "be itself" again when needed, so it can be bound to a c-term it was not previously bound.

3.2 S-Narrowing

The s-narrowing relation is defined in Figure 3. In s-narrowing we work with configurations of the shape $e \mid S$ where e is a goal expression and S is a solution like those used in s-unification. We do this in order to avoid instantiating the variables in the goal, so we could bind them to several c-terms at the same time. In this way, we collect in S the bindings for those variables. The idea of s-narrowing is pretty simple. First we s-unify

$$C[f(\overline{e})] \mid S_1 \leadsto C[r\sigma_p] \mid S_2 \text{ for any fresh variant } (f(\overline{p}) \to r) \in \mathcal{P} \text{ such that:}$$
$$i) \; \{f(\overline{p}) \overset{?}{=} f(\overline{e})\}; S_1 \Rightarrow^* \emptyset; S \quad ii) \; S_p = S|_{var(\overline{p})} \text{ and } S_2 = S|_{\setminus var(\overline{p})} \quad iii) \; \sigma_p = \widehat{\sigma_{S_p}}$$

Fig. 3. S-Narrowing

an expression $f(\overline{e})$ occurring in the goal expression with the left hand-side of a fresh variant of a programa rule. To do that we start s-unification using the solution computed so far, that contains the bindings collected for the goal subexpression. As the variant is fresh then occurs check is not needed. If s-unification succeeds then we take the part S_p of the solution corresponding to the fresh left-hand side and use it for parameter passing. The following result ensures that each s-expressions in the range of S_p is singleton, so $\widehat{\sigma_{S_p}} = \sigma_p \in Subst$:

Lemma 1. *For all* $e_1, e_2 \in Exp$ *if* e_1 *is linear,* $var(e_1) \cap var(e_2) = \emptyset$ *and* $\{e_1 \overset{?}{=} e_2\}; \emptyset \Rightarrow^*$ $\emptyset; S$, *then for* $S_{e_1} = S|_{var(e_1)} \; \forall X \in dom(S_{e_1}) \; S_{e_1}[X]$ *is singleton.*

Then the propagation of the bindings computed for $f(\overline{e})$ is implicitly performed by using S_2 in the resulting s-narrowing configuration, as it is the part of the solution for the s-unification that does not affect the fresh left-hand side. By $\leadsto^*$ we denote the reflexive-transitive closure of $\leadsto$. A successful s-narrowing derivation for an expression e is a derivation $e \mid \emptyset \leadsto^* t \mid S$ where t is a c-term. Then, similarly to s-unification, the *s-subst computed as solution by* that *s-narrowing* derivation is $\sigma_S{}^\circ$.

Note that the application of σ_p to r is needed to ensure soundness, as we can see considering the program $\{f(X) \to g(X), g(1) \to 2\}$. If we drop the application of σ_p at each step, then we can do:

$$f(0) \mid \emptyset \leadsto g(X_1) \mid \{X_1 \mapsto \{0\}\} \qquad \text{as } \{f(X_1) \overset{?}{=} f(0)\}; \emptyset \Rightarrow^* \emptyset; \{X_1 \mapsto \{0\}\}$$
$$\leadsto 2 \mid \{X_1 \mapsto \{0,1\}\} \qquad \text{as } \{g(1) \overset{?}{=} g(X_1)\}; \{X_1 \mapsto \{0\}\} \Rightarrow^* \emptyset; \{X_1 \mapsto \{0,1\}\}$$

but this is clearly unsound because $f(0)[X_1/0?1] \not\rightarrow^* 2$, and in fact there is no $\sigma \in$ *Subst* such that $f(0)\sigma \to^* 2$. Thus the application of σ_p is necessary to respect the restrictions imposed by the symbols of Σ present in the goal expression which, contrary to variables, cannot be replaced by the application of substitutions. Conversely, if we use $\leadsto$ as defined in Figure 3 then the derivation gets stuck after the first step, as expected:

$$f(0) \mid \emptyset \leadsto g(0) \mid \emptyset \qquad \text{as } \{f(X_1) \overset{?}{=} f(0)\} \mid \emptyset \Rightarrow^* \emptyset \mid \{X_1 \mapsto \{0\}\}$$

and we cannot continue as $\{g(1) \overset{?}{=} g(0)\}; \emptyset \Rightarrow \{1 \overset{?}{=} 0\}; \emptyset \Rightarrow fail$. Just like classical narrowing can be rephrased as a unification step followed by a term rewriting step, i.e. as $C[f(\overline{e})] \Rightarrow C\sigma[f(\overline{e})\sigma] \to C\sigma[r\sigma]$, we could similarly rephrase s-narrowing as $C[f(\overline{e})] \mid S_1 \Rightarrow C[f(\overline{e})\sigma_p] \mid S_2 \to C[r\sigma_p] \mid S_2$.

The following example shows why we open the substitution computed as solution. Given the program $\{f(0,1,X) \to X, coin \to 0, coin \to 1\}$ and the goal $f(X,X,X)$ for which we can compute $f(X,X,X) \mid \emptyset \leadsto X \mid \{X \mapsto \{0,1\}\}$. If we use σ_S with $S = \{X \mapsto \{0,1\}\}$ as the computed solution then we could not reach X by term rewriting, as $f(X,X,X)\widehat{[X/\{0,1\}]} \not\rightarrow^* X$, while we can reach it using the non-normalized substitution $[X/coin\ ?\ X]$. But if we open the solution and use σ_{S}° as the computed solution, as we originally proposed, then $f(X,X,X)\widehat{[X/\{0,1\}]^{\circ}} \to^{*} f(0,1,X) \to X$. This is also coherent with our view of free variables in s-narrowing, which are never instantiated and are always implicitly bound to (the singleton set containing) themselves.

In Section 3.1 we saw that s-unification is not a conservative extension of unification because the bindings in the solution computed so far are not reused to solve subsequent equations. The following example illustrates how reusing those bindings would result in computing too specific solutions. Consider the program $\{f(c(X),Y) \to h(X,Y), h(X,c(Y)) \to g(X,Y), g(0,1) \to 2\}$ and the goal expression $f(X,X)$, for which we can do $f(X,X) \mid \emptyset \rightsquigarrow h(U,X) \mid \{X \mapsto c(U)\}$—for the sake of conciseness we drop the bindings for irrelevant variables. Now in order to unify $h(U,X)$ with $h(W,c(V))$—a fresh variant of the left-hand side of the rule for h—we have two options. On the one hand, if we modify the rule ADDBIND in order to reuse the binding in $\{X \mapsto c(U)\}$ then we can perform the step $h(U,X) \mid \{X \mapsto c(U)\} \rightsquigarrow g(U,U) \mid \{X \mapsto c(U)\}$ and then $g(U,U) \mid \{X \mapsto c(U)\} \rightsquigarrow 2 \mid \{X \mapsto c(U), U \mapsto \{0,1\}\}$, thus getting the solution $[X/c(\{0,1\})]^{\circ}$—for conciseness here we restrict the solution to the variables in the starting goal. On the other hand, if we use the proposed definition of s-unification then derivation proceeds as $h(U,X) \mid \{X \mapsto c(U)\} \rightsquigarrow g(U,V) \mid \{X \mapsto \{c(U),c(V)\}\} \rightsquigarrow 2 \mid \{X \mapsto \{c(U),c(V)\}, U \mapsto 0, V \mapsto 1\}$, getting the solution $[X/\{c(0),c(1)\}]^{\circ}$. Although both solutions are sound in the sense that both $f(X,X)\widehat{[X/c(\{0,1\})]^{\circ}} \to^{*} 2$ and $f(X,X)\widehat{[X/\{c(0),c(1)\}]^{\circ}} \to^{*} 2$, the solution computed by the original definition is better in the sense that $[X/\{c(0),c(1)\}]^{\circ} \sqsubseteq [X/c(\{0,1\})]^{\circ}$ while $[X/c(\{0,1\})]^{\circ} \not\sqsubseteq [X/\{c(0),c(1)\}]^{\circ}$. This is also reflected at the term rewriting level, as seen with function g in Section 1. For these reasons we have chosen not to reuse bindings in s-unifications.

We have not obtained any formal result about the adequacy of s-narrowing yet, so we only have some conjectures. Regarding soundness, we think that $e_1 \mid S_1 \rightsquigarrow^{*} e_2 \mid S_2$ implies $e_1\widehat{\sigma_{S_2}^{\circ}} \to^{*} e_2$. For completeness we would like to prove a lifting lemma in the style of Hullot's one, but first we have to find an appropiate order to be used there. That is pretty difficult because that order should be able to express at the same time that the computed substitution neither instantiates too much, nor introduces redundant alternatives in the sets contained in the s-expressions in its range. Therefore it would be a combination of the usual instantiation preorder [4] and the preorder $\sqsubseteq$, that also should treat any expression and its opening as equivalent. Hence, a lot of additional work should be put in developing the theory of s-unification.

4   Maude Prototype and Sample Application

We present in this section our prototype and outline its implementation. Much more information can be found at http://gpd.sip.ucm.es/snarrowing.

4.1   Implementation Notes

We have implemented our prototype in Maude [6], a high-level language and high-performance system supporting both equational and rewriting logic computation for a wide range of applications. Maude modules correspond to specifications in *rewriting logic* [13], a simple and expressive logic which allows the representation of many models of concurrent and distributed systems. This logic is an extension of equational logic; in particular, Maude *functional modules* correspond to specifications in *membership equational logic* [5], which, in addition to equations, allows the statement of *membership axioms* characterizing the elements of a sort. Rewriting logic extends membership equational logic by adding rewrite rules, that represent transitions in a concurrent system. This logic is a good semantic framework for formally specifying programming languages as rewrite theories [14]; since Maude specifications are executable, we obtain an interpreter for the language being specified.

Exploiting the fact that rewriting logic is reflective, an important feature of Maude is its systematic and efficient use of reflection through its predefined META-LEVEL module [6, Chapter 14], a characteristic that allows many advanced metaprogramming and metalanguage applications. This feature allows access to metalevel entities such as specifications or computations as usual data. In this way, we define the syntax of the modules introduced by the user, manipulate them, direct the evaluation of the terms (by using on-demand strategies), and implement the input/output interactions in Maude itself.

An important point of our implementation is the use of an adaptation of the on-demand evaluation strategy natural narrowing [9], which generates a matching definitional trees for each function symbol and then traverses them to decide the position of the current term where narrowing must be applied. However, the description of natural narrowing presented in [9] used syntactic unification while traversing the definitional trees used by the technique, which leads to incompleteness in our approach. For this reason we have slightly modified the algorithm to use s-unification, which implies modifying the application of the unifier to the current term in order to preserve matching.

4.2 Prototype

The prototype is started by typing `loop init-s .`, that initiates an input/output loop where programs and commands can be introduced. These programs have syntax `smod NAME is STMNTS ends`, where `NAME` is the identifier of the program and `STMNTS` is a sequence of constructor-based left-linear rewrite rules, written in the following format:

```
(smod ICTAC is
  f(c(X),Y) -> h(X,Y) .
  h(X, c(Y)) -> g(X,Y) .
  g(0,1) -> 2 . ends)
```

where upper-case letters are assumed to be variables. We can first see how the tool solves s-unification problems with the `=?` command:

```
Maude> (g(0, 1) =? g(X,X) .)
  X -> 0 ? 1
```

We can evaluate terms with variables by using s-narrowing with the natural narrowing strategy, which is used with the command:

```
Maude> (narrowing f(X,X) .)
  {2, X -> c(0) ? c(1)}
```

The narrowing command returns the obtained result (2 in this case) as well as the required substitution, that in this case indicates that the variable X must take the set of values composed of c(0) and c(1). We can ask the system for more solutions with the cont command until no more solutions (as in the current example) are found:

```
Maude> (cont .)
No more solutions.
```

Finally, the system combines the on-demand techniques, that indicate the positions and the rules that must be used, with two different search strategies: depth-first and breadth-first. These strategies can be switched with breadth-first and depth-first.

4.3   The Dolev-Yao Intruder Model Using S-Narrowing

We present an implementation of the Dolev-Yao intruder model [7] in the line of [15] but now using s-narrowing, as proof-of-concept of our system. Note that the different features provided but these languages make the implementation rather different. We first define alice and bob as the possible roles or participants:

```
roles -> alice .
roles -> bob .
```

Decryption of messages is specified by using a ground simulation of the equality constraint, where we use the constructor enc to define the encryption of messages and inv as data constructor for inverting a key:

```
decrypt(enc(M,k1),inv(k1)) -> M .
decrypt(enc(M,k2),inv(k2)) -> M .
```

The protocol function associates to each participant a set of actions, which are the answers he or she returns for a given question. First, alice share a pair with the messages ma1 and ma2, using the key received as parameter to encrypt them. Note that *the same parameter is used in both messages*:

```
protocol(alice, X) -> p(enc(ma1, X), enc(ma2, X)) .
```

When bob receives the message ma1 encrypted with the k1 key he sends mb1; similarly, he sends mb2 when he receives ma2 encrypted with k2. In these rules and the one above lies the novelty of the s-narrowing approach: the variable X above must be bound to both k1 and k2 for bob to send the appropriate messages:

```
protocol(bob, enc(ma1, k1)) -> mb1 .
protocol(bob, enc(ma2, k2)) -> mb2 .
```

Finally, if alice receives a pair with the two messages from bob she sends the inverse of k1, that can be used to decrypt, for example, enc(ma1, k1):

```
protocol(alice, p(mb1, mb2)) -> inv(k1) .
```

The function discover models the messages that can be deduced by the intruder from a starting set of messages, where discStep combines the information generated by the responses of alice and bob to the queries of the intruder, and the one generated by the intruder by combining the starting messages according to the Dolev-Yao model:

```
discover(M) -> M ? discover(discStep(M) ? M) .
discStep(M) -> protocol(roles, M) ? dyStep(M) .
```

The auxiliary dyStep function can generate pairs of the elements, split these pairs, encrypt, and decrypt, thus representing the recombination of information the intruder is able to perform, according to the Dolev-Yao model for the intruder capabilities. Note that in this function the same variable M appears twice in the right-hand side of the first, third, and fourth rules. This variable will be bound to a set of values (built with the ? function symbol) in the s-narrowing, thus allowing the program to use different values:

```
dyStep(M) -> p(M, M) .
dyStep(p(M1, M2)) -> M1 ? M2 .
dyStep(M) -> enc(M, M) .
dyStep(M) -> decrypt(M, M) .
```

Finally, we define a function attack that returns true if the secret, ma1, is found:

```
attack(M) -> secret(discover(M)) .
secret(ma1) -> true .
```

Once this module is loaded into the prototype, we can use s-narrowing to find the initial information required to break the protocol, i.e. the instantiation of X for this goal:

```
Maude> (narrowing attack(X) .)
{true, X -> ma1}
```

This result shows the trivial answer: if we already posses the secret information the attack is successful. We can ask for more interesting answers with the cont command:

```
Maude> (cont .)
{true, X -> p(ma1,V:Exp)}
```

In this case the tool deduces that we can split the pair and use the secret. Using this command we find several other possible attacks, like:

```
{true, X -> p(enc(ma1,k1),V#1:Exp) ? p(inv(k1),V#2:Exp)}
```

which indicates that we can split the pairs and use the inverse of k1 to decrypt ma1. After many other results, the tool answers that the substitution k1 ? k2 allows us to find the secret by using it in the first message sent by alice.

5   Concluding Remarks and Ongoing Work

In this work we propose a new narrowing relation for called s-narrowing that is based on the novel notion of s-unification, a modification of syntactic unification that allows variables to be bound to sets of expressions. It has been devised with the aim of improving the completeness results of classic narrowing. Although we think that s-unification has great potential, we still have to develop the theory of s-unification so we can use it to prove the adequacy of s-unification. This proposal has been implemented in a Maude prototype that allows us to study their expressivity and possible applications. The prototype uses an adaptation to s-narrowing of natural narrowing [9] as its on-demand strategy, thus providing an efficient implementation that allows us to use the tool with complex examples—see http://gpd.sip.ucm.es/snarrowing for more programs.

Regarding future work, our priority is proving the adequacy of s-narrowing, which implies defining an adequate order over s-unifiers. Besides, we should prove that our adaptation of natural narrowing to s-unification is still complete and optimal. We also consider expanding the prototype with search commands in the style of Maude to specify the shape of the solutions, thus avoiding irrelevant results.

References

1. Antoy, S., Hanus, M.: Overlapping Rules and Logic Variables in Functional Logic Programs. In: Etalle, S., Truszczyński, M. (eds.) ICLP 2006. LNCS, vol. 4079, pp. 87–101. Springer, Heidelberg (2006)
2. Antoy, S., Hanus, M.: Functional logic programming. Communications of the ACM 53(4), 74–85 (2010)
3. Baader, F., Nipkow, T.: Term Rewriting and All That. Cambridge University Press (1998)
4. Baader, F., Snyder, W.: Unification theory. In: Robinson, J.A., Voronkov, A. (eds.) Handbook of Automated Reasoning, pp. 445–532. Elsevier and MIT Press (2001)
5. Bouhoula, A., Jouannaud, J.-P., Meseguer, J.: Specification and proof in membership equational logic. Theoretical Computer Science 236, 35–132 (2000)
6. Clavel, M., Durán, F., Eker, S., Lincoln, P., Martí-Oliet, N., Meseguer, J., Talcott, C. (eds.): All About Maude - A High-Performance Logical Framework. LNCS, vol. 4350. Springer, Heidelberg (2007)
7. Dolev, D., Yao, A.C.-C.: On the security of public key protocols. IEEE Transactions on Information Theory 29(2), 198–207 (1983)
8. Durán, F., Eker, S., Escobar, S., Meseguer, J., Talcott, C.L.: Variants, unification, narrowing, and symbolic reachability in maude 2.6. In: Schmidt-Schauß, M. (ed.) RTA. LIPIcs, vol. 10, pp. 31–40. Schloss Dagstuhl - Leibniz-Zentrum fuer Informatik (2011)
9. Escobar, S.: Implementing Natural Rewriting and Narrowing Efficiently. In: Kameyama, Y., Stuckey, P.J. (eds.) FLOPS 2004. LNCS, vol. 2998, pp. 147–162. Springer, Heidelberg (2004)
10. Hanus, M.: Functional logic programming: From theory to Curry. Technical report, Christian-Albrechts-Universität Kiel (2005)
11. Hullot, J.: Canonical Forms and Unification. In: Bibel, W., Kowalski, R. (eds.) Automated Deduction. LNCS, vol. 87, pp. 318–334. Springer, Heidelberg (1980)
12. López-Fraguas, F.J., Rodríguez-Hortalá, J., Sánchez-Hernández, J.: A Fully Abstract Semantics for Constructor Systems. In: Treinen, R. (ed.) RTA 2009. LNCS, vol. 5595, pp. 320–334. Springer, Heidelberg (2009)
13. Meseguer, J.: Conditional rewriting logic as a unified model of concurrency. Theoretical Computer Science 96(1), 73–155 (1992)
14. Meseguer, J., Roşu, G.: The rewriting logic semantics project. Theoretical Computer Science 373(3), 213–237 (2007)
15. Meseguer, J., Thati, P.: Symbolic reachability analysis using narrowing and its application to verification of cryptographic protocols. Higher-Order and Symbolic Computation 20(1-2), 123–160 (2007)
16. Middeldorp, A., Hamoen, E.: Completeness results for basic narrowing. Appl. Algebra Eng. Commun. Comput. 5, 213–253 (1994)
17. Riesco, A., Rodríguez-Hortalá, J.: Generators: Detailed proofs. Technical Report 07/12, DSIC (2012), http://gpd.sip.ucm.es/snarrowing
18. Riesco, A., Rodríguez-Hortalá, J.: S-narrowing for constructor systems: Detailed proofs. Technical report, DSIC (2012), http://gpd.sip.ucm.es/snarrowing
19. Rodríguez-Hortalá, J.: A hierarchy of semantics for non-deterministic term rewriting systems. In: Hariharan, R., Mukund, M., Vinay, V. (eds.) Proceedings Foundations of Software Technology and Theoretical Computer Science, FSTTCS 2008. LIPICS, vol. 2, pp. 328–339. Schloss Dagstuhl–Leibniz-Zentrum fuer Informatik (2008)
20. Runciman, C., Naylor, M., Lindblad, F.: Smallcheck and Lazy Smallcheck: automatic exhaustive testing for small values. In: Gill, A. (ed.) Proceedings of the 1st ACM SIGPLAN Symposium on Haskell, Haskell 2008, pp. 37–48. ACM (2008)
21. Thati, P., Meseguer, J.: Complete symbolic reachability analysis using back-and-forth narrowing. Theoretical Computer Science 366(1-2), 163–179 (2006)

Data Privacy Using MASKETEER™

Sachin Lodha[1], Nikhil Patwardhan[1], Ashim Roy[1], Sharada Sundaram[1],
and Dilys Thomas[2]

[1] Tata Consultancy Services
{sachin.lodha,nikhil.patwardhan,ashim.roy}@tcs.com
[2] Stanford University
{dilys,shas}@cs.stanford.edu

Abstract. Advances in storage, networks, and hardware technology have re-
sulted in an explosion of data and given rise to multiple sources of overlapping
data. This, combined with general apathy towards privacy issues while designing
systems and processes, leads to frequent breaches in personal identity and data
security. What makes this worse is that many of these breaches are committed
by the legitimate users of the data. Major countries like the U.S., Japan, Canada,
Australia and EU have come up with strict data distribution laws which demand
their organizations to implement proper data security measures that respect personal privacy and prohibit dissemination of raw data outside the country.

Since companies are not able to provide real data, they often resort to completely random data. It is obvious that such a data would offer complete privacy,
but would have very low utility. This has serious implications for an IT services
company like Tata Consultancy Services Ltd. (TCS), since application development and testing environments rely on realistic test data to verify that the applications provide the functionality and reliability they were designed to deliver. It
is always desirable that the test data is *similar* to, if not the same as, the production data. Hence, deploying proven tools that make de-identifying production
data easy, meaningful and cost-effective is essential.

Data masking methods came into existence to permit the legitimate use of data
and avoid misuse. In this paper, we consider various such techniques to come up
with a comprehensive solution for data privacy requirements. We present a detailed methodology and solutions for enterprise-wide masking. We also present
the data masking product MASKETEER™ , developed at TCS, which implements these techniques for providing maximum privacy for data while maintaining good utility.

1 Introduction

Suppose that a large corporation wants TCS to develop an application that is going to
use a lot of its sensitive data. Its main concern is about the security and confidentiality
of its data, for it needs to protect the interests of its clients and partners. TCS presents its
security practices and security audit certificates. However, the client corporations senior
management is not convinced. They fear that an application developer with access to
this data may use it maliciously. They suggest that the software development vendor
should use some fictitious data during the application development cycle.

A. Roychoudhury and M. D'Souza (Eds.): ICTAC 2012, LNCS 7521, pp. 151–158, 2012.

Application development and testing environments in TCS rely on realistic test data to verify that the applications provide the functionality and reliability they were designed to deliver. So it is desirable that the test data is similar to, if not same as, the production data. This leads to a deadlock situation, where in TCS needs the original data to develop a good product while owing to the privacy concerns of its clients the large corporation cannot give the data to TCS. One solution is to change or mask the production data when migrating it to the test environment. Masking the production data is *the process of systematically removing or transforming data elements that could be used to gain additional knowledge about the sensitive information.* That is the data is as realistic as possible for the test environment and also as fake as possible to respect privacy.

The objective of data masking is to maximize data utility in such a way that the masked data should have the same characteristics as the original data and at the same time minimize disclosure risks, that is, reduce the ability to identify an individual and reduce the ability to predict the value of confidential attributes. Note that there is a natural trade-off between the data privacy and its utility. An unmasked, original data would naturally have the highest data utility, but no privacy. On the other hand, randomly generated data would guarantee very high privacy, but almost no utility. However, if done properly, data masking should combine the best of both the worlds, that is, high data utility as well as high data privacy.

It is important to note that the results of the data transformation have to be appropriate in the context of the application. Data utility is dependent on the use of the masked data. For example for testing purposes larger volumes of syntactically correct data is needed with all the outliers. While for data mining or knowledge discovery the data needs to be as realistic as possible but completely de-identified.

The need for data masking is, in fact, ubiquitous. The contract software development is just one such striking example. Many useful properties can be extracted from the data even if it is masked. Data Mining is one such example, where certain statistical properties of the data set can be retained even by destroying their association with the original data. Data masking plays a key role when a certain version of privately held data has to be made public. Here goal is to keep the identities of the individuals who are the subjects of the data secret, and yet allow the legitimate users to make perfect use of the released data. This problem is very common in the health sector. Government agencies would need to solve the same problem while releasing census data. One more scenario where data masking is of crucial significance is location-based applications. Here the infrastructure should allow mobile users to avail all possible location-based information services without endangering their location privacy.

2 Masking Approaches

Over the years, statisticians, cryptographers and computer scientists have developed many models and techniques to address the trade-off between data privacy and its utility. We present here techniques that are robust, practical, and have simple quantification of privacy/utility. We explain them using Figures 1 and 2.

Randomization: In this approach, a data-element is replaced by a randomly chosen value from a given range or a dataset. The **Name** column of Figure 1 is replaced by randomly

SSN	Name	Gender	Age	Zipcode	Balance
101	Alice	F	31	94305	100
102	Bob	M	31	94308	24
103	Carol	F	32	94308	35
104	David	M	22	94125	85
105	Evelyn	F	34	90428	12
106	Frank	M	18	94308	73
107	George	M	35	92405	57

Fig. 1. Original Database table

SSN	Name	Gender	Age	Zipcode	Balance
501	Jane	F	31	9430*	110
438	Kurt	M	31	9430*	30
107	Lance	M	31	9430*	45
745	Molly	F	20	94***	75
885	Nancy	F	34	9****	25
990	Oscar	M	20	94***	60
210	Philip	M	34	9****	52

Fig. 2. Masked Database table

chosen names from a dataset of English Names in Figure 2. This technique provides strong identity protection.

Hashing and Encryption: In this approach, the data-element X is replaced by its image $h(X)$ where h is a suitable hash function. Ideally, one would want the hash function h to be collision-free, non-idempotent and one-way. Unfortunately no such h is provably known. But in practice, MD5, SHA-1, or Discrete Log based functions are useful. In the above example, encryption is applied to the **SSN** column. Encryption techniques are often efficient, but they provide low data utility by destroying semantics readily.

Shuffling: Shuffling randomly permutes the data-elements in a column. Thus, it can easily destroy relations between the columns. Shuffling is applied to the **Gender** column in the above example.

Perturbation: Another popular approach is to use perturbation techniques in order to hide the exact values, for example, adding noise to data and its numerous improvements. Here it is possible to capture the richness of data, say, with the covariance matrices . A simple perturbation technique could be addition of Gaussian noise to the input data. Let X be the input column. Then, the resultant Y would be $Y = X + e$, here e is the Gaussian noise taken from a standard distribution. Perturbation is applied to the **Balance** column in the above example.

Perturbation techniques, capable of providing high data utility and low disclosure risk, may require some pre-processing of the data to yield parameter values. Otherwise, they are fairly efficient. They are not very suitable if one wants to draw inferences with 100% confidence.

k-Anonymity: De-identifying the data by masking key attributes like **SSN** and **Name** may not protect identities since linking such a masked database with a publicly available database on non-key attributes like **Gender**, **Date of Birth** and **Zipcode** can uniquely identify an individual [10].

A table provides k-anonymity [10] if any attempt to link the identifying columns by external joins results in k or more matches. It means that each row in the table is forced to be same as at least $k - 1$ other rows in the potentially identifying attributes. Thus, identification of an individual by external join is with a probability of at most $1/k$. k-Anonymity is achieved by blocking all the dissimilar values (suppression) or by replacing them with a less specific common consistent value (generalization). Hence k-anonymity is a trade off between data utility and privacy. A higher value of k enforces a stricter privacy but more data loss. It is important to note that the data loss happens mainly for the potentially identifying attributes only, and the sensitive information (for example, say, medical condition of patients or cash balance) may appear as it is.

In the above example, we have applied 2-Anonymity to **Age** and **Zipcode**. The first three, the 4th and 6th, and the 5th and 7th rows in Figure 2 are identical in these two columns. Non identical values in **Age** are replaced by their average, while those in **Zipcode** are substituted by *. Hence anybody trying to link some known **Age** and **Zipcode** values with those in this table to find the **Balance** value would essentially be confused with *two* balance values. Thus, we are guaranteed 50% privacy.

k-Anonymity provides high data utility since it generalizes or suppresses only the quasi-identifiers. It also quantifies the identity disclosure risk at $1/k$. But the optimal k-anonymity is known to be NP-hard [2]. The known algorithms are either $O(k)$ approximations [2] or super-linear [1] or require time exponential in the number of columns [7] thus making them inefficient or expensive. We have designed and implemented a single pass algorithm that scales linearly in the number of columns [8] in our product.

A comparative overview of the different techniques is given in Figure 3. It is clear from this table that no single technique by itself can provide low disclosure risk, high data utility and work for high data volumes. But good news is that these techniques seem to complement each other. So their right combination may generate *good* data for us. A recent Forrester report [13] also advocates the same.

Technique	**Data Utility**	**Identity Disclosure Risk**	**Value Disclosure Risk**	**Scalability**
Randomization	Low	**Low**	**Low**	**High**
Encryption	Low	Medium	Medium	**High**
Shuffling	Medium	**Low**	High	Medium
Perturbation	Medium	**Low**	Medium	Medium
k-Anonymity	**High**	**Low**	High	Low

Fig. 3. Techniques Overview

3 Masking Challenges

The simple techniques described above are privacy-preserving and amenable to efficient implementations that scale well. Also appropriate choice of parameters for these techniques can help us retain much of the characteristics and patterns from the original data providing sound results. But there are other database constraints that limit the ability of masking. For example theoretically k-anonymity kind of solution would provably provide better privacy [10,8] and preserve some vital statistical properties, but if any one of the columns is declared as unique then a method like k-anonymity cannot be applied at all. This is where theory parts ways with practice and we have to consider the real world restrictions and accommodate them. They bring in serious engineering challenges. The database related constraints can be broadly classified as

Syntactic Constraints: The masked values should be within the limits specified in the database schema.

Uniqueness Constraints: For attributes that are marked as unique or as primary keys of the table, the masked values should be unique.

Relational Integrity: In order to support RDBMS, it is important to make sure that relational integrity constraints are satisfied, that is, the masked data-elements are propagated from the parent table to child tables.

Business Constraints: Much of the known business logic is encoded in company databases by linking multiple columns through some arithmetical or logical operations. The masked data should also satisfy these constraints.

Semantic Constraints: The data values in real life could be clustered around a certain value or have some distinctive association with values in other columns. From the masked value more information about the original values should not be obtained due to some uncharacteristic organization of the data.

4   Information Retrieval from Masked Data

Masking data is important for other purposes like outsourced data mining and remote analysis of data [10,7,9]. It is also useful for sanitizing data before putting it together from multiple sources [3,11,4]. Data put together from multiple sources could be **horizontally partitioned** or **vertically partitioned**. In case of horizontal partitioning the different data sources have data conforming to the same schema but contribute data about different rows or individuals. This allows more information to be learned from the combined data and also allows the discovery of rare facts as there is more data. In the case of vertical partitioning the different data sources provide data about the same rows or individuals. However the different sources provide different aspects, features or columns corresponding to the rows or individuals. This allows the inferring of knowledge correlating different columns, which may not be possible at any single data source.

Extracting information and learning functions from data distributed on multiple sources has been well studied for two decades. The area of secure multiparty computation [12,5] has allowed the computation of an arbitrary function expressed as a circuit on top of the original data sources. This can afford the sources the strongest notion of privacy, semantic security [6]. However more recent research tries to give the data sources weaker notions of privacy [11,3,4] while at the same time provide techniques for easy computation of a large class of useful functions on these distributed data sources.

It is important during data sanitization to retain as many properties of the data so that the data mining algorithm will be able to learn maximum amount of information from the database. For tools like MASKETEER™ we can come up with principles to decide the sanitization to be applied to different columns before giving it out for knowledge discovery. For identifier columns like SSN, drivers license number, voter number etc. randomization or hashing are popular techniques as they provide good data privacy. For other columns which are also available at other sources and are susceptible to join attacks (called quasi-identifiers in contemporary research), like date of birth, gender and zipcode k-anonymity [10,7,8] is the technique to be applied. Sensitive columns which are only available at the data source can be subjected to l-diversity [9] transformation. Perturbation can be applied to numeric columns, and shuffling can be applied to categorical columns.

5 Masking Best Practices

Data masking is not just applying a standard algorithm to all information. The choice of the masking algorithm and its parameters depend on the desired application of masked data, the database constraints and also the actual values present in the production data. There is no single right solution but a slew of things need to be taken care before sending the masked data out. After interacting with many TCS clients from banking, finance, and health sectors, as well as detailed market studies, we recommend these guidelines for achieving the best results:

1. **Analysis** It is important to understand the complexity of the application and data environment. This would help to identify sensitive data at the bare minimum (as opposed to all), understand data relationships and constraints defined both in data as well as in application. Sufficient rigor is needed to understand the flow of data across applications, various assumptions, both at the application and inter-application level. Even all the sources of the data, their flow and their copies needs to be known to avoid unwarranted data leakage. A good knowledge of the applicable regulatory laws is also essential for their compliance and coming up with a masking strategy.
2. **Setup** This part is crucial in the sense that the person, who has the authority to access the original data needs to setup the whole masking strategy of selecting the sensitive data, applying the right masking technique and taking into consideration the risks involved in identifying the data back. We suggest a few guidelines for using the algorithms described above.

   Randomization Useful for performance testing
     - Data is effectively useless
     - Privacy is maximum
     - Domain for randomization needs to carefully defined from some external source.

   Encryption and Hashing Useful for relinking back to original data
     - Semantic information about the data is lost to do any meaningful analysis.
     - Encryption and hashing algorithms should be coded with great care to avoid any possible error.

Shuffling Useful for testing as outliers are maintained
- Bad for non-uniformly distributed data.
- Data associations with other columns are lost.
- Original data is in the clear.

Perturbation Testing statistical analysis and data mining
- The amount of noise depends on the distribution of the data.
- Lot of advance research exist about such techniques and their guarantees.
- Applicable mainly to numerical data.

k-Anonymity Aggregate analysis and data mining
- Good against a weak attacker model
- Not good for unique and sparse data values.

All the data integrity constraints need to be in place for correct masking and only then the masking should be carried out. If the database size is huge then sampling would be a good idea to reduce processing time. If masking is a regular job then based on the strategy a schedule of the test bed creation can programmed.

3. **Masking** The actual masking of the data could be a time consuming process depending on the amount of data to be masked. There needs to be a way to recover from failures if any. At the end of masking, user must verify the quality of masking and identify any unintended variation on the statistical measure or amiss from the specification.

4. **Upload and Final Review** Once the masking is done, there should be some easy way to transfer the masked data to various target systems. A thorough check to ensure the inter-relationships and constraints of data are maintained is necessary so that the data is acceptable the to various applications using it.

6 Conclusion

MASKETEER™ supports most of the RDBMS using, say, JDBC drivers for connectivity. For example, it supports DB2, MS Access, Oracle, MS SQL Server, Sybase, Informix, MySQL, VSAM, TeraData, Advantage, DB2 on AS 400, PostgreSQL, IMX, XLS and also flat files. Its extensible framework allows users to plug-in other databases as well. MASKETEER™ is available on Mainframe, Windows, Linux ,Unix and Mac. The top sixteen customers of MASKETEER™ , including customers in different industry units like BFS, Insurance, Telecom and HiTech have masked totally hundreds of Gigabytes of data, stored in thousands of tables, spanning tens of databases.[1] This simple, intuitive, versatile, user-friendly and easy to use tool has served as a good business enabler for TCS and has won 2010 Golden Peacock Award for Innovation Product.

Acknowledgement. We will like to thank everyone who has helped in the making of MASKETEER™ , namely, Raghava Annaparthi, Yogesh Athavale, Sitaram B, Nandita Babu, Arpita Baheria, Aditya Bahulekar, Vijayanand Banahatti, Munesh Bandaru, Joel

---

[1] For more information and also evaluation copies of MASKETEER™ , please feel free to write to global.toolscare@tcs.com.
Visit our website at: http://www.tcs.com/offerings/technology-products/masketeer-data-privacy-solutions/Pages/default.aspx

C, Siddhartha Chatterjee, Amitesh Chellaramani, Prasenjit Das, Anshula Dhar, Rahul Ghodeswar, Hema Gopalan, Chandrashekhar Hire, Srinivasan Iyengar, Sumit Johri, Kalaiselvan K, Rahul Kanwar, Vijaya Kedar, Aniket Kulkarni, Amol Limaye, Sanooja M, Snigdha Nayak, Jayant Patil, Ellora Praharaj, Ravi Rajamony, Chandrama Ramkumar, Sasanka Roy, Barath S, Rupali Sagade, Aparna Sarnobat, Vinayak Sharma, Manish Shukla, Lovekesh Verma, Kumar Vidhani, Avinash Wagh and Leena Walavalkar. Special thanks to Professor Mathai Joseph ((now retired) Executive Director of TRDDC), K Ananth Krishnan (Chief Technology Officer, TCS), Professor Harrick Vin (Head of Systems Research Lab at TRDDC) and Arun Bahulkar (Head of Software Engineering Lab), Vijayalakshmi Gopal (Head of TCS Tools Group) and Dr. Santosh Mohanty (Head of Component Engineering Group) for their continued guidance, support, and encouragement for this activity. We would like to thank Professors John Mitchell, Rajeev Motwani, Hector Garcia-Molina, Dan Boneh and Jeffrey Ullman for leading the privacy research group at Stanford.

References

1. Aggarwal, G., Feder, T., Kenthapadi, K., Khuller, S., Panigrahy, R., Thomas, D., Zhu, A.: Achieving anonymity via clustering. In: Proceedings of the ACM Symposium on Principles of Database Systems, pp. 153–162 (2006)
2. Aggarwal, G., Feder, T., Kenthapadi, K., Motwani, R., Panigrahy, R., Thomas, D., Zhu, A.: Anonymizing Tables. In: Eiter, T., Libkin, L. (eds.) ICDT 2005. LNCS, vol. 3363, pp. 246–258. Springer, Heidelberg (2005)
3. Agrawal, R., Srikant, R., Thomas, D.: Privacy preserving OLAP. In: Proceedings of the ACM SIGMOD International Conference on Management of Data, pp. 251–262 (2005)
4. Dwork, C., Nissim, K.: Privacy-preserving Datamining on Vertically Partitioned Databases. In: Franklin, M. (ed.) CRYPTO 2004. LNCS, vol. 3152, pp. 134–138. Springer, Heidelberg (2004)
5. Goldreich, O., Micali, S., Wigderson, A.: How to play any mental game – a completeness theorem for protocols with a honest majority. In: Proceedings of the 1987 Annual ACM Symp. on Theory of Computing, pp. 218–229 (1987)
6. Goldwasser, S., Micali, S.: Probablistic encryption. Journal of Computer Security 28, 270–299 (1984)
7. LeFevre, K., DeWitt, D., Ramakrishnan, R.: Incognito: Efficient full-domain k-anonymity. In: Proceedings of the ACM SIGMOD International Conference on Management of Data, pp. 49–60 (2005)
8. Lodha, S.P., Thomas, D.: Probabilistic Anonymity. In: Bonchi, F., Malin, B., Saygın, Y. (eds.) PInKDD 2007. LNCS, vol. 4890, pp. 56–79. Springer, Heidelberg (2008)
9. Machanavajjhala, A., Kifer, D., Gehrke, J., Venkitasubramaniam, M.: l-diversity: Privacy beyond k-anonymity. In: Proceedings of the International Conference on Data Engineering, p. 24 (2006)
10. Sweeney, L.: k-Anonymity: A model for preserving privacy. International Journal on Uncertainty, Fuzziness and Knowledge-based Systems 10(5), 557–570 (2002)
11. Vaidya, J., Clifton, C.: Privacy preserving association rule mining in vertically partitioned data. In: Proceedings of the 2002 ACM SIGKDD International Conference on Knowledge Discovery and Data Mining, pp. 639–644 (2002)
12. Yao, A.: How to generate and exchange secrets. In: Proceedings of the 1986 Annual IEEE Symposium on Foundations of Computer Science, pp. 162–167 (1986)
13. Yuhanna, N.: Protecting private data with data masking: Technology can help meet certain compliance and outsourcing requirements. Technical report, Forrester Research (2006)

A Conformance Checker Tool CSPConCheck

Suman Roy[1], Sidharth Bihary[1], and Jose Alfonso Corso Laos[2,*]

[1] Infosys Lab, Infosys Ltd.,
44 Electronics City, Hosur Road, Bangalore 560 100
{Suman_Roy,Sidharth_Bihary}@infosys.com
[2] College of Engineering, Pontificia Universidad Catolica De Chile,
Libertador Bernardo OHiggins, 340-Santiago-Chile
pepecorso@gmail.com

Abstract. We describe a tool on conformance checking which verifies if the event logs (observed) match/fit the reference (arbitrary) business process, we call this tool "CSPConCheck". We use concepts from Communicating Sequential Processes (CSP), which facilitates automated analysis using PAT toolkit for conformance checking. Our tool takes process diagram and process logs as input and uses PAT tool to check for conformance.

1 Introduction

Process-aware information systems are widely used in industries these days as they provide precise description of business requirements; industrial regulatory business activities need to be monitored for auditing an organization (which is made mandatory by the new Sarbanes-Oxlay (SOX) Act [6]) in conjunction with business process modeling and simulation. A natural question arises - how closely the observed behavior follows or fits the specified behavior of a process. This is known as the problem of *"conformance"*. Our tool aims at checking conformance of business processes *wrt* their executions which can result in balancing 'Business-IT' platform in software development.

Information systems, such as WFM, ERP, CRM, SCM and B2B systems maintain foot prints of execution of the activities of processes, which is also called event logs or transaction logs. Each event log denotes one instance of the process. In this work, we use Business Process Modeling Notation (BPMN) to capture processes, which are modeled using an in-house tool, called InFlux. BPMN allows four types of constructs: event, activity, control-flow gateway and sequence (with their obvious meaning). The event logs of the model are recorded in MXML files as industry standard which provides the execution sequence of the activities, number of instances of the log and some other data.

We use a process algebraic language called *Communicating Sequential Process* (*CSP*) for generating compact representations of both the reference model and the event logs. CSP is a process algebra for describing processes or programs [3,5]

---

* This work was done when the author was an intern with Infosys Lab during Dec'11-Feb'12.

A. Roychoudhury and M. D'Souza (Eds.): ICTAC 2012, LNCS 7521, pp. 159–163, 2012.
© Springer-Verlag Berlin Heidelberg 2012

in which processes communicate via events. The CSP for the reference model is called the specification *(Spec)*. Also, we describe event logs in CSP, which is called the implementation *(Impl)*. Both *Spec* and *Impl* are trace equivalent *wrt* the process and event logs respectively. Moreover, we assume all the activities in event logs appear in the process descriptions also. Then CSP processes are fed into PAT model checker [7,4] and using the notion of trace refinement, it is checked whether the *Impl* trace refines *Spec*. In fact, *Impl* trace refines *Spec* if and only if the event log conforms to the process.

We have implemented these algorithms with PAT tool [7] at the back end. We call this tool "CSPConCheck". The algorithm for generating CSP descriptions for the processes is a modification of the algorithm used for converting UML diagrams to CSP descriptions [2]. The basic methodology of the mapping is to decompose the process model into atomic patterns and generate independent CSP description for each of these patterns. Then using the prefix operator the CSPs are merged to get the complete CSP description of the whole process. For activity and event nodes the CSP is a simple prefix process. For gateway nodes it uses different operators depending upon the type of the gateway. The nodes of the process model are considered as events in the CSP description and the edges of the model are treated as processes. The CSP description for an event log is generated by constructing a single CSP process for each trace in the log set and then aggregating all of them using the external choice operator. The CSP for each trace is a simple prefix process as the traces contain only the sequence of activities [1]. When both the CSP descriptions are fed to the tool it decides whether the logs conform to the process or not. In case of the latter, by using the shortest counterexample produced by PAT tool one can produce all the error traces in separate stages (an error trace is one which cannot replayed on the process). Also this tool can compute metrics related to conformance checking that shows the fitness, closeness, and appropriateness of the event logs with respect to the reference process models.

2   Description of CSPConCheck Tool

CSPConCheck is a JAVA based tool. The menu File is displayed on the GUI and allows the user to open event logs (in MXML format) and to import reference models (in XMI format) into the tool. We use our in-house process modeler (InFlux tool) to draw the process which generates an XMI file. The event logs are assumed to be in MXML format. The tool picks up the process models and relevant logs for further processing as driven by the menu. When the application is run, it generates one CSP file for each process model and event log. We have written Java code to convert XMI representation of processes to CSP descriptions in machine readable format of PAT tool. Similarly, another Java code is used to translate event logs to machine readable CSP description. Both these CSP descriptions are fed into PAT toolkit which is a windows based tool. The tool produces the result for conformance checking. A schematic diagram of this setup is shown in Figure 1. The tool offers a GUI for the visualization of the reference model and replay of logs in the form of path coverage. In case of presence of

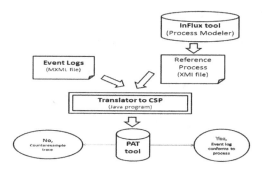

Fig. 1. A schematic diagram of the tool

error traces the tool has a Display module for showing all of them. Moreover, CSPConCheck has a Metric module which computes and displays the metric values for an event log set vis-a-vis the reference model.

3   Functionalities of CSPConCheck

In this section we will illustrate the funtionalities of the tool though a case study. Figure 2 portrays is a typical example of a business process followed in a bank for opening account, modeled using Influx tool. The process is free of control flow related errors like deadlock and lack of synchronization, and contains complex constructs like loops, unstructured gateways etc. We use the convention that an activity is labeled with an alphabet displayed against it. Table 1 shows the event logs for the process which comprise of sequence of activities i.e. traces and the corresponding instances of occurrence.

The reference model and the event logs are fed to CSPConCheck for conformance checking purposes, the tool reports that the event log does not conform to the reference model and displays the shortest counter example as $< A, B, E, C, H >$. The tool further shows all the error traces

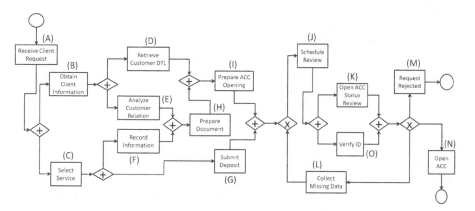

Fig. 2. An example of a bank account opening process

Table 1. Event logs for bank account opening process

No of instances	Log Traces
92	ACBEGFDHIJKOL
34	ACBGFEDHIJKOLJKOM
81	ABCDEGFHIJLKOJKOM
9	ABECHFGDIJKON
80	ACBDEGFHIJKOLJKON
2	ABCEGDFHIJKOLJKOLJKON

which cannot played on the reference model, *e.g.*, {*ACBEGFDHIJKOL, ABCDEGFHIJLKOJKOM, ABECHFGDIJKON*}. Subsequently it computes metrics for conformance checking and displays them in the Metric module.

4   Experimental Results

We perform some experiment related to conformance checking on industrial process models. For experimentation purposes, we use Intel Pentium 4 CPU, 2.8 GHz, a physical memory of 2 GB RAM on Microsoft windows XP Service Pack 3. The business processes which are modeled using InFlux tool arise in different business domains of Infosys, they are seggregated into three libraries A, B, and C depending on the domain. Lib A, B and C contain 20, 12, 18 models thus aggregating 50 models. Some of these models contain 65 XOR gates and a maximum of 5 AND gates. Now we use our tool for conformance checking. The experimental results are given in Table 2 which is accurate. The time taken for conformance checking is negligible, for most of the real life processes conformance checking can be performed quickly.

Table 2. Conformance checking of InFlux processes using PAT

Libraries	A	B	C
Avg no of explored states	38.6	56.78	72
Max no of explored states	84	136	110
Avg length of shortest counterexample	1.4	1.28	0.85
Avg analysis time (in seconds)	0.040	0.034	0.044
Total analysis time (in seconds)	0.807	0.414	0.796

References

1. Bihary, S., Koneti, J., Roy, S.: Process conformance using CSP. In: Proceeding of the 5th ISEC 2012, pp. 139–142. ACM (2012)
2. Bisztray, D., Heckel, R.: Rule-level verification of business process transformations using CSP. ECEASST 6 (2007)
3. Hoare, C.A.R.: Communicating Sequential Processes. Prentice Hall (1985)

4. Liu, Y., Sun, J., Dong, J.S.: PAT 3: An extensible architecture for building multi-domain model checkers. In: IEEE 22nd International Symposium on Software Reliability Engineering (ISSRE 2011), pp. 190–199 (2011)
5. Roscoe, A.W.: The theory and practice of concurrency. Prentice Hall (1997)
6. Sarbanes, P., Oxley, G., et al.: Sarbanes-Oxley act of 2002 (2002)
7. Sun, J., Liu, Y., Roychoudhury, A., Liu, S., Dong, J.S.: Fair Model Checking with Process Counter Abstraction. In: Cavalcanti, A., Dams, D.R. (eds.) FM 2009. LNCS, vol. 5850, pp. 123–139. Springer, Heidelberg (2009)

SmartTestGen+: A Test Suite Booster for Enhanced Structural Coverage

S. Raviram[1], P. Peranandam[2], M. Satpathy[2], and S. Ramesh[2]

[1] GM Powertrain – India, GM Tech Center (India), Bangalore 560066
[2] India Science Lab, Global General Motors R&D, Bangalore 560066

Abstract. Our work concerns with test case generation for structural coverage of Simulink/Stateflow (SL/SF) models. We have developed a tool called SmartTestGen which integrates multiple test generation techniques; experiments show that this tool performs better than some commercial tools. In this paper, we discuss a novel experiment. SmartTestGen uses random testing as one of the testing techniques. The random testing component first generates random test cases; the tool then *extends* these test cases to cover the uncovered targets. In our experiment, instead of using the random test cases as the initial seed, we use the test cases of an existing test suite. We have evaluated the impact of this modified testing process by considering 20 industrial strength SL/SF models.

1 Introduction

The Simulink/Stateflow (SL/SF) modeling notation [1] is widely used in industry. We have performed experiments with many test case generation techniques – random testing, model checking, constraint solving, mix of random testing and constraint solving etc – on a number of industrial-strength models. We observed that the coverage achieved by the individual techniques in a broader sense complement each other. With this aim in mind, we have developed SmartTestGen [5], an integrated test generation environment which uses various test generation engines, each engine implementing a different technique. We have observed that SmartTestGen outperforms some of the commercial tools [5].

Even if SmartTestGen performs better than an existing tool, it is unlikely to replace such a tool in an industrial setting where hundreds of engineers use the existing tool for test case generation. Introduction of such a tool could be seen as a disrupting technology. In this context, we present in this paper a supporting technology involving SmartTestGen which is more likely to be accepted by engineers; this we outline in the following.

SmartTestGen has a random testing component which generates random test sequences; thereafter, other components of the tool extend the traces due to the random test sequences to cover the uncovered targets. We have performed a novel experiment on SmartTestGen. We replace the random test sequences generated by the random testing component of SmartTestGen by the test sequences of an existing test suite – possibly obtained by some other test generator. In other words, the traces due to the test sequences of the existing test suite are extended

A. Roychoudhury and M. D'Souza (Eds.): ICTAC 2012, LNCS 7521, pp. 164–167, 2012.
© Springer-Verlag Berlin Heidelberg 2012

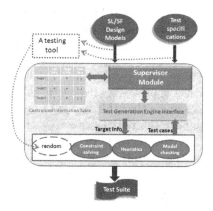

Fig. 1. SmartTestGen architecture: dotted lines show the modifications

by other components of SmartTestGen. We refer to this new use of SmartTestGen
as SmartTestGen+. Our main contributions:

- SmartTestGen+ tool using an existing test suite as its initial seed: we argue
  that this extension is a **supporting technology** and hence can be adapted
  with ease in an industrial testing process.
- Evaluation of SmartTestGen+ on 20 production quality industrial models: for
  our experiments, we have considered the test cases produced by a commercial
  tool, and compared its coverage results with those of SmartTestGen+.

2   SmartTestGen+ Architecture

Figure 1 shows the SmartTestGen architecture. This tool has three major components a) Centralized Information table (CIT) b) a set of test generation engines,
and (c) the Supervisor module.

The CIT contains all the target candidates (based on the coverage criteria),
to what extent they have been covered, what are the uncovered targets, and the
test cases for the covered targets. In addition, the CIT also stores targets which
have been shown to be unreachable.

SmartTestGen uses three test generation engines: (a) the **random** test generation engine to generate the initial test cases, (b) the **constraint solving and
heuristics** engine which essentially extends the traces of the current test sequences by using a combination of constraint solving and heuristics [3], and (c)
a SAL based **model checking engine** which is used to cover some given targets
by using model checking. Heuristics are primarily used to cover targets when the
constraints are non-linear or when the size of a constraint becomes too large [3].

The functionality of the **Supervisor module** is as follows: the **Random
testing** engine produces the initial test cases. Depending on the nature of the
targets, an appropriate test engine is selected for test case generation. This
goes on till all engines are invoked. The **constraint solving and heuristics**

engine extends the earlier test cases (a) by performing constraint solving with
respect to an intermediate point of a given test case [5], or (b) by using heuristics.
Model checking engine has two tasks: (i) it tries to generate test cases to cover
certain targets, and (ii) it also tries to show unreachability of certain targets.

For SmartTestGen+, we deactivate the random testing engine of
SmartTestGen. We now use a pre-generated test suite as the initial cases;
refer to Figure 1. We can assume that this test suite is produced by an existing
testing method. Once we have the initial test cases, the SmartTestGen testing
process is used to generate the subsequent test cases and the unreachability
proofs. In Figure 1, the portion with the dotted lines illustrate this modification.

3   Experimental Results

We consider the test cases already generated by the Reactis tool [2] as our initial
test suite. Note that Reactis is a highly successful tool, widely used in industry
for test case generation [2]. We then use SmartTestGen+ which enhances the
above test suite for additional structural coverage. We have considered twenty
SL/SF design models from various domains of automotive engineering such as
Active safety (AS), Performance traction control (PTC), Powertrain (PT), Heat-
ing ventilation and cooling (HVAC) and Electronic stability control (ESC). The
model sizes vary from 37 blocks to 901 SL/SF blocks. These models contain

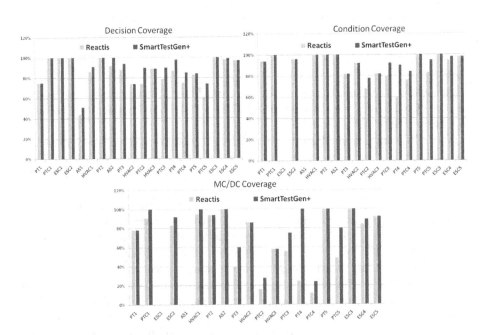

Fig. 2. Comparison of Decision, Condition and MC/DC coverages between Reactis,
SmartTestGen and SmartTestGen+

Stateflow blocks, multi-dimensional inputs, legacy code, non-linear blocks like multiplication and division, dynamic lookup tables and hierarchical triggering of blocks. Simulink Verification & Validation (V & V) tool box [4] is our common measuring platform. All the experiments were carried out on a machine with Intel Xeon 3 GHz and 3.5 GB RAM running Windows XP professional. The tool versions used were: Reactis 2009.2 and Matlab R2011.2.

We have compared the results of SmartTestGen+ with those of Reactis when used independently. The graphs in Figure 2 respectively show the comparison results for the decision, condition and MC/DC coverages of all the 20 models. For each model, the first bar shows the coverage by Reactis, and the second shows the coverage of SmartTestGen+.

SmartTestGen+ achieves (a) better decision coverage than Reactis in 50% cases, (b) better condition coverage than Reactis in 33% of the cases, and (c) better MC/DC coverage than Reactis in 55% of the cases. In the remaining cases the coverage results are equal.

Using the model checking engine, we have verified that the remaining decision targets of *PT1*, *HVAC2* and *PTC3* models are un-reachable. Similar advantages are also observed in case of models *PT1*, *HVAC2* and *PTC3* for condition coverage, and in case of *PT1* and *HVAC2* models for MC/DC coverage. The Reactis tester as of now does not address the issue of unreachability.

4   Summary

- We claim that introduction of SmartTestGen+ in an industrial setting is not a disrupting technology but a supporting technology. Consider a scenario in which the testers use the existing test generation tool to produce test cases. Based on the criticality of the applications, the test cases of this tool could be fed to SmartTestGen+, and test cases with higher coverage would possibly be obtained. All the testers need not learn SmartTestGen+, only a small percentage can use it. In this sense, the original testing process would be minimally affected.
- In case of automotive or aerospace domains, many applications are safety-critical. Therefore the added coverage we obtain would increase the reliability of the applications.

References

1. The Mathworks, http://www.mathworks.com
2. Reactis, http://www.reactive-systems.com
3. Satpathy, M., Yeolekar, A., Ramesh, S.: Randomized Directed Testing (REDIRECT) for Simulink/Stateflow Models. In: ACM EMSOFT 2008, Atlanta (2008)
4. The Mathworks, Verification and Validation Tool Box, http://www.mathworks.com/verification-validation/
5. Paranandam, P., et al.: An Integrated Test Generation Tool for coverage of Simulink/Stateflow Models. In: Proc. of IEEE DATE 2012 (2012)

Model Checking under Fairness in ProB and Its Application to Fair Exchange Protocols

David M. Williams[1], Joeri de Ruiter[2], and Wan Fokkink[1,3]

[1] Department of Computer Science, VU University Amsterdam
[2] Institute for Computing and Information Science, Radboud University Nijmegen
[3] Faculty of Mechanical Engineering, Eindhoven University of Technology

Abstract. Motivated by Murray's work on the limits of refinement testing for CSP, we propose the use of ProB to check liveness properties under assumptions of strong and weak event fairness, whose refinement-closures cannot generally be expressed as refinement checks for FDR. Such properties are necessary for the analysis of fair exchange protocols in CSP, which assume at least some messages are sent over a resilient channel. As the properties we check are refinement-closed, we retain CSP's theory of refinement, enabling subsequent step-wise refinement of the CSP model. Moreover, we improve upon existing CSP models of fair exchange protocols by proposing a revised intruder model inspired by the one of Cederquist and Dashti. Our intruder model is stronger as we use a weaker fairness constraint.

1 Introduction

Hoare's Communicating Sequential Processes (CSP) [1] is a process algebra for describing models of interacting processes in terms of the events that they perform. For two decades the Failures Divergence Refinement (FDR) checker [2] has been the principal tool for verifying properties of models expressed in CSP. FDR tests whether the CSP model of the system being analysed refines some specification of the system's desired behaviour, which is also written in CSP. This differentiates FDR from other model checkers which test whether a system satisfies some predicate expressed in a temporal logic.

In [3], Lowe investigated the extent to which it can be checked that CSP processes satisfy temporal logic specifications using a refinement-based model checker, such as FDR. He defined the atomic formulae of a temporal logic he considered appropriate for specifying communicating processes. Subsequently, as a result of his investigation into the limits of refinement testing for CSP, Murray concluded that alternative verification approaches besides refinement checking for CSP should be further pursued [4]. Murray demonstrated there exist useful predicates that cannot generally be expressed as refinement checks in any semantic model of CSP that FDR can handle. One such class of predicates includes liveness properties under Murray's refinement-closed notions of strong and weak event fairness.

A. Roychoudhury and M. D'Souza (Eds.): ICTAC 2012, LNCS 7521, pp. 168–182, 2012.

We demonstrate how to directly check whether CSP processes satisfy predicates expressed in Lowe's temporal logic using ProB, which is a tool that facilitates LTL model checking for a number of formalisms including CSP [5]. Not all of the operators offered by ProB for LTL model checking match the intended meaning of their counterpart in the grammar defined by Lowe. However, we shall show how one can express Lowe's temporal logic in ProB. By using ProB to check that a CSP process P satisfies a formula S, written in Lowe's grammar, we can be sure that checking $P \sqsubseteq_{\mathcal{RT}} P'$ in FDR guarantees that $P' \models S$. This is necessary when $P \models S$ cannot be expressed as a simple refinement check $Spec(S) \sqsubseteq P$ in $\mathcal{RT}$ or any other semantic model $\mathcal{M}$ that FDR can handle.

Model checking fair exchange protocols against liveness properties constrained by Murray's refinement-closed interpretation of fairness provides a practical setting exemplifying the ability of our approach to verify properties that cannot, in general, be tested for via simple refinement checks in FDR. Typically, a Dolev-Yao (DY) intruder [6], which is limited by perfect cryptography but has complete control over the network, is assumed when analysing security protocols. However, such an intruder model trivially breaks liveness properties, as the DY intruder may choose not to communicate any message sent. Fair exchange protocols often rely upon the assumption that at least some messages are communicated using resilient channels [7], which eventually deliver each message [8]. In this paper we construct a CSP model of an intruder constrained by a resilient communication channel assumption, based on work by Cederquist and Dashti [9], that can be used to verify liveness properties in fair exchange protocols using the fairness constraints proposed by Murray [4].

Following the necessary background on CSP provided in Section 2, Section 3 describes how the atomic formulae of Lowe's temporal logic can be expressed using the temporal operators offered when LTL model checking in ProB. Section 3 can stand alone demonstrating how, in general, one can reason about liveness properties constrained by Murray's refinement-closed interpretation of fairness using ProB, while Section 4 describes its application in the specific setting of fair exchange protocols. In Section 4 we construct an intruder model for reasoning about liveness properties of fair exchange protocols in the presence of resilient channels. Finally, Section 5 and Section 6 describe related and future work.

2   CSP

CSP is a process algebra for describing models of interacting processes in terms of the atomic events that they perform [1]. Processes, denoted by identifiers beginning in uppercase (e.g., P, Q), interact by synchronising on visible events, denoted by lowercase characters (e.g., a, b). The set of all visible (i.e., external) events is denoted by Σ, which does not contain the internal action τ. *Stop* is the deadlocked process that performs no event. The CSP process $a \rightarrow P$ performs the event a and then acts as P. The equation $P = a \rightarrow P$ defines a recursive process that infinitely performs a. The process $P \square Q$ may act as either P or Q, the choice of which is resolved by the environment. Similarly, the process $P \sqcap Q$

may act as either P or Q, but in this case the choice is resolved internally by the system. The difference between the internal and external choice operators is illustrated by processes P_3 and P_4 in Figure 1. The process $P \triangleright Q$ acts as P, although a timeout may occur, represented as an internal action τ, before P performs its first visible event. Following a timeout the process shall then act as Q, as illustrated by process P_5 in Figure 1.

The process $P \parallel_A Q$ runs P and Q in parallel, synchronising each occurrence of an event in A. Parallel composition $P \mathbin{|||} Q$ of processes that do not synchronise on any event are said to be interleaved. Note that prefixing binds tighter than each of the choice operators, which in turn bind tighter than the parallel operators. The process $P \setminus A$ acts as P but with each of the events in A replaced by the internal action τ. Finally, $P[\![^a/_b]\!]$ acts as P but with each occurrence of event b in P replaced by event a.

Various semantic models of CSP [10] enable us to distinguish between processes. The coarsest model is the *traces* model $\mathcal{T}$, which captures the traces of events which a CSP process might exhibit. A sequence of visible events, $\langle e_1, e_2, \ldots, e_n \rangle$, is a *trace* of a process P if there is some execution of P in which exactly that sequence of events is performed. For example, the set of all traces of $P_1 = a \to Stop \ \Box \ b \to Stop$, which offers the environment a choice between performing a or b before reaching deadlock, is the set $\{\langle\rangle, \langle a\rangle, \langle b\rangle\}$. The same set of traces can be generated by the process $P_2 = a \to Stop \triangleright b \to Stop$, although in P_2 a choice between performing an a or b is not offered to the environment. Instead a may be performed unless a timeout first occurs, after which b may be performed. If an internal action τ may be performed from some state, then the state is *unstable* (e.g., the initial state of P_2) otherwise it is *stable*. A process may stabilise by performing successive internal actions until a stable state is reached. A process is divergent if it can perform an infinite succession of internal actions. In this paper we only consider systems that are free of divergence.

Lowe proved that the refusal-traces model $\mathcal{RT}$ is necessary for capturing requirements expressed in the temporal logic defined in [3]. For this reason $\mathcal{RT}$ is the semantic model used in the remainder of the paper. Rather than recording only the traces of events performed by a process, $\mathcal{RT}$ also records the set of actions refused after each event performed, $\langle X_0, e_1, X_1, e_1, X_2, \ldots, e_n, X_n \rangle$. As refusal sets are recorded only in stable states, the null refusal symbol, $\bullet$, is used to denote the absence of refusal information. A null refusal may be recorded should an event occur from an unstable state or should no attempt be made to observe the refusal information. For example, the CSP process P_2 has the refusal trace $\langle \bullet, a, \Sigma \rangle$. Likewise, $\langle \bullet, a, \Sigma \rangle$ is a refusal trace of the process P_1, although $\langle \emptyset, a, \Sigma \rangle$ is a refusal trace of P_1 but not of P_2.

In addition to these denotational semantics of CSP, there exists an operational semantics based upon labelled transition systems (LTS) [10]. Any CSP process can be given as an LTS, consisting of a non-empty set of states, an initial state, a set of labels $\Sigma \cup \{\tau\}$, and a set of labelled transitions, where a labelled transition $S \xrightarrow{a} S'$ denotes that an action a can be taken from the state S to move to state S'. All figures in this paper illustrate a CSP process as an LTS.

CSP has a theory of refinement that enables us to compare the behaviour of processes. If a process S is refined by a process P, then all of the possible behaviours of P must also be possible behaviours of S according to some semantic model, e.g., $S \sqsubseteq_{\mathcal{RT}} P$ states that P refines S in $\mathcal{RT}$. The refinement checker FDR [2] automatically checks whether a specification of a property (S) is satisfied by a proposed model (P). If the result of a check is negative, a refusal trace that leads to the violation of the property is given.

3   Model Checking under Fairness Constraints in ProB

As an alternative to refinement-based model checking, one may directly test whether requirements expressed in a temporal logic are satisfied by the model of the implementation. In [3], Lowe investigated the extent to which it can be checked that CSP processes satisfy temporal logic specifications using a refinement-based model checker, such as FDR. The following grammar, as proposed by Lowe, defines a temporal logic for specifying communicating processes:

$$\phi, \psi ::= true \mid false \mid a \mid available\ a \mid deadlocked \mid$$
$$\phi \wedge \psi \mid \phi \vee \psi \mid \neg \phi \mid \phi \Rightarrow \psi \mid \Diamond \phi \mid \Box \phi \mid \bigcirc \phi \mid \psi \mathcal{U} \phi \mid \phi \mathcal{R} \psi \qquad \text{where } a \in \Sigma$$

Formulae in such a temporal logic regard properties of individual maximal paths of a process, i.e., an infinite refusals-trace of the process or a finite refusals-trace that ends in deadlock. $P \models \phi$ shall denote that a process P satisfies a formula ϕ if every maximal path of P satisfies ϕ. The formula a, for $a \in \Sigma$, states that the event a is guaranteed to be the first visible event performed. The formula $available\ a$ states that the event a is not refused whenever the process stabilises before performing its first visible event, while $deadlocked$ guarantees there is no next visible event. The logical operators $\wedge$, $\vee$ and $\Rightarrow$ have their usual meaning. The formulae $\Diamond \phi$ and $\Box \phi$ denote that eventually ϕ holds and that globally ϕ holds, respectively. $\bigcirc \phi$ guarantees that if there is a next visible action, ϕ holds after its occurrence. $\phi \mathcal{U} \psi$ states that ϕ remains true until ψ becomes true, whereas $\psi \mathcal{R} \phi$ states that ϕ remains true up to and including the state in which ψ becomes true, although ψ may never become true. The meaning each of these temporal operators is described more precisely in [3].

Lowe has shown that the temporal operators eventually $\Diamond$, until $\mathcal{U}$, and negation $\neg$ cannot in general be tested for via simple refinement checks. Furthermore, Murray has investigated the limits of refinement testing for CSP, demonstrating that there exist useful refinement-closed predicates that cannot in general be expressed as refinement checks in any standard CSP model that FDR can handle. Liveness properties under the assumption of strong or weak event fairness constitute one such class of predicates. It is common to make assumptions regarding which infinite behaviours of a system should be deemed fair when analysing an abstract model of a system. Many interpretations of fairness exist in the literature [11]; we shall follow Murray's interpretation of strong (resp. weak) event fairness assumption, which distinguishes itself from other notions of fairness [11–13] in its definition of $available$: an infinitely (resp. constantly) often $available$ event shall occur infinitely often.

$$SEF = \bigwedge_{a \in \Sigma} (\Box \Diamond \text{ available } a \Rightarrow \Box \Diamond a)$$

$$WEF = \bigwedge_{a \in \Sigma} (\Diamond \Box \text{ available } a \Rightarrow \Box \Diamond a)$$

Alternative notions of fairness [11–13], defined in terms of 'available' (or enabled) events without checking the process stabilises before performing its first visible event, consider 'available' a to be satisfied by $a \to Stop \rhd Stop$. Such a process is refined by $Stop$ in each of the semantic models discussed in Section 2, in which a is clearly 'unavailable'. The advantage of Murray's interpretation of SEF and WEF is that they are refinement-closed in $\mathcal{RT}$. As temporal properties constrained by SEF or WEF cannot in general be expressed as refinement checks for FDR [4], we propose the use of ProB [14], which enables LTL model checking of CSP processes using the following grammar [5].

$\phi, \psi ::= \text{true} \mid \text{false} \mid \text{[a]} \mid \text{e(a)} \mid \text{deadlock} \mid$
$\qquad \phi \& \psi \mid \phi \text{ or } \psi \mid \text{not } \phi \mid \phi \text{ => } \psi \mid \text{F}\,\phi \mid \text{G}\,\phi \mid \text{X}\,\phi \mid \phi\text{U}\psi \mid \psi\text{R}\phi \quad$ where $\text{a} \in \Sigma \cup \{\tau\}$

Not all of the above operators offered by ProB for LTL model checking match their counterpart in the grammar defined by Lowe. The temporal operators $\Diamond$, $\Box$, $\mathcal{U}$ and $\mathcal{R}$ can be expressed directly as their counterpart in ProB, i.e., F, G, U and R. The same is true for the boolean logic operators. However, Lowe's operators a, $available\ a$, $deadlocked$ and $\bigcirc \phi$ require further attention.

Note that Lowe's actions range over the set of visible actions, whereas ProB also enables us to express properties in terms of internal events. The formula [a] is satisfied along some linear execution path of a process if the first action taken is an a. This is true also of the internal action τ, i.e., [tau] is satisfied along some path if the first action taken from the current state along the path is the invisible action. A path satisfies e(a), where $a \in \Sigma \cup \{\tau\}$, if a is not refused from the current state, whether a is the next action taken along the path or not. X ϕ states that there is a visible or internal action leading to a next state, in which ϕ holds. Finally, deadlock is satisfied by a state from which no visible or internal actions are offered.

Despite their differences, we can express the four atomic formulae from Lowe's temporal logic that do not match their counterpart in the grammar offered by ProB in the following manner:

a $\to$ [tau] U [a]
$available\ a$ $\to$ [tau] U ((e(tau) & not [tau]) or (e(a) & not e(tau)))
$deadlocked$ $\to$ [tau] U deadlock
$\bigcirc \phi$ $\to$ [tau] U (deadlock or (not [tau] & X ϕ))

We captured the formula a, that states the event a is guaranteed to be the first visible event performed, by asserting that τ events are performed from each state on the path until an a is performed. Similarly, $deadlocked$, which guarantees there is no next visible event, is expressed by asserting that τ events are performed from each state along the path until deadlock is reached. The availability of a, defined as a is enabled whenever the process stabilises before performing its

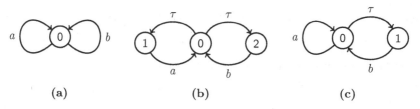

Fig. 1. CSP Processes: (a) $P_3 = a \to P_3 \,\square\, b \to P_3$; (b) $P_4 = a \to P_4 \,\sqcap\, b \to P_4$; and (c) $P_5 = a \to P_5 \rhd b \to P_5$

first event, is captured by stating that τ events are performed, until either some visible action is taken from an unstable state or, if, a stable state is reached, then a must be enabled. Finally, that ϕ is guaranteed to hold after the first visible action is captured as [tau] U (deadlock or (not [tau] & X ϕ)). Note that $\bigcirc\phi$ is vacuously true if there is no next stable state. The stronger statement 'there exists a next state and in it ϕ holds' is expressed by removing deadlock from the formula.

To illustrate his interpretation of strong event fairness, and prove that it cannot be expressed as a simple refinement check for FDR, Murray had us consider the three CSP processes depicted in Figure 1. As a is globally available in P_3, infinite executions in which an a never occurs are considered *unfair*. Likewise, infinite executions of P_3 in which a b never occurs are also unfair. Hence, $P_3 \models SEF \Rightarrow \Diamond a$ and $P_3 \models SEF \Rightarrow \Diamond b$.

Neither *available a* nor *available b* is satisfied in the initial state of P_4, which is visited infinitely many times in each infinite path. Thus, neither a nor b is globally available and so no infinite path of P_4 is considered unfair. Hence, $P_4 \not\models SEF \Rightarrow \Diamond a$ and $P_4 \not\models SEF \Rightarrow \Diamond b$. In process P_5, a can only occur from an unstable state, so infinite paths in which a never occurs must be deemed *fair*. In each state of P_5, whenever the process stabilises before performing its first visible event, only b is offered. Therefore, infinite paths of P_5 in which a never occurs must be deemed *fair*, whereas infinite paths in which b never occurs must be deemed *unfair*. Hence, $P_5 \not\models SEF \Rightarrow \Diamond a$, but $P_5 \models SEF \Rightarrow \Diamond b$.

Processes P_3, P_4 and P_5 can be checked against $SEF \Rightarrow \Diamond a$ and $SEF \Rightarrow \Diamond b$ in ProB using our definitions of a and *available a* above. The same results hold under Murray's interpretation of weak event fairness [4], which was also proved to not be expressible as a simple refinement check for FDR. Thus our definitions of a and *available a* also enable one to use ProB to check CSP processes against properties constrained by weak event fairness.

4   An Intruder Model in CSP for Verifying Liveness

When analysing security protocols it is standard to assume a Dolev-Yao (DY) intruder model in which the intruder has full control over the network [6]. Liveness properties are not satisfiable under this assumption, as the DY intruder may choose not to communicate any message sent. Fair exchange protocols rely upon the assumption that at least some messages are communicated using resilient channels in order to satisfy certain liveness properties [7]. In this section we construct a new intruder model for reasoning about liveness properties of fair exchange protocols in the presence of resilient channels. We analyse our models against fairness constrained properties in ProB, as described in Section 3.

Our intruder model is based upon the one of Cederquist and Dashti [9], who analysed μCRL [15] models of fair exchange protocols against μ-calculus expressions [16] of liveness properties constrained by fairness using CADP [17]. While the properties against which Cederquist and Dashti analysed their models are not refinement-closed, our liveness properties shall be. Should our models satisfy some liveness property constrained under Murray's SEF, then any refinement of our models in $\mathcal{RT}$ shall also necessarily satisfy the property.

We begin, in Section 4.1, with a description of a CSP model of the DY intruder proposed for reasoning about safety properties. We shall demonstrate why such an intruder model is insufficient for reasoning about liveness properties. In Section 4.2, we discuss how this issue was addressed by Cederquist and Dashti [9], but show that their properties are not refinement-closed. We address this issue in Section 4.3 by revising Roscoe's intruder model to enable the intruder to refuse to perform certain events. Finally, in Section 4.4, we propose a CSP model of the intruder that enables us to analyse fair exchange protocols in the presence of resilient channels with use of the fairness constraints described in Section 3.

4.1 Roscoe's Intruder Model for Verifying Safety

In [18], Roscoe's lazy spy was constructed to check whether the Needham-Schroeder public-key protocol satisfies certain safety properties in the presence of a DY intruder. Although written differently to better suit model checking in FDR, Roscoe's spy is $\mathcal{RT}$ equivalent to the following CSP process. The function $Close(X)$, defined in [18], returns the closure of a set of facts X under all deductions that the intruder can perform. The set $\mathcal{M}$ contains all the messages that can be sent or received in the protocol.

$$Spy^S(X) = \left(\begin{array}{c} \square \\ {}_{m \in X \cap \mathcal{M}} \\ \square \quad \square \quad learn.m \to Spy^S(Close(X \cup \{m\})) \\ {}_{m \in \mathcal{M}} \end{array} \right)$$

It is important to appreciate that Spy^S is willing to accept any incoming message on *learn* and is always willing to *say* any message it can construct as a consequence of the use of external choice in its construction. Spy^S cannot refrain from saying a message it can construct, should some other process synchronise on performing such an event. This is of little concern when considering only safety properties, as checked in the traces model of CSP, in which the intruder has little to gain by refraining from performing certain events. However, the same is not true when checking liveness properties. Let us consider the following system, similar to that described in [13], where $\mathcal{A} = \{A, B, I\}$ with A and B being the honest agents and I the intruder.

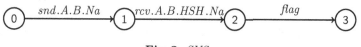

Fig. 2. SYS_1

$SND_1 = snd.A.B.Na \rightarrow Stop$
$RCV_1 = rcv.A.B.HSH.Na \rightarrow flag \rightarrow Stop$
$SYS_1 = (SND_1 \;|||\; RCV_1) \underset{\{|snd,rcv|\}}{\|} Spy^S [\![^{snd.x.y,rcv.y.x}/_{learn,say} \;|_{x \leftarrow \mathcal{A} \backslash \{I\}, y \leftarrow \mathcal{A} \backslash \{x\}}]\!]$

Spy^S allows any message to be sent by the other agents, and is willing to deliver any message it can construct from its current knowledge. We need only assume appropriate deduction rules for hashing and sequence generation for our examples, and in each the initial knowledge of the intruder is assumed empty. Figure 2 illustrates SYS_1, in which SND_1 and RCV_1 synchronise with Spy^S on events in $\{|\; snd, rcv \;|\} = \{snd.a.b.m, rcv.a.b.m \mid a \leftarrow \mathcal{A}, b \leftarrow \mathcal{A} \backslash \{a\}, m \leftarrow \mathcal{M}\}$. The sender, A, who behaves as the process SND_1, is willing to send a single message consisting only of a nonce, Na, to B. Conversely, the process RCV_1, which expresses the behaviour of the recipient B, is willing only to receive the hashed value $HSH.Na$. Clearly, A and B shall fail to communicate should they attempt to do so over any reasonable medium, as B is willing to receive none of the messages sent by A. However, the parallel composition of SND_1 and RCV_1 with the intruder process, Spy^S, fabricates curious behaviour. The signal event, *flag*, occurs in all maximal paths of SYS_1 only because the modelling of the intruder guarantees that it shall.

4.2 Cederquist-Dashti Resilient Channel Assumption

In [13], Dashti demonstrated that the fairness constraint that states that 'each infinitely enabled transition is infinitely taken' is insufficient to resolve this issue. It is important to appreciate the subtle differences between this fairness assumption and Murray's *SEF*, as described in Section 3. Firstly, Dashti's initial fairness assumption is described in terms of transitions, whereas Murray's is described in terms of events. Secondly, external and internal events are treated the same in Dashti's initial fairness assumption, but not in Murray's. Hence, the process P_5, illustrated in Figure 1, satisfies $\Diamond a$ under Dashti's interpretation of fairness but not Murray's.

Regardless of their differences, under either of these fairness constraints, *flag* is guaranteed to eventually occur in SYS_1 only because the modelling of the intruder guarantees that it shall. To resolve this issue, Cederquist and Dashti [9] proposed an alternative fairness constraint and to parameterise the intruder process by the set of all messages sent but not yet delivered, which we shall denote as Y. Initially the set is empty, but following each *snd* action the message, as well as the correct addressing information, is added to Y. Should a message be sent multiple times without being delivered, only one instance of the message is recorded within Y. This intruder satisfies Cederquist and Dashti's resilient communication channel assumption RCC_1 [9]. This assumption states that a resilient channel delivers the message at least once after the message has been sent multiple times.

As an alternative to Dashti's initial fairness assumption described above, Cederquist and Dashti propose the use of the μ-calculus notion of fair reachability of an action, which states that whatever path has been taken previously, there remains a path in which the action finally occurs. By distinguishing those messages sent but not yet received and all others messages delivered by the intruder as rcv and $rcv^\dagger$, respectively, Cederquist and Dashti check that whatever path has been taken previously, there remains a path containing no $rcv^\dagger$'s in which the signal event $flag$ finally occurs. Such a property is not refinement-closed. Consider again the examples illustrated in Figure 1. In each process P_3, P_4 and P_5, no matter what path has been taken previously, there always exist a path in which a occurs. However, removing the nondeterminism from P_4, for example by demanding that the b path is always taken, refines P_4 in each semantic model discussed in Section 2. In particular, $P_4 \sqsubseteq_{\mathcal{RT}} Q$ where $Q = b \rightarrow Q$. Hence, although P_4 satisfies fair reachability, after refinement of P_4 this property may no longer be satisfied.

4.3   An Intruder Model without Resilient Channels

To maintain the use of CSP's theory of refinement, we wish to analyse our models against liveness properties expressed in Lowe's temporal logic constrained by Murray's SEF, as presented in Section 3. Therefore, rather than adopting an alternative fairness constraint, we have adapted the model of the intruder to include behaviour enabling the intruder to refuse to cooperate. Our intruder model enables the intruder to nondeterministically choose the set of messages he is willing to send at any given time, from the set of all subsets of the messages he can construct at that time. CSP's notion of external choice and the use of the semantic model, $\mathcal{RT}$, are well-suited to modelling the intruder behaviour in this way. We begin by revising the process Spy^S to include behaviour enabling the intruder to refuse to cooperate in this manner.

$$Spy^{L_0}(X) = \bigsqcap_{S \in Set(X \cap \mathcal{M})} \left(\begin{array}{l} \square_{m \in S} \; say.m \rightarrow Spy^{L_0}(X) \\ \square \; \square_{m \in \mathcal{M}} \; learn.m \rightarrow Spy^{L_0}(Close(X \cup \{m\})) \end{array} \right)$$

The process $Spy^{L_0}(X)$ presents an initial attempt at modelling the intruder's ability to refuse to cooperate. However, the result of the renaming within the process $Spy^{L_0}(X)[\![^{snd.x.y,rcv.y.x}/_{learn,say} |_{x \leftarrow \mathcal{A}\backslash\{I\}, y \leftarrow \mathcal{A}\backslash\{x\}}]\!]$ is such that the intruder chooses whether or not he is willing to perform a rcv event regarding (for example) Na. It does not give the intruder the ability to offer $rcv.A.B.Na$ whilst also refusing $rcv.B.A.Na$. The process $Spy^L(X)$, constructed directly of snd and rcv events, provides this necessary additional behaviour.

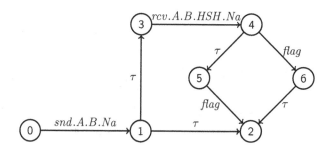

Fig. 3. $(SND_1 \;|||\; RCV_1) \;\underset{\{|snd,rcv|\}}{\|}\; Spy^L$

$$Spy^L(X) =$$

$$\underset{\mathcal{S} \in Set\left(\left\{ (x,y,n) \middle| \begin{matrix} x \leftarrow \mathcal{A} \\ y \leftarrow \mathcal{A} \setminus \{x,I\} \\ n \leftarrow (X \cap \mathcal{M}) \end{matrix} \right\}\right)}{\sqcap} \left(\square \; \underset{(a,b,m) \in \left\{ (x,y,n) \middle| \begin{matrix} y \leftarrow \mathcal{A} \\ x \leftarrow \mathcal{A} \setminus \{y,I\} \\ n \leftarrow \mathcal{M} \end{matrix} \right\}}{\square} \begin{matrix} \underset{(a,b,m) \in \mathcal{S}}{\square} \; rcv.a.b.m \rightarrow Spy^L(X) \\ \\ snd.a.b.m \rightarrow \\ Spy^L(Close(X \cup \{m\})) \end{matrix} \right)$$

Replacing Spy^S with Spy^L in SYS_1 produces the state space illustrated in Figure 3. From the initial state the intruder does not hold enough knowledge to generate any messages, so $snd.A.B.Na$ is guaranteed to be the first action performed. Following $snd.A.B.Na$, the intruder chooses which subset of messages he is willing to deliver from the set of all messages he can construct. Hence, he chooses between performing $rcv.A.B.HSH.Na$ or refusing to perform $rcv.A.B.HSH.Na$. If he chooses to refuse the event, then no further actions are possible, otherwise $rcv.A.B.HSH.Na$ is performed in synchrony with RCV_1. RCV_1 is then able to perform the event $flag$, while the intruder can again resolve his internal choice. Thus the interleaving of $flag$ and τ actions means that they may occur in either order before the system deadlocks. As a consequence of our revisions to the intruder model, the signal event $flag$ no longer occurs in all maximal paths of SYS_1, as was desired.

With full control over the network, the DY intruder may now choose not to communicate any message sent. As a result, liveness properties, such as $\Diamond flag$, can never be guaranteed in this model, even under the assumption of strong event fairness. It is for this reason that fair exchange protocols rely upon the assumption that at least some messages are communicated over resilient channels [7]. Our revised intruder, which can choose not to communicate any message, requires further revision to capture Cederquist and Dashti's resilient channel assumption, RCC_1. First let us motivate such a revision to the intruder model via a second example.

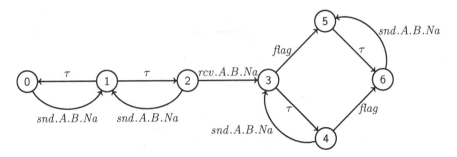

Fig. 4. SYS_2

$$SND_2 = snd.A.B.Na \rightarrow SND_2$$
$$RCV_2 = rcv.A.B.Na \rightarrow flag \rightarrow Stop$$
$$SYS_2 = (SND_2 ||| RCV_2) \underset{\{|snd,rcv|\}}{\|} Spy^L$$

Figure 4 illustrates the state space of such a system. Initially, $snd.A.B.Na$ is guaranteed to be the first action performed, as the intruder does not hold enough knowledge to generate any messages. Following $snd.A.B.Na$, the intruder again chooses which messages he is willing to deliver from the set of all subsets of the messages he can construct. Hence, he chooses between performing or refusing to perform $rcv.A.B.Na$. If he chooses to refuse the event, then the system returns to the initial state, otherwise either $snd.A.B.Na$ is again performed in synchrony with SND_2, returning to a previously visited state, or $rcv.A.B.Na$ is performed in synchrony with RCV_2. In the latter case, RCV_2 is able to perform the event $flag$, while the intruder can again resolve his internal choice. Thus, the interleaving of the $flag$ and τ actions means that they may occur in either order, after which $snd.A.B.Na$ is the only possible event, in each case returning the system to a previously visited state.

Using ProB we can verify that SYS_2 does not satisfy $\Diamond flag$. The system includes infinite execution paths in which (i) the intruder always chooses to refuse the delivery of Na, and (ii) the intruder is willing to perform $rcv.A.B.Na$, but infinitely often $snd.A.B.Na$ is taken instead.

4.4 An Intruder Model with Resilient Channels

We shall revise the intruder model such that he is unable to refuse to deliver messages that have been sent but not yet delivered. Such a revised model can then be analysed under the assumption of strong event fairness.

$$Spy^{L\dagger}(X, Y) =$$

$$\underset{S \in Set\left(\left\{(x,y,n) \middle| \begin{smallmatrix} x \leftarrow A \\ y \leftarrow A \setminus \{x,I\} \\ n \leftarrow (X \cap M) \setminus Y \end{smallmatrix}\right\}\right)}{\bigsqcap} \left(\begin{array}{l} \underset{(a,b,m) \in S \cup Y}{\Box} rcv.a.b.m \rightarrow Spy^L(X, Y \setminus \{(a,b,m)\}) \\ \underset{(a,b,m) \in \left\{(x,y,n) \middle| \begin{smallmatrix} y \leftarrow A \\ x \leftarrow A \setminus \{y,I\} \\ n \leftarrow M \end{smallmatrix}\right\}}{\Box} \begin{array}{l} snd.a.b.m \rightarrow \\ Spy^L(Close(X \cup \{m\}), Y \cup \{(a,b,m)\}) \end{array} \end{array} \right)$$

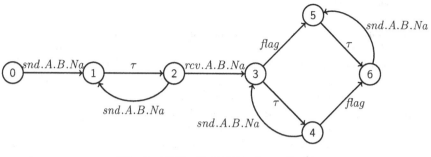

Fig. 5. $(SND_2 \;|||\; RCV_2) \;\underset{\{|snd,rcv|\}}{\|}\; Spy^{L\dagger}$

Like Cederquist and Dashti's intruder model, our process $Spy^{L\dagger}$ is parameterised by the set Y of all messages sent but not yet delivered. Initially the set is empty. Following each $snd.a.b.m$ event, the message as well as the correct addressing information (a, b, m) is added to Y. Should a message be sent multiple times without being delivered, only one instance of the message is recorded within Y, as this is the information required to assure the intruder satisfies RCC_1. As the correct addressing information must be recorded in Y, $Spy^{L\dagger}(X, Y)$ is constructed explicitly of snd and rcv events, rather than renaming a process constructed of simpler $learn$ events. The consequence of the other revisions is that the intruder never refuses the delivery of messages contained in Y, but remains able to refuse any subset of the remaining messages he can construct. We have used ProB to successfully check that the revised model SYS_2, as illustrated in Figure 5, satisfies $SEF \Rightarrow \Diamond flag$ using the definitions from Section 3.

4.5   Conclusion

The intruder model $Spy^{L\dagger}$ constructed in this section is suitable for analysing fair exchange protocols in the presence of resilient channels and a DY intruder. Our analyses needed to be closed under refinement to be sure that the system will be secure under any refinements of the nondeterministic intruder, which represent different attack strategies. Murray's refinement-closed interpretation of strong event fairness SEF was added as a premise of the liveness property being checked. The consequence of this fairness constraint was that paths in which the intruder never delivers some message from Y, supposing that the recipient is always willing to accept it, were disregarded as unfair paths.

A fair exchange protocol may only require certain messages to be sent via resilient channels. Minimal changes to Spy^L are required to model such a system. Distinguishing between messages sent over non-resilient and resilient channels as snd and $sndr$, respectively, is sufficient to record which messages should be contained in Y.

5   Related Work

Building upon Schneider's analysis [19] and drawing from the work of Evans [20], Wei and Heather analysed the Zhou-Gollmann non-repudiation protocol [21] protocol using CSP and FDR [22] as well as the theorem prover PVS [23]. The contribution that distinguishes our CSP intruder model from those that preceded it is the modelling of the resilient channel. Wei and Heather modelled the resilient communication between the trusted third party and the other agents as a synchronous communication over a reliable and secure channel. Originally, Zhou and Gollmann assumed that the channel, over which the third party sends messages, will eventually be available, i.e., that there exists a resilient channel between the third party and other agents. Our intruder model increases the possible behaviours of the intruder, who is able to record which messages are sent over the resilient channel and delay the delivery of such messages. He must only not indefinitely delay the delivery of such messages, assuming the recipient remains willing to receive it. Thus our intruder model aims to more faithfully capture the assumptions of resilience in CSP models of fair exchange protocols.

By adopting Murray's refinement-closed interpretation of fairness [4] we maintain CSP's theory of refinement. Furthermore, such a notion of fairness is weaker than the one of Cederquist and Dashti [9]. Rather than treating all outgoing external and internal actions fairly, we demand only that infinitely often available (visible) events are treated fairly. As we adopt a weaker notion of fairness, our intruder model is stronger, because less of its behaviour is restricted. Even under this stronger intruder model we have been successful in checking the satisfaction of liveness properties in the examples given in this paper.

The Process Analysis Toolkit [24] has specific functionality for model checking CSP processes under various fairness assumptions. However, such notions of fairness do not match the ones proposed by Murray and are not refinement-closed. The process P_4, illustrated in Figure 1, satisfies $\Diamond b$ under the PAT interpretation of strong event fairness, but it also satisfies $\Diamond a$ as the internal event τ is treated the same as visible actions. Refining P_4 by removing the unstable a action would cause the process to no longer satisfy $\Diamond a$, so PAT's interpretation of strong event fairness is not refinement-closed.

6   Discussion and Future Work

In [4] it was shown that Murray's refinement-closed interpretation of strong and weak event fairness cannot be expressed as refinement checks in the semantic models supported by FDR. We therefore propose the use of ProB, as we have shown that its LTL model checker [5] can be used to model check liveness properties under such fairness constraints, which were expressed in Lowe's temporal logic [3]. More generally, we have shown how any formula of Lowe's temporal logic can be expressed in the grammar offered by ProB for LTL model checking, even though the two grammars differ.

Subsequently, using Roscoe's intruder model [18] as a foundation, we proposed a new intruder model for reasoning about liveness properties in security protocols in the presence of resilient channels. Roscoe's intruder model [18] required revision for this purpose, since this model of the intruder can drop all messages, thus trivially violating all liveness properties. Furthermore, an example was provided to demonstrate that Roscoe's intruder model can in some sense help in satisfying liveness properties that would not otherwise be satisfied in the presence of a reliable medium. Such observations were first made in [13], which justified the construction of a new intruder model in [9]. The primary distinction between our approach to that in [9] is the use of Murray's refinement-closed interpretation of strong event fairness. Our analyses needed to be closed under refinement to be sure that the system will be secure under any and all refinements of the nondeterministic intruder, which represent different attack strategies.

The examples provided in this paper to demonstrate and justify our approach were necessarily simplistic to enable ProB to complete the checks in reasonable time. The application of our approach to more meaningful fair exchange protocols, such as those described in [7], remains future research. Murray's fairness constraint was added as a premise of the liveness property, i.e., $SEF \Rightarrow \phi$, where SEF was constructed as the conjunction over the potentially large set of events Σ. This method of model checking under fairness constraints is inefficient, as the time complexity of LTL model checking is exponential in the size of the formula [24]. Rather than incorporating the fairness constraint as a premise of the property being checked, dedicated algorithms have been implemented within PAT to analyse CSP models against LTL properties under fairness. In Section 5 we demonstrated that PAT's interpretation of strong event fairness is not refinement-closed, so investigating how to efficiently check liveness properties under SEF remains an open research question.

When model checking CTL, fairness constraints cannot simply be added as a premise of the property being checked, as they are not typically expressible in branching time logic. It is worth considering how the work in [3] can be adapted to check CSP processes against CTL properties that are closed under refinement. Furthermore, it would be worthwhile to consider the use of more expressive temporal logics when model checking CSP processes. The relationship between LTL, CTL, CTL* and μ-calculus is well documented, but it is unclear precisely how the limits of refinement testing for model checking CSP processes relate.

Acknowledgements. This work is supported by the Netherlands Organisation for Scientific Research (NWO). Our thanks go to Mohammad Torabi Dashti and Toby Murray for discussions relating to their work as well as comments provided on previous drafts of this paper. We also thank Gavin Lowe for discussing his paper. We would like to thank the ProB team, in particular Ivaylo Dobrikov, for providing notable tool support. Finally, we would like to thank the anonymous reviewers for their constructive comments.

References

1. Hoare, C.A.R.: Communicating Sequential Processes. Prentice-Hall (1985)
2. Gardiner, P., Goldsmith, M., Hulance, J., Jackson, D., Roscoe, B., Scattergood, B., Armstrong, P.: FDR Manual. Oxford University (2010)
3. Lowe, G.: Specification of communicating processes: Temporal logic versus refusals-based refinement. Formal Aspects of Computing 20, 277–294 (2008)
4. Murray, T.: On the limits of refinement-testing for model-checking CSP. Formal Aspects of Computing (to appear, 2012)
5. Plagge, D., Leuschel, M.: Seven at one stroke: LTL model checking for high-level specifications in B, Z, CSP, and more. Software Tools for Technology Transfer 12, 9–21 (2010)
6. Dolev, D., Yao, A.: On the security of public key protocols. IEEE Transactions on Information Theory 29, 198–208 (1983)
7. Kremer, S., Markowitch, O., Zhou, J.: An intensive survey of fair non-repudiation protocols. Computer Communications 25, 1606–1621 (2002)
8. Asokan, N.: Fairness in electronic commerce. Technical report, University of Waterloo (1998)
9. Cederquist, J., Torabi Dashti, M.: An intruder model for verifying liveness in security protocols. In: Proc. FMSE 2006, pp. 23–32. ACM (2006)
10. Roscoe, A.: Understanding Concurrent Systems. Springer (2010)
11. Francez, N.: Fairness. Springer (1986)
12. Puhakka, A., Valmari, A.: Liveness and Fairness in Process-Algebraic Verification. In: Larsen, K.G., Nielsen, M. (eds.) CONCUR 2001. LNCS, vol. 2154, pp. 202–217. Springer, Heidelberg (2001)
13. Torabi Dashti, M.: Keeping Fairness Alive. PhD thesis, VU University Amsterdam (2008)
14. Leuschel, M., Butler, M.: ProB: An automated analysis toolset for the B method. Software Tools for Technology Transfer 10, 185–203 (2008)
15. Fokkink, W.J.: Modelling Distributed Systems. Springer (2007)
16. Mateescu, R., Sighireanu, M.: Efficient on-the-fly model checking for regular alternation-free mu-calculus. Science of Computer Programming 46, 255–281 (2003)
17. Garavel, H., Lang, F., Mateescu, R., Serwe, W.: CADP 2010: A Toolbox for the Construction and Analysis of Distributed Processes. In: Abdulla, P.A., Leino, K.R.M. (eds.) TACAS 2011. LNCS, vol. 6605, pp. 372–387. Springer, Heidelberg (2011)
18. Roscoe, A.W.: The Theory and Practice of Concurrency. Prentice-Hall (1998)
19. Schneider, S.: Formal analysis of a non-repudiation protocol. In: Proc. CSF 1998, pp. 54–65. IEEE (1998)
20. Evans, N., Schneider, S.: Verifying security protocols with PVS: Widening the rank function approach. Journal of Logic and Algebraic Programming 64, 253–284 (2005)
21. Zhou, J., Gollman, D.: A fair non-repudiation protocol. In: S&P 1996, pp. 55–61. IEEE (1996)
22. Wei, K., Heather, J.: Towards Verification of Timed Non-repudiation Protocols. In: Dimitrakos, T., Martinelli, F., Ryan, P.Y.A., Schneider, S. (eds.) FAST 2005. LNCS, vol. 3866, pp. 244–257. Springer, Heidelberg (2006)
23. Wei, K., Heather, J.: A Theorem-Proving Approach to Verification of Fair Non-repudiation Protocols. In: Dimitrakos, T., Martinelli, F., Ryan, P.Y.A., Schneider, S. (eds.) FAST 2006. LNCS, vol. 4691, pp. 202–219. Springer, Heidelberg (2007)
24. Sun, J., Liu, Y., Dong, J.S., Pang, J.: PAT: Towards Flexible Verification under Fairness. In: Bouajjani, A., Maler, O. (eds.) CAV 2009. LNCS, vol. 5643, pp. 709–714. Springer, Heidelberg (2009)

Model Checking of OSEK/VDX OS Design Model Based on Environment Modeling

Kenro Yatake and Toshiaki Aoki

Japan Advanced Institute of Science and Technology,
1-1 Asahidai, Nomi, Ishikawa 923-1292, Japan
{k-yatake,toshiaki}@jaist.ac.jp

Abstract. This paper presents a model-checking experiment for a design model of a practical real-time operating system (RTOS) based on environment modeling. In previous work, we developed a tool called the environment generator to generate environments for model-checking general RTOS models in Spin. This tool takes a general model of the environments, called the environment model, as an input and generates all possible environments within the bounds of the model. Here, we applied the tool to verify the design model of an OSEK/VDX OS, the RTOS for controlling automotive systems. In this paper, we explain the details of constructing the environment models for verifying various aspects of the RTOS. We also show the results of an experiment using our tool.

1 Introduction

Nowadays, many embedded systems are using real-time operating systems (RTOSs) to realize high functionality and responsiveness. RTOSs are required to have high reliability because they are commonly used in a wide variety of systems. Since failures in embedded systems lead to huge recalling costs, and can even endanger human lives, it is important to ensure the correctness of their behavior. Currently, we are working on a project to verify the design model of an OSEK/VDX OS [8] (hereinafter, the RTOS model) by model checking. OSEK/VDX is the OS specification for controlling automotive systems. The RTOS model that we have developed is described in Promela, the input language of the Spin model checker [6]. We focus on the verification of the task scheduling algorithm. This algorithm is based on priorities, and its correctness is critically important for the safety of automobiles. Specifically, high-priority tasks such as life-saving units must always be activated before all low priority tasks.

To apply model checking to the RTOS model, we need to construct an *environment* that provides function calls to the RTOS model. Such an environment is an application consisting of tasks and resources, and is necessary as a driver to close the behavior of the RTOS model. According to the number of tasks and resources and their priorities, there are a number of environmental variations. For example, one environment may consist of 2 tasks with priorities 1 and 2, whereas another environment consists of 3 tasks with priorities 1, 2 and 3,

A. Roychoudhury and M. D'Souza (Eds.): ICTAC 2012, LNCS 7521, pp. 183–197, 2012.

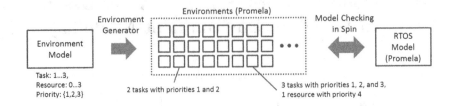

Fig. 1. Environment generator

and a resource with priority 4. Since exhaustively constructing all variations by hand is infeasible, we have developed a tool called the *environment generator* to automate the process. Fig. 1 summarizes the concepts behind the tool. The environment generator first takes a general model of the environments, called the *environment model*, as an input. This model consists of class and statechart models, whose notations are based on the unified modeling language (UML) [7], to describe the structure and behavior of the environment. The environment generator then generates all possible environments within the bounds of the model. Finally, each generated environment is model-checked in combination with the RTOS model in Spin.

For the current study, we applied this tool to verify the RTOS model. During verification, we had to construct various environment models to clarify various aspects of the RTOS such as task management, resource management, event control, and interrupt handling. In this paper, we explain the details of constructing the environment models and show experimental verification results.

This paper is organized as follows. In Section 2, we describe the RTOS model and how an environment is used to verify it. In Section 3, we explain the environment model and the environment generator. In Section 4, we explain the verification procedure of the RTOS model by using the environment generator. In Section 5, we discuss the effectiveness of our method. In Section 6, we outline related work. In Section 7, we conclude this paper.

2   RTOS Model and Its Environment

Let us first introduce the RTOS model and explain how it is checked using an environment. The RTOS model is constructed based on the OSEK OS specification, and is described in about 2800 lines of Promela code, following the approach in [2]. The main functionalities of the OS are modeled, including its task management, resource management, event mechanism, and interrupt processing. Fig. 2 (left) shows the basic structure of the code. The first part defines the data structures such as tasks, resources, and the ready queue. Here, tasks are the entities that compete for a central processing unit (CPU), and the currently running task is represented by the variable `turn`. The ready queue is used to manage the execution order of tasks, and is represented by a two-dimensional array (i.e., a set of queues assigned for each task priority level). When a task is

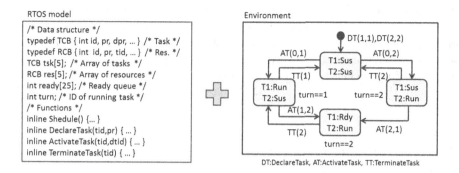

Fig. 2. RTOS model and an environment

activated, it is pushed onto the queue with corresponding priority. The next task to be executed is then the one at the head of the highest priority queue. The second part of the code defines a number of functions. The function `Schedule` corresponds to the activation of the scheduler, and is called only from inside of the OS. When `Schedule` is called, the next task to be executed is dispatched from the ready queue and the identifier (ID) of the task is stored in `turn`. In contrast, the functions `DeclareTask`, `ActivateTask`, and `TerminateTask` are called from outside the OS. `DeclareTask` registers a new task for the RTOS model. `ActivateTask` and `TerminateTask` activate and terminate a task, respectively, and the main role of these two functions is to enqueue and dequeue tasks for the ready queue. At the end of the execution of these functions, `Schedule` is called to activate the scheduler. Including these three functions, a total of 13 external OS functions are defined. Their executions all follow the same procedure, namely, after conducting their operation, the scheduler is activated.

To apply model checking to the RTOS model, we need an environment that provides function calls to the RTOS model. Fig. 2 (right) shows an example of an environment. In actuality, this environment is implemented in Promela; however, we show it here as a state model for readability. This example environment consists of two tasks: T1 with priority 1 and T2 with priority 2. It describes a sequence of function calls to the RTOS model, as well as the state transitions of the tasks expected by the function calls. The environment starts in an initial state constructed by declaring the two tasks using `DeclareTask`. Both tasks are expected to be suspended in this state. When `ActivateTask(0,1)` (activation of T1 by the OS) is called in this initial state, the environment moves to the left state in which T1 and T2 are expected to be running and suspended, respectively. When `ActivateTask(1,2)` (activation of T2 by T1) is called in the left state, the environment moves to the bottom state in which T1 and T2 are expected to be ready and running, respectively. T2 hence preempts the execution of T1. In this way, the environment describes the state transitions of tasks expected by the function calls. To ensure that this expectation is actually satisfied, we check the consistency of the environment and the RTOS model by using assertions. In this example, we check that the task running in the environment is also running in the RTOS model by inspecting the variable turn of the RTOS model in each state of the environment. For instance, for the left state in which T1 is expected to be running, we check that turn is equal to the ID of T1 (= 1). In this way, we ensure the correctness of the RTOS model by applying model checking in combination with an environment.

3   Environment Generator

The example in the previous section is so simple that we can construct it even by hand. However, as stated in Section 1, there are many environmental variations considering the number of tasks and resources and their priorities. To automate the construction of environmental variants, we previously developed the environment generator tool. We briefly introduce this tool here. For more details, please refer to our earlier work [17].

Environment models are input models of the environment generator. An environment model consists of a class model and statechart models. In the class model, we describe structural variations of the environment. In the statechart models, we describe the state transitions of environment objects, which are expected by the function calls to the target system. Fig. 3 shows an example environment model. The class model defines the following two classes. The first class RTOS represents the verification target and defines two types of functions: trigger functions (defined in the upper box of the figure) and reference functions (defined in the lower box). Trigger functions cause state transitions to the environment, and their arguments are defined with a range that characterizes the call variations. Reference functions refer to the internal values of the target system and are used to define assertions. The second class Task represents the environment of the target system. It is defined in terms of attributes and associations. For example, the attribute pr represents the priority of a task, and the association from RTOS to Task represents the number of tasks. Such attributes and associations are also defined with ranges that characterize the value and multiplicity variations, respectively. The detailed structure of the environments is constrained by invariants. For example, the invariant of Task forces the priorities of tasks to be different from one another. The properties under examination are defined by assertions, which are checked in all states of each object. For example, the assertion of Task checks the consistency of the running task between the environment and the RTOS model (as explained in Section 2). The function GetTurn is used to reference the value of turn in the RTOS model. Invariants and assertions are described in object constraint language (OCL) [16].

The figure also shows the statechart model of Task. A transition is caused by calling a trigger function, for example, the transition AT1 is caused by ActivateTask such that when a suspended task is activated, this task runs if no other tasks are running. The expression in the square brackets ([]) beneath AT1 is a guard condition. Simultaneous transitions among multiple objects are defined by

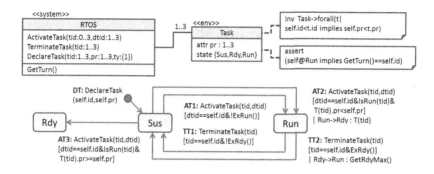

Fig. 3. Example environment model

synchronous transitions. For example, the transition AT2 defines a synchronous transition |Run->Rdy:GetRun(). During the main transition, the task transits from suspended to running. In combination with this transition, the task expressed by GetRun() (i.e., the running task GetRun()=Task->select(t|t@Run)) transits from running to ready. Guard conditions and the objects in synchronous transitions are also described in OCL.

The environment generator generates all possible environments of the environment model. It is implemented as a LINUX command line tool that takes an environment model as a text file input and outputs environments as Promela files. Environment generation is conducted in three steps. Firstly, all possible object graphs are generated within the bounds of the class model. In [17], we performed this generation by using an elementary algorithm that enumerated all of the object graphs in alphabetical order. However, we have now updated the generator to use a satisfiability modulo theories (SMT) solver Yices. The problem of finding object graphs that satisfy the invariants can be considered as a constraint solving problem against the class diagram [3,4]. We follow this approach, and enumerate all of the object graphs efficiently using Yices [1]. Secondly, for each object graph, we generate a labeled transition system (LTS) by composing the statechart models of all objects in the object graph. Finally, we generate the environments by translating each LTS into a Promela file.

4 Verification of RTOS Model

4.1 Approach

To verify the RTOS model, we constructed environment models based on the OSEK/VDX OS specification. For this construction, we followed two approaches: (1) separation of environment models and (2) use case analysis of state transitions.

Separation of Environment Models. We first constructed separate environment models based on the individual functionality of the OS. Fig. 4 summarizes

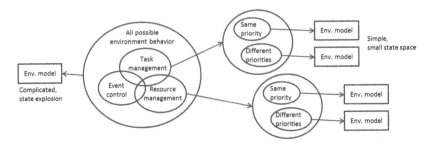

Fig. 4. Separation of environment (Env.) models

this concept. The OS has various functionalities such as task management, resource management, event control, and interrupt processing, and we constructed multiple environment models to independently check each of these. There are two reasons for separating the models. Firstly, each environment model is simplified. In actuality, it is possible to construct a single environment model that covers all aspects of the OS. However, we avoided this because the environment model becomes so complicated that the reliability of the verification is reduced. Since the environment model describes the OS properties, it must be simple so as to clearly reflect the intention of the verification. However, if all aspects of the OS are placed into a single environment model, the complexity of the model becomes equivalent to that of the RTOS model. Creating such a model for verification makes little sense because the correctness of the environment model becomes as uncertain as that of the RTOS model. Therefore, we constructed the environment models separately such that each model was as simple as possible. Secondly, the models are separated to reduce the risk of state explosion. If we check all aspects of the OS at once, state explosion can easily occur. However, by separating the environment models, we can check each of them within a relatively small state space. As a result, we can check the entire environment without causing state explosion.

In addition to separation according to functionality, we separated the environment models based on the priority of tasks. Specifically, for each functionality, we constructed two environment models: one consisting of tasks with different priorities and the other consisting of tasks with the same priority. This separation also retains the simplicity of the environment models. To deal with tasks having arbitrary priorities, we would need to define a data structure similar to a ready queue that precisely defines the order of task executions. (For example, let us consider the case where T1 with priority 2 is running and T2 and T3, both with priority 1, are ready. When T1 terminates, we cannot tell which of T2 and T3 will run next unless we record their activation order.) However, this again increases the complexity of the environment model such that it is equivalent to that of the RTOS model because the RTOS model uses the ready queue. Thus, we divided the environment models into above two cases. In the different priority case, we can check the preemptive mechanism of task execution, namely, that a task with higher priority is executed before those with lower priorities. Here,

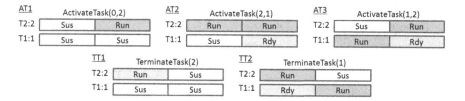

Fig. 5. Use cases for ActivateTask and TerminateTask

we do not need a ready queue because the order of task execution is simply determined by comparing their priorities. In the same priority case, we can check the first-in-first-out order of task execution, that is, tasks with the same priority are executed in activation order. Here, we still need a ready queue to record the order of task activation. However, a single array is adequate to represent the ready queue because there is only one level of priority. This simplifies the environment model compared with the RTOS model, where the ready queue is represented by a two dimensional array.

Use Case Analysis of State Transitions. Second, before constructing the environment models, we constructed use case models to understand the specification correctly. In actuality, the behavior of functions is described in various ways in the specification such as by plain text, diagrams, tables, and so on. This variety makes direct conversion of the specification into environment models prone to errors. Hence, we introduced use case models as intermediate models to fill the notational gaps between the specification and environment models. Fig. 5 shows an example of use case models. In such models, we describe the state transition patterns caused by function calls by using concrete objects in the environment. For example, AT3 presents the state transitions of two tasks, T1 with priority 1 and T2 with priority 2, caused by ActivateTask(1,2) (activation of T2 by T1). Initially, T1 is running and T2 is suspended. After the function call, T1 then becomes ready and T2 becomes running. When constructing use case models, it is important to exhaustively cover all state transition patterns. The five cases in the figure are all of the state transition patterns caused by ActivateTask and TerminateTask in which the tasks have different priorities. Specifically, the three cases of ActivateTask are divided into AT1, and {AT2, AT3} based on the existence of a running task. Furthermore, AT2 and AT3 are divided based on the relation between the priorities of the running and activated tasks, namely, AT2 with T1.pr<T2.pr and AT3 with T1.pr>T2.pr. The two cases of TerminateTask are divided based on the existence of a ready task. Through such a case analysis, we exhaustively extract all state transition patterns from the specification.

We constructed environment models by generalizing the use case models using OCL expressions. For instance, the five cases in the example in Fig. 5 are generalized as the statechart model shown in Fig. 3. The initial conditions are defined by guard conditions and the state transitions of multiple objects are defined by synchronous transitions. Although we have not developed a formal way

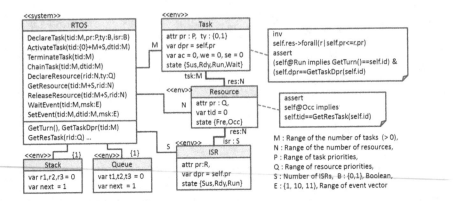

Fig. 6. Class model

of analyzing and generalizing use case models, we consider that the case analysis employed to construct the use case models is an important activity for correctly ascertaining the behavior of functions.

4.2   Environment Models

Following the approach outlined in the Section 4.1, we defined a total of 12 environment models to check each aspect of the RTOS model. The class model commonly defined for these environment models, is shown in Fig. 6. The ranges of the parameters, invariants, and statechart models are defined individually for each environment model.

Fig. 7 shows the configuration of each environment model. The environment models are divided into six groups based on which the functionalities of the OS are being checked. Each group is further divided into two cases based on the equality of task priorities. For example, environment models No. 1 (TaskDiff) and No. 2 (TaskEq) check the task management functions. They represent the cases with different priorities and the same priority, respectively. The table lists the parameter ranges in the class model. For example, in model No.1, we define the range of task priorities (P) as 1..3 and add an invariant to specify that the priorities are different for each task. On the other hand, in model No. 2, we simply define the range as {1} to make the priority equal for all tasks. The table also lists the number of transitions in the statechart model. For example, the statechart model of model No. 1, which we have already shown in Fig. 3, consists of six transitions: 1 for DeclareTask, 3 for ActivateTask, and 2 for TerminateTask. As we can see, these functions are used commonly by all of the other models. This is because tasks are necessary to compose the minimum behavior of the environment. We thus treated models No. 1 and No. 2 as core environment models and defined all of the other models by extending these core models. For example, Fig. 8 shows the statechart models of models No. 5, 7, and 9, which are defined by extending model No.1. These three models check the functions associated

No.	Env. model	Class model						Statechart model												
		M	P	N	Q	S	R	DT	AT	TT	CT	DR	GR	RR	WE	SE	CE	DI	SI	RI
1	TaskDiff	1..3	1..3					1	3	2										
2	TaskEq	1..3	1					1	2	2										
3	CtDiff	1..3	1..3					1	3	2	6									
4	CtEq	1..3	1					1	2	2	4									
5	MultDiff	1..3	1..3					1	5	3										
6	MultEq	1..3	1					1	4	5										
7	ResDiff	1..3	1..3	1..3	1..3			1	3	3		1	1	2						
8	ResEq	1..3	1	1..3	1..3			1	2	2		1	1	1						
9	EvDiff	1..3	1..3					1	3	2					2	3	1			
10	EvEq	1..3	1					1	2	2					2	2	1			
11	IsrDiff	1..3	1..3			1..3	4..6	1	4	2								1	4	3
12	IsrEq	1..3	1			1..3	4..6	1	3	2								1	4	3

DT:DeclareTask,AT:ActivateTask,TT:TerminateTask,CT:ChainTask,DR:DeclareResource, GR:GetResource, RR:ReleaseResource,WE:WaitEvent,SE:SetEvent,CE:ClearEvent,DI:DeclareInter,SI:SetInter,RI:ResetInter

Fig. 7. Configuration of environment models

with multiple activation of tasks, resource management, and event control, respectively. Model No. 5 adds the state transitions AT4 and AT5, which occur when a ready task or a running task is activated multiple times, respectively. Model No. 7 adds the statechart model of the resource, and state transitions TT1 and TT2 are updated to include a guard condition that prohibits a task from terminating while occupying resources. Model No. 9 adds the state Wait for waiting events. In this way, we constructed each environment model by adding the relevant behaviors to the core models.

Let us explain more about the class model. The attribute ty of Task represents two types of tasks (basic tasks and extended tasks) defined in the OS. The accessibility of a task to functions is defined based on this type. For example, WaitEvent is called only by extended tasks. We check this accessibility in the guard condition of state transitions by referring the attribute. The variable dpr of Task represents the dynamic priority of a task. Under the priority ceiling protocol of the OSEK/VDX OS, all resources are defined with a ceiling priority (the attribute pr or Resource). When a task acquires a resource, its priority is changed to the ceiling priority of the resource. In the class model, such dynamic data is defined as a variable, and its value can be changed by actions that are defined along with the state transitions. The invariant of Task defines the constraint on the association between Task and Resource whereby a task can only access resources whose priorities are greater than or equal to that of the task. The classes Queue and Stack are utility functions for defining the precise behavior of tasks. Queue is the single ready queue that we explained in Section 4.1, and is used to record the activation order of tasks for models with the same priority. Stack is used to control the last-in-first-out order of resource accessing, specifically, when a task releases a resource, that resource must be the last one acquired by the task. The class ISR represents the interrupt service routines. ISRs are those entities besides tasks that compete for the CPU. Interrupt processing is checked in models No. 11 and12, which use the functions DeclareInterrupt, SetInterrupt and ResetInterrupt. These functions are

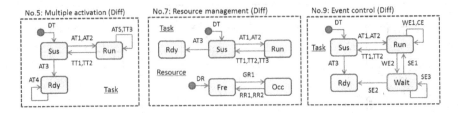

Fig. 8. Statechart models of models No. 5, 7, and 9

not defined in the specification; however, we included them in the RTOS model to represent the activation and termination of ISRs. Interruption is then realized by calling these functions from the environment model. Since the processing level of ISRs is higher than that of tasks, the range of the ISR priorities (R) is set to be higher than that of the task priorities. For the assertions, we checked the consistency of running tasks between the RTOS model and the environment for all models. We also checked the consistency of the dynamic priority of tasks and the consistency of the owner task of a resource in the resource management models (No. 7 and 8).

4.3 Verification Results

Fig. 9 shows the results of environment generation and model checking. The environment generation results show the number of environments generated from each environment model, the time taken for generation, the average length of the Promela files, and the average number of states and transitions contained in each environment. The model checking results show the time taken for checking all of the environments and the number of environments in which errors were detected. From Fig. 7, we limited the number of tasks, resources, and ISRs to a maximum of 3. With these ranges, we were able to generate a total of 620 environments in about 1 min, which is quite efficient since only about 0.1 s was needed to generate each environment. This result demonstrates the effectiveness of using the SMT solver. For model checking, we were able to check the RTOS model using all of the environments without state explosion occurring due to the separation of the environment models. The entire model checking took 106 min such that about 10 s per environment was required on average. Most of this time was used for compilation, which grows exponentially with the length of the Promela file. The cost of model checking can therefore be improved by using PC clusters, that is, checking all of the environments in parallel.

The results show that errors were found in the environments of models No. 3, 4, 7, and 8. The RTOS model and the environment models were constructed by different researchers. Hence, when an error was discovered, we needed to identify which model had caused it. The results show both situations. For models No. 3 and 4, the errors were caused by the environment models. Specifically, the errors were contained in the state transition of ChainTask. When ChainTask(t1,t2) is

No.	Env. model	Environment Generation					Model Check			No.7			
		Num	Time(s)	Lines	States	Trans	Time(s)	Errors	Task	Res	Num	Errors
1	TaskDiff	26	0.5	153	4	9	113.8	0	1	1	8	0
2	TaskEq	14	0.4	273	10	19	70.7	0	1	2	22	14
3	CtDiff	26	0.6	183	4	17	116.3	19	1	3	62	54
4	CtEq	14	0.5	343	10	37	76.4	13	2	1	9	0
5	MultDiff	26	0.7	199	8	19	119.1	0	2	2	27	18
6	MultEq	14	1.6	597	50	99	106.3	0	2	3	81	72
7	ResDiff	248	38.3	878	44	110	2904.0	188	3	1	3	0
8	ResEq	98	15.4	1079	53	136	1702.0	56	3	2	9	6
9	EvDiff	26	1.2	336	15	47	143.0	0	3	3	27	24
10	EvEq	14	2.3	1271	78	251	253.6	0				
11	IsrDiff	182	10.3	502	17	49	1249.7	0				
12	IsrEq	98	9.6	903	40	117	1964.4	0				

Fig. 9. Verification results (CPU: 2.4 GHz, Memory: 4.0 GB)

called, it first terminates task t1 and then activates task t2. If task t2 is already running or is ready, however, then the task is activated twice. Such multiple activation is allowed only for basic tasks. Nevertheless, the environment models did not check this condition and allowed multiple activation also for extended tasks. As a result, the RTOS model flagged an error to notify the violation of this condition. For models No. 7 and 8, the errors were caused by the RTOS model. Under the priority ceiling protocol, the priority of the task is changed only when it acquires a resource whose priority is higher than that of the task. However, the RTOS model was defined to change the priority every time a task acquired a resource. As a result, the assertion in the environment was violated due to the inconsistency between the dynamic priority of the tasks of the RTOS model and those of the environment. In both of the above cases, when errors were found, we held a discussion to identify the cause of the errors. This activity allowed us to understand the specification correctly, and led us to construct an error-free RTOS model within the bounds of the environment models.

The results also show a feature of our method: *structural difference analysis of errors*. The table on the right-hand side of Fig. 9 lists the number of errors found in the environments of model No. 7 grouped according to the number of tasks and resources. For example, among the 27 environments containing 2 tasks and 2 resources, 18 environments caused errors. From this table, we can see that errors were caused by environments containing more than one resource. This result leads us to infer that an error occurs when a task tries to acquire multiple resources, and we further infer that changes in the dynamic priority are not performed correctly. From structural information such as this, we can predict the cause of errors before analyzing counterexample traces.

5 Discussion

5.1 Effectiveness

In the environment model, we can declare the structural variation of the environment in OCL using the ranges of the parameter and invariants. From this model, we can then exhaustively generate all environmental variants using the environment generator within the given bounds. As shown in the experiment, the number of environments can become so large that it is almost impossible to correctly construct them all by hand. However, the environment generator enables automatic and effective generation of environments with leveraging the SMT solver. The generator can also exhaustively enumerate all structural variations, which is important for obtaining a full coverage of verification with respect to all environment structures. Thanks to this exhaustiveness, we were able to find an error in the resource manipulation without missing the case in which a task is linked to multiple resources.

Our method is also effective for avoiding state explosion. The act of generating all structural variations of the environment is equivalent to structurally decomposing the entire environment into smaller environments. This enables us to check each environment independently within a small state space. As a result, we can check the entire environment without causing state explosion. We further benefit from this decomposition since it facilitates structural difference analysis of errors. The effect of the decomposition is thus notable, especially when it is applied to the verification of systems that have various environmental structures. In this sense, our method is most effective when applied to the domains of OSs and middleware.

5.2   Verification Coverage

In our method, the verification coverage must be evaluated with respect to the structure and behavior of the environment. For the structural coverage, we limited the numbers of tasks, resources, and ISRs to a maximum of 3. We consider that this number is sufficient to check the critical properties of the OS. For example, to check that the priority ceiling protocol is satisfied, we need to examine the following properties. (1) When a task occupies multiple resources, its dynamic priority is set to the maximum priority of the resources. (2) A task with higher dynamic priority must be executed before that with lower dynamic priority. To check (1), we need to create a situation in which a task can access at least two resources. To check (2), we need to create a situation in which two tasks occupy at least one resource. Therefore, we need at least 2 tasks and 2 resources and must define the ranges accordingly to cover these numbers. Basically, the sufficient ranges depend on the system under verification. Thus, when defining the ranges, it is important to identify which properties to check and the structure that needs to be created to check them. The ranges must initially be defined to at least cover that structure. Then, they should be extended further to raise the structural verification coverage depending on the machine power. Currently, the environment generator efficiently generates environments for up to 8 objects on a PC with average specifications. For a greater number of objects, the composition of the statechart models becomes the bottleneck and generation takes hours.

For the behavioral coverage, we have so far defined statechart models for checking normal execution sequences of the OS. However, for such execution sequences, we still need to check the interaction between functionalities. For example, we need to check the case where ISRs can access resources and set events. When we check many functionalities simultaneously, we risk complicating the statechart models. We consider that the combination of 2 functionalities is a limitation for maintaining the simplicity of the model. For checking further combinations, a simple and specific environment should be constructed directly by hand on the Promela level by abondoning the generarity of the environment model. For abnormal execution sequences, we can construct statechart models for verifying them by extending those of normal execution sequences. For example, when `ActivateTask` is called for a running task, an error must be flagged by the OS. This can be checked by adding a transition from the running state to an error state that is entered when `ActivateTask` is called for a running task. In the error state, we check that the error is actually flagged in the RTOS model by referring the variable representing the error code.

Moreover, we need to strengthen the verification of interrupt processing. We modeled the activation and termination of ISRs by calling the functions `SetInter` and `ResetInter` from the environment. However, we only call them before and after other functions calls, and we have not checked the case where they are called *within* a function execution. To enable such a check, we need to define ISRs as different processes from the process of the environment. This then allows ISRs to interleave the functions of the environment. Still, the difficulty remains of how to realize the nested activation of ISRs and the function call from ISRs. Furthermore, allowing interleaving at any point of a function execution can increase the risk of state explosion. Considering these problems, we need to develop an effective way to verify interrupt processing.

6   Related Work

Tkachuk et al. [15] proposed the Bandera Environment Generator (BEG) to automatically generate environments for the verification of Java programs in Bandera. BEG has been used to verify commercial software and a web application [14,12]. BEG generates environments from specifications written by the user, called environment assumptions, or by analyzing the programs that implement the environment. The environment assumptions are described through regular expressions as sequences of method calls. Their approach corresponds to describing a single instance of the environment model in our method; however, by expressing the set of instances as a class model, we can automatically generate all possible instances based on variations of this model.

Penix et al. [11] validated the time partitioning of DEOS RTOS by using Spin. In their method, environments are obtained by filtering a nondeterministic environment with linear temporal logic (LTL) assumptions [10]. The method uses a top-down approach, where an over-approximated environment is gradually reduced by LTL assumptions toward the ideal environment. In comparison, our approach is bottom-up, that is, we start with an under-approximated environment and gradually extend it toward the ideal environment. Our method enables execution of this process by using statechart models, which are a familiar concept for general software engineers. In this sense, we consider that our method is more effective in practical settings.

Dhaussy et al. [5] proposed a formal language called context description language (CDL) for describing system environments. In their method, environment behavior is defined by using actors and sequence diagrams. Through CDL, a set of traces representing the interaction between the environment and the system are generated. Each trace is checked in combination with the system, and the property automata are examined by model checking. Raji et al. [13] extended Dhaussy et al.fs method by introducing use case diagrams to facilitate the description of an environment. Similar to those works, we also make use of UML to describe environments. However, we address the problem of structural variation by using a class model, which is crucial for the verification of OSs.

Parizek et al. [9] proposed a method that combines the Java PathFinder and Protocol Checker model checkers. Their method targets the validation of Java components whose protocols are described in architecture description language (ADL). Model checking is conducted by searching the program states using Java PathFinder in the Java parts and Protocol Checker in the ADL parts. Although the environment in their method can be modeled in ADL, environmental variation cannot be expressed using classes as in our method.

7   Conclusion

In this paper, we presented a model-checking experiment for an OSEK/VDX OS design model based on environment modeling. In the environment model, we define the structure and behavior of the environment using class and statechart models. From this environment model, the environment generator generates all possible environmental variations within the bounds of the model. To verify various individual aspects of the RTOS model, we constructed separate environment models. By this separation, each model was simplified and the risk of state explosion was avoided. By using the environment generator, we were able to efficiently generate a sufficient range of environments to verify the critical properties of the RTOS model. By checking the RTOS model using the generated environments, we have shown that the correctness of the RTOS model can be guaranteed within the given experimental bounds. As future work, we need to verify other aspects of the RTOS model including abnormal execution sequences and interrupt processing. We will also consider the development of a formal way to analyze use case models and to extend the environment models.

References

1. Yices: An SMT Solver, http://yices.csl.sri.com/
2. Aoki, T.: Model Checking Multi-Task Software on Real-Time Operating Systems. In: ISORC, pp. 551–555. IEEE Computer Society (2008)
3. Cabot, J., Clarisó, R., Riera, D.: Verification of UML/OCL Class Diagrams using Constraint Programming. In: Proceedings of the 2008 IEEE International Conference on Software Testing Verification and Validation Workshop, pp. 73–80. IEEE Computer Society, Washington, DC (2008)

4. Clavel, M., Egea, M., de Dios, M.A.G.: Checking Unsatisfiability for OCL Constraints. ECEASST 24 (2009)
5. Dhaussy, P., Pillain, P.-Y., Creff, S., Raji, A., Le Traon, Y., Baudry, B.: Evaluating Context Descriptions and Property Definition Patterns for Software Formal Validation. In: Schürr, A., Selic, B. (eds.) MODELS 2009. LNCS, vol. 5795, pp. 438–452. Springer, Heidelberg (2009)
6. Holzmann, G.J.: The Spin Model Checker - Primer and Reference Manual. Addison-Wesley (2004)
7. OMG. Unified Modeling Language (1989), http://www.uml.org/
8. OSEK/VDX. OSEK/VDX Operating System Specification 2.2.3 (2005), http://portal.osek-vdx.org/
9. Parizek, P., Plasil, F.: Partial Verification of Software Components: Heuristics for Environment Construction. In: EUROMICRO-SEAA, pp. 75–82. IEEE Computer Society (2007)
10. Pasareanu, C.S.: DEOS Kernel: Environment Modeling using LTL Assumptions. Nasa ames technical report nasa-arc-ic-2000-196, NASA Ames Research Center (2000)
11. Penix, J., Visser, W., Park, S., Pasareanu, C.S., Engstrom, E., Larson, A., Weininger, N.: Verifying Time Partitioning in the DEOS Scheduling Kernel. Formal Methods in System Design 26(2), 103–135 (2005)
12. Rajan, S.P., Tkachuk, O., Prasad, M.R., Ghosh, I., Goel, N., Uehara, T.: WEAVE: WEb Applications Validation Environment. In: ICSE Companion, pp. 101–111. IEEE (2009)
13. Raji, A., Dhaussy, P.: Use Cases Modeling for Scalable Model-Checking. In: APSEC 2011, Minh City, Viet Nam (December 2011)
14. Tkachuk, O., Dwyer, M.B.: Environment generation for validating event-driven software using model checking. IET Software 4(3), 194–209 (2010)
15. Tkachuk, O., Dwyer, M.B., Pasareanu, C.S.: Automated Environment Generation for Software Model Checking. In: ASE, pp. 116–129. IEEE Computer Society (2003)
16. Warmer, J., Kleppe, A.: The Object Constraint Language: Precise Modeling with UML. Addison-Wesley (1999)
17. Yatake, K., Aoki, T.: Automatic Generation of Model Checking Scripts Based on Environment Modeling. In: van de Pol, J., Weber, M. (eds.) SPIN 2010. LNCS, vol. 6349, pp. 58–75. Springer, Heidelberg (2010)

A Cure for Stuttering Parity Games

Sjoerd Cranen, Jeroen J.A. Keiren, and Tim A.C. Willemse

Department of Computer Science and Mathematics
Eindhoven University of Technology
PO Box 513, 5600MB Eindhoven, The Netherlands

Abstract. We define governed stuttering bisimulation for parity games, weakening stuttering bisimulation by taking the ownership of vertices into account only when this might lead to observably different games. We show that governed stuttering bisimilarity is an equivalence for parity games and allows for a natural quotienting operation. Moreover, we prove that all pairs of vertices related by governed stuttering bisimilarity are won by the same player in the parity game. Thus, our equivalence can be used as a preprocessing step when solving parity games. Governed stuttering bisimilarity can be decided in $\mathcal{O}(n^2 m)$ time for parity games with n vertices and m edges. Our experiments indicate that governed stuttering bisimilarity is mostly competitive with stuttering equivalence on parity games encoding typical verification problems.

1 Introduction

Parity games [11,22,27] are played by two players (represented by $\diamond$ and $\square$) on a directed graph in which every vertex is owned by one of the players, and vertices are assigned a priority. The game is played by moving a single token along the edges in the graph; the choice where to move next is dictated by the player owning the vertex on which the token currently resides. Both players try to play such that the resulting infinite path is *winning* for them, and a vertex is won by the player that can play such that, however the opponent plays, every path from that vertex is won by her. The winner of a vertex is uniquely determined [11,22,27] and partitioning the graph in vertices that are won by player $\diamond$ and those won by player $\square$ is referred to as *solving* the parity game.

The parity game framework is a key instrument in solving practical verification and synthesis problems, see [11,2]. Its practical significance is mirrored by its role in searching for the true complexity of model checking: modal μ-calculus model checking is polynomially reducible to parity game solving, and *vice versa* [25]. Despite the apparent simplicity of the latter problem, the precise complexity of solving parity games is still open: the problem is known to be in NP $\cap$ coNP, and more specifically in UP $\cap$ coUP [17], suggesting there just might exist a polynomial time algorithm. Indeed, non-trivial classes of parity games have been identified that admit polynomial time solving algorithms, see *e.g.* [4,23].

In the past decade, several advanced algorithms for solving parity games have been designed. These include algorithms exponential in the number of priorities, such as Jurdziński's *small progress measures* algorithm [18] and Schewe's *bigstep* algorithm [24], as well as the sub-exponential algorithm due to Jurdziński *et al.* [19]. Orthogonally to

A. Roychoudhury and M. D'Souza (Eds.): ICTAC 2012, LNCS 7521, pp. 198–212, 2012.

the algorithmic improvements, heuristics have been devised that may speed up solving parity games that occur in practice [12]. Such heuristics work particularly well for verification problems, which give rise to games with only few different priorities.

The heuristic that we consider in this paper, following, *e.g.*, Fritz and Wilke's study of *delayed simulation* [14], is based on the use of fine-grained equivalence relations that approximate the solution to a parity game. The idea is to recast the solving problem as the problem of deciding *winner equivalence* between vertices: two vertices in a parity game are equivalent whenever they are won by the same player. Finding equivalence relations that refine winner equivalence and that are decidable in polynomial time yields a preprocessing step that can be used to reduce games prior to solving.

From a practical viewpoint, we are particularly interested in those simulation and equivalence relations that strike a favourable balance between their power to compress the game graph and their computational complexity. Stuttering bisimulation [7] for Kripke Structures is among a select number of candidates worth considering, with an $\mathcal{O}(nm)$ time complexity (n being the number of vertices and m the number of edges). Observe that stuttering bisimulation only preserves a fragment of the μ-calculus when applied to Kripke Structures. It may therefore be surprising that it does preserve the winner of parity games, including those that stem from encodings of arbitrary μ-calculus model checking problems. As earlier experiments [10] indicate, off-the-shelf stuttering bisimulation reduction algorithms can be competitive when compared to modern available parity game solvers. Stuttering bisimulation, however, is inadequate when faced with alternations between players along the possible plays: it cannot relate vertices belonging to different players. Controller synthesis problems *e.g.* [2], and constructs such as $\Box\Diamond\phi$ and $\Diamond\Box\phi$ in μ-calculus verification, give rise to such parity games.

A natural question is, therefore, whether stuttering bisimulation can at all be modified so that it is able to relate vertices that belong to different players. We answer this question in this paper by defining a relation, which we dub *governed stuttering bisimulation* (reflecting that a player's ruling capabilities are taken as primitive), which we show to be strictly weaker than stuttering bisimilarity. In addition, we prove that governed stuttering bisimilarity:

- is an equivalence relation on parity games.
- refines winner equivalence.
- is decidable in $\mathcal{O}(n^2m)$ time using a partition refinement algorithm.

The time complexity for deciding governed stuttering bisimilarity is a factor n worse than that for stuttering bisimilarity; this is due to finding a splitter, for which our algorithm requires $\mathcal{O}(mn)$ rather than $\mathcal{O}(m)$ time. Our experiments, however, indicate that this factor does not manifest itself in practice; in fact, our algorithm is mostly competitive with the one for stuttering bisimilarity.

Structure of the paper. Section 2 briefly introduces the parity game framework. We recall the definition of stuttering bisimulation and we define governed stuttering bisimulation in Section 3. In Section 4, we show that governed stuttering bisimulation is an equivalence relation, we show it refines winner equivalence, and we address its decidability. We discuss our experiments with a prototype implementation of our algorithm for deciding governed stuttering bisimulation in Section 5. Related work is discussed in

Section 6, and future work is described in Section 7. Note that, due to space restrictions, details of the proofs have been omitted. Detailed proofs are provided in [9].

2 Preliminaries

A parity game is a two-player graph game, played by two players on a directed graph. The game is formally defined as follows.

Definition 1 (Parity game). *A parity game is a directed graph* $(V, \rightarrow, \Omega, \mathcal{P})$, *where*

- *V is a finite set of vertices,*
- *$\rightarrow \subseteq V \times V$ is a total edge relation* (i.e., *for each $v \in V$ there is at least one $w \in V$ such that $(v, w) \in \rightarrow$*),
- *$\Omega : V \rightarrow \mathbb{N}$ is a priority function that assigns priorities to vertices,*
- *$\mathcal{P} : V \rightarrow \{\diamond, \square\}$ is a function assigning vertices to players.*

If i is a player, then $\neg i$ denotes the opponent of i, i.e., $\neg \diamond = \square$ and $\neg \square = \diamond$. A sequence of vertices $v_1, \ldots, v_n$ for which $v_m \rightarrow v_{m+1}$ for all $1 \leq m < n$ is a *path*, and may be denoted using angular brackets: $\langle v_1 \ldots v_n \rangle$. The concatenation $p \cdot q$ of paths p and q is again a path. Infinite paths are defined in a similar manner. We use p_n to denote the nth vertex in a path p.

A game starts by placing a token on vertex $v \in V$. Players move the token indefinitely according to the following simple rule: if the token is on some vertex v, player $\mathcal{P}(v)$ moves the token to some vertex w such that $v \rightarrow w$. The result is an infinite path p in the game graph. The *parity* of the lowest priority that occurs infinitely often on p defines the *winner* of the path. If this priority is even, then player $\diamond$ wins, otherwise player $\square$ wins.

A *strategy* for player i is a partial function $\sigma : V^* \rightarrow V$, that is defined only for paths ending in a vertex owned by player i and determines the next vertex to be played onto. The set of strategies for player i in a game $\mathcal{G}$ is denoted $\mathbb{S}^*_{\mathcal{G},i}$, or simply $\mathbb{S}^*_i$ if $\mathcal{G}$ is clear from the context. If a strategy yields the same vertex for every pair of paths that end in the same vertex, then the strategy is said to be *memoryless*. The set of memoryless strategies for player i in a game $\mathcal{G}$ is denoted $\mathbb{S}_{\mathcal{G},i}$, abbreviated to $\mathbb{S}_i$ when $\mathcal{G}$ is clear from the context. A memoryless strategy is usually given as a partial function $\sigma : V \rightarrow V$.

A path p of length n is *consistent* with a strategy $\sigma \in \mathbb{S}^*_i$, denoted $\sigma \Vdash p$, if and only if for all $1 \leq j < n$ it is the case that if σ is defined for $\langle p_1 \ldots p_j \rangle$, then $p_{j+1} = \sigma(\langle p_1 \ldots p_j \rangle)$. The definition of consistency is extended to infinite paths in the obvious manner. A strategy $\sigma \in \mathbb{S}^*_i$ is said to be a *winning strategy* from a vertex v if and only if i is the winner of every path consistent with σ. A vertex is won by i if i has a winning strategy from that vertex. Parity games are memoryless determined [11], i.e. each vertex in the game is won by exactly one player, and it suffices to play a memoryless strategy.

In this paper, we are concerned with relations partitioning the vertices in a parity game such that all related vertices are won by the same player. Let R be a relation over a set V. For $v, w \in V$ we write $v \mathrel{R} w$ for $(v, w) \in R$. For an equivalence relation R, and vertex $v \in V$ we define $[v]_R$, the equivalence class of v under R, as $\{v' \in V \mid v \mathrel{R} v'\}$. The set of equivalence classes of V under R is denoted $V_{/R}$. A collection $\{B_i \mid i \in I\}$, with $\emptyset \neq B_i \subseteq V$, is called a *partition* of V if $\bigcup_{i \in I} B_i = V$ and for $i \neq j : B_i \cap B_j = \emptyset$. An element B_i of a partition is called a *block*. If P and Q are partitions of V then Q *refines* P if $\forall B_i \in Q : \exists B_j \in P : B_i \subseteq B_j$. We use the notions of equivalence relation and partition interchangeably, and occasionally write $v \, P \, v'$ rather than $v, v' \in B$ for some $B \in P$.

Determinacy of parity games effectively induces a partition on the set of vertices V in those vertices won by player $\diamond$ and those vertices won by player $\square$. This partition is the natural equivalence relation on V.

Definition 2 (Winner equivalence). *Let* $(V, \rightarrow, \Omega, \mathcal{P})$ *be a parity game. Vertices* $v, w \in V$ *are* winner equivalent, *denoted* $v \sim w$ *iff* v *and* w *are won by the same player.*

3 Governed Stuttering Bisimulation

In [10] we introduced *stuttering bisimulation* for parity games. Informally, stuttering bisimulation compresses subsequences of "identical" vertices, *i.e.* vertices with the same priority, owned by the same player, along a path p in a parity game, such that the path retains the essentials of the graph's branching structure.

Before we give the formal definition of stuttering bisimulation, we first introduce some notation. Let $(V, \rightarrow, \Omega, \mathcal{P})$ be a parity game. In the following, let $U \subseteq V$ be arbitrary sets of vertices; we write $v \rightarrow U$ if there exists a $u \in U$ such that $v \rightarrow u$.

Let $R \subseteq V \times V$ be a relation on the set of vertices. The generalised transition relation $v \mapsto_R U$, defined below, formalises that U is eventually reached from v by some computation path through R-related nodes. Likewise, $v \mapsto_R$ expresses that v is the start of an infinite computation path along vertices related through R.

$$v \mapsto_R U \overset{\mu}{=} \exists u : v \rightarrow u \wedge (u \in U \vee (v \, R \, u \wedge u \mapsto_R U))$$
$$v \mapsto_R \overset{\nu}{=} \exists u : v \rightarrow u \wedge v \, R \, u \wedge u \mapsto_R$$

We next formalise the notion of stuttering bisimulation, deviating notationally from [10]; the definitions, however, are easily seen to coincide and the modifications are standard. Our main reason for deviating from [10] is that the presented definition facilitates explaining the intuition of its generalisation to governed stuttering bisimulation.

Definition 3 (Stuttering bisimulation for parity games [10]). *Let* $(V, \rightarrow, \Omega, \mathcal{P})$ *be a parity game. Let* $R \subseteq V \times V$ *be an equivalence relation on vertices;* R *is a* stuttering bisimulation *if* $v \, R \, v'$ *implies*

a) $\Omega(v) = \Omega(v')$ *and* $\mathcal{P}(v) = \mathcal{P}(v')$;
b) $v \rightarrow C$ *implies* $v' \mapsto_R C$, *for all* $C \in V_{/R} \setminus \{[v]_R\}$.
c) $v \mapsto_R$ *iff* $v' \mapsto_R$;

Two states v *and* v' *are said to be* stuttering bisimilar, *denoted* $v \simeq v'$ *iff there is a stuttering bisimulation relation* R, *such that* $v \, R \, v'$.

Our objective is to weaken stuttering bisimulation so that it will be able to relate vertices of different players. However, we cannot simply weaken clause *a)* to $\Omega(v) = \Omega(v')$ without modifying the remaining clauses, as this would enable us to relate vertices won by different players, as the following parity game demonstrates:

The suggested weakening of clause *a)* would allow us to relate all vertices with priority 2; the two left vertices, however are won by player $\diamond$, whereas the other vertices are won by player $\square$.

The problem in the above example is that the computation paths that appear in clauses *b)* and *c)* may consist of vertices owned by different players. This means that a fixed player is at the mercy of her opponent to stay on a computation path: the opponent may simply choose an alternative next vertex if that would better suit her. We are therefore forced to reason about computation trees, taking all the opponent's choices into account. Effectively, clause *b)* must be strengthened to ensure that a player eventually reaches class $\mathcal{C}$ along some computation tree, and clause *c)* must be strengthened to ensure that a player can construct an infinite computation tree not leaving its own class.

We first extend our notation to facilitate reasoning about computation trees rather than computation paths. Given a memoryless strategy σ for some player, the ability to move from vertex v to another vertex u depends on this strategy.

$$v_\sigma \to u = \begin{cases} v \to u \wedge \sigma(v) = u, & \text{if } \sigma(v) \text{ is defined} \\ v \to u, & \text{otherwise} \end{cases}$$

From the viewpoint of a fixed player and her memoryless strategy σ, a token may be moved along the edges of a computation tree that only branches at vertices owned by her opponent. This notation $v_\sigma \mapsto_R U$, defined below, formalises that all plays allowed by σ eventually reach the set of vertices U immediately when they follow an edge to a vertex that is no longer related under relation R. The notation $v_\sigma \mapsto_R$ is dual; it expresses that all plays allowed by σ can reach only vertices related under R to the previous vertex in that play:

$$v_\sigma \mapsto_R U \overset{\mu}{=} \forall u : v_\sigma \to u \implies u \in U \vee (v \, R \, u \wedge u_\sigma \mapsto_R U)$$
$$v_\sigma \mapsto_R \overset{\nu}{=} \forall u : v_\sigma \to u \implies v \, R \, u \wedge u_\sigma \mapsto_R$$

If the strategy is unimportant to the purpose at hand, we abstract from the specific strategy that is used and reason only in terms of a player i having a strategy with the capability of forcing a play to a set of vertices U, and, dually, for i to be able to force the play to *diverge* within a class of R:

$$x_i \mapsto_R U = \exists \sigma \in \mathbb{S}_i : x_\sigma \mapsto_R U$$
$$x_i \mapsto_R = \exists \sigma \in \mathbb{S}_i : x_\sigma \mapsto_R$$

We omit R if it is the relation $V \times V$. Note that $v_i \mapsto_R \emptyset$ never holds. On the other hand, $v_i \mapsto_R V$ and $v_i \mapsto$ are trivially true. We write $v_i \not\mapsto_R U$ for $\neg(v_i \mapsto_R U)$; likewise for all other arrows. If $\mathcal{U} \subseteq V_{/R}$, then we write $v_i \mapsto_R \mathcal{U}$ to denote $v_i \mapsto_R \bigcup_{\mathcal{C} \in \mathcal{U}} \mathcal{C}$.

Definition 4 (Governed stuttering bisimulation). *Let* $(V, \to, \Omega, \mathcal{P})$ *be a parity game. Let* $R \subseteq V \times V$ *be an equivalence relation. Then* R *is a* governed stuttering bisimulation *if* $v \, R \, v'$ *implies*

a) $\Omega(v) = \Omega(v')$;
b) $v \to C$ implies $v'\ _{\mathcal{P}(v)}\!\mapsto_R C$, for all $C \in V_{/R} \setminus \{[v]_R\}$.
c) $v\ _i\!\mapsto_R$ iff $v'\ _i\!\mapsto_R$ for $i \in \{\Diamond, \Box\}$.

Vertices v and v' are governed stuttering bisimilar, *denoted* $v \simeq v'$, *iff a governed stuttering bisimulation* R *exists such that* $v\ R\ v'$.

If we additionally require that $\mathcal{P}(v) = \mathcal{P}(v')$, we find that $v \mapsto_R U$ iff $v\ _{\mathcal{P}(v)}\!\mapsto_R U$, and, likewise, $v \mapsto_R$ iff $v\ _{\mathcal{P}(v)}\!\mapsto_R$. This is the basis for the following proposition.

Proposition 1. *Let* $R \subseteq V \times V$ *be a governed stuttering bisimulation, such that* $v\ R\ v'$ *implies* $\mathcal{P}(v) = \mathcal{P}(v')$. *Then* R *is a stuttering bisimulation.*

Example 1. Consider the parity game depicted in Figure 1a. The equivalence relation that relates vertices with equal priorities is a governed stuttering bisimulation. Stuttering bisimulation does not relate any of the vertices.

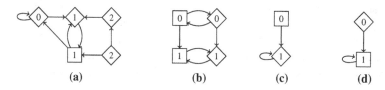

(a)   (b)   (c)   (d)

Fig. 1. All vertices in (a) with the same priorities can be related using governed stuttering bisimilarity. Both (c) and (d) are minimal representations of (b).

4 Properties of Governed Stuttering Bisimulation

We next study three key properties of governed stuttering bisimulation, *viz.*, governed stuttering bisimilarity is an equivalence on parity games, it refines winner equivalence and it is decidable in polynomial time.

4.1 Governed Stuttering Bisimilarity is an Equivalence

Proving that $\simeq$ is an equivalence relation on parity games is far from straightforward: transitivity no longer bows to the standard proof strategies that work for stuttering bisimilarity and branching bisimilarity [26]. As a result of the asymmetry in the use of two different transition relations in clause *b)* of Definition 4, proving that the equivalence closure of the union of two governed stuttering bisimulation relations is again a governed stuttering bisimulation relation is equally problematic.

The strategy we pursue is as follows. We characterise governed stuttering bisimulation, in two steps, by a set of symmetric requirements. The obtained alternative characterisation is then used in our equivalence proof. These alternative characterisations do not facilitate the reuse of standard proof strategies, but they are instrumental in the technically involved proof that the equivalence closure of two governed stuttering bisimulation relations is again a governed stuttering bisimulation relation. Apart from being convenient technically, the characterisations offer more insight into the nature of governed stuttering bisimilarity. Hence, instead of providing the details of our equivalence proof, we focus on the alternative characterisations of governed stuttering bisimulation.

Our result below states that we can rephrase condition *b)* of governed stuttering bisimulation by requiring that a fixed player must have the same power to force the play from any pair of related vertices to reach an arbitrary class. Thus, we abstract from the player that takes the initiative to leave its class in one step.

Theorem 1. *Let $R \subseteq V \times V$ and $v, v' \in V$. Then R is a governed stuttering bisimulation iff R is an equivalence relation and $v \, R \, v'$ implies:*

a) $\Omega(v) = \Omega(v')$;
b) $v \,_i\!\!\mapsto_R C$ iff $v' \,_i\!\!\mapsto_R C$ for all $i \in \{\diamond, \square\}, C \in V_{/R} \setminus \{[v]_R\}$;
c) $v \,_i\!\!\mapsto_R$ iff $v' \,_i\!\!\mapsto_R$ for all $i \in \{\diamond, \square\}$.

While the above alternative characterisation of governed stuttering bisimulation is now fully symmetric, the restriction on the class C that is considered in clause *b)* turns out to be too strong to facilitate our proof that $\simeq$ is an equivalence relation. We therefore generalise this clause once more to reason about sets of classes. A perhaps surprising side-result of this generalisation is that the divergence requirement of clause *c)* becomes superfluous. Note that this last generalisation is not trivial, as $v \,_i\!\!\mapsto_R \{C_1, C_2\}$ is in general neither equivalent to saying that $v \,_i\!\!\mapsto_R C_1$ and $v \,_i\!\!\mapsto_R C_2$, nor $v \,_i\!\!\mapsto_R C_1$ or $v \,_i\!\!\mapsto_R C_2$.

Theorem 2. *Let $R \subseteq V \times V$ and $v, v' \in V$. Then R is a governed stuttering bisimulation iff R is an equivalence relation and $v \, R \, v'$ implies:*

a) $\Omega(v) = \Omega(v')$;
b) $v \,_i\!\!\mapsto_R \mathcal{U}$ iff $v' \,_i\!\!\mapsto_R \mathcal{U}$ for all $i \in \{\diamond, \square\}, \mathcal{U} \subseteq V_{/R} \setminus \{[v]_R\}$.

Note that the divergence requirement $v \,_i\!\!\mapsto_R$ iff $v' \,_i\!\!\mapsto_R$ can be recovered by instantiating set $\mathcal{U}$ by $V_{/R} \setminus \{[v]_R\}$ for player $\neg i$ in the above theorem. The last characterisation enables us to prove the following theorem.

Theorem 3. $\simeq$ *is an equivalence relation.*

As a side-result of the proof of Theorem 3, we find that the *equivalence closure* of the union of two governed stuttering bisimulations is again a governed stuttering bisimulation. The union of *all* governed stuttering bisimulations is again a governed stuttering bisimulation, which coincides with governed stuttering bisimilarity.

4.2 Quotienting

The main reason for studying equivalence relations for parity games is that they may offer the prospect of minimising the parity game by collapsing vertices that are considered equivalent. The resulting minimised structure is referred to as the quotient. However, not all equivalence relations admit such a quotienting operation; in particular, the delayed simulation [14] for parity games fails to have a natural quotienting operation.

Quotienting for governed stuttering bisimulation can be done efficiently. Due to the nature of governed stuttering bisimulation, we have some freedom in the definition of the quotient, in particular when assigning vertices to players. We therefore first define a notion of minimality, and we subsequently define the quotient in terms of that notion.

Definition 5 (Minimality). *A $\approx$-minimal representation of a parity game $(V, \rightarrow, \Omega, \mathcal{P})$ is defined as a game $(V_m, \rightarrow_m, \Omega_m, \mathcal{P}_m)$, that satisfies the following conditions (where $c, c', c'' \in V_m$):*

$$V_m = \{ [v]_\approx \mid v \in V \}$$
$$\Omega_m(c) = \Omega(v) \text{ for all } v \in c$$
$$\mathcal{P}_m(c) = i, \text{ if for all } v \in c, \text{ and some } c' \neq c \text{ we have } v \; {}_i\!\!\mapsto_\approx c' \text{ and } v \; {}_{\neg i}\!\!\not\mapsto_\approx V \setminus c'$$
$$c \rightarrow_m c \text{ iff } v \; {}_i\!\!\mapsto_\approx \text{ for all } v \in c \text{ for some player } i$$
$$c \rightarrow_m c' \text{ iff } v \; {}_i\!\!\mapsto_\approx c' \text{ for all } v \in c \text{ for some player } i \text{ and } c' \neq c$$

Observe that for the third clause above, if from some vertex v the play could be forced to c' by i without $\neg i$ having the opportunity to diverge, player i is in charge of the game when the play arrives in c. This requires the representative in the quotient to be owned by player i.

Note that a parity game may have multiple $\approx$-minimal representations. It is not hard to verify that every parity game contains at least as many vertices and edges as its $\approx$-minimal representations. Moreover, any parity game is governed stuttering bisimulation equivalent to all its $\approx$-minimal representations. As a result, the governed stuttering bisimulation quotient of a graph can be defined as its least $\approx$-minimal representation, given some arbitrary ordering on parity games. A natural ordering would be one that is induced by an ordering on players, *e.g.*, $\square < \Diamond$.

Example 2. Consider the parity game in Figure 1b. Two of its four minimal representations are in Figure 1c and 1d. Observe that the particular player chosen for the 0 and 1 vertices is arbitrary and does not impact the solution to the games.

4.3   Governed Stuttering Bisimilarity Refines Winner Equivalence

In this section, we prove that governed stuttering bisimilarity is strictly finer than winner equivalence. That is, vertices that are won by different players are never related by governed stuttering bisimilarity. In order to prove this result, we must first lift the concept of governed stuttering bisimilarity to paths.

Paths of length 1 are equivalent if the vertices they consist of are equivalent. If paths p and q are equivalent, then $p \cdot \langle v \rangle \approx q$ iff v is equivalent to the last vertex in q, and $p \cdot \langle v \rangle \approx q \cdot \langle w \rangle$ iff $v \approx w$. An infinite path p is equivalent to a path q if for all finite prefixes of p there is an equivalent prefix of q and *vice versa*.

We define $\Pi_\varphi^n(v)$ to be the set of paths of length n that start in v and that are allowed by some strategy φ. $\Pi_\varphi^\omega(v)$ is then the set of all infinite paths allowed by φ, starting in v. In a similar fashion, we also define $\Psi_\varphi^n(v)$, which contains those paths starting in v that are allowed by φ and that consist of exactly n segments in which all vertices in a segment are related by $\approx$, except the last vertex. Also included in $\Psi_\varphi^n(v)$ are infinite paths that stay in the same class forever after n or less such segments.

Definition 6 (Levels). *Formally we define the nth* level paths $\Psi_\varphi^n(v)$ *of a strategy* φ *from root vertex* v *for all paths* p *as follows:*

$$p \in \Psi_\varphi^0(v) \text{ iff } p = \langle v \rangle$$
$$p \cdot q \in \Psi_\varphi^{n+1}(v) \text{ iff } p \in \Psi_\varphi^n(v) \wedge \varphi \Vdash p \cdot q \wedge$$
$$((p \cdot q \eqsim p \wedge |q| = \infty) \vee$$
$$(\exists \bar{q}, v : q = \bar{q} \cdot \langle v \rangle \wedge p \cdot \bar{q} \eqsim p \wedge p \cdot q \not\eqsim p))$$

Note that $\Pi_\varphi^\omega(v) = \Psi_\varphi^\omega(v)$. The following lemma is the basis for establishing that governed stuttering bisimilarity refines winner equivalence.

Lemma 1. *Given some* $v, w \in V$ *such that* $v \eqsim w$, *then for every strategy* $\varphi \in \mathbb{S}_i$ *we have a strategy* $\psi \in \mathbb{S}_i^*$ *such that* $\forall n \in \mathbb{N} : \forall p \in \Psi_\psi^n(w) : \exists p' \in \Psi_\varphi^n(v) : p \eqsim p'$

We are now in a position to prove that governed stuttering bisimilarity refines winner equivalence.

Theorem 4. *Governed stuttering bisimulation strictly refines winner equivalence.*

Proof. Let φ be a strategy for player i that wins from $v \in V$. Without loss of generality assume that φ is memoryless, and let $w \in V$ such that $v \eqsim w$. By Lemma 1, we know that there is some strategy ψ such that for every path in $\Psi_\psi^\omega(w)$ there is a related path in $\Psi_\varphi^\omega(v)$. As $\Pi_\varphi^\omega(v) = \Psi_\varphi^\omega(v)$, this means that for every path starting in w that is allowed by ψ, we have an equivalent path starting in v that is allowed by φ. Equivalent paths have the same set of infinitely often recurring priorities. Any priority that may be visited infinitely often under ψ could therefore also have been visited infinitely often under φ. Therefore, ψ must be a winning strategy. The strictness of the refinement follows from, *e.g.*, the example in Figure 1.c, in which player $\square$ wins both vertices. □

4.4 Decidability

Our algorithm for deciding governed stuttering bisimilarity is based on Groote and Vaandrager's $\mathcal{O}(nm)$ algorithm for deciding stuttering bisimilarity [16]. Before we provide the details, we introduce the necessary additional concepts.

Our algorithm requires a generalisation of the well-known notion of *attractor sets* [22] along the lines of the generalisation used for the computation of the *Until* in the alternating-time temporal logic ATL [1]. The generalisation introduces a parameter restricting the set of vertices that are considered in the attractor sets.

$$
\begin{aligned}
{}_BAttr_i^0(U) &= U \\
{}_BAttr_i^{n+1}(U) &= {}_BAttr_i^n(U) \\
&\cup \{v \in B \mid \mathcal{P}(v) = i \wedge \exists v \to v' : v' \in {}_BAttr_i^n(U)\} \\
&\cup \{v \in B \mid \mathcal{P}(v) \neq i \wedge \forall v \to v' : v' \in {}_BAttr_i^n(U)\} \\
{}_BAttr_i(U) &= {}_BAttr_i^\omega(U) \\
Leave_i(B, W) &= {}_BAttr_i(W) \cap B
\end{aligned}
$$

The set $Leave_i(B, W)$ captures the subset of B from which player i can force the game to $W \subseteq V$. The formal correspondence between *Leave* and $_i\mapsto$ is formalised below; this allows for restating the criteria from Definition 4 in terms of *Leave*.

Lemma 2. *Let P be a partition of V, and let $B \in P$ be a block. Then for all $u \in B$:*
$u_i \mapsto_P$ *if and only if* $u \notin Leave_{\neg i}(B, V \setminus B)$.

Lemma 3. *Let P partition V, and let $B, B' \in P$ such that $B \neq B'$. Let $v \in B$ such that $v \rightarrow B'$. Then for all $w \in B$ it holds that $w_{\mathcal{P}(v)} \mapsto_P B'$ if and only if $w \in Leave_{\mathcal{P}(v)}(B, B')$.*

Groote and Vaandrager's algorithm for stuttering bisimulation repeatedly refines a carefully chosen initial partition P_0 using a so-called *splitter*. We apply the same principle, choosing P_0 such that for all $v, v' \in V$, $v\ P_0\ v'$ if and only if $\Omega(v) = \Omega(v')$ as our initial partition. As our splitter, we define a function *pos* that returns the set of vertices in B from which a given player i can force the play to reach B', or, in case $B = B'$, force the play to diverge:

$$pos_i(B, B') = \begin{cases} \{v \in B \mid v_i \mapsto_P\} & \text{if } B = B' \\ \{v \in B \mid v_i \mapsto_P B'\} & \text{if } B \neq B' \end{cases}$$

In line with [16], we say that B' is a *splitter* of B if and only if $\emptyset \neq pos_i(B, B') \neq B$ for some player i. A partition P is *stable with respect to a block* $B \in P$ if B is not a splitter of any block in P. The partition itself is stable if it is stable with respect to all its blocks. A high-level description of our algorithm for governed stuttering bisimulation,

---

Algorithm 1. Decision procedure for $\approx$

$n \leftarrow 0$
repeat
    splitter $\leftarrow \perp$
    for each $B \in P_n$ and player i **do** { Find splitter in $\mathcal{O}(nm)$ }
      if there exists $v \in B$ with $v \rightarrow B'$ and $\emptyset \neq pos_i(B, B') \neq B$ for $B' \in P_n$ **then**
        splitter $\leftarrow (B, pos_i(B, B'))$
      end if
    end for
    if *splitter* $= (B, Pos)$ **then** { Refine partition in $\mathcal{O}(m)$ }
      $P_{n+1} \leftarrow (P_n \setminus \{B\}) \cup \{Pos, B \setminus Pos\}$
    end if
    $n \leftarrow n + 1$
until $P_{n-1} = P_n$

---

is given as Algorithm 1. Note that this does not compute the quotient. Correctness of the algorithm follows the same line of reasoning as in [16]. Based on this algorithm, we obtain the following complexity result.

Theorem 5. *Algorithm 1 decides $\approx$ in $\mathcal{O}(n^2m)$ time for a parity game that contains n vertices and m edges.*

Our time complexity is worse than the $\mathcal{O}(nm)$ achieved by the original algorithm for deciding stuttering bisimulation. The extra factor $\mathcal{O}(n)$ is due to the complexity required to search for a splitter which, in our case, requires $\mathcal{O}(nm)$ time, instead of the original $\mathcal{O}(m)$ time.

5   Experiments

While the running time of our algorithm for governed stuttering bisimilarity is theo-retically worse than that of the algorithm for stuttering bisimilarity, we expect that for solving parity games, in practice both are comparable. We test this hypothesis on a set of over 200 real-life model checking problems, part of which was previously used to study the effect of stuttering bisimilarity for parity games, see [10].

Whereas in [10] a signature based approach [5] was used, in the present paper we use the Groote-Vaandrager algorithm for computing stuttering bisimilarity in order to an-swer our hypothesis. For computing governed stuttering bisimilarity we have modified the implementation of Groote-Vaandrager to include the changes presented in Algo-rithm 1.

For running our experiments we reuse the setup of [10] for solving parity games, *i.e.*, we use an optimised C++ implementation of the *small progress measures* algo-rithm [18], and the optimised variants of the small progress measures, recursive [22,27] and *bigstep* algorithms [24] offered by the PGSolver [12] toolset.

All experiments were conducted on a machine consisting of 28 Intel® Xeon© E5520 Processors running at 2.27GHz, with 1TB of shared main memory, running a 64-bit Linux distribution using kernel version 2.6.27. None of our experiments employ multi-core features.

5.1   Test Sets

The parity games that were used for our experiments are clustered into four test sets. We give a brief description of each of the sets below.

Model checking. Our main interest is in the practical implications of governed stutter-ing bisimilarity reduction on solving model checking problems. To this end, a num-ber of model checking problems have been selected from the literature [21,3,15]. The properties that have been checked include fairness, liveness and safety proper-ties.

Games. The second test set considers a number of turn-based, two player board games. For each of these games, and for each player, we have encoded the property that said player can play the game in such a way that, regardless of the play of the opponent, she can win the game.

PGSolver. The third test set was taken from [12] and consists of the elevator problem and the Hanoi towers problem described in that paper. It also includes alternative encodings of these problems, taken from [10].

Equivalence checking. The last test set consists of a number of equivalence checking problems encoded into parity games as described in [8].

The problems in these test sets are scalable. In every test set, a number of instances of every problem is included. Each problem gives rise to a parity game with at most 4 different priorities, which is typical for practical verification problems.

The model checking, PGSolver and equivalence checking problems were studied before in the setting of stuttering bisimilarity [10]. We extended that test set to include more examples of parity games with alternations between players and priorities. We can expect improved reductions compared to stuttering bisimilarity in these cases.

5.2 Measurements: Size and Time

To analyse the performance of our reduction, we measured the difference in the sizes (computed as the sum of the number of vertices and the number of edges) of the stuttering and governed stuttering minimal games. A reduction of 0% means that the governed stuttering bisimilarity reduced game has the same size as the stuttering bisimilarity reduced game.

For every problem in the test set, we compute the reduction as the average reduction over all instances of that problem. We do this in order to measure the reduction rate for the different problems, rather than for the instances. Figure 2a shows the average reduction for problems in each test set, together with the minimal and maximal reduction achieved within that set.

In addition, we measured the times needed to reduce the parity games plus the time needed to solve the reduced game using the fastest solver. That is, the sum of these two is the *total solving time* for a parity game. This way, our results can be compared to those listed in [10]. In Figure 2b, every data point represents a problem instance, of which the total solving time of the stuttering minimal game determines the x-coordinate, and the total solving time for the governed stuttering bisimilarity minimal game determines the y-coordinate.

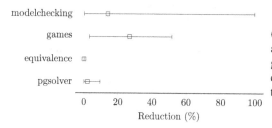

(a) Minimum, maximum and average reduction of parity games using governed stuttering bisimulation reduction, as percentage of the size after stuttering bisimilarity reduction

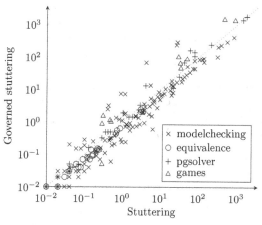

(b) Solving times (=sum of reduction time and subsequent solving) in seconds using governed stuttering bisimilarity set out against the solving times using stuttering bisimilarity. The dotted line is defined as $x = y$ and serves as a reference. Note that the axes are in log scale.

Fig. 2. Comparison of sizes and times of reductions

5.3 Discussion

Figure 2b shows that solving times for governed stuttering bisimilarity are generally comparable to those for stuttering bisimilarity, confirming our hypothesis.

Whether governed stuttering bisimilarity offers additional reductions over stuttering bisimilarity depends largely on the kind of property that is checked, and the resulting structure of the parity game. On average, a modest additional reduction is achieved, and there are practical cases in which the additional reduction is almost 100%.

For several model checking cases, stuttering bisimilarity already reduces the parity game to a graph with one vertex per priority. Obviously, governed stuttering bisimilarity cannot improve on that. However, in one of our problems (model checking a leadership protocol) a reduction of almost 100% is achieved, increasing the average reduction for this test set.

The properties that we considered on two-player games naturally give rise to alternations between players in the parity game. For these type of properties, the reduction achieved using governed stuttering bisimilarity surpasses that of stuttering bisimilarity by about 20% on average. Similar results for parity games obtained for controller synthesis (see *e.g.* [2]) may be obtained as these exhibit similar structures.

For the equivalence cases, stuttering bisimilarity reduction already yields games of a small size and governed stuttering bisimilarity does not reduce any further.[1]

Interestingly, one of the PGSolver cases taken from [12] shows a better reduction using governed stuttering bisimilarity, in contrast to an alternative encoding also used in [10].

Summarising, we conclude that governed stuttering bisimilarity reduces slightly better than stuttering bisimilarity, without noticable loss of performance.

6 Related Work

As observed in Fritz' thesis [13], *direct simulation* for parity games led to disappointing reductions, spurring Fritz and Wilke to investigate a weaker notion, called *delayed simulation* [14] and its induced equivalence. Delayed simulation equivalence is incomparable to governed stuttering bisimilarity. Contrary to governed stuttering bisimilarity, delayed simulation equivalence has the capability to relate vertices with different priorities. On the other hand, governed stuttering bisimilarity can relate vertices with the same priority in cases that delayed simulation equivalence cannot, as illustrated by the two parity games below, in which governed stuttering bisimulation relates all vertices with equal priority whereas delayed simulation equivalence does not:

Contrary to governed stuttering bisimulation, the definition of the simulation relation is entirely in terms of a *simulation game*, *viz.*, a game graph equipped with Büchi winning conditions. The simulation game gives rise to an $\mathcal{O}(d^2 n^3 m)$ algorithm for deciding

---

[1] [10] reports a poor reduction for stuttering equivalence in these cases. This was caused by "optimisations" that were used during generation of the parity games.

delayed simulation (here, n is the number of vertices, m the number of edges, and d the number of different priorities in the game), significantly exceeding our $\mathcal{O}(n^2m)$ complexity for governed stuttering bisimulation.

Apart from delayed simulation, in the setting of Boolean equation systems, the notion of *idempotence-identifying bisimilarity* was defined and investigated [20]. This equivalence relation enables one to relate conjunctive equations to disjunctive equations. In parity games, this translates to being able to relate □ vertices and ◇ vertices, respectively. Idempotence-identifying bisimilarity is much finer than governed stuttering bisimulation, as the former is based on strong bisimulation. Interestingly, the complexity of deciding idempotence-identifying bisimilarity is the same as for strong bisimilarity.

7 Concluding Remarks

We have described a non-trivial modification of stuttering bisimulation that allows relating vertices that belong to different players. The resulting relation, dubbed *governed stuttering bisimulation*, is an equivalence relation that can be decided in $\mathcal{O}(n^2m)$ time using a partition refinement algorithm. Although this complexity is worse than the $\mathcal{O}(nm)$ time complexity for deciding stuttering bisimulation, our experiments indicate that this factor does not manifest itself in practice. In fact, the algorithm is largely competitive with the one for stuttering bisimilarity.

An obvious question is whether elements of Fritz and Wilke's delayed simulation [14] and governed stuttering bisimulation can be combined. Given the complexity of the proofs of most of our results for governed stuttering bisimulation and our attempts to weakening governed stuttering bisimulation along these lines, we are rather sceptical about the chances of success. Even if one would manage to define such a relation, it would likely have little practical significance due to the prohibitive complexity of delayed simulation.

An interesting extension of our work could be to generalise the concepts of governed stuttering bisimilarity to games with other payoff functions that are insensitive to stuttering. We expect such a generalisation to be reasonably straightforward.

Finally, we observe that stuttering bisimulation (also known as *branching bisimulation* in labelled transition systems) underlies several confluence reduction techniques for syntactic system descriptions, see [6]. Such reductions partly side-step the state-space explosion. We believe that our study offers the required foundations for bringing similar-spirited confluence reduction techniques to a setting of symbolic representations of parity games.

References

1. Alur, R., Henzinger, T.A., Kupferman, O.: Alternating-time temporal logic. J. ACM 49(5), 672–713 (2002)
2. Arnold, A., Vincent, A., Walukiewicz, I.: Games for synthesis of controllers with partial observation. TCS 303(1), 7–34 (2003)
3. Badban, B., Fokkink, W., Groote, J.F., Pang, J., van de Pol, J.: Verification of a sliding window protocol in μCRL and PVS. FAC 17, 342–388 (2005)

4. Berwanger, D., Dawar, A., Hunter, P., Kreutzer, S.: DAG-Width and Parity Games. In: Durand, B., Thomas, W. (eds.) STACS 2006. LNCS, vol. 3884, pp. 524–536. Springer, Heidelberg (2006)

5. Blom, S.C.C., Orzan, S.: Distributed branching bisimulation reduction of state spaces. Electronic Notes in Theoretical Computer Science 89(1), 99–113 (2003)

6. Blom, S., van de Pol, J.: State Space Reduction by Proving Confluence. In: Brinksma, E., Larsen, K.G. (eds.) CAV 2002. LNCS, vol. 2404, pp. 596–694. Springer, Heidelberg (2002)

7. Browne, M.C., Clarke, E.M., Grumberg, O.: Characterizing finite Kripke structures in propositional temporal logic. TCS 59, 115–131 (1988)

8. Chen, T., Ploeger, B., van de Pol, J., Willemse, T.A.C.: Equivalence Checking for Infinite Systems Using Parameterized Boolean Equation Systems. In: Caires, L., Vasconcelos, V.T. (eds.) CONCUR 2007. LNCS, vol. 4703, pp. 120–135. Springer, Heidelberg (2007)

9. Cranen, S., Keiren, J.J.A., Willemse, T.A.C.: A cure for stuttering parity games. Technical Report 12-05, Eindhoven University of Technology, Eindhoven (2012), http://alexandria.tue.nl/repository/books/732149.pdf

10. Cranen, S., Keiren, J.J.A., Willemse, T.A.C.: Stuttering Mostly Speeds Up Solving Parity Games. In: Bobaru, M., Havelund, K., Holzmann, G.J., Joshi, R. (eds.) NFM 2011. LNCS, vol. 6617, pp. 207–221. Springer, Heidelberg (2011)

11. Emerson, E.A., Jutla, C.S.: Tree automata, mu-calculus and determinacy. In: FOCS 1991, pp. 368–377. IEEE Computer Society, Washington, DC (1991)

12. Friedmann, O., Lange, M.: Solving Parity Games in Practice. In: Liu, Z., Ravn, A.P. (eds.) ATVA 2009. LNCS, vol. 5799, pp. 182–196. Springer, Heidelberg (2009)

13. Fritz, C.: Simulation-Based Simplification of omega-Automata. PhD thesis, Christian-Albrechts-Universität zu Kiel (2005)

14. Fritz, C., Wilke, T.: Simulation Relations for Alternating Parity Automata and Parity Games. In: Ibarra, O.H., Dang, Z. (eds.) DLT 2006. LNCS, vol. 4036, pp. 59–70. Springer, Heidelberg (2006)

15. Groote, J.F., Pang, J., Wouters, A.G.: Analysis of a distributed system for lifting trucks. In: JLAP, vol. 55, pp. 21–56. Elsevier (2003)

16. Groote, J.F., Vaandrager, F.W.: An Efficient Algorithm for Branching Bisimulation and Stuttering Equivalence. In: Paterson, M. (ed.) ICALP 1990. LNCS, vol. 443, pp. 626–638. Springer, Heidelberg (1990)

17. Jurdziński, M.: Deciding the winner in parity games is in UP ∩ co-UP. IPL 68(3), 119–124 (1998)

18. Jurdziński, M.: Small Progress Measures for Solving Parity Games. In: Reichel, H., Tison, S. (eds.) STACS 2000. LNCS, vol. 1770, pp. 290–301. Springer, Heidelberg (2000)

19. Jurdziński, M., Paterson, M., Zwick, U.: A Deterministic Subexponential Algorithm for Solving Parity Games. In: SODA 2006, pp. 117–123. ACM/SIAM (2006)

20. Keiren, J.J.A., Willemse, T.A.C.: Bisimulation Minimisations for Boolean Equation Systems. In: Namjoshi, K., Zeller, A., Ziv, A. (eds.) HVC 2009. LNCS, vol. 6405, pp. 102–116. Springer, Heidelberg (2011)

21. Luttik, S.P.: Description and formal specification of the link layer of P1394. In: Workshop on Applied Formal Methods in System Design, pp. 43–56 (1997)

22. McNaughton, R.: Infinite games played on finite graphs. APAL 65(2), 149–184 (1993)

23. Obdrzálek, J.: Clique-Width and Parity Games. In: CSL, pp. 54–68 (2007)

24. Schewe, S.: Solving Parity Games in Big Steps. In: Arvind, V., Prasad, S. (eds.) FSTTCS 2007. LNCS, vol. 4855, pp. 449–460. Springer, Heidelberg (2007)

25. Stirling, C.: Bisimulation, Model Checking and Other Games. In: Notes for Mathfit Workshop on Finite Model Theory, University of Wales Swansea (1996)

26. van Glabbeek, R.J., Weijland, W.P.: Branching time and abstraction in bisimulation semantics. J. ACM 43(3), 555–600 (1996)

27. Zielonka, W.: Infinite games on finitely coloured graphs with applications to automata on infinite trees. TCS 200(1-2), 135–183 (1998)

Ensuring Reachability by Design*

Benoît Caillaud[1] and Jean-Baptiste Raclet[2]

[1] INRIA, Campus de Beaulieu, F-35042 Rennes cedex, France
Benoit.Caillaud@inria.fr
[2] IRIT/CNRS, 118 Route de Narbonne, F-31062 Toulouse cedex 9, France
Jean-Baptiste.Raclet@irit.fr

Abstract. This paper studies the independent implementability of reachability properties, which are in general not compositional. We consider modal specifications, which are widely acknowledged as suitable for abstracting implementation details of components while exposing to the environment relevant information about cross-component interactions. In order to obtain the required expressivity, we extend them with marked states to model states to be reached. We then develop an algebra with both logical and structural composition operators ensuring reachability properties by construction.

1 Introduction

In order to face the intrinsic complexity of automotive, aeronautic and consumer electronics embedded systems, but also of web-based service oriented architectures, modular design aims at organizing systems as a set of distinct components that can be developed independently and then assembled together. This is best achieved using interfaces which abstract superfluous implementation details of a component and expose cross-component protocol informations that are essential to a correct use of a component. Component reuse in different contexts is thus made possible, not only reducing design time, but also enabling the amortization of design costs over several different projects.

Component interoperability or compatibility is then a major issue: when can we safely compose two (or more) components? Compatibility is often considered at a signature level. In this simple case, interfaces consist in function or method types and compatibility consists in a type-checking, performed either at compile-time or at run-time. This paper deals with a richer notion of interfaces capable of capturing behavioral properties.

The first work on behavioral compatibility of interfaces has been proposed in [1]. This paper considers an automata-based formalism for interfaces in which transitions are labeled with output (produced by the component) or input (produced by the environment) actions. Then, a run-time error occurs whenever a component produces an output that is not accepted as input by one of its peers. The fact that a runtime error may occur does not necessarily lead to deem the

---

* A long version is available as a research report [5].

A. Roychoudhury and M. D'Souza (Eds.): ICTAC 2012, LNCS 7521, pp. 213–227, 2012.
© Springer-Verlag Berlin Heidelberg 2012

214   B. Caillaud and J.-B. Raclet

interfaces incompatible. Indeed, the authors promote an optimistic approach of composition in which two interfaces are compatible if there exists a restriction of the permitted actions of the environment in order to prevent the reachability of a runtime error. They show that this form of compatibility is preserved in the design flow provided alternating refinement [2] is used. More precisely, starting from initial interfaces whose product satisfies a particular *safety* property (i.e., a runtime error cannot be reached), they can be refined independently and then composed, their product will also satisfy the same safety property. This principle, called *independent implementability*, is of key importance [11] and enables the concurrent design of systems that are then assembled in a bottom-up manner.

This paper now studies the case of *reachability* properties and proposes results regarding their satisfaction by design. Basically, a reachability property states that some particular situation can be reached. Examples abound in practice. For instance, consider Service Oriented Architectures (SOA) formed of several interacting services; they should always have the possibility to reach a termination state, by delivering a response to all service activation. However, termination is in general not preserved by service composition. Although reachability properties are easy to verify in this context [4], model-checking may not be an appropriate solution. First, because it requires to construct the reachability graph of a system which may lead to a state explosion problem. Moreover, in case model-checking reveals a violation of the reachability property, designers have to iterate the design cycle by re-coding and re-validating their components, therefore extending time to market. The alternative approach advocated in this paper consists in controlling the design flow of components, that is, the evolution of interfaces through compositions and refinements, in order to ensure a reachability property by construction. Now, what specification formalism capturing some behavioral aspects of components is convenient for interface-based design? Modal specifications [16,14,3] are widely acknowledged as a suitable proposal [12,20,21]. Basically, they consist in labeling interface transitions with modalities, either *must* if the transition has to be enabled in any refinement, or *may* if the transition is allowed. In [12,20,21], modal specifications are shown to have many benefits comparing the specification formalism introduced in [1]; they are not only equipped with an optimistic composition operator and a refinement relation but also with a conjunction and a quotient operator. As reachability properties cannot be expressed, in general, with modal specifications, we first consider in this paper modal specifications enriched with marked states, in the same fashion as it is done in [6]. We show that, in this framework, we can develop a theory ensuring reachability properties by design.

2   Modeling with Marked Modal Specifications

2.1   Background on Automata

Let Σ be a finite alphabet of actions, a *deterministic* automaton over Σ is a tuple $\mathcal{M} = (R, r^0, \Sigma, \lambda, G)$ where R is a finite set of states, $r^0 \in R$ is the unique initial state, λ is a partial map from $R \times \Sigma$ to R called the *labeled transition map* and $G \subseteq R$ is a non-empty set of *marked* states. The set of *firable* actions from $r \in R$ is $ready(r) = \{a \in \Sigma \mid \lambda(r, a) \text{ is defined}\}$.

Transition map λ is extended to its transitive and reflexive closure: let ϵ denote the empty word, for all $r \in R$, $\lambda(r, \epsilon) = r$ and for all $u \in \Sigma^*$, $a \in \Sigma$, $r_1, r_2, r_3 \in R$, $\lambda(r_1, u) = r_2$ and $\lambda(r_2, a) = r_3$ imply $\lambda(r_1, u.a) = r_3$. Define $\mathcal{L}_\mathcal{M} = \{u \in \Sigma^* \mid \exists r' \in R, \lambda(r^0, u) = r'\}$ to be the *language* of $\mathcal{M}$. If $\lambda(r, u) = r'$ for some u then r' is said to be *reachable* from r.

Given $P \subseteq R$, define $pre^*(P)$ and $post^*(P)$ to be the set of states that are respectively coreachable and reachable from any state $r \in P$: it is the least set such that for $r \in P$, $r \in pre^*(P)$ and $r \in post^*(P)$ and for every $\lambda(r', a) = r''$, if $r'' \in pre^*(P)$ then $r' \in pre^*(P)$ and if $r' \in post^*(P)$ then $r'' \in post^*(P)$. With a slight abuse, we may write $pre^*(r)$ and $post^*(r)$ for $pre^*(\{r\})$ and $post^*(\{r\})$.

If modeling a service, it is desirable to set that a service session eventually terminates; this is often refered in SOC as weak termination. To capture this kind of requirement, we define *terminating* automata: an automaton $\mathcal{M}$ is said to be *terminating* whenever $R = pre^*(G)$ meaning that it is always possible to reach a marked state from any state of the automaton. In other words, $\mathcal{M}$ is terminating if and only if for any $u \in \mathcal{L}_\mathcal{M}$, there exists a v such that $uv \in \mathcal{L}_\mathcal{M}$ and $\lambda(r^0, uv) \in G$. In the temporal logic CTL, this property can be written $AG(EF\ G)$.

Given two automata $\mathcal{M}_1 = (R_1, r_1^0, \Sigma_1, \lambda_1, G_1)$ and $\mathcal{M}_2 = (R_2, r_2^0, \Sigma_2, \lambda_2, G_2)$, their product is the automaton $\mathcal{M}_1 \times \mathcal{M}_2 = (R_1 \times R_2, (r_1^0, r_2^0), \Sigma_1 \cup \Sigma_2, \lambda, G_1 \times G_2)$ where $\lambda((r_1, r_2), a)$ is defined as $(\lambda_1(r_1, a), r_2)$ for $a \in \Sigma_1 \setminus \Sigma_2$, $(r_1, \lambda_2(r_2, a))$ for $a \in \Sigma_2 \setminus \Sigma_1$ and $(\lambda_1(r_1, a), \lambda_2(r_2, a))$ for $a \in \Sigma_1 \cap \Sigma_2$.

2.2   Marked Modal Specifications

Following [6], we enrich modal specifications [16,14,3] with marked states in order to model *states to be reached*. For instance, if a designer specifies a service, this enables to represent session terminations. The obtained formalism allows to specify a (possibly infinite) set of automata called *implementations*.

Definition 1 (Marked Modal Specification). *A marked modal specification over Σ is a tuple $\mathcal{C} = (Q, q^0, \Sigma, \delta, must, may, F)$, where Q is a finite set of states, $q^0 \in Q$ is the unique initial state, $\delta : Q \times \Sigma \to Q$ is a partial labeled transition map; $must, may : Q \to 2^\Sigma$ map to each state q the set of required and allowed actions from q, $F \subseteq Q$ is a non-empty set of marked states.*

It is assumed that a transition is associated to any allowed action, that is for every state $q \in Q$ and every action $a \in \Sigma$, $a \in may(q)$ if and only if $\delta(q, a)$ is defined. The mapping $may : Q \to 2^\Sigma$ can thus be reconstructed from the transition relation δ. However, this distinction simplifies the definition of satisfaction and refinement relations and compositions operators.

In this paper, marked modal specifications are taken *deterministic*, that is: for any $a \in \Sigma$ and any state q there is at most one state q' such that $\delta(q, a) = q'$. The reason for this will be given later in Sec. 3.

The *underlying automata* associated to C is $\mathrm{Un}(C) = (Q, q^0, \Sigma, \delta, F)$. The language $\mathcal{L}_C$ is then $\mathcal{L}_{\mathrm{Un}(C)}$. As previously for automata, we extend δ to words by taking its transitive and reflexive closure. Moreover, we define $pre_M^*(P)$ and $pre_m^*(P)$ with $P \subseteq Q$ as the set of states that are coreachable from any state $q \in Q$ by following transitions labeled by required and allowed actions, respectively: $pre_m^*(P)$ corresponds to $pre^*(P)$ in $\mathrm{Un}(C)$; $pre_M^*(P)$ is the least set such that for $r \in P$, $r \in pre_M^*(P)$ and for every $\lambda(r', a) = r''$ with $a \in must(r')$ and $r'' \in pre_M^*(P)$ then $r' \in pre_M^*(P)$. Last, $post_m^*(P)$ is $post^*(P)$ in $\mathrm{Un}(C)$.

Any terminating automaton can be seen as a marked modal specification with no design choice left open, that is, for any state r, the optional action set $may(r) \setminus must(r)$ is empty. More formally, the *embedding* of a terminating automaton $\mathcal{M} = (R, r^0, \Sigma, \lambda, G)$ into the class of the marked modal specifications is $\mathrm{Em}(\mathcal{M}) = (R, r^0, \Sigma, \lambda, must, may, G)$ with, for all $r \in R$, $may(r) = must(r) = ready(r)$. Now, the semantics of marked modal specifications is given in terms of terminating automata:

Definition 2 (Satisfaction). *A terminating automaton $\mathcal{M} = (R, r^0, \Sigma, \lambda, G)$ satisfies the marked modal specification $C = (Q, q^0, \Sigma, \delta, must, may, F)$, denoted $\mathcal{M} \models C$, if and only if there exists a simulation relation $\pi \subseteq R \times Q$ such that $(r^0, q^0) \in \pi$ and for all pairs $(r, q) \in \pi$:*
- *$must(q) \subseteq ready(r) \subseteq may(q)$;*
- *$r \in G$ implies $q \in F$;*
- *for every $a \in \Sigma$ and every $r' \in R$, $\lambda(r, a) = r'$ implies $\big(r', \delta(q, a)\big) \in \pi$.*

The set of models (or implementations) of C is denoted $[\![C]\!]$. A marked modal specification is said *satisfiable* if and only if $[\![C]\!] \neq \emptyset$. Two marked modal specifications C and C' are said *equivalent*, written $C \equiv C'$, if and only if they admit the same implementations: $[\![C]\!] = [\![C']\!]$. Any unsatisfiable specification is mapped on a special specification denoted $C_\perp$, with $[\![C_\perp]\!] = \emptyset$.

Example 1. Consider the terminating automaton $\mathcal{M}$ in Fig. 1(a) and the marked modal specification C in Fig. 1(b) where transitions from q labeled by a are dashed when $a \in may(q) \setminus must(q)$ and plain when $a \in must(q)$; marked states are double-circled. $\mathcal{M}$ satisfies C because of the simulation relation $\pi = \{(0, 0'), (1, 1'), (2, 2'), (3, 1')\}$.

Observe that, in state $2'$, although none of the two outgoing transition is *must*, at least one of the two has to be present in any model in order to preserve the reachability of a marked state. Such restricted disjunction cannot be expressed with traditional unmarked modal specifications. Observe also that, according to the second item of the Def. 2, the reachability of a marked state may be delayed: $1'$ is marked, $(3, 1') \in \pi$ but 3 is not marked; however, a marked state can be eventually reached from 3 thanks to the state 1.

According to Def. 2, only reachable states of C are semantically meaningful. We thus suppose from now on, and without loss of generality, that C is reachable, that is: $\forall q \in Q$, $q^0 \in pre^*(q)$.

(a) A terminating automaton $\mathcal{M}$ (b) A marked modal spec. $\mathcal{C}$

Fig. 1. $\mathcal{M}$ is a model of $\mathcal{C}$

A marked state $q \in F$ is said *delayable* if q can be reached again, that is, there exists a word $u \neq \epsilon$ such that $\delta(q, u) = q$; it is said *undelayable* otherwise. Denote by D the set of delayable states of a marked modal specification.

A marked state $q \in F$ is a bottleneck of $\mathcal{C}$ if it is the only marked state reachable from some state $q' \in Q$ that is, $post_m^*(q') \cap F = \{q\}$. Intuitively, this notion allows to identify the states that will be marked in any model of the specification.

Lemma 1. *Given a terminating automaton $\mathcal{M}$ and a marked modal specification $\mathcal{C}$ s.t. $\mathcal{M} \models \mathcal{C}$ then: $\mathcal{L}_{\mathcal{M}} \subseteq \mathcal{L}_{\mathcal{C}}$, and, for all $u \in \mathcal{L}_{\mathcal{M}}$, $\left(\lambda(r^0, u), \delta(q^0, u)\right) \in \pi$.*

The introduced semantics induces some simplifications in the structure of the marked modal specifications that we discuss now. At the end of this section, this will lead to the definition of an associated normal form.

Must-saturation. Observe that any terminating automaton model of the marked modal specification in Fig. 1 includes the starting transition labeled by a stemming from the initial state. It is thus a required transition that can be assigned a must modality in the specification. We therefore introduce the *must-saturation* of marked modal specifications.

Definition 3 (Must-saturation). *A marked modal specification is* must-saturated *if for all $q \notin F$ such that there is a unique $a \in may(q)$, we have $a \in must(q)$. Such a must-mapping is then said to be* saturated.

Lemma 2. *Any must-mapping can be saturated without changing the set of marked implementations.*

Consistency and attractability. Given a marked modal specification $\mathcal{C} = (Q, q^0, \Sigma, \delta, must, may, F)$ and a state $q \in Q$, $\mathcal{C}$ is said *consistent* in q if and only if $must(q) \subseteq may(q)$. $\mathcal{C}$ is said *attracted* in q if and only if $q \in pre_m^*(F)$.

Lemma 3. *If $\mathcal{M} \models \mathcal{C}$ then $\mathcal{C}$ is consistent and attracted in every state $\delta(q^0, u)$ with $u \in \mathcal{L}_{\mathcal{M}}$.*

As a consequence, only consistent and attracting states of $\mathcal{C}$ are semantically meaningful. This now leads us to define a reduced form:

Definition 4 (Reduced marked modal specification). *$\mathcal{C}$ is reduced iff every state is reachable and it is consistent and attracted in every state $q \in Q$.*

Proposition 1 (Reducibility). *Every satisfiable marked modal specification is equivalent to a reduced marked modal specification.*

Proof of this proposition is by construction of a reduced marked specification $\rho\mathcal{C}$ and then proving that $\mathcal{C}$ and $\rho\mathcal{C}$ are equivalent. This construction makes use of a pruning operation. We denote by $Q_\Psi \subseteq Q$ the set of all states $q \in Q$ such that q is inconsistent or unattracting, that is: $must(q) \nsubseteq may(q)$ or $q \notin pre^*(F)$.

Definition 5 (Reduction operation). *Given a marked modal specification $\mathcal{C} = (Q, q^0, \Sigma, \delta, must, may, F)$: if $q^0 \in pre^*_M(Q_\Psi)$ then the reduction of $\mathcal{C}$ is $\mathcal{C}_\perp$; otherwise, it is the marked modal specification $(Q \setminus pre^*_M(Q_\Psi), q^0, \Sigma, \delta', must', may', F \setminus pre^*_M(Q_\Psi))$ where: $\delta'(r,a) = r'$ if and only if $\delta(r,a) = r'$ and $r, r' \notin pre^*_M(Q_\Psi)$; as indicated in right after Def. 1, may' can be recovered from δ' whereas must' is the restriction of must to the domain $Q \setminus pre^*_M(Q_\Psi)$.*

Normal form. This now leads us to define the normal form of any marked modal specification:

Definition 6 (Normal form). *A marked modal specification is in normal form if it is both must-saturated and reduced.*

According to Lem. 2 and Prop. 1, any marked modal specification $\mathcal{C}$ can be put in normal form $\eta\mathcal{C}$ without altering its set of models. As a result, from now on, we always suppose that marked modal specifications are in normal form.

At this point, the reader may wonder why must-saturation, consistency and attractability are not fully part of the definition of marked modal specification (as it is the case for the consistency requirement in the original papers on unmarked modal specifications [16,14]). The reason for this is because, in what follows, we propose composition operators on marked modal specifications and it is easier to define these constructions without trying to preserve these different requirements. Now if the combination of two marked modal specifications (which are now implicitly supposed to be in normal form) gives rise to a specification violating one of the above requirements then a step of normalization has to be applied on the result in order to have an iterative process.

3   Refinement of Marked Modal Specifications

A refinement relation aims at relating interfaces at different stages of their design. Basically, it should correspond to refine the set of allowed implementations of an interface. Moreover, we shall see later that refinement should entail *substitutability*, meaning that the substitution of an interface $\mathcal{C}_2$ by a refined version $\mathcal{C}_1$ must not impact the possible and actual cooperation with other components, that have been previously declared as legal for $\mathcal{C}_2$.

Definition 7 (Refinement). *Given two marked modal specifications $\mathcal{C}_1 = (Q_1, q_1^0, \Sigma, \delta_1, must_1, may_1, F_1)$ and $\mathcal{C}_2 = (Q_2, q_2^0, \Sigma, \delta_2, must_2, may_2, F_2)$, $\mathcal{C}_1$ is a refinement of $\mathcal{C}_2$, noted $\mathcal{C}_1 \leq \mathcal{C}_2$, if and only if there exists a simulation relation $\Pi \subseteq Q_1 \times Q_2$ such that $(q_1^0, q_2^0) \in \Pi$ and, for all pairs $(q_1, q_2) \in \Pi$:*

- $may_1(q_1) \subseteq may_2(q_2)$ and $must_1(q_1) \supseteq must_2(q_2)$;
- $q_1 \in F_1$ implies $q_2 \in F_2$;
- for every $a \in may_1(q_1)$, we have: $\big(\delta_1(q_1, a), \delta_2(q_2, a)\big) \in \Pi$.

Intuitively, refining an interface corresponds to possibly changing a transition with a *may* modality into either a required or a proscribed transition while potentially delaying the reachability of a marked state. This relation is reflexive and transitive and is thus a preorder.

Theorem 1. *Given two marked modal specifications C_1 and C_2, $C_1 \leq C_2$ if and only if, $[\![C_1]\!] \subseteq [\![C_2]\!]$.*

Theorem 1 holds provided the marked modal specifications are deterministic. If nondeterminism is allowed, refinement becomes correct but not fully abstract (the implication from right to left in Theorem 1 is not true in general). This is discussed for *unmarked* modal specifications in [15]; their counterexample can be immediately adapted to our context. Moreover, as argued in [8], nondeterministic modal specifications are not really suitable to characterize a set of *deterministic* automata.

When the left counterpart is ultimately refined, the refinement relation coincide with the implementation relation: given a terminating automaton $\mathcal{M}$ and a marked modal specification C, $\mathcal{M} \models C$ if and only if $Em(\mathcal{M}) \leq C$.

4   Conjunction of Marked Modal Specification

It is a current practice, when modeling complex systems, to associate several specifications with a same system, sub-system, or component, each of them describing a different aspect of it. These so-called *viewpoints* may be engineered independently, and possibly by different teams. It is then natural to question whether different viewpoints are not contradictory and how to realize all of them. This leads to define a conjunction operator. Moreover in [7], the authors point out that, during the design cycle, a designer may be tempted to merge two interfaces which share some similarities in order to use a same implementation for the two interfaces. More formally, this corresponds to look for a shared refinement of the interfaces, if it exists.

We now define a conjunction operator which enjoy the expected properties to solve the two above problems.

Definition 8 (Conjunction). *Given two marked modal specifications $C_1 = (Q_1, q_1^0, \Sigma, \delta_1, must_1, may_1, F_1)$ and $C_2 = (Q_2, q_2^0, \Sigma, \delta_2, must_2, may_2, F_2)$, the conjunction of C_1 and C_2, noted $C_1 \wedge C_2$, is the normal form $\eta(C_1 \& C_2)$ of $C_1 \& C_2 = (Q, q^0, \Sigma, \delta, must, may, F)$ with:*

- *$Q = Q_1 \times Q_2$ and $q^0 = (q_1^0, q_2^0)$;*
- *for any $q_1 \in Q_1$, $q_2 \in Q_2$ and $a \in \Sigma$, $\delta\big((q_1, q_2), a\big) = (q_1', q_2')$ if and only if $\delta_1(q_1, a) = q_1'$ and $\delta_2(q_2, a) = q_2'$;*
- *$may(q_1, q_2) = may_1(q_1) \cap may_2(q_2)$ and $must(q_1, q_2) = must_1(q_1) \cup must_2(q_2)$;*

– $(q_1, q_2) \in F$ *if and only if* $q_1 \in F_1$ *and* $q_2 \in F_2$.

Considering the manipulations done on the may/must-maps and on the transition map to obtain C_1 & C_2, the must-saturation and the consistency may not be respected. We thus impose a normalization step in order to have an iterative process as explained at the end of Sec. 2.

Theorem 2. *Given some marked modal specifications* C_1, C_2, C_3 *and* C:
- $[\![C_1 \wedge C_2]\!] = [\![C_1]\!] \cap [\![C_2]\!]$;
- $C_1 \wedge C_2$ *is the greatest lower bound of* C_1 *and* C_2 *for the refinement relation:* $C \leq C_1$ *and* $C \leq C_2$ *iff* $C \leq C_1 \wedge C_2$;
- $\wedge$ *is associative:* $C_1 \wedge (C_2 \wedge C_3) \equiv (C_1 \wedge C_2) \wedge C_3$.

5   Product of Marked Modal Specifications

Reachability is not preserved by product in general. Fig. 2 shows a simple example: $\mathcal{M}_1 \models C_1$ and $\mathcal{M}_2 \models C_2$; however the product of $\mathcal{M}_1 \times \mathcal{M}_2$ is a single non-marked state, hence the reachability of a marked state is not possible.

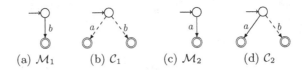

(a) $\mathcal{M}_1$ (b) C_1 (c) $\mathcal{M}_2$ (d) C_2

Fig. 2. Reachability is not compositional

This leads us to consider the following problem: given two marked modal specifications, can they be implemented concurrently i.e., such that the product of any model of the first specification with any model of the second one will always have the ability to reach a marked state of the product?

Similarly to [1], we distinguish a pessimistic from an optimistic view of composition and solve the previous problem in this two contexts.

First, in order to represent the cooperation between subsystems, a signature over Σ is now associated to any terminating automaton or marked modal specification over Σ:

Definition 9 (Signature). *Given a set of actions* Σ, *a signature over* Σ *is a mapping* $\mu : \Sigma \to \{?, !\}$ *which associates to any action either* ? *when the action is an input or* ! *when it is an output.*

Now, transitions are either labeled $!a$ (for $\mu(a) = !$) when the entity responsible for the occurrence of a is the system, or $?a$ (for $\mu(a) = ?$) if a stems from the environment of the system. The resulting formalism is thus suited to model protocols between a system and an unknown partner belonging to the system environment. Contrarily to the input/output automata of [18] and following the interface automata of [1], terminating automata and marked modal specifications are not required to be input-enabled, meaning that some actions $?b$ of the environment may not be permitted in some state q. More formally, this situation occurs in state q if there is no outgoing transition from q labeled by $?b$. This allows to restrict, from the point of view of the system, the behavior of its environment.

Example 2. Fig. 3(a) depicts the specification of a service which can receive requests $?r$ from an unidentified subsystem in its environment and then answers by producing $!a$ until it is stopped with $?f$. It may also produce $!b$ when set in an enhanced mode by $?e$. Fig. 3(b) depicts the specification of a client which expects to receive $?a$ as an answer to any request $!r$ and is ready to receive remitted $?a$. Although $?b$ is in the signature of $\mathcal{C}_2$, there is no transition labeled $?b$ meaning that the client rejects this inputs.

We write $\Sigma^?$ and $\Sigma^!$ for the set of input and output actions, respectively, thus forming a partition of Σ. A system is then *closed* if its associated signature is such that $\Sigma^? = \emptyset$ and *open* otherwise. In this paper, we assume that if $\mathcal{M} \models \mathcal{C}$ then the signature associated to $\mathcal{M}$ and $\mathcal{C}$ is identical. Similarly, if $\mathcal{C}_1 \leq \mathcal{C}_2$ then $\mathcal{C}_1$ and $\mathcal{C}_2$ have the same signature[1].

A first condition to product is the *composability* of signatures. Given two signatures μ_1 and μ_2 over Σ_1 and Σ_2 respectively, defining two partitions $(\Sigma_1^?, \Sigma_1^!)$ and $(\Sigma_2^?, \Sigma_2^!)$, they are *composable* if no output actions is shared: $\Sigma_1^! \cap \Sigma_2^! = \emptyset$. For composable signatures, we let the *communication* actions be the set $\Sigma_{co}(\mu_1, \mu_2) = (\Sigma_1^? \cap \Sigma_2^!) \cup (\Sigma_2^? \cap \Sigma_1^!)$ which corresponds to the shared actions on which a synchronization will be possible. The set of *private* actions is $\Sigma_{pr}(\mu_1, \mu_2) = (\Sigma_1 \cup \Sigma_2) \setminus (\Sigma_1 \cap \Sigma_2)$.

Definition 10 (Product of signatures). *The product of two composable signatures μ_1 and μ_2 is $\mu = \mu_1 \times \mu_2$ defined over $\Sigma_1 \cup \Sigma_2$ such that: $\Sigma^? = (\Sigma_1^? \cup \Sigma_2^?) \setminus \Sigma_{co}(\mu_1, \mu_2)$ and $\Sigma^! = \Sigma_1^! \cup \Sigma_2^!$.*

The product of two terminating automata $\mathcal{M}_1$ and $\mathcal{M}_2$ with respective composable signatures μ_1 and μ_2 is then $\mathcal{M}_1 \times \mathcal{M}_2$ as defined in Sec. 2.1 with signature $\mu_1 \times \mu_2$.

5.1 Pessimistic Composition of Marked Modal Specifications

We first consider the case of *pessimistic*[2] composition; we define a sufficient and necessary condition such that two marked modal specification can be independently implemented, the product of any of their implementations being terminating.

This condition corresponds to the existence of a joint path to a marked state, for every reachable state of the product of arbitrary implementations. We then

---

[1] This assumption is taken to simplify the presentation. Refinement of signature as defined in [21] can be handled in the presented theory.

[2] The pessimistic view of this approach will be made clearer in the next section.

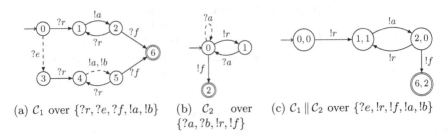

(a) $\mathcal{C}_1$ over $\{?r, ?e, ?f, !a, !b\}$ (b) $\mathcal{C}_2$ over $\{?a, ?b, !r, !f\}$ (c) $\mathcal{C}_1 \parallel \mathcal{C}_2$ over $\{?e, !r, !f, !a, !b\}$

Fig. 3. Example of composition

consider the less cooperative situation in which any optional behavior is disabled and check if such paths exist. However, the minimal behavior associated to a state of a marked modal specification is not unique in general. Consider $\mathcal{C}_1$ in Fig. 2(b), the minimal number of outgoing transition stemming from the initial state among all the models of $\mathcal{C}_1$ is 1 and can be either a transition label by a or by b. To represent the different minimal possibilities, we thus use an intermediate structure called *minimal constraint automaton*. First we define the set of minimal constraints associated to a state:

Definition 11 (Minimal constraints). *For any state q of a marked modal specification $\mathcal{C}$ defined over Σ, we associate the set $\zeta(q) \in 2^{2^{\Sigma}}$ defined by:*

$$\zeta(q) = \begin{cases} \{ \ must(q) \ \} & \text{if } must(q) \neq \emptyset \\ \{ \ \{a\} \mid a \in may(q) \ \} & \text{if } must(q) = \emptyset \text{ and } q \notin F \\ \{ \ \emptyset \ \} & \text{if } must(q) = \emptyset \text{ and } q \in F \end{cases}$$

Definition 12 (Minimal constraints automaton). *Given a state q of a marked modal specification $\mathcal{C}$ over Σ, the minimal constraints automaton $Min(\mathcal{C}, q)$ is the automaton over Σ whose initial state is q; its labeled transition map is λ_{Min} such that $\lambda_{Min}(q', a) = q''$ if and only if $a \in X$ with $X \in \zeta(q')$ and $\delta(q', a) = q''$; its set of final states G_{Min} is the set of undelayable bottlenecks of $\mathcal{C}$.*

We identify potential dead-ends, that is pairs of states of two marked modal specifications $\mathcal{C}_1$ and $\mathcal{C}_2$ to be composed from which no outgoing transition may be available in a product of two respective implementations:

Definition 13 (Dead-end). *Given q_1 and q_2 two states respectively from the marked modal specifications $\mathcal{C}_1$ and $\mathcal{C}_2$ defined over Σ_1 and Σ_2, the pair (q_1, q_2) is a dead-end if:*

- *$q_1 \notin (F_1 \setminus D_1)$ or $q_2 \notin (F_2 \setminus D_2)$ and,*
- *there exists $X_1 \in \zeta_1(q_1)$ and $X_2 \in \zeta_2(q_2)$ such that: $(X_1 \cup (\Sigma_2 \setminus \Sigma_1)) \cap (X_2 \cup (\Sigma_1 \setminus \Sigma_2)) = \emptyset$.*

Example 3. The minimal constraints associated to the initial states of $\mathcal{C}_1$ and $\mathcal{C}_2$ from Fig. 2 and defined over the same alphabet of actions $\{a, b\}$ are respectively

$\{\{a\}, \{b\}\}$ and $\{\{a\}\}$. The pair formed by this two states is thus a dead-end as for $X_1 = \{b\}$ and $X_2 = \{a\}$, we have $X_1 \cap X_2 = \emptyset$.

This now leads us to a definition of *exception state pairs* from which a joint path to a marked state pair cannot be ensured independently of the implementation choices to be made:

Definition 14 (Exception state pair). *Given q_1 and q_2 two states respectively from two marked modal specifications $\mathcal{C}_1$ and $\mathcal{C}_2$, the pair (q_1, q_2) is an exception if:*

- *$Min(\mathcal{C}_1, q_1) \times Min(\mathcal{C}_2, q_2)$ is not terminating or,*
- *there exists a reachable dead-end[3] (q_1', q_2') in $Min(\mathcal{C}_1, q_1) \times Min(\mathcal{C}_2, q_2)$.*

We denote by $Ex(\mathcal{C}_1, \mathcal{C}_2)$ the set of exception state pairs from $\mathcal{C}_1$ and $\mathcal{C}_2$. Then we can define the following criterion characterizing marked modal specifications having compatible reachability:

Definition 15 (Compatible reachability). *Two marked modal specifications $\mathcal{C}_1$ and $\mathcal{C}_2$ have a compatible reachability, noted $\mathcal{C}_1 \sim_\mathcal{T} \mathcal{C}_2$, if there is no exception state pair that is reachable in $Un(\mathcal{C}_1) \times Un(\mathcal{C}_2)$.*

The soundness and the completeness of the previous definition are then stated by the following Theorem:

Theorem 3 (Independent implementability). *Given two marked modal specifications $\mathcal{C}_1$ and $\mathcal{C}_2$, $\mathcal{C}_1 \sim_\mathcal{T} \mathcal{C}_2$ if and only if for any $\mathcal{M}_1 \models \mathcal{C}_1$ and $\mathcal{M}_2 \models \mathcal{C}_2$, the product $\mathcal{M}_1 \times \mathcal{M}_2$ is terminating.*

We now define the product of two marked modal specifications with compatible reachability.

Definition 16 (Pessimistic product). *Given two marked modal specifications $\mathcal{C}_1 = (Q_1, q_1^0, \Sigma_1, \delta_1, must_1, may_1, F_1)$ and $\mathcal{C}_2 = (Q_2, q_2^0, \Sigma_2, \delta_2, must_2, may_2, F_2)$ with compatible reachability, the product $\mathcal{C}_1 \otimes \mathcal{C}_2$ is the marked modal specification $(Q, q^0, \Sigma_1 \cup \Sigma_2, \delta, must, may, F)$ with:*

- *$Q = Q_1 \times Q_2$ and $q^0 = (q_1^0, q_2^0)$;*
- *for any $q_1 \in Q_1$, $q_2 \in Q_2$ and $a \in \Sigma_1 \cup \Sigma_2$, $\delta((q_1, q_2), a)$ is defined as $(\delta_1(q_1, a), \delta_2(q_2, a))$ for $a \in \Sigma_1 \cap \Sigma_2$, $(\delta_1(q_1, a), q_2)$ for $a \in \Sigma_1 \setminus \Sigma_2$ and $(q_1, \delta_2(q_2, a))$ for $a \in \Sigma_2 \setminus \Sigma_1$;*
- *$may((q_1, q_2)) = \big(may_1(q_1) \cup (\Sigma_2 \setminus \Sigma_1)\big) \cap \big(may_2(q_2) \cup (\Sigma_1 \setminus \Sigma_2)\big)$;*
- *$must((q_1, q_2)) = \big(must_1(q_1) \cup (\Sigma_2 \setminus \Sigma_1)\big) \cap \big(must_2(q_2) \cup (\Sigma_1 \setminus \Sigma_2)\big)$;*
- *$(q_1, q_2) \in F$ if and only if $q_1 \in F_1$ and $q_2 \in F_2$.*

Now, the product of any models $\mathcal{M}_1$ of $\mathcal{C}_1$ and $\mathcal{M}_2$ of $\mathcal{C}_2$ is model of $\mathcal{C}_1 \otimes \mathcal{C}_2$:

---

[3] As the set of states of $Min(\mathcal{C}_i, q_i)$ is a subset of these of $\mathcal{C}_i$, we can refer to (q_1', q_2') in $Min(\mathcal{C}_1, q_1) \times Min(\mathcal{C}_2, q_2)$ as a pair of states of $\mathcal{C}_1$ and $\mathcal{C}_2$ and then test if it is a dead-end in the sense of Def. 13.

Proposition 2. *Given two marked modal specifications C_1 and C_2, if $C_1 \sim_T C_2$ then for any $\mathcal{M}_1 \models C_1$ and $\mathcal{M}_2 \models C_2$, $\mathcal{M}_1 \times \mathcal{M}_2 \models C_1 \otimes C_2$.*

Moreover, $C_1 \otimes C_2$ gives the most precise characterization of the behavior of the product of any models $\mathcal{M}_1$ of C_1 and $\mathcal{M}_2$ of C_2:

Proposition 3. *Given two marked modal specifications C_1 and C_2, if $C_1 \sim_T C_2$ and if there exists a marked modal specification C such that for any $\mathcal{M}_1 \models C_1$ and $\mathcal{M}_2 \models C_2$ we have $\mathcal{M}_1 \times \mathcal{M}_2 \models C$ then $C_1 \otimes C_2 \leq C$.*

One important principle in modular and concurrent design of systems is the fact that a property checked on a primary version of some system artifacts remains true on any refined version of them. This is what allows to guarantee that the system parts corresponding to compatible interfaces can be designed concurrently. This is respected for compatible reachability:

Proposition 4. *For all marked modal specifications C_1, C_1' and C_2, if $C_1 \sim_T C_2$ and $C_1' \preceq C_1$ then $C_1' \sim_T C_2$ and $C_1' \otimes C_2 \preceq C_1 \otimes C_2$.*

Last, the product is a commutative and associative operator, meaning that interfaces can be assembled in any order without affecting the result.

Proposition 5. *The product of marked modal specifications is commutative and associative. Given three marked modal specifications C_1, C_2 and C_3: $C_1 \otimes C_2 \equiv C_2 \otimes C_1$ and $C_1 \otimes (C_2 \otimes C_3) \equiv (C_1 \otimes C_2) \otimes C_3$.*

5.2 Optimistic Composition of Marked Modal Specifications

Consider again C_1 and C_2 from Fig. 3. They do not have a compatible reachability as $(3,0)$ is an exception state pairs because $(4,1)$ is a reachable dead-end from it. It is however pessimistic to declare C_1 and C_2 as not composable. Indeed, the system potentially formed by any model of C_1 and C_2 would not be closed as the occurence of $?e$ would still be under the control of the environment. Now by preventing the environment from producing $!e$ when C_1 and C_2 are in their initial state, the reachability of the exception state pairs $(4,1)$ can be avoided. In this section, let us now be optimistic and declare composable any C_1 and C_2 if there exists *at least one* environment, closing the system and preventing the reachability of the *bad* states of C_1 and C_2 in which the reachability property cannot be guaranteed.

Definition 17 (Legal environment). *Given $\mathcal{M}$ and $\mathcal{E}$ two terminating automata, $\mathcal{E}$ is said to be a* legal *environment for $\mathcal{M}$, if and only if: the signature of $\mathcal{M}$ and $\mathcal{E}$ are composable; $\mathcal{M} \times \mathcal{E}$ is closed; $Em(\mathcal{M}) \sim_T Em(\mathcal{E})$, that is $\mathcal{M} \times \mathcal{E}$ is terminating.*

Next, we define, for any automaton $\mathcal{M}$ (terminating or not) with $r^0 \in pre^*(G)$, the subautomaton $\mathcal{M}^\star = (pre^*(G), r^0, \Sigma, \lambda^\star, G)$ where $\lambda^\star(r,a) = r'$ if and only if $\lambda(r,a) = r'$ and $r, r' \in pre^*(G)$. It corresponds to the potential reachable part of $\mathcal{M}$ when interacting with a legal environment.

Definition 18 (Optimistic compatible reachability). *Two marked modal specifications C_1 and C_2 have an optimistic compatible reachability, noted $C_1 \sim_\mathcal{O} C_2$ if the pair of initial states (q_1^0, q_2^0) is not an exception state pairs.*

This criterion is sound and complete as stated by the following Theorem:

Theorem 4 (Independent implementability). *Given two marked modal specifications C_1 and C_2, $C_1 \sim_\mathcal{O} C_2$ if and only if for any $\mathcal{M}_1 \models C_1$ and $\mathcal{M}_2 \models C_2$ there exists a legal environment $\mathcal{E}$ for $\mathcal{M}_1 \times \mathcal{M}_2$.*

Definition 19 (Optimistic product). *Given two marked modal specifications C_1 and C_2 over composable signatures μ_1 and μ_2 and with optimistic compatible reachability, the optimistic product $C_1 \parallel C_2$ is the normal form of the marked modal specification $(Q, q^0, \Sigma_1 \cup \Sigma_2, \delta, must, may, F)$ over $\mu_1 \times \mu_2$ with:*

- $Q = (Q_1 \times Q_2) \setminus Ex(C_1, C_2)$ *and* $q^0 = (q_1^0, q_2^0)$;
- *for any* $q_1 \in Q_1$, $q_2 \in Q_2$ *and* $a \in \Sigma_1 \cup \Sigma_2$:
  - *if* $a \in \Sigma_1 \setminus \Sigma_2$ *and* $(\delta_1(q_1, a), q_2) \notin Ex(C_1, C_2)$: $\delta((q_1, q_2), a) = (\delta_1(q_1, a), q_2)$;
  - *if* $a \in \Sigma_2 \setminus \Sigma_1$ *and* $(q_1, \delta_2(q_2, a)) \notin Ex(C_1, C_2)$: $\delta((q_1, q_2), a) = (q_1, \delta_2(q_2, a))$;
  - *if* $a \in \Sigma_1 \cap \Sigma_2$ *and* $(\delta_1(q_1, a), \delta_2(q_2, a)) \notin Ex(C_1, C_2)$: $\delta((q_1, q_2), a) = (\delta_1(q_1, a), \delta_2(q_2, a))$.
- $a \in must((q_1, q_2))$ *if* $a \in \big(must_1(q_1) \cup (\Sigma_2 \setminus \Sigma_1)\big) \cap \big(must_2(q_2) \cup (\Sigma_1 \setminus \Sigma_2)\big)$ *and* $\delta\big((q_1, q_2), a\big)$ *is defined;*
- $(q_1, q_2) \in F$ *if and only if* $q_1 \in F_1$ *and* $q_2 \in F_2$.

Example 4. The optimistic product of C_1 and C_2 from Fig. 3 is depicted in Fig. 3(c). The action $?e$ is not allowed in the initial state as a legal environement would never produce $!e$ to prevent the reachability of the exception states $(3, 0)$.

Proposition 6. *Given two marked modal specifications C_1 and C_2, if $C_1 \sim_\mathcal{O} C_2$ then for any $\mathcal{M}_1 \models C_1$ and $\mathcal{M}_2 \models C_2$, $(\mathcal{M}_1 \times \mathcal{M}_2)^\star \models C_1 \parallel C_2$.*

The next proposition states that $C_1 \parallel C_2$ is the minimal marked modal specification w.r.t. refinement enjoying the independent implementability property:

Proposition 7. *Given two marked modal specifications C_1 and C_2, if $C_1 \sim_\mathcal{O} C_2$ and if there exists a marked modal specification C such that for any $\mathcal{M}_1 \models C_1$ and $\mathcal{M}_2 \models C_2$ there exists a legal environment $\mathcal{E}$ for $\mathcal{M}_1 \times \mathcal{M}_2$ and $(\mathcal{M}_1 \times \mathcal{M}_2)^\star \models C$, then $C_1 \parallel C_2 \preceq C$.*

Optimistic compatible reachability is preserved by refinement hence allowing concurrent design of sub-systems. Moreover, the optimistic product is monotonic with respect to the refinement relation and is also associative which guarantees independence in the design flow.

Proposition 8. *For all marked modal specifications C_1, C_1' and C_2, if $C_1 \sim_\mathcal{O} C_2$ and $C_1' \preceq C_1$ then $C_1' \sim_\mathcal{O} C_2$ and $C_1' \parallel C_2 \preceq C_1 \parallel C_2$.*

Proposition 9. *The optimistic product of marked modal specifications is commutative and associative. Given three marked modal specifications C_1, C_2 and C_3:*
$C_1 \parallel C_2 \equiv C_2 \parallel C_1$ *and* $C_1 \parallel (C_2 \parallel C_3) \equiv (C_1 \parallel C_2) \parallel C_3$.

6 Related Works and Conclusion

Marked modal specifications can be used to express, in a modular manner, that a system should be capable of reaching one or several marked states representing either the completion of a composition of services or the quiescence of a network of interacting agents. They improve the expressive power of deterministic modal specifications that corresponds to the conjunctive ν-calculus [10] which does not allow to capture reachability properties.

The same goal can be achieved with automata-theoretic specifications in which states are annotated with propositional formulas expressing implementation
variants and, possibly, an obligation of progress. This is the case of *annotated automata* [22] and *operating guidelines* [19,17]. While both formalisms have a product (or parallel) composition operator, they are missing the optimistic view of composition and also the conjunction operator that turns out to be instrumental as soon as components are described according to several distinct but interacting viewpoints [21].

The disjunctive variants of modal specifications [13,9] allows to constraint progress and thus to inductively express reachability. However no implementation relations including marked states nor optimistic composition have been proposed for these variants of modal specifications.

Marked modal specifications look similar to the modal specifications with marked states introduced in [6]. However, these two formalisms are very different because the satisfaction relation in [6] admits implementations having final states corresponding to a state of the specification that is not final. This is appropriate in the context of supervisory control synthesis. However, this semantics does not seem well-suited to a specification algebra with a refinement preorder, which explains why a different satisfaction relation is used for marked modal specifications.

References

1. de Alfaro, L., Henzinger, T.A.: Interface automata. In: Proc. of the 9th ACM SIGSOFT Inter. Symp. on Foundations of Software Engineering (FSE 2001). pp. 109–120. ACM Press (2001)
2. Alur, R., Henzinger, T.A., Kupferman, O., Vardi, M.Y.: Alternating Refinement Relations. In: Sangiorgi, D., de Simone, R. (eds.) CONCUR 1998. LNCS, vol. 1466, pp. 163–178. Springer, Heidelberg (1998)
3. Antonik, A., Huth, M., Larsen, K.G., Nyman, U., Wasowski, A.: 20 years of modal and mixed specifications. Bulletin of the EATCS 1(94) (2008)

4. Bérard, B., Bidoit, M., Finkel, A., Laroussinie, F., Petit, A., Petrucci, L., Schnoebelen, P.: Systems and Software Verification. Model-Checking Techniques and Tools. Springer (2001)
5. Caillaud, B., Raclet, J.B.: Ensuring reachability by design. Tech. rep., INRIA Research Report 7928 (2012), http://hal.inria.fr/hal-00696151
6. Darondeau, P., Dubreil, J., Marchand, H.: Supervisory control for modal specifications of services. In: Workshop on Discrete Event Systems (WODES 2010), Berlin, Germany, pp. 428–435 (August 2010)
7. Doyen, L., Henzinger, T.A., Jobstmann, B., Petrov, T.: Interface theories with component reuse. In: Proc. of the 8th Inter. Conf. on Embedded Software (EMSOFT 2008), pp. 79–88. ACM Press (2008)
8. Fecher, H., de Frutos-Escrig, D., Lüttgen, G., Schmidt, H.: On the Expressiveness of Refinement Settings. In: Arbab, F., Sirjani, M. (eds.) FSEN 2009. LNCS, vol. 5961, pp. 276–291. Springer, Heidelberg (2010)
9. Fecher, H., Schmidt, H.: Comparing disjunctive modal transition systems with an one-selecting variant. J. Log. Algebr. Program. 77(1-2), 20–39 (2008)
10. Feuillade, G., Pinchinat, S.: Modal specifications for the control theory of discrete-event systems. Discrete Event Dynamic Systems 17(2), 181–205 (2007)
11. Henzinger, T.A., Sifakis, J.: The discipline of embedded systems design. IEEE Computer 40(10), 32–40 (2007)
12. Larsen, K.G., Nyman, U., Wąsowski, A.: Modal I/O Automata for Interface and Product Line Theories. In: De Nicola, R. (ed.) ESOP 2007. LNCS, vol. 4421, pp. 64–79. Springer, Heidelberg (2007)
13. Larsen, K.G., Xinxin, L.: Equation solving using modal transition systems. In: Proc. of the 5th IEEE Symp. on Logic in Computer Science, LICS 1990, pp. 108–117. IEEE Computer Society Press (1990)
14. Larsen, K.G.: Modal Specifications. In: Sifakis, J. (ed.) CAV 1989. LNCS, vol. 407, pp. 232–246. Springer, Heidelberg (1990)
15. Larsen, K.G., Nyman, U., Wąsowski, A.: On Modal Refinement and Consistency. In: Caires, L., Vasconcelos, V.T. (eds.) CONCUR 2007. LNCS, vol. 4703, pp. 105–119. Springer, Heidelberg (2007)
16. Larsen, K.G., Thomsen, B.: A modal process logic. In: Proc. of the 3rd Annual Symp. on Logic in Computer Science (LICS 1988), pp. 203–210. IEEE (1988)
17. Lohmann, N., Wolf, K.: Compact representations and efficient algorithms for operating guidelines. Fundam. Inform. 108(1-2), 43–62 (2011)
18. Lynch, N., Tuttle, M.R.: An introduction to Input/Output automata. CWI-quarterly 2(3), 219–246 (1989)
19. Massuthe, P., Schmidt, K.: Operating guidelines - an automata-theoretic foundation for the service-oriented architecture. In: QSIC, pp. 452–457. IEEE Computer Society (2005)
20. Raclet, J.B., Badouel, E., Benveniste, A., Caillaud, B., Legay, A., Passerone, R.: Modal interfaces: unifying interface automata and modal specifications. In: Proc. of the 9th Int. Conf. on Embedded Software (EMSOFT 2009), pp. 87–96. ACM (2009)
21. Raclet, J.B., Benveniste, A., Caillaud, B., Legay, A., Passerone, R.: A modal interface theory for component-based design. Fundam. Inform. 107, 1–32 (2011)
22. Wombacher, A., Mahleko, B., Neuhold, E.J.: IPSI-PF - a business process matchmaking engine based on annotated finite state automata. Inf. Syst. E-Business Management 3(2), 127–150 (2005)

Approximate Verification and Enumeration Problems

Sylvain Peyronnet[1], Michel De Rougemont[2], and Yann Strozecki[1]

[1] LRI, Université Paris-Sud XI, Orsay, F-91405
[2] Université Paris II & LIAFA, Université Paris 7, Paris, F-75005

Abstract. We study enumeration problems using probabilistic methods, with application to verification problems. We consider the enumeration of monomials of a polynomial given as a black box, and the enumeration of discrete points which separate two polytopes in a space of dimension n, using a random walk which provides witnesses if the volume of the difference of the polytopes is large enough. The first method allows to enumerate all words of a given size which distinguish two probabilistic automata with a polynomial delay. The second method enumerates words which ε-distinguish two nondeterministic finite automata. We also enumerate strategies which ε-distinguish two Markov Decision Processes in time polynomial in the dimension of their statistical representation.

1 Introduction

An enumeration problem consists in generating all structures that satisfy a given property. It can be defined for any NP problem: instead of deciding if there is one correct solution among an exponential number of candidates, one should list all the solutions. Enumeration is better understood as a dynamic process which produces the solutions one at a time. One wants to bound the *delay* between two solutions. Enumeration problems can also be defined for large objects given as a black box. The number of solutions to enumerate can then be infinite and we either restrict the solutions set or sample them uniformly at random.

We study two enumeration problems with direct applications to verification. First, the enumeration of the monomials of a large multivariate polynomial given as a black box, *i.e.*, the polynomial can be evaluated on specific values for the variables, in one call. One of the monomials of a polynomial can be produced with a number of calls polynomial in the number of variables and the degree [13]. Also, if the polynomial is multilinear, the polynomial can be interpolated with a polynomial number of calls to the black box between each produced monomial [20]. Second, the enumeration of points which separate two polytopes whose difference has a large enough volume. The *Polytope Separator* algorithm solves this problem, and is based on a random walk as the one used to compute the volume of a polytope [11] and is polynomial in the dimension of the space.

In model checking, we compare schemas, such as regular expressions or Büchi automata on words. One may ask to enumerate all the words which distinguish two regular expressions or Büchi automata: they represent the counter-examples.

A. Roychoudhury and M. D'Souza (Eds.): ICTAC 2012, LNCS 7521, pp. 228–242, 2012.
© Springer-Verlag Berlin Heidelberg 2012

Given formulas ψ_1 and ψ_2 in some logic, we want to enumerate the structures $\mathcal{U}$ such that ψ_1 and ψ_2 disagree on $\mathcal{U}$. This may be computationally hard, so we study if we can realize it with high probability. If it is still hard, we relax the exact enumeration to an approximate enumeration. We set a distance on the structures and define, for $\varepsilon \in [0,1]$, $\mathcal{U} \models_\varepsilon \psi$ if there exists a structure $\mathcal{U}'$, ε-close to $\mathcal{U}$ such that $\mathcal{U}' \models \psi$. The approximate ε-version is to enumerate $\mathcal{U}$ such that $\mathcal{U} \models \psi_1$ and $\mathcal{U} \not\models_\varepsilon \psi_2$ (or symmetrically).

In probabilistic model checking, given two probabilistic automata $\mathcal{A}_1$ and $\mathcal{A}_2$, we want to enumerate the words w such that $Pr[w \in \mathcal{A}_1] \neq Pr[w \in \mathcal{A}_2]$. There is a deterministic polynomial algorithm to distinguish two probabilistic automata [21] and a recent more efficient probabilistic algorithm [12] based on polynomials associated to the automata. We apply enumeration methods to these structured multilinear polynomials and obtain probabilistic algorithms to generate all the words which distinguish the two automata.

It is computationally hard to separate nondeterministic automata or Markov Decision Processes (MDPs), even with probabilistic methods, unless PSPACE = BPP. We thus only solve approximate versions of these problems. In both cases, we represent the objects to compare by polytopes and apply our Polytope Separator algorithm to generate counter-examples. On nondeterministic automata, we use the word embedding introduced in [8]. We want to ε-distinguish (for the distance introduced in [5]) two MDPs with traces on the same alphabet Σ. We represent them by the k-gram (for $k = 1/\varepsilon$) of the stationary distributions of their traces, i.e. vectors of dimension $|\Sigma|^k$. We show how to find strategies which ε-distinguish the MDPs in polynomial time in the size of the MDPs and the dimension, whereas previous methods were exponential in the dimension.

Our main results are probabilistics methods for:

- Enumerating efficiently points in the difference of two polytopes (Theor. 4).
- Enumerating words that ε-distinguish nondeterministic automata (Theor. 5).
- Enumerating strategies which ε-distinguish two MDPs (Theor. 6).

In section 2, we show how to enumerate words which distinguish two probabilistic automata. Section 3 presents the Polytope Separator algorithm. We apply it in section 4, to enumerate words which ε-distinguish two regular expressions and in section 5 to enumerate strategies which ε-distinguish two MDPs.

2   Enumeration of Monomials and Separation of Probabilistic Automata

2.1   Equivalence Testing

In this section, we compare two probabilistic automata denoted by A and B.

Definition 1. *A probabilistic automaton is a tuple $A = (S, \Sigma, M, \alpha, \eta)$ where S is a set of n states, Σ a finite alphabet, M is a collection of transition matrices M for each letter $\sigma \in \Sigma$: $M : \Sigma \to \mathbb{R}^{n \times n}$ where each $M(\sigma)$ is a probabilistic* *transition matrix, α is an initial probabilistic distribution of states, η is the final vector in $\mathbb{R}^n$.*

Let $w = w_1 w_2 \ldots w_k$ be a word, we let $A(w) = \alpha(\prod_{i=1 \ldots k} M(w_i))\eta$ denote the probability that w is accepted by A. The number of states of A and B is bounded by n and their number of transitions is bounded by m.

We associate a classical polynomial P_A to the automaton A. The set of its $|\Sigma|n$ variables is $\{X_{\sigma,i}\}_{\sigma \in \Sigma, i \leq n}$. It encodes the words of size less or equal to n and their probability to be accepted by A:

$$P_A(x) = \sum_{k=0}^{n} \sum_{w \in \Sigma^k} A(w) X_{w_1,1} X_{w_2,2} \ldots X_{w_k,k}.$$

The polynomial P_A has an exponential number of monomials and thus seems hard to evaluate. We give another form of P_A, which allows to evaluate it in polynomial time since it involves only polynomial size sums and products:

$$P_A = \alpha \left(\sum_{k=0}^{n} \prod_{j=1}^{k} \sum_{\sigma \in \Sigma} X_{\sigma,j} M(\sigma) \right) \eta$$

Given two probabilistic automata A and B, we wish to decide if $A \equiv B$, *i.e.* if all words are accepted with the same probability. The deterministic algorithm of [21] decides this property with complexity in $O(n^3 |\Sigma|)$. It is also possible to use the polynomial representation of A and B to design a probabilistic algorithm to test if A and B have the same language (see [12]). Indeed, deciding whether P_A is equal to P_B is equivalent to deciding whether $A \equiv B$. To do that, it is enough to compute $P_A - P_B$ on random integer points by the Schwarz-Zippel Lemma.

Lemma 1. *[Schwarz-Zippel [18,22]] Let P be a nonzero polynomial with n variables of total degree D, if $x_1, \ldots, x_n$ are randomly chosen integers in a set S of size $\frac{D}{\varepsilon}$ then the probability that $P(x_1, \ldots, x_n) = 0$ is bounded by ε.*

The complexity of this testing procedure is equal to the one of the evaluation of P_A and P_B, which can be done very efficiently by a succession of products of a vector by the matrices representing the transitions of A and B. Since the transition probabilities are in $\mathbb{R}$ we count the number of arithmetic operations in the complexity of the following algorithms. It can be turned into roughly the same boolean complexity by considering transition matrices with small rational numbers as coefficients.

Theorem 1 (In [12]). *Let A and B be two automata with at most n states and m transitions. We can decide with probability $1 - \varepsilon$ whether $A \equiv B$ in $O(nm \log(\varepsilon^{-1}))$ arithmetic operations. If A and B are not equivalent, a minimal counter-example can be produced in the same time.*

The algorithm which produces a counter-example, that is a word which has not the same probability to be accepted by A and B, is given in Section 2.4 of [12]. It can also be seen as a specialization of Alg. 1 given in [20] which produces a monomial of any multilinear polynomial.

2.2 Producing All Counter-Examples

In some practical context it is interesting to produce many counter-examples which will be used as a test bed to separate a program from its specification.

We leverage the polynomial representation to design an algorithm which enumerates all counter-examples: the monomials of $P_A - P_B$ are the words which separate A from B and their coefficient is the difference of accepting probability for A and B. Since $P_A - P_B$ is multilinear, all its monomials can be enumerated with a polynomial delay thanks to Theorem 2 of [20]. We describe here a specialization of this algorithm to the polynomial $P_A - P_B$, which is simpler and has a better complexity. It is easy to change the definition of P_A and P_B so that they represent the words of size l accepted by A and B for any given integer l. As a consequence, we can state the following theorem.

Theorem 2. *Let A and B be two probabilistic automata with at most m transitions and n states. There is a probabilistic algorithm to enumerate with probability $1 - \varepsilon$ all words of size less than l which separate A and B. The delay between the production of two counter-examples is in $O(ml^3 \log(|\Sigma|\varepsilon^{-1}))$ arithmetic operations and the time to produce all of them is linear in their number.*

Proof. Let P be the polynomial $P_A - P_B$ and let $w = w_1 w_2 \ldots w_k$ be a word. We denote by P_w the polynomial P where for each $i \leq k$ we have substituted 1 to X_{i,w_i} and 0 to $X_{i,\sigma}$ for $\sigma \neq w_i$. The algorithm relies on the fact, that for each $i \leq l$, a monomial of P contains exactly one of the variables of $\{X_{i,\sigma}\}_{\sigma \in \Sigma}$. Therefore we have $P_w = \sum_{\sigma \in \Sigma} X_{k+1,\sigma} P_{w\sigma}$.

Let T be the tree whose nodes are labeled by a prefix of a word which separates A from B. The children of a node labeled by w are all nodes labeled by $w\sigma$ for some $\sigma \in \Sigma$. Therefore the leaves of this tree are labeled by all the separating words. A node of label w is in T if and only if P_w is not zero, which can be tested thanks to the Schwarz-Zippel lemma. Therefore a depth-first traversal of T generates all the separating words.

Now, let study the complexity of this procedure. First, the error in the Schwarz-Zippel Lemma can be bounded by ε', if we do $\log(\varepsilon'^{-1})$ independent random evaluations of the polynomial, so that we only use random integers less than $2l$. Note that we can test whether $P_{w\sigma}$ is identically zero for each $\sigma \in \Sigma$ at once. We substitute the same random integers to the variables $\{X_{i,\sigma}\}_{i > k+1}$, in all $P_{w\sigma}$. With probability $1 - |\Sigma|\varepsilon'$, all $P_{w\sigma}$ will evaluate to some non zero value if they are not identically zero. Thanks to the particular structure of P, we can compute all $P_{w\sigma}$ on these random values in time $O(ml \log(\varepsilon'^{-1}))$.

The probabilistic test is used in the algorithm at most $|\Sigma|^l$ times which is the maximal number of leaves in T. Therefore, we must choose $\varepsilon' = \varepsilon \Sigma^{-l-1}$ so that the whole algorithm succeeds with probability $1 - \varepsilon$.

When we traverse a leaf, we find a counter-example, but we still have to compute its coefficient in P that is the difference of probability to be accepted by A and B. This can be done by a single evaluation of P in $O(ml)$ operations. Finally the delay between the production of two counter-examples is bounded by the time to visit at most $2l$ nodes since l is the depth of T, hence it is in $O(ml^3 \log(|\Sigma|\varepsilon^{-1})$ arithmetic operations.

Producing all the words which separate two automata, can be helpful to compute a distance between automata, at least when it depends on all accepted words of a given size. We show that computing such a distance or an approximation of it is usually hard. Enumeration may thus be the best way to approach this problem. Indeed the delay of the algorithm is polynomially bounded, thus any increase in computing time enables to produce more counter-examples which in turn allow to compute a better approximation of the distance.

The maximal distance is defined as the maximum of $|A(w) - B(w)|$ over all words w. The problem to decide whether a probabilistic automaton computes a word with a probability greater than some given positive rational is called the *Emptiness* problem. The emptiness problem is undecidable [17], and can be reduced to the computation of the maximal distance. Indeed, if one wants to decide whether an automaton A accepts a word with probability larger than $q \in \mathbb{Q}$, it is equivalent to test whether the maximal distance of A and B is larger than q, where B accepts all words with probability 0.

To overcome the undecidability, we have to change the distance: we consider the bounded maximal distance that is the maximum of $|A(w) - B(w)|$ over all words w of size n. The n-*Emptiness* problem is the Emptiness problem restricted to words of size n, where n is part of the instance and given in unary. Note that the n-*Emptiness* problem can be reduced to the computation of the bounded maximal distance in the same way as the unbounded version.

Some relaxed version of the n-*Emptiness* problem is proved to be NP-hard in [5]. Hence the bounded maximal distance is hard to compute, in fact approximating this distance is still hard. The hardness of the bounded maximal distance together with the representation of a probabilistic automata by a multilinear polynomial can be used to show that enumeration in some order may be hard, a result of self interest.

Proposition 1. *Let P be a multilinear polynomial given by a black box. There is no polynomial delay algorithm to produce the monomials in decreasing order of coefficient unless* P = NP.

In this section, we have seen that we can distinguish two probabilistic automata in polynomial time, while deciding if they are far for the bounded maximal distance is hard. In the next sections, we are interested with the separation of non-deterministic automa or MDPs which is hard, and to make these problems tractable, we choose to assume some properties on distances between these objects. Moreover, the algorithms for producing one or all counter-example to the equivalence of two automata are Bellagio algorithms: They are probabilistic but they always produce the same objects in the same order (see [9]). The randomness is useful only to make them polynomially faster. The algorithms presented in the next sections rely on a random walk and by their very nature they produce counter-examples which depend on the randomness.

3   Separation of Two Polytopes

This section considers polytopes and their geometric difference. A polytope can be represented by a set of points, of which it is the convex hull, it is then called a $\mathcal{V}$-polytope. It can also be represented by a set of linear inequalities, it is then called a $\mathcal{H}$-polytope. In general, the number of extremal vertices can be exponential in the number of inequalities and vice-versa. One way to abstract away the representation is to represent a polytope by a so-called strong membership oracle: the oracle is given a point and answers whether it belongs to the polytope.

From a $\mathcal{H}$-polytope or a $\mathcal{V}$-polytope, we can simulate a strong membership oracle. For a $\mathcal{V}$-polytope, defined by a set of points S, we check if the point given to the oracle is in the convex hull of S, that is the point is a convex combination of points in S. This problem can be reduced to solving a system of linear inequalities in a time polynomial in S. For a $\mathcal{H}$-polytope, defined by a system of linear inequalities, we only have to test if the input point satisfies the inequalities in time linear in the size of the system.

From an algorithmic point of view, the representation is crucial. The problem to separate two polytopes is easy for $\mathcal{H}$-polytopes. Let K_1 and K_2 be two $\mathcal{H}$-polytopes represented respectively by the sets of inequalities S and $\{e_1, \ldots e_m\}$. Let $\bar{e}_i$ denote the negation of e_i. The set of inequalities $S \cup \{\bar{e}_i\}$ defines a polytope, from which a point can be found in polynomial time. Since $K_1 \setminus K_2$ is equal to the union of the points satisfying $S \cup \{\bar{e}_i\}$ for all i, we have a polynomial time algorithm to decide whether $K_1 \setminus K_2 = \emptyset$ and to produce one of its elements.

However, we need another method when the representation is different. This is why we design a complex algorithm to find a point in the difference of two polytopes through a random walk. Moreover, the random walk method enables us to sample almost uniformly the difference of two polytopes. This should be seen as the best approximation to the enumeration of all points, an unfeasible task since the difference of two polytopes has an infinite number of points.

3.1   Hardness and Relation between Distances

Let $K \in \mathbb{R}^n$ be a polytope, we denote by $\mathcal{V}(K)$ the volume of the polytope. Let $d(x, y)$ be the L_1 distance on $\mathbb{R}^n$. The distance of a point x to a compact K is $d(x, K) = \min_{y \in K} d(x, y)$, and this minimum is realized by some point of K. We denote by $diam(K)$ the diameter of K, that is the largest distance between two points of K. Let K_1 and K_2 be two convex polytopes in $\mathbb{R}^n$, we consider the two following distances between these objects:

1. Hausdorff pseudo-distance: $d_H(K_1, K_2) = \max_{x \in K_1} d(x, K_2)$
   We symmetrize and normalize this distance:

$$d_h(K_1, K_2) = \max \left\{ \frac{d_H(K_1, K_2)}{diam(K_1)}, \frac{d_H(K_2, K_1)}{diam(K_2)} \right\}$$

2. Volume of the difference as a pseudo-distance: $d_{\mathrm{VOL}}(K_1, K_2) = \mathcal{V}(K_1 \setminus K_2)$

We symmetrize and normalize this distance:

$$d_{vol}(K_1, K_2) = \max \left\{ \frac{d_{\mathrm{VOL}}(K_1, K_2)}{\mathcal{V}(K_1)}, \frac{d_{\mathrm{VOL}}(K_2, K_1)}{\mathcal{V}(K_2)} \right\}$$

Remark that d_{vol} is not defined when K_1 and K_2 are of volume 0 which happens if their dimensions are lower than the dimension of the space in which they are embedded. It is always possible to assume that at least one of the polytope is of positive volume (if it is not a singleton): we compute an affine subspace generated by the points of the polytope and restrict the whole space to this subspace. The two distances are related, as the following lemma states (proof in appendix).

Lemma 2. *For all polytopes K_1 and K_2 such that $K_1 \cap K_2 \neq \emptyset$ we have:*

$$d_h(K_1, K_2)^n \leq d_{vol}(K_1, K_2)$$

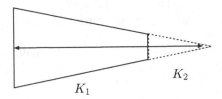

Fig. 1. The polytopes: K_1 in hard lines and K_2 in hard lines and dotted lines

The inequality is tight, see for instance Fig. 1 in dimension two, a situation easily generalizable to any dimension. Moreover, $d_{vol}(K_1, K_2)$ cannot be bound by some continuous increasing function of $d_h(K_1, K_2)$. Indeed, in Fig. 2, $d_{vol}(K_1, K_2) = \frac{1}{2}$ while $d_h(K_1, K_2) = \frac{1}{2l^2}$ where l can be made arbitrarily large.

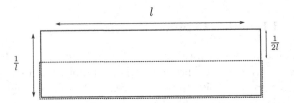

Fig. 2. The polytope K_1 in hard lines and the polytope K_2 in dotted lines

In fact, the Hausdorff distance is hard to compute, while it is possible to approximate the volume distance (if it is not too small). The proof that the Hausdorff distance is hard to approximate relies on the hardness to approximate the diameter of a polytope, as stated in Theorem 3.

Theorem 3 (Theorem 1.2 of [2]). *The diameter of a $\mathcal{H}$-polytope is NP-hard to approximate within a factor polynomial in the dimension.*

In Prop. 2 (proof in appendix), we show that the Hausdorff distance and its normalized version are hard to compute. This motivates our choice of the volume distance to design an algorithm to separate two sufficiently different polytopes.

Proposition 2. *The approximation of the functions d_H or d_h within a factor polynomial in the dimension over $\mathcal{H}$-polytopes is NP-hard.*

3.2   Sampling the Difference

Our goal is to design an algorithm that provides a witness to the fact that two polytopes K_1 and K_2 are different. To do so, our algorithm is sampling points in each polytope. If $d_{vol}(K_1, K_2)$ is large enough, the algorithm samples points in the difference between K_1 and K_2 with high probability. Sampling uniformly points of a convex body is a well-studied algorithmic problem. Our algorithm is based on known results [14,11,19].

To sample points, we use the *Ball Walk*. The idea of this walk is to pick a uniform random point y from the ball of a given radius centered at the current point x. If y is in the polytope, we proceed from y, otherwise from x.

In order to speed up the convergence of random walks within polytopes, it is convenient to pre-process the polytopes by putting them into *quasi-isotropic position* [19]. Once this is done, sampling becomes easier. Finding the exact isotropic position is hard, so we consider algorithms for putting a convex body into nearly isotropic position (see for instance [14,11]).

Definition 2. *Let K be a polytope with center of gravity $b(K)$. Let $0 < \gamma < 1$. K is in γ-nearly isotropic position if $||b(K)|| \leq \gamma$, and if $\forall v \in \mathbb{R}^n$, we have:*

$$(1 - \gamma)||v||^2 \leq \frac{1}{vol(K)} \int_{K-b(K)} (v^\top x)^2 dx \leq (1 + \gamma)||v||^2.$$

Th. 6 of [19] states that, for $0 < \gamma < 1$, there is a randomized algorithm that finds an affine transformation A such that AK is γ-nearly isotropic, with probability at least $2/3$. The number of oracle calls of the algorithm is $O(n^5|\ln \gamma| \ln n)$. This algorithm to put a convex body K into γ-nearly isotropic position is called *QISO*. $QISO(K, \gamma)$ is a γ-nearly isotropic version of K, with prob. at least $2/3$. We sketch the idea of this algorithm. First, pairwise "nearly" independent points are "nearly" uniformly drawn from K. Then, an affine transformation A brings K into nearly isotropic position. A depends mainly on the barycenter of the sampled points. The idea is to center the polytope around the origin by translating the center of gravity, but also to "round" it. If the sampling is close to the uniform distribution, then with high probability we obtain the nearly isotropic position. However, sampling pairwise "nearly" independent points is a difficult task, for which a bootstrapping step is required (thus the overall complexity).

Once the nearly isotropic position has been computed, we can use the Ball Walk in order to efficiently sample points uniformly at random from our polytope. To do so, we use the algorithm $P-B$: $P-B(x, \delta)$ is a random point, distributed uniformly in $\mathbb{B}(x, \delta)$ ($\delta \in \mathbb{R}$). Then, Alg. 1 picks at random a point of

Algorithm 1. B-W(S, x, k, δ)

> **Input:** S : set (as a strong membership oracle) ; x : point ; k : int
> **Output:** a point of S
> **begin**
> > **if** $k = 0$ **then**
> > > ∟ **return** x
> >
> > $y = $P-B$(x, \delta)$;
> > **if** $y \in S$ **then**
> > > ∟ B-W$(S, y, k - 1, \delta)$
> >
> > B-W$(S, x, k - 1, \delta)$
> **end**

a set given by a strong membership oracle (SMO). The parameter k in Alg. 1 is set at the mixing time of a Ball Walk, thus Alg. 1 outputs a point almost uniformly distributed in S. The parameter δ is the step size of the Ball Walk. Finally, by using Alg. 2 twice (*i.e.*, on $(K_1, K_2, \gamma, \varepsilon)$ and $(K_2, K_1, \gamma, \varepsilon)$) we find with high probability a witness that $K_1 \neq K_2$ if $d_{vol}(K_1, K_2) \geq \varepsilon$. The use of Alg. 2 on both $(K_1, K_2, \gamma, \varepsilon)$ and $(K_2, K_1, \gamma, \varepsilon)$ is called the *Polytope Separator*.

Algorithm 2. E-C$(J, K, \gamma, \varepsilon)$

> **Input:** J, K : polytopes ; $\gamma, \varepsilon \in]0, 1[$
> **Output:** x such that $x \in J$ and $x \notin K$
> **begin**
> > $k = n^3 \cdot (2 + \ln(2n)) \cdot \ln(2/\varepsilon)$;
> > $J_{iso} = $QISO$(J, \gamma)$;
> > **for** $m = 1$ **to** $\frac{2}{\varepsilon} \ln(3)$ **do**
> > > y=B-W$(J_{iso},$P-B$(0, 1), k, 1/\sqrt{n})$;
> > > Compute $x \in J$ corresponding to $y \in J_{iso}$;
> > > **if** $x \in J$ *and* $x \notin K$ **then**
> > > > ∟ **return** x
> >
> > **return** *FAIL*
> **end**

Theorem 4. *Let K_1 and K_2 be two polytopes, given as SMOs. For all $\varepsilon > 0$, if $d_{vol}(K_1, K_2) \geq \varepsilon$, then the Polytope Separator outputs a point x such that $x \in K_1 \wedge x \notin K_2$ or $x \in K_2 \wedge x \notin K_1$ with probability greater than $2/3$. Moreover, the running time of this algorithm is polynomial in n and ε^{-1}.*

Proof. Without loss of generality, we consider only the case $(K_1, K_2, \gamma, \varepsilon)$ and not the symmetric case $(K_2, K_1, \gamma, \varepsilon)$. First, we prove the correctness. Since the parameter $k = n^3 \cdot (2 + \ln(2n)) \cdot \ln(2/\varepsilon)$ is the mixing time for a Ball Walk [10] when $\delta = 1/\sqrt{n}$, the algorithm outputs a point $\frac{\varepsilon}{2}$-nearly uniform in K_1. Since $d_{vol}(K_1, K_2) \geq \varepsilon$, there is a fraction ε of K_2 which is not in K_1. Thus the probability of not finding a point $x \in K_1$ such that $x \notin K_2$ after sampling m points is $(1 - \frac{\varepsilon}{2})^m$ (the Ball Walk is $\frac{\varepsilon}{2}$-nearly uniform with high probability). By taking $m = \frac{2}{\varepsilon} \ln(3)$ the probability of not finding a point $x \in K_1$ such that $x \notin K_2$ is upper bounded by $1/3$. So the algorithm is correct. The complexity can be decomposed as follows. To put a polytope in quasi-isotropic position, we need $O(n^5|\ln\gamma|\ln n)$ oracle calls (see [19]). The mixing time of the Ball Walk is essentially $O(n^3)$ when $\delta = 1/\sqrt{n}$ (see [11,10]). The Ball Walk is repeated $\frac{4}{\varepsilon}\ln(3)$ at most. Thus the complexity in terms of oracles calls is polynomial in n and ε^{-1}. The cost of a call depends on the representation of the polytope, but is always polynomial. The running time is then polynomial in n and ε^{-1}.

4   Approximate Separation of Regular Languages

We apply the Polytope Separator to a verification problem: the approximate separation of regular languages given by non deterministic regular automata.

4.1   Statistical Embeddings on Words

We recall how certain polytopes can be associated with regular expressions in the context of approximate verification [8]. For a word w, let $\mathsf{ustat}_k(w)$ be the density vector of all the $n - k + 1$ subwords of length k of the word w, also called the k-gram of w or the shingles's density vector in [3]. For example, for binary words and $k = 2$ there are 4 possible subwords of length 2, which we take in lexicographic order. For the binary word $w = 000111$, $\mathsf{ustat}_2(w) = (2/5, 1/5, 0, 2/5)$ as there are 2 subwords 00, 1 subword 01, no 10 subword and 2 subword 11 among the possible 5 subwords. We extend the definition of ustat to cyclic words of length $n > k$ by considering all the n subwords of length k. This representation is useful to design property testers [8] which approximately decide if two words are close or far, or if a word is close or far to a regular expression.

The *edit distance* between two words is the minimal number of insertions, deletions and substitutions of a letter required to transform one word into the other. The *edit distance with moves* (*EDM*) allows one additional operation: Moving one arbitrary substring to another position in a single step. More information on these distances can be found in [4]. Two words are ε-close if $\mathsf{dist}(w, w') = \frac{EDM(w,w')}{\max\{|w|,|w'|\}} \leq \varepsilon$. They are ε-far if they are not ε-close. The distance of a word w to a regular expression r is $\min_{w' \in r}\{\mathsf{dist}(w, w')\}$.

Note that for the 2^n binary words of length n, there are only a polynomial number of possible ustat_k vectors. An ε-tester to decide if $w \in r$ or if w is ε-far from r uses this property as it constructs $H_r = \{\mathsf{ustat}_k(w) : w \in r\}$ for $k = 1/\varepsilon$, which is a finite union of polytopes. Consider the nondeterministic automaton A associated with the regular expression r, and A^k the automaton where a transition is made of k transitions in A. A finite set of A^k loops is A^k compatible if all the loops can occur one after the other (in any order) in one accepting path of A^k. Each polytope is the convex hull of $\mathsf{ustat}_k(l)$ vectors of compatible loops l of A^m for $m \geq k$. The distance of a word w to r is approximately the L_1-distance between $\mathsf{ustat}_k(w)$ and H_r (see [8] for the proofs of what is stated in this paragraph).

As an example, let $r = (0110)^*(11)^*$, A an automaton for r, and $k = 2$. The A^k-loops of r are $(0110)^l$ and $(11)^l$, for any l. These loops are A^k-compatible. Let $\mathsf{ustat}_2((0110)^l) = (\frac{l-1}{4l-1}, \frac{l}{4l-1}, \frac{l}{4l-1}, \frac{l}{4l-1})$ which converges to

$s_1 = (1/4, 1/4, 1/4, 1/4)$ when $l \to \infty$ and $s_2 = \mathsf{ustat}_2((11)^l) = (0, 0, 0, 1)$. Then we have $H_r = \mathsf{Convex} - \mathsf{Hull}(s_1, s_2)$, which is a segment. Although the dimension of the s_i's is large (2^k), each vector is sparse and has at most $|A|$ nonzero entries.

4.2   Construction and Separation of the Statistical Polytopes

Given two regular languages r_1, r_2, we want to enumerate the words which are in r_1 but not in r_2, or in r_2 but not in r_1. Since the equivalence of two regular languages is PSPACE-complete, the enumeration of one word is hard. We relax the problem: we wish to enumerate words in r_1 but ε-far from r_2, or in r_2 but ε-far from r_1 using the relative *edit distance with moves* between words.

To compare two regular expressions r_1 and r_2, we construct the polytopes H_{r_1} and H_{r_2}. We show how to use the Polytope Separator of section 3 to generate ustat vectors which separate r_1 from r_2. In particular the Polytope Separator has a complexity polynomial in the dimension, while previous techniques introduced in [8], were exponential in the dimension. This approach generalizes to infinite words, to context-free properties and also to unranked ordered trees.

Let A be an automaton with n states and M its transition matrix, *i.e.*, $M(i, j) = a$ if there is an a-transition between state i and state j. For simplicity let us assume that A is strongly connected. If it is not, we have to construct the graph of strongly connected components and to associate a polytope to each components. Let $k = 1/\varepsilon$, we consider A^k the automaton with k transitions in A. The transition matrix M^k of A^k is defined by $M^k(i, j) = \{u_1, \dots, u_p\}$ where each u_l is a word of length k such that j can be reached from i following u_l in A. We do not iterate $M^{k+1}, \dots, M^n$ since their coefficients are sets that may grow exponentially large. Instead, we replace the words by their ustat_k. Let $U^1 = \mathsf{ustat}_k[M^k]$, *i.e.*, $U^1(i, j) = \{\mathsf{ustat}_k(u_1), \dots, \mathsf{ustat}_k(u_p)\}$. In addition to the ustat vector of a word, we need to remember its prefix w_i and suffix v_i of length $k - 1$. Let p denotes the function prefix (resp. suffix s) which remove the last (resp. first) letter of a word, *i.e.*, $w_i = p(u_i)$ and $v_i = s(u_i)$. Let us define the extended U as: $U_e^1(i, j) = \{(\mathsf{ustat}_k(u_1), w_1, v_1), \dots (\mathsf{ustat}_k(u_p), w_p, v_p)\}$.

For $m = 1, \dots, n - k + 1$, let U_e^{m+1} be the matrix such that for each pair of states (i, j), $U_e^{m+1}(i, j)$ contains the ustat_k vectors of words of length $k + m + 1$ linking state i to state j. We build U_e^{m+1} from U_e^m: in each coefficient, we remove the first letter of the suffix v and add the new letter a, that is the new suffix is $v' = s(v).a$. We also modify the ustat to take into account the addition of a letter. Formally U_e^{m+1} is defined as follows:

$$U_e^{m+1}(i, j) = \{(\tfrac{m \cdot \mathsf{ustat}_k}{m+1} + \tfrac{\mathsf{ustat}_k(v.a)}{m+1}, w, v') \mid \exists l \ (\mathsf{ustat}_k, w, v) \in U_e^m(i, l),$$
$A(l, j) = a\}$.

When $i = j$, we reached a loop. We define H^{m+1} as the ustat_k of the loops seen as cyclic words: we adjust the ustat_k in U_e^m with the ustat_k of the k extra words. It is possible, as we kept the prefix w and the suffix v of length $k - 1$.

$$H^{m+1} = \{\mathsf{ustat}_k \cdot \tfrac{m}{k+m+1} + \mathsf{ustat}_k(v.a) \cdot \tfrac{1}{k+m+1} + \mathsf{ustat}_k(a.w) \cdot \tfrac{1}{k+m+1} + \dots +$$
$\mathsf{ustat}_k(s(v).a.w[1]) \cdot \tfrac{1}{k+m+1} \mid \exists i, l \ (\mathsf{ustat}_k, w, v) \in U_e^m(i, l), A(l, i) = a\}$

We stop at U_e^n, and build the polytope H which is the convex hull of all the H^m for all $m \leq n$. H contains all the ustat of the loops of length less than n.

Algorithm 3. Construction of the ustat polytope

Input: A: automata; k: integer
Output: The polytope H associated with A
begin

    Compute A^k; U_e^1; H^1;
    for $m = 1$ **to** $n - k + 1$ **do**
        Compute U_e^{m+1} and H^m
    return $H = Hull\{\cup_m H^m\}$
end

Lemma 3. *We can construct a $\mathcal{V}$-representation of H of size $poly(n, k)$ in time $poly(n, k)$.*

Proof. Being of length less than n, basic loops appear at some stage m in U_e^m. Each entry of the matrix is a set of polynomial size, since the set of possible ustat vectors is polynomially bounded. The time to build H is polynomially bounded.

Theorem 5. *Given two regular expressions r_1, r_2 on words and ε, if $d_{vol}(H_{r_1}, H_{r_2}) \geq \lambda$ we can generate ε-separating words in time polynomial in the dimension and $1/\lambda$.*

Proof. Construct H_{r_1} and H_{r_2} as explained in the previous lemma. From each polytope, we build a membership oracle which takes a ustat vector x and answers YES if the L_1 distance of x to the polytope is greater than ε and NO otherwise. We apply the Polytope Separator on these two oracles. It outputs a separating ustat vector with high probability if it exists.

Given a separating ustat vector x in H_{r_1}, which is not in H_{r_2}, we can generate a large word w from x as follows: pick a starting word u of length k according to the x distribution, and let v be its suffix of length $k - 1$. Then pick the next letter according to the conditional distribution $x(u|v)$, *i.e.*, the distribution of words which have v as a prefix. We repeat this process to obtain a word w of size n, for a large enough n, such that $\mathrm{ustat}_k(w)$ is ε-close to x. By the completeness of the edit distance with moves [8], the word w is ε'-far from r_2.

Notice that the process has two probabilistic components: the random walk in the polytopes to find a separator x and then the generator to find w from x.

5   Approximate Separation of MDPs

In this section, we give a second application of the Polytope Separator algorithm to verification: the approximate separation of MDPs.

5.1   Statistical Analysis of MDPs

We recall how certain polytopes can be associated with MDPs in the context of (state, action) frequencies [5]. Let Σ be a finite alphabet (set of actions) and S the set of states. If S is finite, $\Delta(S)$ denotes the set of distributions over S.

Definition 3. *A Markov Decision Process is a tuple* $\mathcal{S} = (S, \Sigma, P, \Delta_0(S))$. S *is a finite set of states,* Σ *is a set of actions, and* $P : S \times \Sigma \times S \rightarrow [0; 1]$ *is the transition relation. The probability to go from state* s *to state* t, *when action* $a \in \Sigma$ *is chosen, is denoted* $P(s, a, t)$ *or* $P(t|s, a)$. $\Delta_0(S)$ *is the initial distribution.*

If there is no action a from s, $P(t|s, a) = 0$ for all $t \in S$. A *run* on $\mathcal{S}$ is a finite or infinite alternating sequence of states and actions, which begins and ends with a state. We write Ω^* for the set of finite runs, Ω for the set of infinite runs on $\mathcal{S}$. If $n \in \mathbb{N}$ and $r \in \Omega$, we write $r_{|n}$ for the sequence of the first $n - 1$ state-action couples in r and the n-th state in r. The *trace* $Tr(r)$ of a run r is the sequence of actions. If $n \in \mathbb{N}$, X_n and Y_n are the random variables which associate to a run r its n-th state and its n-th action. A *policy* on $\mathcal{S}$ is a function $\sigma : \Omega^* \rightarrow \Delta(\Sigma)$. A policy resolves the non determinism of the system by choosing a distribution on the set of available actions from the last state of the given run. We write HR for the set of History dependent and Randomized policies.

Let σ be a policy on $\mathcal{S}$, $k \in \mathbb{N}$ and $T \geq 0$. Let $\hat{y}_k^T$ be the random variable which associates to all $r \in \Omega$ the k-gram of its prefix of length T, i.e. $\hat{y}_k^T = \mathsf{ustat}_k(r_{|T}) \in [0; 1]^{(S \times \Sigma)^k}$. Given an initial distribution α, the expected state-action frequency vector $y_{\sigma, \alpha, k}^T$ is $\mathbb{E}_{\sigma, \alpha}[\hat{y}_k^T]$, i.e. the expectation of $\hat{y}_k^T$. It may converge as $T \rightarrow +\infty$, to the limit point $y_{\sigma, \alpha, k}$. Consider the set of possible $y_{\sigma, \alpha, k}$ over all the strategies in HR,

$$H_k(\alpha) = \bigcup_{\sigma \in HR} y_{\sigma, \alpha, k}.$$

The analysis of MDPs with this state action frequency vector was initiated in [6] and [16] for $k = 1$ and generalized in [5] for an arbitrary k, by introducing the new MDP $\mathcal{S}^k = (S', \Sigma, P', \alpha)$ which iterates k transitions in $\mathcal{S}$, i.e. $S' = (\prod_{i=1}^{k-1} S \times \Sigma) \times S$ and with probabilities adjusted to k transitions. The polytope H_k associated to $\mathcal{S}$ is equal to the polytope H_1 associated to $\mathcal{S}^k$ and they are independent of the initial distribution α. The polytope H_1 has an efficient representation by the following system of linear equalities and inequalities, for each $s' \in S'$:

$$\sum_{s \in S'} \sum_{a \in \Sigma} P'(s'|s, a) \cdot y(s, a) = \sum_{a' \in \Sigma} y(s', a') \tag{1}$$

Each equation corresponds to the conservation of densities in state s', and we have $|S'|$ such equations.

We are interested in the set of possible traces of an MDP, as we want to compare two MDPs with entirely different states but with the same action set. Hence, we consider the similar vector on the traces $\hat{x}_{\sigma, \alpha, k}^T = \mathsf{ustat}_k(Tr(r_{|T})) \in [0; 1]^{\Sigma^k}$ and its limit $x_{\sigma, \alpha, k}$ when $T \rightarrow +\infty$. For all $v \in \Sigma^k$ we have:

$$x_{\sigma, \alpha, k}[v] = \sum_{u \in (S \times \Sigma)^k \ s.t. \ Tr(u) = v} y_{\sigma, \alpha, k}[u] \tag{2}$$

i.e., the projection vector on the actions. We are mainly interested in the projection of the polytope H_k, also independent of α, that we denote by $\pi(H_k)$ and which is defined as follows: $\pi(H_k) = \{x_{\sigma, \alpha, k}\}$.

The ε-distance between two weakly communicating MDPs $\mathcal{S}_1, \mathcal{S}_2$, introduced in [5], is the the Haussdorf distance between $\pi(H_{1,k})$ and $\pi(H_{2,k})$ for $k = 1/\varepsilon$. A vector x ε-distinguishes two MDPs if it is inside one polytope and ε-far from the other one. It corresponds to strategies which separate the most the traces of the MDPs for the edit distance with moves between traces. Precisely, let $\text{dist}_k(x, \mathcal{S}) = \text{Inf}_{z \in \pi(H_k)} ||x - z||_1$. Then

$$\text{dist}_k(\mathcal{S}_1, \mathcal{S}_2) = \max_{\substack{x_1 \in \pi(H_{1,k}) \\ x_2 \in \pi(H_{2,k})}} \{\text{dist}_k(x_1, \mathcal{S}_2), \text{dist}_k(x_2, \mathcal{S}_1)\}$$

We can easily compute $\text{dist}_k(x, \mathcal{S})$ with a linear program while $\text{dist}_k(\mathcal{S}_1, \mathcal{S}_2)$ is hard (in the dimension), even to approximate, as we could otherwise approximate the diameter which is hard [2]. Other metrics to compare probabilistic systems are related to bisimulation [7,1], L_1 or L_2 distances between distributions, Kullback–Leibler divergence, and $\bar{D}$ distance [15].

5.2   Construction and Separation of the Statistical Polytopes

We want to apply the separator algorithm to ε-distinguish two MDPs on the same action set. We construct the polytopes $\pi(H_{k,1})$ and $\pi(H_{k,2})$ as defined previously. We then define an oracle which takes x, $\pi(H_{k,1})$ and ϵ and answers YES if $\text{dist}(x, \pi(H_{k,1})) \leq \varepsilon$. Let us recall how to efficiently compute $\text{dist}_k(x, \mathcal{S}) = \text{Min}_{z \in \pi(H_k)} ||x-z||_1$ with a linear program. Let $y \in [0; 1]^{(S \times \Sigma)^k}$ and its projection $x \in [0; 1]^{(\Sigma)^k}$. Let us write $A.y = b$ for the equations (1) of section 5.1 and the equality $\sum_u y[u] = 1$. Let $x = C.y$ the equations (2) of section 5.1 and let us assume that all variables are ≥ 0 and ≤ 1.

We want to compute $\text{Min}_{z \in \pi(H_k)} ||x - z||_1$ such that $z = C.y$ and $A.y = b$.

We have to consider the sum of the absolute values of $x[u] - z[u]$, so let $t[u] = |x[u] - z[u]|$ where $t \in [0; 1]^{(\Sigma)^k}$ is a new vector. Then $t[u] \geq x[u] - z[u]$ and $t[u] \geq -x[u] + z[u]$. If e is the vector in $[0; 1]^{(\Sigma)^k}$ with all components equal to 1, we can write: $\text{Min}_{t \in R^{(\Sigma)^k}} \, e^t \cdot t$ s.t. $t \geq x - C.y$; $t \geq -x + C.y$; $A.y = b$.

The Oracle necessary for the separator algorithm takes $x, \pi(H_{k,1}), \varepsilon$ as inputs and answers YES if $\text{dist}_k(x, \pi(H_{k,1}))$ computed by the above linear program is larger than ε and NO otherwise.

Theorem 6. *Given two communicating MDPs on the same action set Σ, $\pi(H_{k,1})$, $\pi(H_{k,2})$ and ε, if $d_{vol}(\pi(H_{k,1}), \pi(H_{k,2})) \geq \lambda$ we can generate ε-separating x vectors in polynomial time in the dimension and $1/\lambda$.*

Notice that the separator algorithm outputs a separating x, the statistics of the stationary distribution of a strategy in one of the MDP which is outside of the polytope of the other MDP. The set of saturating constraints in the linear system gives some information on the strategies whose statistics are close to x.

References

1. Baier, C.: Polynomial Time Algorithms for Testing Probabilistic Bisimulation and Simulation. In: Alur, R., Henzinger, T.A. (eds.) CAV 1996. LNCS, vol. 1102, pp. 38–49. Springer, Heidelberg (1996)

2. Brieden, A.: Geometric optimization problems likely not contained in apx. Discrete and Computational Geometry 28(2), 201–209 (2002)
3. Broder, A.: On the resemblance and containment of documents. In: SEQUENCES 1997: Proceedings of the Compression and Complexity of Sequences (1997)
4. Cormode, G., Muthukrishnan, S.: The string edit distance matching problem with moves. In: Proceedings of the ACM-SIAM Symposium on Discrete Algorithms, pp. 667–676. Society for Industrial and Applied Mathematics (2002)
5. de Rougemont, M., Tracol, M.: Statistic analysis for probabilistic processes. In: Proc. of the 24th Annual IEEE Symposium on Logic in Computer Science (LICS), pp. 299–308. IEEE Computer Society (2009)
6. Derman, C.: Finite State Markovian Decision Processes. Academic Press, Inc., Orlando (1970)
7. Desharnais, J., Gupta, V., Jagadeesan, R., Panangaden, P.: Metrics for labelled Markov processes. Theoretical Computer Science 318(3), 323–354 (2004)
8. Fischer, E., Magniez, F., de Rougemont, M.: Approximate satisfiability and equivalence. SIAM J. Comput. 39(6), 2251–2281 (2010)
9. Gat, E., Goldwasser, S.: Probabilistic search algorithms with unique answers and their cryptographic applications. Electronic Colloquium on Computational Complexity (ECCC) 18, 136 (2011)
10. Kannan, R., Lovász, L., Montenegro, R.: Blocking conductance and mixing in random walks. Comb. Probab. Comput. 15, 541–570 (2006)
11. Kannan, R., Lovász, L., Simonovits, M.: Random walks and an o*(n5) volume algorithm for convex bodies. Random Structures and Algorithms 11(1), 1–50 (1997)
12. Kiefer, S., Murawski, A.S., Ouaknine, J., Wachter, B., Worrell, J.: Language Equivalence for Probabilistic Automata. In: Gopalakrishnan, G., Qadeer, S. (eds.) CAV 2011. LNCS, vol. 6806, pp. 526–540. Springer, Heidelberg (2011)
13. Klivans, A.R., Spielman, D.: Randomness efficient identity testing of multivariate polynomials. In: Proceedings of the 33rd Annual ACM Symposium on Theory of Computing, pp. 216–223. ACM, New York (2001)
14. Lovász, L., Simonovits, M.: Random walks in a convex body and an improved volume algorithm. Random Structures & Algorithms 4(4), 359–412 (1993)
15. Ornstein, D., Weiss, B.: How sampling reveals a process. Annals of Probability 18, 905–930 (1990)
16. Puterman, M.L.: Markov Decision Processes: Discrete Stochastic Dynamic Programming. John Wiley & Sons (1994)
17. Rabin, M.O.: Probabilistic automata. Information and Control 6(3), 230–245 (1963)
18. Schwartz, J.T.: Fast probabilistic algorithms for verification of polynomial identities. Journal of the ACM (JACM) 27(4), 717 (1980)
19. Simonovits, M.: How to compute the volume in high dimension? Mathematical Programming 97(1), 337–374 (2003)
20. Strozecki, Y.: Enumeration of the Monomials of a Polynomial and Related Complexity Classes. In: Hliněný, P., Kučera, A. (eds.) MFCS 2010. LNCS, vol. 6281, pp. 629–640. Springer, Heidelberg (2010)
21. Tzeng, W.G.: A polynomial-time algorithm for the equivalence of probabilistic automata. SIAM Journal on Computing 21, 216 (1992)
22. Zippel, R.: Probabilistic Algorithms for Sparse Polynomials. In: Ng, K.W. (ed.) EUROSAM 1979 and ISSAC 1979. LNCS, vol. 72, pp. 216–226. Springer, Heidelberg (1979)

Undecidability of Quantized State Feedback Control for Discrete Time Linear Hybrid Systems

Federico Mari, Igor Melatti, Ivano Salvo, and Enrico Tronci

Computer Science Department, Sapienza University of Rome, Italy
{mari,melatti,salvo,tronci}@di.uniroma1.it

Abstract. We show that the existence of a quantized controller for a given *Discrete Time Linear Hybrid System* (DTLHS) is undecidable. This is a relevant class of controllers since *control software* always implements a quantized controller. Furthermore, we investigate the relationship between dense time modelling and discrete time modelling by showing that any *Rectangular Hybrid Automaton* (and thus, any *Timed Automaton*) can be modelled as a DTLHS.

1 Introduction

Many embedded systems are software based control systems. A software based control system consists of two main subsystems: the *controller* and the *plant*. Typically, the plant is a physical system consisting, for example, of mechanical or electrical devices while the controller consists of *control software* running on a microcontroller. In an endless loop, each T seconds (sampling time), the controller, after an *Analog-to-Digital* (AD) conversion (*quantization*), reads sensor outputs from the plant and, possibly after a *Digital-to-Analog* (DA) conversion, sends commands to plant actuators. The controller selects commands in order to guarantee that the closed loop system (that is, the system consisting of both plant and controller) meets given safety and liveness properties, i.e. system level specifications.

Formal verification of system level specifications for software based control systems requires modelling both continuous systems (typically, the plant) as well as discrete systems (the controller). This is typically done using *Hybrid Systems* (e.g., see [3,2,11,14,9]).

In [15], we presented a constructive necessary condition and a constructive sufficient condition for the existence of a (*quantized sampling*) controller for a software based control system when the plant is modelled using a *Discrete Time Linear Hybrid System* (DTLHS).

From [12] we know that the existence of a sampling controller is undecidable even for relatively simple linear hybrid automata. Considering that, given a *quantization schema* (i.e. number of bits used in AD conversion), the number of quantized sampling controllers is finite and that when using DTLHSs also the plant is modelled using a discrete model of time, one may be led to think that the existence of a quantized sampling controller might be decidable. In this paper we show that this problem is also undecidable.

A. Roychoudhury and M. D'Souza (Eds.): ICTAC 2012, LNCS 7521, pp. 243–258, 2012.

Furthermore, we investigate the relationship between dense time modelling and discrete time modelling by showing that the class of *Rectangular Hybrid Automata* (RHA) [13] (and thus, the class of *Timed Automata* (TA) [3,14]) can be encoded into the class of DTLHSs.

Our Main Contributions. A DTLHS (e.g., see [5,15] and citations thereof) is a discrete time hybrid system whose dynamics is defined as a linear predicate, i.e. a boolean combination (without negation) of linear constraints on its continuous as well as discrete variables. A large class of hybrid systems, including mixed-mode analog circuits, can be modelled using DTLHSs. System level safety as well as liveness specifications may be modelled as sets of states defined in turn as linear predicates. In our setting, as always in control problems, liveness constraints define the set of states that any evolution of the closed loop system should eventually reach (*goal states*). Our main contributions are the following.

First, we show that the existence of a quantized sampling controller for DTLHSs, meeting given safety and liveness specifications is undecidable (Section 5). We prove such a result by showing that any two-counter machine can be coded as a DTLHS thereby extending to DTLHSs the proof technique in [12].

Despite that, the non-complete algorithm in [15] usually succeeds in control software synthesis for meaningful hybrid systems. The main ingredient of our approach in [15] is to reduce the nondeterminism of a finite state abstraction of a given DTLHS: in Section 6, we show that also finding the "best" abstraction (in order to maximize the possibilities of finding a controller) involves to solve an undecidable problem.

Finally, we show that any RHA can be modelled as a DTLHS (Section 7). Since a TA is also an RHA, this implies that any TA can be modelled as a DTLHS. Such an embedding sheds light on how, by exploiting availability of real valued state and input variables, dense time behaviours can be modelled using discrete time behaviours.

Related Work. TAs [3,14] are a subset of RHAs [13] which, in turn, are a subset of *Linear Hybrid Automata* (LHA) [2,11]. Undecidability results of the control synthesis problem for dense as well as discrete time linear hybrid systems have been presented in [13,12,19,4]. A more general problem is considered in [7], namely the discrete time control with unknown sampling rate, that is undecidable even for TA. Moreover, we note that none of the above papers addresses the issue of quantized control. In [15], we presented a non-complete algorithm for DTLHS quantized sampling control synthesis from formal system level specifications, without addressing the issue of decidability.

Indeed, to the best of our knowledge, no previously published work has addressed the issue of decidability of existence of a quantized sampling controller for DTLHSs.

The relationship between dense time models and discrete time models has been extensively studied in control engineering (e.g., see [6]) with the goal of *approximating* dense time dynamics with discrete time ones. Here we present an *exact* representation of RHA as DTLHSs thus showing that, as long as real valued variables are available, interesting dense time behaviors can also be *exactly* modelled using a discrete time approach.

2   Background

We denote with $[n]$ the initial segment $\{1, \ldots, n\}$ of the natural numbers. We denote with $X = x_1, \ldots, x_n$ a finite sequence of distinct variables, that we may regard, when convenient, as a set. Each variable x ranges on a known (bounded or unbounded) interval $\mathcal{D}_x$ either of the reals (*continuous variables*) or of the integers (*discrete variables*). We denote with $\mathcal{D}_X$ the set $\prod_{x \in X} \mathcal{D}_x$. If $X = \varnothing$ then $\mathcal{D}_X = \{\epsilon\}$, where ϵ is an arbitrary constant. Boolean variables are discrete variables ranging on the set $\mathbb{B} = \{0, 1\}$. If x is a boolean variable, we write $\bar{x}$ for its complement. We denote with X^r (resp. X^d, X^b) the sequence of real (resp. discrete, boolean) variables in X.

A *linear expression* $L(X)$ over a sequence of variables X is a linear combination $\sum_i a_i x_i$ of variables in X with rational coefficients. A *linear constraint* over X (or simply a *constraint*) is an expression of the form $L(X) \bowtie b$ where $L(X)$ is a linear expression over X, $\bowtie$ is one of $\leq, \geq, =$ and b is a rational constant.

Predicates are inductively defined as follows. A constraint $C(X)$ over a sequence of variables X is a predicate on X. If $A(X)$ and $B(X)$ are predicates on X, then $(A(X) \wedge B(X))$ and $(A(X) \vee B(X))$ are predicates on X. Parentheses may be omitted, assuming usual associativity and precedence rules of logical operators. A *conjunctive predicate* is a conjunction of constraints.

Let $P(X)$ be a predicate. A variable $x \in X$ is said to be *bounded* in P if there exist $a, b \in \mathcal{D}_x$ such that $P(X)$ implies $a \leq x \leq b$. In such a case, we denote a with $\inf(x)$ and b with $\sup(x)$. A predicate P is *bounded* if all its variables are bounded. Let a be a rational number and x be a bounded variable. We write $\sup(ax)$ (resp. $\inf(ax)$) for $a \sup(x)$ (resp. $a \inf(x)$) if $a \geq 0$ and for $a \inf(x)$ (resp. $a \sup(x)$) if $a < 0$. We write $\sup(L(X))$ for $\sum_{i=1}^n \sup(a_i x_i)$ and $\inf(L(X))$ for $\sum_{i=1}^n \inf(a_i x_i)$.

A *valuation* over a sequence of variables X is a function v that maps each variable $x \in X$ to a value $v(x)$ in $\mathcal{D}_x$. We also call valuation the sequence of values $X^* = v(x_1), \ldots, v(x_n)$. A *satisfying assignment* to a predicate P over X is a valuation X^* such that $P(X^*)$ holds. Two predicates P and Q over X are *equivalent* if they have the same set of satisfying assignments. They are equisatisfiable, if P is satisfiable if and only if Q is satisfiable.

Given a constraint $C(X)$ and a fresh boolean variable $y \notin X$, the *guarded constraint* $y \to C(X)$ (if y then $C(X)$) denotes the predicate $((y = 0) \vee C(X))$. Similarly, we use $\bar{y} \to C(X)$ to denote the predicate $((y = 1) \vee C(X))$. A *guarded predicate* is a conjunction of either constraints or guarded constraints. A bounded guarded predicate can be transformed into a conjunctive predicate, by observing that a guarded constraint $z \to (L(X) \leq b)$ (resp. $\bar{z} \to (L(X) \leq b)$) is equivalent to the constraint $(\sup(L(X)) - b)z + L(X) \leq \sup(L(X))$ (resp. $(b - \sup(L(X)))z + L(X) \leq b$). Therefore, the following proposition holds.

Proposition 1. *For each bounded guarded predicate $P(X)$, there exists an equivalent conjunctive predicate $Q(X)$.*

3   Labeled Transition Systems

In this section we define the reachability and the control problem for *Labeled Transition Systems* (LTSs), by extending to possibly infinite LTSs the definitions in [18,8] for finite LTSs.

An LTS $\mathcal{S}$ is a tuple (S, A, T) where S is a possibly infinite (even possibly uncountable) set of *states*, A is a possibly infinite (even possibly uncountable) set of *actions*, and $T : S \times A \times S \rightarrow \mathbb{B}$ is the *transition relation* of $\mathcal{S}$. Given a state $s \in S$ and an action $a \in A$, we denote with $\mathrm{Adm}(\mathcal{S}, s)$ the set of actions admissible in s, that is $\mathrm{Adm}(\mathcal{S}, s) = \{a \in A \mid \exists s' T(s, a, s')\}$ and with $\mathrm{Img}(\mathcal{S}, s, a)$ the set of next states from s via a, that is $\mathrm{Img}(\mathcal{S}, s, a) = \{s' \in S \mid T(s, a, s')\}$. $\mathcal{S}$ is said to be *deterministic* if, for all $s \in S, a \in A$, $|\mathrm{Img}(\mathcal{S}, s, a)| \leq 1$. We call *self-loop* a transition of the form $T(s, a, s)$.

Given two LTSs $\mathcal{S}_1 = (S_1, A_1, T_1)$ and $\mathcal{S}_2 = (S_2, A_2, T_2)$, we say that $\mathcal{S}_1$ and $\mathcal{S}_2$ are *isomorphic*, notation $\mathcal{S}_1 \simeq \mathcal{S}_2$, if there exist two bijective maps $f_S : S_1 \rightarrow S_2$ and $f_A : A_1 \rightarrow A_2$ such that for all $s \in S_1$, for all $a \in A_1$ $T_1(s, a, s')$ holds if and only if $T_2(f_S(s), f_A(a), f_S(s'))$ holds.

Given two LTSs $\mathcal{S}_1 = (S, A, T_1)$ and $\mathcal{S}_2 = (S, A, T_2)$, we say that $\mathcal{S}_1$ *refines* $\mathcal{S}_2$ (notation $\mathcal{S}_1 \sqsubseteq \mathcal{S}_2$) iff $T_1(s, a, s')$ implies $T_2(s, a, s')$ for each state $s, s' \in S$ and action $a \in A$. The refinement relation is a partial order on LTSs. Informally speaking, the LTS $\mathcal{S}_1$ refines the LTS $\mathcal{S}_2$ if the set of transitions of $\mathcal{S}_1$ is a subset of the set of transitions of $\mathcal{S}_2$.

A *run* or *path* for an LTS $\mathcal{S}$ is a sequence $\pi = s_0, a_0, s_1, a_1, s_2, a_2, \ldots$ of states s_t and actions a_t s. t. $\forall t \geq 0$ $T(s_t, a_t, s_{t+1})$. The length $|\pi|$ of a finite run is the number of actions in π. The t-th state element of π is denoted by $\pi^{(S)}(t)$, and $\pi^{(A)}(t)$ denotes the t-th action element of π, that is $\pi^{(S)}(t) = s_t$, and $\pi^{(A)}(t) = a_t$.

Definition 1. *A* reachability problem *is a triple* $(\mathcal{S}, I, G)$, *where* $\mathcal{S}$ *is an LTS* (S, A, T), *and* $I, G \subseteq S$. G *is reachable from* I *if there exists a run* π *of* $\mathcal{S}$ *such that* $\pi^{(S)}(0) \in I$ *and* $\pi^{(S)}(t) \in G$ *for some* $t \in \mathbb{N}$.

3.1   LTS Control Problem

A *controller* for an LTS $\mathcal{S}$ is used to restrict the dynamics of $\mathcal{S}$ so that all states in the initial region will reach in one or more steps the goal region. A *strong controller* ensures that the closed loop system meets liveness specifications under a pessimistic view of nondeterminism (worst case distance J_s defined below), whereas a *weak controller* assumes an optimistic view of nondetermism (best case distance J_w defined below). In the following, we formalize such concepts by defining strong and weak solutions to an LTS control problem. In what follows, let $\mathcal{S} = (S, A, T)$ be an LTS, $I, G \subseteq S$ be, respectively, the *initial* and *goal* regions of $\mathcal{S}$.

Definition 2. *A controller for S is a function $K : S \times A \to \mathbb{B}$ such that $\forall s \in S$, $\forall a \in A$, if $K(s, a)$ then $\exists s'\ T(s, a, s')$. The domain of K is the set $\mathrm{dom}(K)$ of all states for which at least a control action is enabled. Formally, $\mathrm{dom}(K) = \{s \in S \mid \exists a\ K(s, a)\}$.*

$S^{(K)}$ denotes the closed loop system, *that is the LTS $(S, A, T^{(K)})$, where $T^{(K)}(s, a, s') = T(s, a, s') \wedge K(s, a)$.*

We call a path π *fullpath* if either it is infinite or its last state $\pi^{(S)}(|\pi|)$ has no successors (i.e. $\mathrm{Adm}(S, \pi^{(S)}(|\pi|)) = \varnothing$). We denote with $\mathrm{Path}(s, a)$ the set of fullpaths starting in state s with action a, i.e. the set of fullpaths π such that $\pi^{(S)}(0) = s$ and $\pi^{(A)}(0) = a$.

Given a path π in S, we define $j(S, \pi, G)$ as follows. If there exists $n > 0$ such that $\pi^{(S)}(n) \in G$, then $j(S, \pi, G) = \min\{n \mid n > 0 \wedge \pi^{(S)}(n) \in G\}$. Otherwise, $j(S, \pi, G) = +\infty$. We require $n > 0$ since our systems are non-terminating and each controllable state (including a goal state) must have a path of positive length to a goal state. Taking $\sup \varnothing = +\infty$ and $\inf \varnothing = +\infty$, the *worst case distance* (pessimistic view) of a state s from the goal region G is $J_s(S, G, s) = \sup\{j_s(S, G, s, a) \mid a \in \mathrm{Adm}(S, s)\}$, where $j_s(S, G, s, a) = \sup\{j(S, G, \pi) \mid \pi \in \mathrm{Path}(s, a)\}$. The *best case distance* (optimistic view) of a state s from the goal region G is $J_w(S, G, s) = \sup\{j_w(S, G, s, a) \mid a \in \mathrm{Adm}(S, s)\}$, where $j_w(S, G, s, a) = \inf\{j(S, G, \pi) \mid \pi \in \mathrm{Path}(s, a)\}$.

Definition 3. *A* control problem *for S is a triple $\mathcal{P} = (S, I, G)$. A* strong *(resp.* weak*) solution to $\mathcal{P}$ is a controller K for S, such that $I \subseteq \mathrm{dom}(K)$ and for all $s \in \mathrm{dom}(K)$, $J_s(S^{(K)}, G, s)$ (resp. $J_w(S^{(K)}, G, s)$) is finite.*

Example 1. Let $S_1 = (S_1, A_1, T_1)$ be the LTS in Fig. 1 and let $S_2 = (S_2, A_2, T_2)$ be the LTS in Fig. 2. S_1 is the integer interval $[-1, 2]$ and $S_2 = [-2, 5]$. $A_1 = A_2 = \{0, 1\}$ and the transition relations T_1 and T_2 are defined by all continuous arrows in the pictures (dotted arrows will be considered later in Example 4). Let $I_1 = S_1$, $I_2 = S_2$ and let $G = \{0\}$.

There is no strong solution to the control problem (S_1, I_1, G). Because of the self-loops of the state 1, we have that both $j_s(S_1, G, 1, 0) = +\infty$ and $j_s(S_1, G, 1, 1) = +\infty$. On the other hand, the controller K_1, defined by $K_1(s, a) \equiv a = 0$, that enables action 0 in all states, is a weak solution.

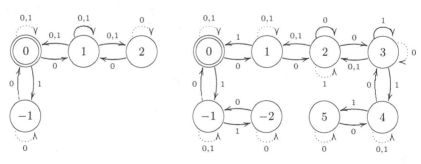

Fig. 1. The LTS S_1 in Example 1   **Fig. 2.** The LTS S_2 in Example 1

The controller K_2, defined by $K_2(s,a) \equiv ((s = 2 \vee s = 1) \wedge a = 1) \vee (s \neq 1 \wedge s \neq 2 \wedge a = 0)$ is a the most general optimal strong solution to the control problem (S_2, I_2, G).

We end this section, by recalling a well-known result that relates strong and weak solutions that will be useful in the sequel.

Proposition 2. *Let (S, I, G) be a control problem. Then each strong solution is also a weak solution. If S is deterministic, then each weak solution is also a strong solution.*

4   Discrete Time Linear Hybrid Systems

Discrete Time Linear Hybrid Sytems (DTLHSs) can effectively model linear algebraic constraints involving both continuous as well as discrete variables. Many embedded control systems can be modeled as DTLHSs. As an example, in [15] it is provided a DTLHS model of a buck DC-DC converter, i.e. a mixed-mode analog circuit that converts the DC input voltage to a desired DC output voltage. The dynamics of a DTLHS is given in terms of a suitable LTS.

Definition 4. *A DTLHS $\mathcal{H}$ is a tuple (X, U, Y, N) where:*
  $X = X^r \cup X^d$ is a finite sequence of real (X^r) and discrete (X^d) present state variables. We denote with X' the sequence of next state variables obtained by decorating with $'$ all variables in X.
  $U = U^r \cup U^d$ is a finite sequence of input variables, that models controllable inputs.
  $Y = Y^r \cup Y^d$ is a finite sequence of auxiliary variables. Auxiliary variables are typically used to model modes (e.g., from switching elements such as diodes) or uncontrollable inputs (e.g., disturbances).
  $N(X, U, Y, X')$ is a predicate over $X \cup U \cup Y \cup X'$ defining the transition relation (next state) of the system.

$\mathcal{H}$ *is* bounded *if N is a bounded predicate. It is* conjunctive *if N is a conjunctive predicate. It is* deterministic *iff $N(x, u, y, x') \wedge N(x, u, \tilde{y}, \tilde{x}')$ implies $x' = \tilde{x}'$.*

Definition 5. *Let $\mathcal{H} = (X, U, Y, N)$ be a DTLHS. The dynamics of $\mathcal{H}$ is defined by the labeled transition system $\mathrm{LTS}(\mathcal{H}) = (\mathcal{D}_X, \mathcal{D}_U, \bar{N})$ where: $\bar{N} : \mathcal{D}_X \times \mathcal{D}_U \times \mathcal{D}_X \to \mathbb{B}$ is a function s.t. $\bar{N}(x, u, x') = \exists y \in \mathcal{D}_Y\ N(x, u, y, x')$. A state x for $\mathcal{H}$ is a state x for $\mathrm{LTS}(\mathcal{H})$ and a path for $\mathcal{H}$ is a path for $\mathrm{LTS}(\mathcal{H})$.*

4.1   DTLHS Reachability and Control Problem

Definition 6. *Let $\mathcal{H} = (X, U, Y, N)$ be a DTLHS and let I and G be linear predicates over X. The DTLHS reachability problem $\mathcal{R} = (\mathcal{H}, I, G)$ is defined as the LTS reachability problem $(\mathrm{LTS}(\mathcal{H}), I, G)$.*
  Similarly, the DTLHS control problem $(\mathcal{H}, I, G)$ is defined as the LTS control problem $(\mathrm{LTS}(\mathcal{H}), I, G)$.

Example 2. Let T be the positive constant $1/10$ (sampling time). We define the DTLHS $\mathcal{H} = (\{x\}, \{u\}, \varnothing, N)$ where x is a continuous variable, u is a boolean variable, and $N(x, u, x') \equiv [\bar{u} \rightarrow x' = x + (5/4 - x)T] \wedge [u \rightarrow x' = x + (x - 7/4)T]$. Finally, let $I(x) \equiv -1 \leq x \leq 5/2$ and $G(x) \equiv 0 \leq x \leq 1/2$.

Let us consider the control problem $\mathcal{P} = (\mathcal{H}, I, G)$. A controller may drive the system into the goal G, by enabling a suitable action in such a way that $x' < x$ when $x > 1/2$ and $x' > x$ when $x < 0$. Indeed, the controller: $K(x, u) = (-1 \leq x < 0 \wedge \bar{u}) \vee (0 \leq x < 2 \wedge u) \vee (1 \leq x \leq 5/2 \wedge \bar{u})$ is a weak solution to P. K is not a strong controller, because it allows infinite paths to be executed. For example, K enables the action $u = 0$ in the state $x = 5/4$. Since $N(5/4, 0, 5/4)$ holds, the closed loop system $\mathcal{H}^{(K)}$ may loop forever along the path $5/4, 0, 5/4, 0 \dots$.

A strong controller K' for $\mathcal{H}$ is $K'(x, u) = (-1 \leq x < 0 \wedge \bar{u}) \vee (0 \leq x < 3/2 \wedge u) \vee (3/2 \leq x \leq 5/2 \wedge \bar{u})$.

4.2   Quantized Control Problem

In order to manage real variables, in classical control theory the concept of *quantization* is introduced (e.g., see [10]). Quantization is the process of approximating a continuous interval by a set of integer values. A quantized feedback control system uses two converters to translate continuous variables into discrete variables (AD converter) and vice versa (DA converter). In the following we formally define a quantized feedback control problem for DTLHSs.

A *quantization function* $\gamma : \mathbb{R} \mapsto \mathbb{Z}$ is a non-decreasing function, such that for any bounded interval $I = [a, b] \subset \mathbb{R}$, $\gamma(I)$ is a bounded integer interval. We will denote $\gamma(I)$ as $\hat{I} = [\gamma(a), \gamma(b)]$. For ease of notation, we extend quantizations to integer intervals, by stipulating that in such a case the quantization function is the identity function.

Definition 7. *Let $\mathcal{H} = (X, U, Y, N)$ be a DTLHS, and let $W = X \cup U \cup Y$. A quantization $\mathcal{Q}$ for $\mathcal{H}$ is a pair $(\mathcal{A}, \Gamma)$, where:*

$\mathcal{A}$ is a predicate over W that explicitly bounds each variable in W. For each $w \in W$ $\mathcal{A}_w = \{w^* \mid \exists w_1, \dots, w_n \mathcal{A}(w_1, \dots, w^*, \dots, w_n)\}$ denotes the admissible region of w, and $\mathcal{A}_W = \prod_{w \in W} \mathcal{A}_w$ denotes the admissible region of Γ.

Γ is a set of maps $\{\gamma_w \mid w \in W$ and γ_w is a quantization function $\}$.

Let $W = [w_1, \dots w_k]$ and $v = [v_1, \dots v_k] \in \mathcal{A}_W$. We write $\Gamma(v)$ for the tuple $[\gamma_{w_1}(v_1), \dots \gamma_{w_k}(v_k)]$.

A control problem admits a *quantized* solution if control decisions can be made by just looking at quantized values. This enables a software implementation for a controller.

Definition 8. *Let $\mathcal{H} = (X, U, Y, N)$ be a DTLHS, $\mathcal{Q} = (\mathcal{A}, \Gamma)$ be a quantization for $\mathcal{H}$ and $\mathcal{P} = (\mathcal{H}, I, G)$ be a DTLHS control problem. A $\mathcal{Q}$ Quantized Feedback Control (QFC) strong (resp. weak) solution to $\mathcal{P}$ is a strong (resp. weak) solution $K(x, u)$ to $\mathcal{P}$ such that $K(x, u) = \hat{K}(\Gamma(x), \Gamma(u))$ where $\hat{K} : \Gamma(\mathcal{A}_X) \times \Gamma(\mathcal{A}_U) \rightarrow \mathbb{B}$.*

Example 3. Let $\mathcal{P}$, K and K' be as in Example 2. Let us consider the quantizations $\mathcal{Q}_1 = (\mathcal{A}_1, \Gamma_1)$, where $\mathcal{A}_1 = I$, $\Gamma_1 = \{\gamma_x\}$ and $\gamma_x(x) = \lfloor x \rfloor$. The set $\Gamma_1(\mathcal{A}_x)$ of quantized states is the integer interval $[-1, 2]$. Let $\hat{K}(s, a) = (a = 0 \land s \neq 0) \lor (a = 1 \land s \in \{0, 1\})$. The controller $K''(x, u) = \hat{K}(\Gamma_1(x), \Gamma_1(u))$ is exactly K, and therefore it is a QFC weak solution to $\mathcal{P}$.

No $\mathcal{Q}$ QFC strong solution can exist, because in state 1 either enabling action 1 or action 0 allows infinite loops to be potentially executed in the closed loop system.

The strong controller K' in Example 2 can be obtained as a quantized controller decreasing the quantization step, for example, by considering the quantization $\mathcal{Q}_2 = (\mathcal{A}_2, \Gamma_2)$, where $\mathcal{A}_2 = \mathcal{A}_1$, $\Gamma_2 = \{\tilde{\gamma}_x\}$ and $\tilde{\gamma}_x(x) = \lfloor 2x \rfloor$.

5   Quantized Feedback Control Problem Undecidability

In this section we prove the undecidability of the DTLHS quantized feedback control problem. Along the same lines of similar undecidability proofs [13,12], we first show that a two-counter machine M can be encoded as a deterministic DTLHS $\mathcal{H}_M$ without controllable inputs in such a way that M halts if and only if $\mathcal{H}_M$ reaches a goal region. This immediately implies that DTLHS reachability is undecidable. Since $\mathcal{H}_M$ has no controllable inputs, existence of a weak controller is equivalent to a reachability problem. For the same reason, actions enabled by any controller for $\mathcal{H}_M$ do not depend on state variables. As a consequence, a quantized weak control problem is equivalent to a DTLHS control problem. Finally, by Proposition 2, weak solutions to deterministic LTS control problems are also strong solutions. Therefore, since $\mathcal{H}_M$ is deterministic, the quantized strong control problem for DTLHS is undecidable, too.

Two-Counter Machines. A *two-counter machine* [16] M consists of two counters that store unbounded natural numbers and a finite control that is a finite sequence of statements $\langle 1 : stmt_1, \ldots, n : stmt_n \rangle$, where $stmt ::= \text{inc } i \ k \mid \text{dec } i \ k \mid \text{beq } i \ k \mid \text{halt}$, with $i \in \{0, 1\}$. Computations start from the statement labeled 1. The execution of $j : \text{inc } i \ k$ increments the counter i and then jumps to the statement labeled k. Similarly, the execution of $j : \text{dec } i \ k$ decrements the counter i (leaving it unchanged if it is 0) and then jumps to the statement labeled k. If the counter i is 0, the execution of $j : \text{beq } i \ k$ causes a jump to the statement labeled k. Otherwise, the statement labeled $j + 1$ will be executed. Finally, the execution stops if a halt statement is executed. The halting problem for two-counter machine is undecidable [16].

Lemma 1. *For any two-counter machine M, there exists a bounded, conjunctive, and deterministic DTLHS $\mathcal{H}_M$, and two predicates I and G such that M halts if and only if G is reachable from I in $\mathcal{H}_M$.*

Proof. Let M be a two-counter machine and let $\mathcal{H}_M$ be the DTLHS (X, U, Y, N), where $X^r = \{x_0, x_1\}$, $X^d = \{l, g\}$, and $U = Y = \varnothing$. Since we are dealing with bounded DTLHSs, we use two real variables x_0 and x_1 to encode values stored in counters. Each natural number m is encoded by the rational number $1/2^m$. Variables x_i are both bounded by the predicate $0 \leq x_i \leq 1$. A discrete variable l stores the label of the statement currently under execution and it is bounded by $0 \leq l \leq n$, where n is the number of statements in the finite control of M. Finally, the boolean variable g encodes termination of the computation of M. The transition relation N encodes the execution of the control program. Let $U(X)$ be the predicate $\bigwedge_{x \in X} x' = x$. A program $\langle 1 : stmt_1, \ldots, n : stmt_n \rangle$ is encoded by the predicate $N = \bigwedge_{j=1}^{n} [\![j : stmt_j]\!]$, where:

$$[\![j : \mathsf{dec}\ i\ k]\!] \equiv (l \neq j) \vee (((x_i = 1) \vee (x_i' = 2x_i)) \wedge$$
$$\wedge ((x_i \neq 1) \vee (x_i' = 1)) \wedge (l' = k) \wedge U(x_{1-i}, g))$$
$$[\![j : \mathsf{inc}\ i\ k]\!] \equiv (l \neq j) \vee ((x_i' = x_i/2) \wedge (l' = k) \wedge U(x_{1-i}, g))$$
$$[\![j : \mathsf{beq}\ i\ k]\!] \equiv (l \neq j) \vee (((x_i \neq 1) \vee (l' = k)) \wedge$$
$$\wedge ((x_i = 1) \vee (l' = l + 1)) \wedge U(x_{1-i}, g))$$
$$[\![j : \mathsf{halt}]\!] \equiv (l \neq j) \vee ((l' = j) \wedge (g' = 1) \wedge U(x_0, x_1))$$

We observe that we use negation as syntactic sugar to improve readability. Indeed, since x_i can assume only values of the form $1/2^m$ for some $m \in \mathbb{N}$, the condition $x_i \neq 1$ can be replaced by the constraint $x_i \leq 1/2$. Moreover, since l is a discrete variable, the condition $l \neq j$ can be replaced by the predicate $(l \leq j - 1) \vee (l \geq j + 1)$.

It is possible to check that $N(\{l, 1/2^m, 1/2^p, g\}, \epsilon, \{l', 1/2^{m'}, 1/2^{p'}, g'\})$ if and only if after executing the statement labeled l with m and p as counter values, M will execute the statement labeled l' with m' and p' as counter values. Moreover if $g = 0$, g' will be 1 if and only if the statement labeled l is a halt statement.

Let I be the predicate $l = 1 \wedge g = 0$ and G be the predicate $g = 1$. G is reachable from I in $\mathcal{H}_M$ if and only if the computation of M terminates.

Finally, we show that N can be written as a conjunctive predicate. Any predicate $P(X)$ can be written as an equivalent DNF $\bigvee_{i=1}^{q} \bigwedge_{j=1}^{m_i} C_{ij}(X)$, where $C_{ij}(X)$ are constraints. By introducing q fresh boolean auxiliary variables $z_1, \ldots, z_q$ this is equisatisfiable to $\bigwedge_{i=1}^{q}(z_i \rightarrow \bigwedge_{j=1}^{m_i} C_{ij}(X)) \wedge \sum_{i=1}^{q} z_i \geq 1$, which in turn is equivalent to $\bigwedge_{i=1}^{q} \bigwedge_{j=1}^{m_i}(z_i \rightarrow C_{ij}(X)) \wedge \sum_{i=1}^{q} z_i \geq 1$. Since N is bounded, by Proposition 1 this can be transformed into a conjunctive predicate.

For example we have:

$$[\![j : \mathsf{halt}]\!] \equiv (z_{j,1} \rightarrow (l \geq j + 1)) \wedge (z_{j,2} \rightarrow (l \leq j - 1)) \wedge (z_{j,3} \rightarrow (l' = j)) \wedge$$
$$\wedge (z_{j,3} \rightarrow (g' = 1)) \wedge (z_{j,3} \rightarrow (x_0' = x_0)) \wedge (z_{j,3} \rightarrow (x_1' = x_1)) \wedge \sum_{i=1}^{3} z_{j,i} \geq 1$$

An immediate consequence of Lemma 1 is the undecidability of the DTLHS reachability problem.

Theorem 1. *The reachability problem for bounded and conjunctive DTLHSs is undecidable.*

Theorem 2. *Existence of strong and weak solutions to a control problem for a bounded and conjunctive DTLHS is undecidable.*

Proof. For any two-counter machine M, the DTLHS $\mathcal{H}_M$ has no controllable actions. Let K be the controller that enables all actions, i.e. such that $\forall x \in \mathcal{D}_X$

$K(x, \epsilon)$ holds. K is a weak solution to the control problem $(\mathcal{H}_M, I, G)$ if and only if G is reachable from I (observe that states in G are controlled by K). Moreover, since the transition relation of $\mathcal{H}_M$ is deterministic, by Proposition 2, K is a weak solution to $(\mathcal{H}_M, I, G)$ if and only if it is a strong solution.

Theorem 3. *Existence of QFC strong and weak solutions to a DTLHS control problem is undecidable.*

Proof. The controller K considered in the proof of Theorem 2 is a quantized controller. Indeed, for any quantization $\mathcal{Q} = (A, \Gamma)$, let $\hat{K}$ be defined by $\forall s \in \Gamma(A_X)$ $\hat{K}(s, \epsilon)$. We have that $K(x, \epsilon) = \hat{K}(\Gamma(x), \epsilon)$.

6   Abstraction Based Control Synthesis

A typical approach to the automatic synthesis of controllers consists of building a suitable finite state abstraction $\hat{\mathcal{H}}$ of a hybrid system $\mathcal{H}$, computing an abstraction $\hat{I}$ (resp. $\hat{G}$) of the initial (resp. goal) region I (resp. G) so that any solution to the LTS control problem $(\hat{\mathcal{H}}, \hat{I}, \hat{G})$ is a finite representation of a solution to $(\mathcal{H}, I, G)$. For example, this can be done by giving conditions ensuring that the abstract system satisfies some equivalence relation with respect to the concrete system (e.g. see [17] or [1]).

In our approach, the abstraction induced by a quantization is a design constraint rather than a methodological tool, since it depends on the number of bits used by AD/DA conversions. In [15], we give a constructive sufficient condition ensuring that the controller computed for $\hat{\mathcal{H}}$ is indeed a quantized controller for $\mathcal{H}$. Such a condition stems from the notion of *control abstraction*. Control abstractions form a family of abstractions induced by a given quantization.

In this section, we show that finding the "best" control abstraction (in order to maximize the possibilities of finding a solution to the original control problem) is also undecidable.

We start by briefly summarizing some definitions and results of [15].

Definition 9. *Let* $\mathcal{H} = (X, U, Y, N)$ *be a DTLHS and* $\mathcal{Q} = (A, \Gamma)$ *be a quantization for* $\mathcal{H}$.

An action $u \in \mathcal{A}_U$ *is* A-admissible *in* $x \in \mathcal{A}_X$ *if for all* x', $(\exists y \in \mathcal{A}_Y : N(x, u, y, x'))$ *implies* $x' \in \mathcal{A}_X$.

An action $a \in \Gamma(\mathcal{A}_U)$ *is* $\mathcal{Q}$-admissible *in* $s \in \Gamma(\mathcal{A}_X)$ *if for all* $x \in \Gamma^{-1}(s)$, $u \in \Gamma^{-1}(a)$, u *is* A-admissible for x in $\mathcal{H}$.

The $\mathcal{Q}$-abstraction *of* $\mathcal{H}$ *is the LTS* $\hat{\mathcal{H}} = (S, A, T)$ *such that* $\Gamma(\mathcal{A}_X) = S$, $\Gamma(\mathcal{A}_U) = A$, *and for all* $s, s' \in S$, $a \in A$ *we have* $T(s, a, s')$ *iff there exists* $x \in \Gamma^{-1}(s)$, $x' \in \Gamma^{-1}(s')$, $u \in \Gamma^{-1}(a)$, $y \in \mathcal{D}_y$ *such that* $N(x, u, y, x')$ *and* a *is* $\mathcal{Q}$-admissible *in* s.

The $\mathcal{Q}$ abstraction could be a highly non-deterministic LTS, thus making problematic the existence of a strong solution to the (abstract) control problem. In particular, for small values of the sampling time, the $\mathcal{Q}$-abstraction may contain a large number of self-loops.

Example 4. Let $\mathcal{H}$ be the DTLHS of Example 2, and let $\mathcal{Q}_1 = (\mathcal{A}_1, \Gamma_1)$ and $\mathcal{Q}_2 = (\mathcal{A}_2, \Gamma_2)$ be quantizations in Example 3. Then, the $\mathcal{Q}_1$-abstraction of $\mathcal{H}$ is the LTS $\mathcal{S}_1'$, obtained from the LTS $\mathcal{S}_1$ in Example 1, by adding all dotted self-loops in Fig. 1. The $\mathcal{Q}_2$-abstraction of $\mathcal{H}$ is the LTS $\mathcal{S}_2'$, obtained from the LTS $\mathcal{S}_2$ in Example 1, by adding all dotted self-loops in Fig. 2.

Let I_1, I_2, and G as in Example 1. Because of self-loop nondeterminism, no strong solution exists for control problems $(\mathcal{S}_1', I_1, G)$ and $(\mathcal{S}_2', I_2, G)$.

On the other hand, if by repeatedly performing an action a in an abstract state s, it is guaranteed that the system will leave the region represented by s after a finite number of steps, a self-loop $T(s, a, s)$ can be eliminated and the action a can be enabled by a strong controller in state s.

Definition 10. *Let $\mathcal{H} = (X, U, Y, N)$ be a DTLHS, and let $\hat{\mathcal{H}} = (S, A, T)$ be its $\mathcal{Q}$-abstraction.*

A self-loop $T(s, a, s)$ is non-eliminable *if there exists at least an infinite run $\pi = x_0 u_0 x_1 u_1 x_2 \ldots$ in $\mathcal{H}$ such that $\forall t \in \mathbb{N}\ x_t \in \Gamma^{-1}(\hat{s})$ and $a_t \in \Gamma^{-1}(\hat{a})$.*

Otherwise, a self-loop $T(s, a, s)$ not satisfying the above property is said to be an eliminable self loop.

Definition 11. *Given the $\mathcal{Q}$-abstraction $\hat{\mathcal{H}}$ of $\mathcal{H}$, we call $\mathcal{Q}$-control abstraction any refinement $C \sqsubseteq \hat{\mathcal{H}}$ that omits some eliminable self-loops.*

The following theorem [15] states that it is correct to consider control abstractions when looking for a QFC strong solution to a DTLHS control problem.

Theorem 4. *Let $\mathcal{H} = (X, U, Y, N)$ be a DTLHS, $\mathcal{Q} = (\mathcal{A}, \Gamma)$ be a quantizantion and let the LTS $\hat{\mathcal{H}}$ be a $\mathcal{Q}$ control abstraction of $\mathcal{H}$. If $I \subseteq \Gamma^{-1}(\hat{I})$ and $G \supseteq \Gamma^{-1}(\hat{G})$, then a strong solution $\hat{K}$ to the control problem $(\hat{\mathcal{H}}, \hat{I}, \hat{G})$ is a quantized solution to $(\mathcal{H}, I, G)$.*

Since self-loop nondeterminism is an obstruction in finding a strong solution to an LTS control problem, and the set of control abstractions is a finite lattice with respect to the refinement relation $\sqsubseteq$, it would be convenient considering the *minimum control abstraction* when looking for a quantized strong solution to a DTLHS control problem.

Theorem 5. *Finding the minimum control abstraction is undecidable.*
Proof. We will show that it is undecidable to state if a self-loop is non-eliminable.

Let M be a two-counter machine. We encode M in a DTLHS $\mathcal{H}_M = (X, U, Y, N)$, where $X^r = \{x_0, x_1, l\}$, $X^d = \{g\}$, and $U = Y = \varnothing$. $N = (\bigvee_{j=1}^n l = j) \wedge (\bigvee_{j=1}^n l' = j) \wedge \bigwedge_{j=1}^n [\![j : stmt_j]\!]$, where $[\![j : stmt_j]\!]$ is defined as in the proof of Lemma 1.

Let $\mathcal{Q} = (\mathcal{A}, \Gamma)$ be the quantization defined as follows: $A_{x_0} = A_{x_1} = [0, 1]$, $A_l = [1, n]$, $A_g = \mathbb{B} = \{0, 1\}$, $A_U = \{0\}$, $\gamma_{x_0}(x) = \gamma_{x_1}(x) = \gamma_l(x) = 1$. Note that we have only two abstract states: $\langle \hat{x}_0, \hat{x}_1, \hat{l}, g \rangle = \langle 1, 1, 1, 0 \rangle$ and $\langle \hat{x}_0, \hat{x}_1, \hat{l}, g \rangle = \langle 1, 1, 1, 1 \rangle$. Then, the self-loop $(\langle 1, 1, 1, 0 \rangle, 0, \langle 1, 1, 1, 0 \rangle)$ is non-eliminable iff there exists an infinite run on M. Being the latter an undecidable problem, we cannot decide if a self-loop is eliminable or non-eliminable.

Example 5. Let us consider again the DTLHS $\mathcal{H}$, and the quantizations $\mathcal{Q}_1$ and $\mathcal{Q}_2$ in Example 4. The LTS $\mathcal{S}_1$ (resp. $\mathcal{S}_2$) in Example 1 is the minimal $\mathcal{Q}_1$ (resp. $\mathcal{Q}_2$) control abstractions of $\mathcal{H}$, where all eliminable self-loops have been eliminated.

Self loops $T(1,0,1)$ and $T(1,1,1)$ in $\mathcal{S}_1$ are not eliminable because of the infinite paths $5/4, 0, 5/4, 0, 5/4 \ldots$ and $7/4, 1, 7/4, 1, 7/4 \ldots$. The same concrete paths make abstract self-loops $T(2,0,2)$ and $T(3,1,3)$ not eliminable in $\mathcal{S}_2$.

7   Dense Time Rectangular Hybrid Automata as DTLHSs

In this section we show that DTLHSs are expressive enough to faithfully encode a relevant class of dense time hybrid systems, namely *Rectangular Hybrid Automata* (RHA) [13], a proper superclass of Timed Automata [3]. More precisely, we show that for every RHA $\mathcal{A}$ there exists a DTLHS $\mathcal{H}_{\mathcal{A}}$ that has the same dynamics, i.e. such that $LTS(\mathcal{H}_{\mathcal{A}}) \simeq LTS(\mathcal{A})$ (Theorem 6). As a byproduct of this encoding, we obtain alternative proofs of Theorems 1 and 2.

Rectangular Hybrid Automata. We define RHA following the presentation in [13]. Given a positive $n > 0$, a subset of $\mathbb{R}^n$ is called a *region*. A closed and bounded region is called a *compact*. A region $R \subseteq \mathbb{R}^n$ is *rectangular* if it is a cartesian product of (possibly unbounded) intervals (finite endpoints are rationals). We write R_i for the projection of R on the i-th coordinate, so that $R = \prod_{i \in [n]} R_i$. The set of rectangular regions in $\mathbb{R}^n$ is denoted by $\mathcal{R}^n$.

An n-dimensional RHA $\mathcal{A}$ consists of a finite directed multigraph (V, E), a finite *observation alphabet* Σ, three vertex labeling functions $init : V \to \mathcal{R}^n$, $inv : V \to \mathcal{R}^n$, and $flow : V \to \mathcal{R}^n$, and four edge labeling functions $pre : E \to \mathcal{R}^n$, $post : E \to \mathcal{R}^n$, $jump : E \to \mathcal{P}([n])$, and $obs : E \to \Sigma$. The set V of vertices is the set of *control modes*, and the set E of edges is the set of *control switches*.

A variable x_i is *bounded* if for every control mode v, the region $inv(v)_i$ is a bounded interval. A variable x_i is *monotone* if for every control mode v, either $flow(v)_i \subset \mathbb{R}_{<0}$ or $flow(v)_i \subset \mathbb{R}_{>0}$. A variable x_i is *closed* if for every control mode and every control switch e, the intervals $inv(v)_i$, $flow(v)_i$, $init(v)_i$, $pre(e)_i$, and $post(e)_i$ are closed intervals. A rectangular automata is bounded (resp. monotone, closed) if all its variables are bounded (resp. monotone, closed).

The rectangular automaton $\mathcal{A}$ defines a labeled transition system $LTS(\mathcal{A}) = (S, A, T)$, where:

States: The set of states S is $V \times \mathbb{R}^n$. Each subset $Z \subseteq S$ is called a *zone* of $\mathcal{A}$. A state (v, x) is an *initial state* of $\mathcal{A}$ if $x \in init(v)$. The *initial zone* of $\mathcal{A}$, denoted by $Init(\mathcal{A})$, is the set of all initial states of $\mathcal{A}$.

Actions: The set of actions A is $\Sigma \cup \mathbb{R}^+$. Each transition labeled with $a \in \Sigma$ corresponds to a jump step, whose observation is a. Each transition labeled with $t \in \mathbb{R}^+$ corresponds to a flow step, whose duration is $t \geq 0$.

Transition Relation: The transition relation T is defined by *jump* and *flow* transitions as follows. For each edge $e = (v, w)$ of $\mathcal{A}$, $T^e((v, x), a, (w, y))$ holds iff $x \in pre(e)$, $y \in post(e)$, for every $i \notin jump(e)$ we have $x_i = y_i$, and $a = obs(e)$. For all $t \in \mathbb{R}^+$, $T^{flow}((v, x), t, (v, y))$ holds iff either $t = 0$ and $x = y$ or $t > 0$ and $(y - x)/t \in flow(v)$. Finally, the transition relation T of $\mathcal{A}$ is $\bigcup_{e \in E} T^e \cup T^{flow}$.

We observe that, thanks to convexity of rectangular regions, we have that a flow transition $T^{flow}((v, x), t, (v, y))$ can be performed if and only if there exists a smooth function $f : [0, t] \rightarrow inv(v)$ with first derivative f' such that $f(0) = x$, $f(t) = y$, and for all $s \in (0, t)$ $f'(s) \in flow(v)$. In the following, for the sake of readability, we consider the case $\Sigma = E$ and $obs(e) = e$.

Theorem 6. *For any closed RHA $\mathcal{A}$ there exists a DTLHS $\mathcal{H}_{\mathcal{A}}$ such that $LTS(\mathcal{A}) \simeq LTS(\mathcal{H}_{\mathcal{A}})$.*

Proof. Let $\mathcal{A}$ be a closed n dimensional RHA. First, we define a DTLHS $\mathcal{H}_{\mathcal{A}}$ that encodes $\mathcal{A}$. Let V be the set of m vertices, and E be the set of l edges of $\mathcal{A}$. Let $|\cdot|_V : V \rightarrow [m]$ and $|\cdot|_E : E \rightarrow [l]$ be two encoding functions of the set of vertices and the set of edges into initial segments of natural numbers. Since both vertex and edge labeling functions define rectangular regions, they can be easily represented as conjunctive predicates. Let $inv(v) = \prod_{i \in [n]} [\underline{\alpha}_{v,i}, \overline{\alpha}_{v,i}]$, $init(v) = \prod_{i \in [n]} [\underline{\beta}_{v,i}, \overline{\beta}_{v,i}]$, $pre(e) = \prod_{i \in [n]} [\underline{\beta}_{v,i}, \overline{\beta}_{v,i}]$, and $post(e) = \prod_{i \in [n]} [\underline{\alpha}_{e,i}, \overline{\alpha}_{e,i}]$. We define the following predicates:

$$\mathsf{inv}_v(x) \equiv \bigwedge_{i \in [n]} \underline{\alpha}_{v,i} \leq x_i \leq \overline{\alpha}_{v,i} \qquad \mathsf{init}_v(x) \equiv \bigwedge_{i \in [n]} \underline{\beta}_{v,i} \leq x_i \leq \overline{\beta}_{v,i}$$

$$\mathsf{pre}_e(x) \equiv \bigwedge_{i \in [n]} \underline{\alpha}_{e,i} \leq x_i \leq \overline{\alpha}_{e,i} \qquad \mathsf{post}_e(x) \equiv \bigwedge_{i \in [n]} \underline{\beta}_{e,i} \leq x'_i \leq \overline{\beta}_{e,i}$$

The DTLHS $\mathcal{H}_{\mathcal{A}} = (X, U, Y, N)$ is defined as follows:

State Variables: The set of present state variables is $X = X^r \cup X^d$, where $X^r = \{x_1, \ldots, x_n\}$ and $X^d = \{q\}$. Each x_i encodes one continuous variable of $\mathcal{A}$, and q encodes the set of vertices V of $\mathcal{A}$. Continuous variables are bounded by inv_v (see the definition of N below), and q ranges over $[m]$.

Input Variables: The set of input variable is $U = U^r \cup U^d$, where $U^r = \{t\}$ and $U^d = \{r\}$. The variable $t \geq 0$ encodes flow transition durations. The variable $r \in \{0, \ldots, l\}$ encodes the edge taken in a jump transition. The variable r assumes the value 0 when a flow transition is taken.

Transition Relation: The transition relation predicate N is defined as follows. Let $flow(v) = \prod_{i \in [n]} [\underline{\gamma}_{v,i}, \overline{\gamma}_{e,i}]$. For each vertex $v \in V$, we define the predicate flow_v as follows:

$$\mathsf{flow}_v(q, x, t, q', x') \equiv \mathsf{inv}_v(x') \wedge q' = q \wedge \bigwedge_{i \in [n]} x_i + \underline{\gamma}_{v,i} t \leq x'_i \leq x_i + \overline{\gamma}_{v,i} t$$

For each edge $e = (v, w) \in E$, we define the predicate jump_e as follows:

$$\mathsf{jump}_e(q, x, q', x') \equiv q = |v|_V \wedge q' = |w|_V \wedge \mathsf{pre}_e(x) \wedge \mathsf{post}_e(x') \\ \wedge \bigwedge_{i \notin jump(e)} x_i = x'_i$$

Finally, we define the transition relation N as follows:

$$N(x,q,t,x',q') \equiv ((r \neq 0) \vee (\bigwedge_{v \in V}(q \neq |v|_V) \vee \mathsf{flow}_v(q,x,t,q',x')))$$
$$\wedge \bigwedge_{e \in E}((r \neq |e|_E) \vee \mathsf{jump}_e(q,x,q',x'))$$

Now we show that $LTS(\mathcal{A}) = (S,A,T)$ is isomorphic to $LTS(\mathcal{H}_\mathcal{A}) = (\mathcal{D}_X, \mathcal{D}_U, N)$. Let us consider the map $f_S : V \times \mathbb{R}^n \to [m] \times \mathbb{R}^n$ defined by $f_S(v,x) = (|v|_V, x)$ and the map $f_A : \Sigma \cup \mathbb{R} \to \{0,\dots,l\} \times \mathbb{R}$ defined by $f_A(a) = (0,a)$ if $a \in \mathbb{R}$ and $f_A(a) = (|a|_E, 0)$ if $a \in E$. We have:

Flow Transitions: For all $v \in V$, $t \geq 0$ we have $T^{flow}((v,x),t,(w,y))$ if and only if $v = w$ and either $t = 0$ and $x = y$ or $t > 0$ and $(y-x)/t \in flow(v)$, i.e. for all $i \in [n]$ $(y_i - x_i)/t \in flow(v)_i$. In turn, this is equivalent to $\mathsf{flow}_v(|v|_V, x, t, |w|_V, y)$ (observe that $t = 0$ implies $x = x'$), and hence if and only if $N((|v|_V, x), (0,t), (|w|_V, y))$.

Jump Transitions: For all $e = (v,w) \in E$ we have $T^e((v,x),t,(v,y))$ if and only if $x \in pre(e)$, $y \in post(e)$, and for all $i \in [n]$ such that $i \notin jump(e)$, $x_i = y_i$. Again, this is equivalent to $\mathsf{jump}_e(|v|_V, x, |w|_V, y)$ and hence if and only if $N((|v|_V, x), (|e|_E, 0), (|w|_V, y))$.

Corollary 1. *Let $\mathcal{A}$ be a closed RHA and let $\mathcal{H}_\mathcal{A}$ be the DTLHS that encodes $\mathcal{A}$. If $\mathcal{A}$ is bounded, then $\mathcal{H}_\mathcal{A}$ is bounded and conjunctive.*

Proof. If the RHA $\mathcal{A}$ is monotone and bounded, then the DTLHS $\mathcal{H}_\mathcal{A}$ is bounded. Each continuous variable x_i is bounded by $\bigwedge_{v \in V} \mathsf{inv}_v(x_i)$. If $inv(v)_i$ is bounded, then $\mathsf{inv}_v(x_i)$ is bounded.

If $\mathcal{A}$ is monotone and bounded, for every mode v there is an upper bound T to flow transition durations. Therefore, the predicate N implies the constraint $0 \leq t \leq T$.

If $\mathcal{A}$ is bounded but not monotone, a bit more involved definition of $\mathcal{H}_\mathcal{A}$ is required. Without going into details, in such a case the definition of $\mathcal{H}_\mathcal{A}$ stems from the fact that a flow transition $T^{flow}((v,x),t,(v,y))$ is equivalent to a sequence of flow transitions $T^{flow}((v,x_1),t_1,(v,x_2))$, $T^{flow}((v,x_2),t_2,(v,x_3))$, ..., $T^{flow}((v,x_n),t_n,(v,x_{n+1}))$, with $x_1 = x$, $x_{n+1} = y$, and $\sum_{i=1}^n t_i = t$.

If $\mathcal{H}_\mathcal{A}$ is bounded, then N can be transformed into a conjunctive predicate as discussed in the proof of Lemma 1.

Undecidability Results Revisited

The reachability problem for RHAs is a pair $(\mathcal{A}, Z)$ where $\mathcal{A}$ is an RHA and Z is a zone of $\mathcal{A}$ and it is defined as the LTS reachability problem $(LTS(\mathcal{A}), init(\mathcal{A}), Z)$.

The reachability problem is undecidable for a restricted class of RHA, namely *Simple Rectangular Automata* (SRA) [13]. Since SRA are bounded rectangular automata, Corollary 1 gives immediately an alternative proof of Theorem 1.

Given an SRA $\mathcal{S}$, the DTLHS $\mathcal{H}_\mathcal{S}$ obtained by applying the encoding in the proof of Theorem 6 has a unique initial state and it is deterministic. In such a case, finding weak and strong solutions can be easily reduced to a reachability problem, thus obtaining an alternative proof of Theorem 2. On the other hand, a proof for Theorem 3 does not follow immediately.

8   Conclusions

We have shown that, for DTLHSs, existence of a quantized sampling controller meeting given (safety and liveness) system level specifications is undecidable. The relevance of such a problem stems from the fact that the *control software* implementing the controller in a software based control system always yields a quantized sampling controller.

Furthermore, we have shown that *Rectangular Automata* (RA), and thus *Timed Automata* (TA), can be modelled as DTLHSs. This shows how, by exploiting availability of real valued variables, dense time behaviors can be modelled using discrete time behaviors.

Investigating interesting classes of (discrete time) hybrid systems for which quantized sampling control is decidable appears to be an interesting future work.

Acknowledgments. We are grateful to our anonymous referees for their helpful comments. Our work has been partially supported by: MIUR project DM24283 (TRAMP) and by the EC FP7 project GA218815 (ULISSE).

References

1. Agrawal, M., Thiagarajan, P.S.: The Discrete Time Behavior of Lazy Linear Hybrid Automata. In: Morari, M., Thiele, L. (eds.) HSCC 2005. LNCS, vol. 3414, pp. 55–69. Springer, Heidelberg (2005)
2. Alur, R., Courcoubetis, C., Halbwachs, N., Henzinger, T.A., Ho, P.H., Nicollin, X., Olivero, A., Sifakis, J., Yovine, S.: The algorithmic analysis of Hybrid Systems. Theoretical Computer Science 138(1), 3–34 (1995)
3. Alur, R.: Timed Automata. In: Halbwachs, N., Peled, D.A. (eds.) CAV 1999. LNCS, vol. 1633, pp. 8–22. Springer, Heidelberg (1999)
4. Asarin, E., Bouajjani, A.: Perturbed Turing Machines and Hybrid Systems. In: LICS, pp. 269–278 (2001)
5. Bemporad, A., Morari, M.: Verification of Hybrid Systems via Mathematical Programming. In: Vaandrager, F.W., van Schuppen, J.H. (eds.) HSCC 1999. LNCS, vol. 1569, pp. 31–45. Springer, Heidelberg (1999)
6. Brogan, W.L.: Modern Control Theory, 3rd edn. Prentice-Hall, Inc., Upper Saddle River (1991)
7. Cassez, F., Henzinger, T.A., Raskin, J.-F.: A Comparison of Control Problems for Timed and Hybrid Systems. In: Tomlin, C.J., Greenstreet, M.R. (eds.) HSCC 2002. LNCS, vol. 2289, pp. 134–148. Springer, Heidelberg (2002)
8. Cimatti, A., Roveri, M., Traverso, P.: Strong planning in non-deterministic domains via Model Checking. In: AIPS, pp. 36–43 (1998)
9. Frehse, G.: Phaver: algorithmic verification of Hybrid Systems past HyTech. Int. J. Softw. Tools Technol. Transf. 10(3), 263–279 (2008)
10. Fu, M., Xie, L.: The sector bound approach to quantized feedback control. IEEE Trans. on Automatic Control 50(11), 1698–1711 (2005)
11. Henzinger, T., Ho, P.H., Wong-Toi, H.: Hytech: A model checker for Hybrid Systems. STTT 1(1), 110–122 (1997)
12. Henzinger, T.A., Kopke, P.W.: Discrete-time Control for Rectangular Hybrid Automata. In: Degano, P., Gorrieri, R., Marchetti-Spaccamela, A. (eds.) ICALP 1997. LNCS, vol. 1256, pp. 582–593. Springer, Heidelberg (1997)

13. Henzinger, T.A., Kopke, P.W., Puri, A., Varaiya, P.: What's decidable about Hybrid Automata? J. of Computer and System Sciences 57(1), 94–124 (1998)
14. Larsen, K.G., Pettersson, P., Yi, W.: Uppaal: Status & Developments. In: Grumberg, O. (ed.) CAV 1997. LNCS, vol. 1254, pp. 456–459. Springer, Heidelberg (1997)
15. Mari, F., Melatti, I., Salvo, I., Tronci, E.: Synthesis of Quantized Feedback Control Software for Discrete Time Linear Hybrid Systems. In: Touili, T., Cook, B., Jackson, P. (eds.) CAV 2010. LNCS, vol. 6174, pp. 180–195. Springer, Heidelberg (2010)
16. Minsky, M.L.: Recursive unsolvability of Post's problem of "tag" and other topics in theory of Turing Machines. The Annals of Mathematics 74(3), 437–455 (1961)
17. Pola, G., Girard, A., Tabuada, P.: Approximately bisimilar symbolic models for nonlinear control systems. Automatica 44(10), 2508–2516 (2008)
18. Tronci, E.: Automatic synthesis of controllers from formal specifications. In: ICFEM, pp. 134–143. IEEE (1998)
19. Vidal, R., Schaffert, S., Shakernia, O., Lygeros, J., Sastry, S.: Decidable and semi-decidable controller synthesis for classes of Discrete Time Hybrid Systems. In: CDC, pp. 1243–1248. IEEE Computer Society (2001)

Author Index